Fodor's
1st EDITION

Moscow,
St. Petersburg,
Kiev

Fodor's Travel Publications, Inc.
New York • Toronto • London • Sydney • Auckland

First Edition

ISBN 0–679–02544–8

Fodor's Moscow, St. Petersburg, Kiev

Editor: Christopher Billy
Contributors: Steven Amsterdam, Robert Blake, Sam Lardner, Linda K. Schmidt, Katherine Semler, Juliette Shapland
Creative Director: Fabrizio La Rocca
Cartographer: Eureka Cartography
Illustrator: Karl Tanner
Cover Photograph: Jeffrey Aaronson

Design: Vignelli Associates

Special Sales

MANUFACTURED IN THE UNITED STATES OF AMERICA
10 9 8 7 6 5 4 3 2 1

Contents

Maps

Foreword

While every care has been taken to ensure the accuracy of the information in this guide, the passage of time will always bring change, and, consequently, the publisher cannot accept responsibility for errors that may occur.

All prices and opening times quoted here are based on information supplied to us at press time. Hours and admission fees may change, however, and the prudent traveler will avoid inconvenience by calling ahead.

Fodor's wants to hear about your travel experiences, both pleasant and unpleasant. When a hotel or restaurant fails to live up to its billing, let us know, and we will investigate the complaint and revise our entries where the facts warrant it.

Send your letters to the editors of Fodor's Travel Publications, 201 East 50th Street, New York, NY 10022.

Highlights and Fodor's Choice

Highlights

At press time, images of the fiery attack on Moscow's parliament building were still fresh. The violent showdown in October 1993 brought the long battle between conservatives and reformists to a dramatic conclusion. With the stalemate that had virtually paralyzed the nation now broken, Russia is again pushing ahead along its bumpy, eight-year road to democracy. Preparations were well under way for national elections in December 1993 at the local and federal levels and for a national referendum on the proposed new constitution. In the weeks following the October confrontation, new economic initiatives were enacted, paving the way for private ownership of land for the first time since the Bolshevik revolution. President Yeltsin had promised to put himself on the ballot for re-election in June 1994, but in November 1993 he surprised the world by declaring he would not run. These are exciting, uncertain times in Russia, and although no one expects a repeat of the violent events of last October, tourists should stay tuned to political developments and traveler's advisories.

The economic reforms begun by Mikhail Gorbachev and continued by Yeltsin have met with dubious success as far as the average Russian is concerned, but one area in which the reforms have produced tangible results is the tourist industry. In the past three years, more than a dozen new hotels, most of them foreign-owned and -managed, have opened in the Russian capital alone, reintroducing, for the first time since the Bolshevik revolution, the concept of luxury accommodations. The tourist industry has also shifted its focus, from group to individual travel. If in the past the Soviet tourist industry frowned upon individual tourists, encouraging foreigners to travel in groups by giving them preferential treatment and discount rates, today the situation has been reversed. In 1994 tourists will discover that there is now a direct correlation between what you pay for and what you get.

At the end of 1993 the Russian and Ukrainian economies continued to be plagued by rampant inflation, and the situation is not likely to change much in the next year or two. Foreign tourists, however, will find themselves largely immune to the fluctuating exchange rates and plummeting value of the local currency, because the many hotels, restaurants, and shops catering to foreigners generally price their goods according to the world market. Goods and services aimed at the general population, such as public transportation, remain incredibly inexpensive for the foreign tourist.

Moscow Arguably the most symbolic change in Moscow after the "October events" of 1993 was the dismissal, by presidential decree, of the military guards keeping watch over Lenin's embalmed body on Red Square. The ceremonial changing of the guards in front of the **Lenin Mausoleum** every hour had been a popular tourist attraction with Russians and foreigners alike. In a country that loves symbols, the dismissal of the guards is in many ways the most decisive break yet with Russia's Soviet past. Yeltsin's advisors are even talking about burying the Soviet Union's founder, who has lain in state in his granite showcase since his death in 1924. The graves of such discredited Communist-party leaders as Stalin, Brezhnev, and Chernenko are to be moved to another location, possibly to Moscow's Novodevichy Cemetery, and the communist luminaries who had been granted the honor of having their ashes sealed in the Kremlin wall are to be given a proper burial.

St. Petersburg Tourists planning to attend the 1994 **Goodwill Games**, scheduled for July 23–August 7, would be wise to make arrangements for accommodations well in advance, as hotels are likely to fill up quickly. More than 2,000 athletes from more than 50 countries are expected to participate in the events. St. Petersburg's many sports stadiums, including the Kirov Stadium, the Yubileiny Palace of Sports, and the Lenin Sports Complex, will be the setting for approximately 200 events in 24 sports.

In May 1993, during celebrations of St. Petersburg's 200th anniversary, the city proclaimed the next 10 years the **"decade of St. Petersburg."** Major refurbishment projects are already under way, to be completed by 2003, when the city will celebrate its tricentennial. Many of the architectural masterpieces once occupied by Communist-party officials, the KGB, and the Soviet military are now being reallocated to public organizations. Two examples are the **Stroganov Palace**, which has been made into a branch of St. Petersburg's Russian Museum, and the **Beloselsky-Belozersky Palace**, once Communist-party headquarters and now St. Petersburg's Municipal Cultural Center.

Kiev The rebirth of Kiev as the capital of a sovereign state has led to the establishment of foreign embassies and an influx of businesspeople from Eastern and Western Europe. Although **tourist facilities** are still relatively limited, restaurants catering to the growing foreign community are opening, and hotels are being refurbished to approach Western standards. Tense relations between Russia and Ukraine are having a direct impact on the struggling Ukrainian economy. Oil and gas are in short supply, and public buildings tend to be poorly heated in winter. At press time the Ukrainian government had announced plans to sell to Russia Ukraine's share of the Black Sea Fleet, for which it had fought bitterly, in order to pay for oil imports from Russia.

Fodor's Choice

No two people will agree on what makes a perfect vacation, but it's fun and helpful to know what others think. We hope you'll have a chance to experience some of Fodor's Choices yourself while visiting Moscow, St. Petersburg, and Kiev. For more information about each entry, refer to the appropriate chapters within this guidebook.

Churches and Monasteries

Alexander Nevsky Lavra, St. Petersburg

Donskoy Monastery, Moscow

Monastery of the Caves, Kiev

New Maiden's Convent and Cemetery, Moscow

St. Andrew's Cathedral, Kiev

St. Basil's Cathedral, Moscow

St. Sophia's Cathedral, Kiev

Smolny Convent and Cathedral, St. Petersburg

Zagorsk (Sergyev Posad), Moscow

Historical Buildings and Sites

Armory Palace, Moscow

Babi Yar, Kiev

Catherine Palace, Pushkin

Kremlin, Moscow

Maria's Palace, Kiev

Palace Square, St. Petersburg

Pavlovsk, St. Petersburg

Petrodvorets, St. Petersburg

Red Square, Moscow

Strelka, St. Petersburg

Winter Palace, St. Petersburg

Museums

Chernobyl Museum, Kiev

Hermitage, St. Petersburg

Kolomenskoye Estate Museum, Moscow

Museum of Historical Treasures, Kiev

Pushkin Museum of Fine Arts, Moscow

State Museum of Russian Art, St. Petersburg

Tretyakov Art Gallery, Moscow

Parks and Gardens

Gidro Park, Kiev

Gorky Park, Moscow

Kirovsky Park on Yelagin Island, St. Petersburg

Summer Gardens, St. Petersburg

Monuments

Bronze Horseman, St. Petersburg

Egyptian Sphinxes, St. Petersburg

Monument to the Baptism of Russia, Kiev

Hotels

Europe, St. Petersburg *(Very Expensive)*

Metropole, Moscow *(Very Expensive)*

Savoy, Moscow *(Very Expensive)*

Restaurants

Europe, St. Petersburg *(Very Expensive)*

Glazur, Moscow *(Very Expensive)*

Savoy, Moscow *(Very Expensive)*

U Pirosmani, Moscow *(Moderate)*

Special Moments

Red Square at night

Your first glimpse of St. Basil's Cathedral

An evening of classical music at the Tchaikovsky Conservatory

A midnight cruise along the Neva River during the White Nights

Kiev in spring

European Russia and Ukraine

KEY
— Rail Lines

0 — 300 miles
0 — 400 km

NORWAY

Barents Sea

Nike

Murmansk

Kozhva

Pechora

SWEDEN

N

White Sea

Arkhangelsk

Vendenga

Mikun

Syktyvkar

Gulf of Bothnia

Yushkózero

Kimasozero

Severnaya Dvina

FINLAND

Kotlas

Petrozavodsk

RUSSIA

Kirov

Vyatka

Lake Ladoga

Helsinki

Vologda

St. Petersburg

Tallinn

Gulf of Finland

Cherepovets

Yaroslavl

Nizhniy Novgorod

Volga

Kazan

Baltic Sea

ESTONIA

Novgorod

Gulf of Riga

Pskov

Tver

Vladimir

Simbirsk

Saransk

Riga

LATVIA

Moscow

Oka

LITHUANIA

Vitsyebsk

Kaunas

Smolensk

Kaluga

Ryazan

Penza

Kaliningrad

Vilnius

Tambov

RUSSIA

Minsk

Mahilyow

Bryansk

Oka

Lipetsk

Saratov

Warsaw

BELARUS

Orel

KAZAKHSTAN

Homyel

Kursk

POLAND

Voronezh

Don

Volga

Belgorod

L'viv

UKRAINE

Kiev

Kharkiv

Volgograd

SLOVAKIA

Dnieper

Donets

Vinnytsya

Dnipropetrovsk

HUNGARY

Rostov na Donu

MOLDOVA

Chisinau

Kherson

Sea of Azov

Stavropol

Odesa

Krasnodar

ROMANIA

Bucharest

Sevastopol

Black Sea

GEORGIA

YUGOSLAVIA

Danube

BULGARIA

Europe

NORWAY
Bergen

Reykjavik
ICELAND

SCOTLAND

NORTHERN
IRELAND
Edinburgh

North
Sea

Skagerrat

Belfast
IRELAND Irish
Sea UNITED

DENMARK

Dublin

KINGDOM

WALES

Hamburg

Cardiff ENGLAND NETHERLANDS
Amsterdam

ATLANTIC
OCEAN

London The Hague
Rotterdam GERM

English Channel

Brussels Bonn
BELGIUM
Frankfurt

Paris LUXEMBOURG

FRANCE Zürich Munich

Bern
SWITZERLAND

Lyon LIECHTENSTEIN

Milan Venice

Monte
Carlo
Marseille Nice MONACO

PORTUGAL Madrid ANDORRA Florence

Lisbon Barcelona Corsica

SPAIN

Sardinia

Seville Granada Balearic
Islands Tyrrhenian

Gibraltar Mediterranean Sea

MOROCCO ALGERIA 0   400 miles

0   600 km TUNISIA

World Time Zones

Numbers below vertical bands relate each zone to Greenwich Mean Time (0 hrs.).
Local times frequently differ from these general indications,
as indicated by light-face numbers on map.

Algiers, **29**
Anchorage, **3**
Athens, **41**
Auckland, **1**
Baghdad, **46**
Bangkok, **50**
Beijing, **54**

Berlin, **34**
Bogotá, **19**
Budapest, **37**
Buenos Aires, **24**
Caracas, **22**
Chicago, **9**
Copenhagen, **33**
Dallas, **10**

Delhi, **48**
Denver, **8**
Djakarta, **53**
Dublin, **26**
Edmonton, **7**
Hong Kong, **56**
Honolulu, **2**

Istanbul, **40**
Jerusalem, **42**
Johannesburg, **44**
Lima, **20**
Lisbon, **28**
London (Greenwich), **27**
Los Angeles, **6**
Madrid, **38**
Manila, **57**

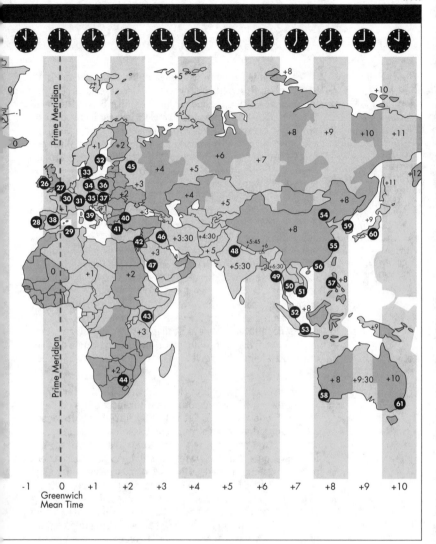

Introduction

By Juliette Shapland

A freelance writer and translator, Juliette Shapland has spent many years in Russia, first with Novosti Publishing House in Moscow and most recently with the Council on International Educational Exchange in St. Petersburg.

Russia is a land of extremes, in its vastness and in its diversity, in its history and in its present. Stretching across 10 time zones, from the Baltic Sea to the Pacific Ocean, Russia is one of the world's largest countries. Its northern borders reach into the Arctic Circle, and its southern territory contains subtropical resorts. With one foot in Europe and the other in Asia, Russia is home to more than 100 distinct ethnic groups. Throughout the long years of the Cold War, we in the West viewed this vast and diverse land as a monolithic empire. We used the terms "Russia" and "Soviet Union" interchangeably and spoke of the region in sweeping generalizations. For some, the country was a definition of evil. Then, suddenly, almost overnight, Russia became a friend, and a needy one at that. The lifting of the Iron Curtain revealed a far different nation than the one we had been taught for decades to loathe and fear. We discovered that the Soviets were not in fact about to "bury" us with their economic achievements, as Nikita Khrushchev had threatened, but rather had buried themselves in their economic failures. So we shifted gears, realigned our world outlook, and discovered, much to our dismay, that a new set of problems had emerged now that the Cold War had been won.

In terms of everyday life, the collapse of the Soviet Union was not a particularly happy event for most of its citizens. However oppressive Soviet rule may have been, its death has been undeniably painful. The present economic crisis, which grew worse as the Soviet Union disintegrated, has left many people nostalgic for the old days. Back in the "era of stagnation" (a term Mikhail Gorbachev coined to describe the Brezhnev years of slow growth and complacency), there was a certain comforting security in knowing that everyone's poverty was guaranteed, that there was no chance of getting ahead, but no chance of being left behind, either. In the past there were strict rules regulating nearly every aspect of life, but today there are no rules at all. Everything that used to be a given—from the price of bread to the impossibility of obtaining an exit visa—has become unpredictable. What was wrong is now right; what was right, wrong. For 70 years Soviet propaganda preached about the pernicious ways of capitalists. Today it is the capitalists who survive—even thrive—in the new world of competition, spiraling inflation, and swelling unemployment. This new group of entrepreneurs may be despised by some, yet it seems most people realize that Russia's future depends on the entrepreneurs' success.

As a tourist in Russia, you will be exposed to the excitement and hope of these times of change and to the despair that goes along with them. A new world has opened, and tours of sights previously off limits to foreigners—including KGB headquarters and the notorious Lubyanka prison—are now available through enterprising tourist agencies. The days when Russians were afraid of contact with Westerners are long gone; you will find people eager to meet you and share their opinions with you and eager for you to like their country. You will be exposed to the raw capitalism of Russian youth every time you step off the tourist bus. Young boys with rabbit-fur hats, military watches, and tins of black caviar await the arrival of foreign tourists at every major destination, ready to pounce and force their goods on potential customers.

The charm of Russia lies in the odd paradoxes of its present and past. The Russian enigma may have been unraveled by the collapse of the Soviet Union, but there is still much about the country that intrigues the foreigner. When you visit Moscow's Kremlin, you may by surprised to discover that the atheist Soviet leaders ran their government from a fortress full of ancient churches. The Soviet technological advances that scared the West into an arms race did not always filter into the everyday lives of the Russian people. As a result, Russia often seems caught in a time warp, suspended somewhere between the 19th and 20th centuries. Store clerks still calculate change with wood abaci. Gardeners use old-fashioned scythes to clip the grass around a monument to Soviet space achievements. In Russia, people still use carbon paper, and televisions and refrigerators often explode in the night due to faulty wiring.

Much of what is true for Russia holds true for Ukraine, as well. The histories of the two countries are intertwined, the two languages and cultures are closely related, and both countries are struggling as newly independent states to reverse the effects of 70 years of Soviet rule. Lately Russia and Ukraine treat each other as estranged relatives. Forced for years to live under one roof and now setting up their own households, they squabble over shared capital. Ukraine refuses to sell its wheat to Russia; Russia refuses to sell its oil to Ukraine. Both lay claim to the Crimea, the Black Sea paradise that was for centuries a part of the Russian empire but was given to Ukraine in the 1950s by Khrushchev.

Kiev, the capital of modern-day Ukraine, is known historically as the Mother of All Russia, for it was in Kiev, some 11 centuries ago, that Russian civilization began. From the late 9th century to the mid-12th century, Kiev flourished as the center of the city-state known as Kievan Rus. Its demise came in the 13th century, when the city was ravaged by Mongol invaders. By the time Russia reemerged as a unified state, in the 15th century, the capital had shifted to Moscow. In the early 19th century, Moscow, in turn, lost its capital status to St. Petersburg, only to have it returned again by the Bolsheviks in the 20th century. As former capitals, all three cities offer a slice of Russian history to the traveler. It is through the monuments of their past—from Kiev's majestic Pechersky Monastery, to St. Petersburg's magnificent imperial palaces, to Moscow's mystical Kremlin and Red Square—that Russian history comes into focus.

In 1931, American journalist Lincoln Steffens, back from a trip to the young Soviet Union, said to Bernard Baruch, "I have been over into the future, and it works." Well, it didn't in the end. As a witness to the current dramatic chapter being played out in Russia and Ukraine, you can judge for yourself whether the future will work. But be cautious in your judgment, for if the collapse of the Soviet Union proved anything, it proved that Russia defies prediction. And, just as Russia itself is unpredictable, a visit to this land of change is full of welcome surprises and unexpected disappointments. A trip to Russia is not likely to give you rest and relaxation, but it offers a glimpse of history in the making. Pack your patience—and your curiosity—and a new world will unfold.

1 Essential Information

Before You Go

Government Information Offices

Tourist Information In the United States **Intourist,** the former Soviet government agency for tourism, splintered into several private organizations in 1991. **Intourist-USA, Inc.** (620 5th Ave., New York, NY 10111, tel. 212/757–3884) can provide information about traveling in Russia and assist with some travel arrangements. The **Russian Consulate General** (9 E. 91st St., New York, NY, tel. 212/348–0926) can also provide some assistance with travel plans. For information about Kiev, contact the **Ukrainian Consulate** (3350 M St., NW, Washington, D.C. 20007, tel. 202/333–7507).

In Canada **Russian Consulate General** (3655 Ave. du Musée, Montreal, Quebec H3G 2E1, tel. 514/843–5901).
Ukrainian Consulate (331 Metcalfe St., Ottawa, Ontario K2P 1S3, tel. 613/230–8015 or 613/235–8214).

In the United Kingdom **Russian Consulate General** (Kensington Palace Gardens 5, London W8, tel. 071/229–32–15).

U.S. Government Travel Briefings The Department of State's **Citizens Emergency Center** issues Consular Information Sheets, which cover crime, security, and health risks as well as embassy locations, entry requirements, currency regulations, and other routine matters. Travel Warnings, which counsel travelers to avoid a country entirely, are issued in extreme cases. For the latest information, stop in at any passport office, consulate, or embassy; call the interactive hotline (tel. 202/647–5225); or, with your PC's modem, tap into the Bureau of Consular Affairs's computer bulletin board (tel. 202/647–9225).

Tour Groups

Should you buy your travel arrangements to Russia and Ukraine packaged or do it yourself? There are advantages either way. Buying packaged arrangements saves you money, particularly if you can find a program that includes exactly the features you want. You also get a pretty good idea of what your trip will cost from the outset. Generally, you have two options: escorted tours and independent packages. Escorted tours are most often via motorcoach, with a tour director in charge. They're ideal if you don't mind having limited free time and traveling with strangers. Your baggage is handled, your time rigorously scheduled, and most meals planned. Such tours are therefore the most hassle-free way to see a destination, as well as generally the least expensive. Independent packages allow plenty of flexibility. They generally include airline travel and hotels, with certain options available, such as sightseeing, car rental, and excursions. Such packages are usually more expensive than escorted tours, but your time is your own.

Although you can book directly through tour operators, you will pay no more to go through a travel agent, who will be able to tell you about tours and packages from a number of operators. Whatever program you ultimately choose, be sure to find exactly what is included: taxes, tips, transfers, meals, baggage handling, ground transportation, entertainment, excursions, sports and recreation (and rental equipment if necessary). Ask about the level of hotel used, its location, the size of its rooms, the kind of beds, and its amenities, such as pool, room service, or programs for children, if these things are important to you. Find out the operator's cancellation penalties. Nearly everyone charges them, and the only way to avoid them is to buy trip-cancellation insurance (*see* Trip Insurance, *below*). Also ask about the single supplement, a surcharge assessed to solo travelers. Some operators do not make you pay if you agree to be matched up with a roommate of the same sex, even if one is not found by departure time. Remember that a program that has features you won't use, whether for rental sporting equipment or discounted museum admissions, may not be the most costwise choice for you.

Fully Escorted Tours Escorted tours are usually sold in three categories: deluxe, first-class, and tourist or budget class. The most important differences are the price, of course, and the level of accommodations. Some operators specialize in one category, and others offer a range. Most itineraries are jam-packed with sightseeing, so you see a lot in a short amount of time (usually one place per day). To judge just how fast-paced the tour is, review the itinerary carefully. If you are in a different hotel each night, you will be getting up early each day to head out, travel to your next destination, do some sightseeing, have dinner, and go to bed; then you'll start all over again. If you want some free time, make sure it's mentioned in the tour brochure; if you want to be escorted to every meal, confirm that any tour you consider does that. Also, when comparing programs, be sure to find out if the motorcoach is air-conditioned and has a rest room on board. Make your selection based on price and stops on the itinerary.

Contact **Abercrombie & Kent** (1520 Kensington Rd., Oak Brook, IL 60521, tel. 708/954–2944 or 800/323–7308) and **Maupintour** (Box 807, Laurence, KS 66044, tel. 913/843–1211 or 800/255–4266) in the deluxe category; **American Express Vacations** (300 Pinnacle Way, Norcross, GA 30093, tel. 800/241–1700), **British Airways** (tel. 800/247–9297), **Caravan Tours** (401 N. Michigan Ave, Suite 3325, Chicago, IL 60611, tel. 312/321–9800 or 800/227–2826), **Delta Dream Vacations** (tel. 800/872–7786), **Globus** (95–25 Queens Blvd., Rego Park, NY 11374, tel. 718/268–7000 or 800/221–0090), **Lufthansa** (tel. 800/645–3880), **Olson-Travelworld** (Box 10066, Manhattan Beach, CA 90226, tel. 310/546–8400 or 800/421–5785), and **Trafalgar Tours** (21 E. 26th St., New York, NY 10010, tel. 212/689–8977 or 800/854–0103) in the first-class category; and **Cosmos,** Globus's sister company (at the same number) in the budget category.

Independent Packages Independent packages, which travel agents call FITs (for foreign Independent Travel), are offered by airlines, tour operators who may also do escorted programs, and any number of other companies from large, established firms to small, new entrepreneurs.

Their programs come in a range of prices based on levels of luxury and options—in hotel and airfare, sightseeing, car rental, transfers, admission to local attractions, and other extras. Note that when pricing different packages, it sometimes pays to purchase the same arrangements separately, as when a rock-bottom promotional airfare is being offered, for example. Again, base your choice on what's available for your budget for the destinations you want to visit.

Special-Interest Travel Special-interest programs may be fully escorted or independent. Some require a certain amount of expertise, but most are for the average traveler with an interest and are usually hosted by experts in the subject matter. When the program is escorted, it enjoys the advantages and disadvantages of all escorted programs; because your fellow travelers are apt to be passionate or knowledgeable about the subject, they can prove as enjoyable a part of your travel as the destination itself. The price range is wide, but the cost is usually higher—sometimes a lot higher—than that of ordinary escorted tours and packages, because of the expert guidance and special activities.

When to Go

The climate in Russia and Ukraine changes dramatically with the seasons. All three cities are best visited in late spring or early autumn, just before and after the peak tourist season. The weather is always unpredictable, but you are most apt to encounter pleasantly warm and sunny days in late May and late August. In Moscow summers tend to be hot, although thunderstorms and heavy rainfall are common in July and August. In St. Petersburg, on the other hand, it rarely gets very hot, even at the height of summer. If this maritime city is your only destination, the ideal time to visit is during the White Nights (mid-June to early July), when the northern day is virtually endless. The Ukrainian climate is milder than the Russian one; spring comes earlier to Kiev than to Moscow and St. Petersburg, and summer lasts longer. In winter months all three cities are covered in an attractive blanket of snow. But only the hardiest tourists should visit between late November and early February, when the days are short and dark, extremely so in St. Petersburg, and the weather is often bitterly cold.

Climate Below are the average daily maxium and minimum temperatures for Moscow.

Jan.	16F	– 9C	May	67F	19C	Sept.	61F	16C
	4	–16		47	8		45	7
Feb.	22F	– 6C	June	70F	21C	Oct.	49F	9C
	7	–14		52	11		38	3
Mar.	32F	0C	July	74F	23C	Nov.	36F	2C
	18	– 8		56	13		27	– 3
Apr.	50F	10C	Aug.	72F	22C	Dec.	23F	– 5C
	34	1		54	12		14	–10

Information Sources For current weather conditions for cities in the United States and abroad, plus the local time and helpful travel tips, call the **Weather Channel Connection** (tel. 900/932–8437; 95¢ per minute) from a touch-tone phone.

Holidays and Festivals

With the demise of the Soviet Union and the accompanying religious revival, church holidays are now more widely celebrated than the traditional political holidays. These days November 7, the anniversary of the Bolshevik Revolution, merits only a minor military parade in Moscow. The date goes by virtually unnoticed in Kiev, while in St. Petersburg November 7 is now celebrated as the anniversary of the city's renaming from Leningrad back to St. Petersburg. Listed below are the current major holidays celebrated in Russia and Ukraine.

January. New Year's Eve is celebrated twice — first on December 31, with the rest of the world, and then again on January 13, "Old" New Year's Eve (according to the Julian calendar used in Russia until the revolution). Russian Orthodox Christmas is celebrated on January 7.

February. February 23, Soviet Army Day, is somewhat similar to Father's Day in the United States. Since just about every male ends up in the army, the holiday traditionally honors all men, not just members of the military. In recent years the holiday—whose name has not changed despite the fact that the Soviet Army no longer exists—has acquired political significance for Communists and nationalists who want the Soviet Union back. The day is celebrated with fireworks in the evening.

March. March 8, International Women's Day, is a popular holiday similar to Mother's Day.

March/April. Orthodox Easter is a major national holiday in both Russia and Ukraine. Visitors should attend the festive services, which begin at midnight and run through the night.

May. May 1, formerly International Labor Day, has in recent years turned into a celebration of spring (in Russian, *Prazdnik Vesny*). May 9, Victory Day, is one of the country's most important holidays; World War II veterans appear on the streets decked out in their medals and are honored throughout the day at open-air festivals and parades. Moscow Stars, a music and dance festival, is held in Moscow on May 5–13.

June. In Kiev, Ivan Kupallo Day (June 6) is a celebration of Mid-Summer's Night that dates from Kiev's pagan days. In St. Petersburg, the White Nights Music Festival is held during the last two weeks of June.

August. August 24 is Ukrainian Independence Day.

November. November 7 and 8, the Anniversary of the Bolshevik Revolution, were, at press time, still public holidays in Russia.

December. December 31, New Year's Eve, is a favorite holiday marked by merrymaking and family gatherings. Friends and family exchange small gifts, putting them under a New Year's tree, a tradition that began when Christmas and other religious holidays were not tolerated by the Soviet authorities. December Nights is a month-long festival of music, dance, theater and art held in Moscow.

What to Pack

Clothing No matter what time of year you visit, bring a sweater. St. Petersburg especially can be unexpectedly cold in summer. A raincoat and fold-up umbrella are also musts. Since you will probably be doing a lot of walking outdoors, bring warm, comfortable clothing, and be sure to pack a pair of sturdy walking shoes. Russians and Ukrainians favor fashion over variety in their wardrobes, and it is perfectly acceptable to wear the same outfit several days in a row. Be sure to pack one outfit for dress-up occasions, such as theater events. Coat-check attendants at theaters and restaurants will scold you if you do not have a hook sewed into the back of your coat for hanging. The layer system works well in the unpredictable weather of fall and spring; wear a light coat with a sweater that you can put on and take off as the weather changes. If you visit in winter you will of course need to prepare for the cold. Take heavy sweaters, warm boots, a wool hat, a scarf and mittens, and a heavy coat. Woolen tights or long underwear are essential during the coldest months. Russian central heating can be overly efficient, so you'll use the layer system again to avoid sweltering in an overheated building or train.

Miscellaneous Local shortages are common. The hard-currency stores (especially those in Moscow) are well stocked, but certain items still disappear periodically and may be hard for passing tourists to find. Bring all your own toiletries and personal hygiene products with you. Women should bring a supply of sanitary napkins or tampons. Of course you'll want to pack as light as possible, but consider whether you might want any of the difficult or impossible-to-find items: ball-point pens, insect repellent (in summer and fall mosquitoes can be a serious problem), film, camera batteries, laxatives, antidiarrhea pills, travel-sickness medicine, aspirin, and any over-the-counter medicine or prescription drug you take regularly. Bring small packages of tissue paper to carry around with you (you'll find toilet paper in most hotels, but rarely in restaurants and public buildings). If you're a stickler for cleanliness and you are staying in one of the old Intourist hotels, bring disinfectant spray for the bathroom. Premoistened cleansing tissues will also come in handy, especially if you are traveling by train. A small flashlight may also prove useful, since streets are often dimly lit at night. Laundry facilities in hotels are unpredictable, so you will probably end up washing some clothes by hand. Bring your own laundry detergent and a round sink stopper (not always provided in hotel rooms). If you're a coffee drinker, bring some instant coffee with you; when the restaurant runs out of coffee, you can ask for a cup of hot water and make your own.

If you meet any Russians, chances are they will give you something; Russians tend to give small gifts even on short acquaintance. You may want to be prepared to reciprocate with souvenirs from your hometown or state, such as postcards, pens, or pins.

Bring an extra pair of eyeglasses or contact lenses. If you have a health problem that may require you to purchase a prescription drug, pack enough to last the duration of the trip, or have your doctor write a prescription using the drug's generic name, since brand names vary from country to country. And don't forget to pack a list of the addresses of offices that supply refunds for lost or stolen traveler's checks.

Electricity The electrical current in Russia and Ukraine is 220 volts, 50 cycles alternating current (AC); the United States runs on 110-volt, 60-cycle AC current. Unlike wall outlets in the United States, which accept plugs with two flat prongs, outlets in Russia and Ukraine take Continental-type plugs, with two round prongs.

Adapters, To plug in U.S.-made appliances abroad, you'll need an
Converters, adapter plug. To reduce the voltage entering the appliance
Transformers from 220 to 110 volts, you'll also need a converter unless it is a dual-voltage appliance made for travel. There are converters for high-wattage appliances (such as hair dryers), low-wattage items (such as electric toothbrushes and razors), and combination models. Hotels sometimes have outlets marked FOR SHAVERS ONLY near the sink; these are 110-volt outlets for low-wattage appliances; don't use them for a high-wattage appliance. If you're traveling with a laptop computer, especially a fairly old one, you may need a transformer—a type of converter used with electronic-circuitry products. Newer laptop computers are auto-sensing, operating equally well on 110 and 220 volts (so you need only the appropriate adapter plug). When in doubt, consult your appli-

ance's owner's manual or the manufacturer. Or get a copy of the free brochure "Foreign Electricity Is No Deep Dark Secret," published by adapter-converter manufacturer Franzus (Murtha Industrial Park, Box 142, Beacon Falls, CT 06403, tel. 203/723–6664; send a stamped, self-addressed envelope when ordering).

Luggage Free baggage allowances on an airline depend on the air-
Regulations line, the route, and the class of your ticket. In general, on domestic and international flights between the United States and foreign destinations, you are entitled to check two bags—neither exceeding 62 inches, or 158 centimeters (length + width + height), or weighing more than 70 pounds (32 kilograms). A third piece may be brought aboard as a carryon; its total dimensions are generally limited to less than 45 inches (114 centimeters), so it will fit easily under the seat in front of you or in the overhead compartment. There are variations, so ask in advance. The single rule, a Federal Aviation Administration safety regulation that pertains to carry-on baggage on U.S. airlines, requires that carryons be properly stowed and allows the airline to limit allowances and tailor them to different aircraft and operational conditions. Charges for excess, oversize, or overweight pieces vary, so inquire before you pack.

If you are flying between two foreign destinations, note that baggage allowances may be determined not by the piece method but by the weight method, which generally allows 88 pounds (40 kilograms) of luggage in first class, 66 pounds (30 kilograms) in business class, and 44 pounds (20 kilograms) in economy. If your flight between two cities abroad *connects* with your transatlantic or transpacific flight, the piece method still applies.

Safeguarding Your Before leaving home, itemize your bags' contents and their
Luggage worth; this list will help you estimate the extent of your loss if your bags go astray. To minimize that risk, tag bags inside and out with your name, address, and phone number. (If you use your home address, cover it so that potential thieves can't see it.) At check-in, make sure that the tag attached by baggage handlers bears the correct three-letter code for your destination.

If your bags do not arrive with you when you land in Russia, or if you detect damage, do not leave the airport until you've filed a written report.

In Russia or Ukraine, regardless of which airline you arrived on, you first have to file your claim for lost luggage with Aeroflot, *before* leaving customs. Aeroflot then theoretically informs your airline of the loss. Aeroflot officials will tell you that you are responsible for retrieving the luggage yourself (that is, by coming back to the airport), but in fact most non-Russian airlines will deliver your luggage to you. In any case, it's best to track down a representative of your carrier after you have filed your claim with Aeroflot to confirm that they received your claim in proper order with all the relevant phone numbers and addresses. But be warned, the local staff of your airline won't talk to you until you've filed your claim with Aeroflot.

Taking Money Abroad

Traveler's Checks Unfortunately, traveler's checks are close to useless in Russia and Ukraine, even in the capital cities. It's best to rely on cash and credit cards. The following information is relevant if you want to keep extra cash in reserve or if your itinerary includes other European countries. The most widely recognized traveler's checks are **American Express, Barclay's, Thomas Cook,** and those issued by such major commercial banks as **Citibank** and **Bank of America.** American Express also issues *Traveler's Cheques for Two,* which can be signed and used by you or your traveling companion. Some checks are free; usually the issuing company or the bank at which you make your purchase charges 1% of the checks' face value as a fee. Be sure to buy a few checks in small denominations to cash toward the end of your trip, when you don't want to be left with more foreign currency than you can spend. Always record the numbers of checks as you spend them, and keep this list separate from the checks.

Currency Exchange Official state-run or bank exchange offices are few and far between in Russia and Ukraine, though more unofficial exchange offices open all the time. The best places to change money are the service bureaus of hotels. (*See* Russian and Ukrainian Currency, *below*, for details.)

Getting Money from Home

American Express Cardholder Services The company's **Express Cash** system lets you withdraw cash and/or traveler's checks from a worldwide network of 57,000 American Express dispensers and participating bank ATMs. You must *enroll first* (call 800/227–4669 for a form and allow two weeks for processing). Withdrawals are charged not to your card but to a designated bank account. You can withdraw up to $1,000 per seven-day period on the basic card, more if your card is gold or platinum. There is a 2% fee (minimum $2.50, maximum $10) for each cash transaction and a 1% fee for traveler's checks (except for the platinum card), which are available only from American Express dispensers.

At AmEx offices, cardholders can also cash personal checks for up to $1,000 in any seven-day period (21 days abroad); of this $200 can be in cash, more if available, with the balance paid in traveler's checks, for which all but platinum cardholders pay a 1% fee. Higher limits apply to the gold and platinum cards.

Wiring Money   You don't have to be a cardholder to send or receive an **American Express MoneyGram** for up to $10,000. To send one, go to an American Express MoneyGram agent, pay up to $1,000 with a credit card and anything over that in cash, and phone a transaction reference number to your intended recipient, who only needs to present identification and the reference number to the nearest MoneyGram agent in order to pick up the cash. There are MoneyGram agents in more than 60 countries (call 800/543–4080 for locations). Fees range from 5% to 10%, depending on the amount and how you pay. You can't use American Express, which is really a convenience card—only Discover, MasterCard, and Visa credit cards.

You can also use **Western Union.** To wire money, take either cash or a check to the nearest office. (Or you can call and use a credit card.) Fees are roughly 5%–10%. Money sent from the United States or Canada will be available for pick up at agent locations in Moscow within minutes. Service is not available to St. Petersburg or Kiev. There are approximately 20,000 agents worldwide (call 800/325–6000 for locations).

Russian and Ukrainian Currency

The national currency in Russia is the ruble, which is divided into 100 kopecks. There are paper notes of 1,3,5, 10, 25, 50, 100, 200, 500, 1,000, 5,000, 10,000, and 50,000 rubles. Until the early 1990s, the highest denomination was the 100-ruble note; new, larger notes were added recently to keep up with inflation. Inflation is so high these days that kopecks are no longer in circulation, and 1-, 3-, and 5-ruble notes have become the equivalent of small change.

Rubles cannot be obtained outside the country, and it is illegal to import or export them. There is no limit, however, on the amount of foreign currency you may bring in with you. The ruble is not a freely convertible currency; many establishments (hotels, stores and restaurants) do not accept rubles but instead trade exclusively in foreign or "hard" currency. You will also find that street artists and vendors often prefer payment in dollars. You should never change more money than you expect to need immediately, since, in addition to the ruble's limited acceptance, it is often difficult to change unspent rubles back into dollars; this can be done only at the airport and only if you have saved your original exchange receipts. Russia is a cash society; traveler's checks can be cashed at only a limited number of banks and hard-currency establishments. Major credit cards (American Express, Diners Club, Eurocard, JCB, MasterCard and Visa) are more widely accepted, but often the only accepted form of payment is cash. Of course it is safest to carry your money in traveler's checks, but you will want to have at least $100 in cash (in tens and twenties). If you don't mind the risk of theft or loss, bring more; you are bound to need it. Make sure your bills are crisp and clean, since worn or torn bills are often refused by Russian merchants.

You can exchange your money at banks and at all the major hotels. You will be constantly approached by people on the streets, in your hotel, and particularly by waiters in state-run restaurants, offering to exchange money at more advantageous rates. These unofficial currency-exchange activities, commonly referred to as the black market, are now legal under Russian law, but only the foolhardy engage in them. Your chances of being shortchanged are extremely high, and the savings are hardly worth the risk.

As in Russia, Ukraine has a two-tiered, predominantly cash economy. Dollars (cash) and major credit cards are accepted at many restaurants, stores and hotels; as in Russia, many establishments accept only foreign currency. Traveler's checks are almost impossible to cash. The Russian ruble—once the only currency throughout the former Soviet Union—is gradually being replaced by the Ukrainian "coupon." The coupon was originally introduced as a ration card to prevent the sale of Ukrainian goods to non-Ukrainian residents and has gradually acquired the status of a national currency. Its value decreases on a daily basis, and you should never exchange more money than you expect to need in the next day or so. The inflation rate in Ukraine has outpaced Russia's, and by press time (fall 1993), one ruble would buy approximately six coupons. You can exchange rubles or dollars for coupons at banks and all major hotels. As in Russia, the black market is a thriving business, and again you are advised to stay away from it.

What It Will Cost

Russians talk about prices in much the same way Americans talk about weather. The inflation rate is mind-boggling, but so far the exchange rate vis-à-vis the dollar has kept pace. In November 1989, when the Soviet government relaxed the strict regulations controlling exchange rates, one ruble was worth approximately $1.50; by the summer of 1993, one dollar was worth more than 1,000 rubles. You can find some incredible bargains for rubles, but you will have to search for them. Goods and services aimed at foreigners are as expensive as anywhere in Western Europe. A cup of coffee in a foreign-run hotel will cost around $3; in a stand-up café dealing in rubles, around 10¢. A ride on the subway is less than a penny and a pass for the entire month costs around a dollar. Taxi rates are also incredibly low, but as soon as the driver realizes that you are a foreigner, the rate goes up, and you will most likely be asked to pay in dollars. Some museums, such as the Armory Palace in the Kremlin and St. Basil's Cathedral on Red Square, have instituted special, hard-currency fees for foreign tourists, but tickets for Russians, in rubles, are incredibly inexpensive. An evening of classical music at one of Russia's many symphonic concert halls can cost less than a dollar if you buy the tickets in rubles, but if you order them through a tourist agency, the cost rises significantly. The price discrimination against foreigners is particularly prevalent in Moscow.

Passports and Visas

If your passport is lost or stolen abroad, report it immediately to the nearest embassy or consulate and to the local police. If you can provide the consular officer with the information contained in the passport, you will probably get a new one. For this reason, it is a good idea to keep a copy of the data page of your passport in a separate place, or to leave the passport number, date, and place of issuance with a relative or friend at home.

U.S. Citizens All U.S. citizens, even infants, need a valid passport to enter Russia or Ukraine for stays of up to 90 days. You can pick up new and renewal application forms at any of the 13 U.S. Passport Agency offices and at some post offices and courthouses. Although passports are usually mailed within two weeks of your application's receipt, it's best to allow three weeks for delivery in low season, five weeks or more from April through summer. Call the Department of State Office of Passport Services' information line (1425 K St. NW, Washington, DC 20522, tel. 202/647–0518) for fees, documentation requirements, and other details.

U.S. citizens traveling to Russia and Ukraine are also required to obtain a visa for each country. For a Russian visa, you will need to submit the following items to the Russian Consulate at least 14 days before departure: a completed application, a copy of the signed page(s) of your passport, three photos, reference numbers from the hotels you'll be staying at (to prove that you have confirmed reservations), a self-addressed stamped envelope, and a $20 application fee. The fee is higher if you need a faster turn-around time ($30 for 2–14 days, $60 for 48 hours). Requirements vary slightly if you'll be staying as a guest in a private home or if you're traveling on business. Contact the **Russian Consulate General** (9 E. 91st St., New York, NY 10128, tel. 212/348–0926) for application forms and more details.

The requirements for obtaining a visa to Ukraine are similar: an application form, copy of your passport, three photos, confirmation of hotel bookings, and the fee ($20 for a single-entry visa, $40 for a double-entry visa, and $100 for a multiple-entry visa). Contact the **Ukrainian Consulate** (3350 M St., NW Washington, D.C. 20007, tel. 202/333–7505) for more information.

Canadian Citizens Canadian citizens need a valid passport to enter Russia or Ukraine for stays of up to 90 days. Application forms are available at 23 regional passport offices as well as post offices and travel agencies. Whether applying for a first or a subsequent passport, you must apply in person. Children under 16 may be included on a parent's passport but must have their own passport in order to travel alone. Passports are valid for five years and are usually mailed within two weeks of an application's receipt. For fees, documentation requirements, and other information in English or French, call the passport office (tel. 514/283–2152).

Canadian citizens are required to obtain a visa to enter either Russia or Ukraine. Requirements are very similar to those outlined above for U.S. citizens. For application forms and details, contact the **Russian Consulate General** (3655 Avenue du Musee, Montreal, Quebec, H3G 2E1, tel. 514/843–5901) and the **Ukrainian Consulate** in Ottawa (tel. 613/230–8015 or 613/235–8214).

U.K. Citizens Citizens of the United Kingdom need a valid passport to enter Russia or Ukraine for stays of up to 90 days. Applications for new and renewal passports are available from main post offices as well as at the six passport offices, located in Belfast, Glasgow, Liverpool, London, Newport, and Peterborough. You may apply in person at all passport offices, or by mail to all except the London office. Children under 16 may travel on a parent's passport when accompanying them. All passports are valid for 10 years. Allow a month for processing.

To obtain application forms and details about visa requirements for Russia, contact the **Russian Consulate General** (Kensington Palace Gardens 5, London W8, tel. 071/229–32–15). For information about visas to Ukraine, contact the **Ukrainian Consulate** (tel. 071/727–6312).

Customs and Duties

On Arrival Upon arrival, you first pass through passport control, where a border guard will carefully examine your passport and visa, and retain one sheet of your Russian visa. The procedure in Ukraine is similar, except that the Ukrainian visa is actually stamped in your passport. After retrieving your luggage, you fill out a customs form that you must keep until departure, when you will be asked to present it again. You may import free of duty and without special license any articles intended for personal use, including clothing, food, tobacco and cigarettes, alcoholic drinks, perfume, sports equipment, and camera. One video camera and one laptop computer per person are allowed. Importing weapons and ammunition, as well as opium, hashish, and pipes for smoking them, is prohibited. The punishment for carrying illegal substances is severe. You should write down on the customs form the exact amount of currency you are carrying (in cash as well as traveler's checks); you may enter the country with any amount of money, but you cannot leave the country with more money than you had when you entered. You should also include on your customs form any jewelry (particularly silver, gold, and amber) as well as any electronic goods (cameras, personal tape recorders, computers, etc.) you have. It is important to include any valuable items on the form to ensure that you will be allowed to export them, but beware that you are expected to take them with you, so you cannot leave them behind as gifts. If an item included on your customs form is stolen, you should obtain a police report to avoid being questioned upon departure.

Returning Home When leaving the country you will fill out a customs form again and present it, along with the original customs form filled out upon arrival, to the customs agent. Your bags will be x-rayed again and perhaps opened for examination. Russian and Ukrainian customs regulations are vague, change frequently, and seem to depend more than anything on the whim of the individual custom's official checking your bags. Anything deemed of "value to the nation" is liable to confiscation at the border. This applies to icons, antiques and art work dated prior to 1945. The rules on modern art are typically vague. Items that are clearly souvenirs of little value (such as wooden Matroshka dolls and black, lacquered boxes) usually clear customs with no problem. To export a canvas, however, you are likely to need permission from the Ministry of Culture. For purchases made in rubles, ask the art salon or shop where you made the purchase to handle the necessary paperwork for you. If they refuse or tell you it's not necessary, stop for a moment before spending a lot of money and think hard about how you would feel if you couldn't take your purchase home with you. Save receipts for everything purchased in a hard-currency store; theoretically customs officials cannot confiscate or impose duty on anything purchased for dollars. Sometimes just showing them a wad of hard-currency receipts is impressive enough to stop them from inquiring further. A duty is sometimes imposed on purchases made in rubles (especially for porcelain, samovars, and other items of obvious value); there are no official written rules governing this policy and the customs official probably keeps at least a part of the "fine." If you have more than two tins of caviar, be prepared to forfeit them or pay a fine—the metal containers show up on the X-ray machine and the customs officers keep their eyes peeled for them.

U.S. Customs Provided you've been out of the country for at least 48 hours and haven't already used the exemption, or any part of it, in the past 30 days, you may bring home $400 worth of foreign goods duty-free. So can each member of your family, regardless of age; and your exemptions may be pooled, so one of you can bring in more if another brings in less. A flat 10% duty applies to the next $1,000 of goods; above $1,400, the rate varies with the merchandise. (If the 48-hour or 30-day limits apply, your duty-free allowance drops to $25, which may not be pooled.) Please note that these are the *general* rules, applicable to most countries; more generous allowances are in effect for certain developing countries benefiting from the Generalized System of Preferences (GSP).

Travelers 21 or older may bring back 1 liter of alcohol duty-free, provided the beverage laws of the state through which they reenter the United States allow it. In addition, 100 non-Cuban cigars and 200 cigarettes are allowed, regardless of your age. Antiques and works of art that are more than 100 years old are duty-free.

Gifts valued at less than $50 may be mailed duty-free to stateside friends and relatives, with a limit of one package per day per addressee (do not send alcohol or tobacco products, or perfume valued at more than $5). These gifts do not count as part of your exemption, unless you bring them home with you. Mark the package "Unsolicited Gift" and include the nature of the gift and its retail value.

For a copy of "Know Before You Go," a free brochure detailing what you may and may not bring back to the United States, rates of duty, and other pointers, contact the **U.S. Customs Service** (Box 7407, Washington, DC 20044, tel. 202/927–6724). A copy of "GSP and the Traveler" is available from the same source.

Canadian Customs Once per calendar year, when you've been out of Canada for at least seven days, you may bring in $300 worth of goods duty-free. If you've been away for less than seven days but more than 48 hours, the duty-free exemption drops to $100 but can be claimed any number of times (as can a $20 duty-free exemption for absences of 24 hours or more). You cannot combine the yearly and 48-hour exemptions, use the $300 exemption only partially (to save the balance for a later trip), or pool exemptions with family members. Goods claimed under the $300 exemption may follow you by mail; those claimed under the lesser exemptions must accompany you on your return.

Alcohol and tobacco products may be included in the yearly and 48-hour exemptions but not in the 24-hour exemption. If you meet the age requirements of the province through which you reenter Canada, you may bring in, duty-free, 1.14 liters (40 imperial ounces) of wine or liquor *or* two dozen 12-ounce cans or bottles of beer or ale. If you are 16 or older, you may bring in, duty-free, 200 cigarettes, 50 cigars or cigarillos, and 400 tobacco sticks or 400 grams of manufactured tobacco. Alcohol and tobacco must accompany you on your return.

Gifts may be mailed to friends in Canada duty-free. These do not count as part of your exemption. Each gift may be worth up to $60—label the package "Unsolicited Gift—Value under $60." There are no limits on the number of gifts that may be sent per day or per addressee, but you can't mail alcohol or tobacco.

For more information, including details of duties on items that exceed your duty-free limit, ask the Revenue Canada Customs and Excise Department (Connaught Bldg., Mac-Kenzie Ave., Ottawa, Ont., K1A OL5, tel. 613/957–0275) for a copy of the free brochure "I Declare/Je Déclare."

U.K. Customs From countries outside the EC, you may import duty-free 200 cigarettes, 100 cigarillos, 50 cigars or 250 grams of tobacco; 1 liter of spirits or 2 liters of fortified or sparkling wine; 2 liters of still table wine; 60 millileters of perfume; 250 millileters of toilet water; plus £36 worth of other goods, including gifts and souvenirs.

For further information or a copy of "A Guide for Travellers," which details standard customs procedures as well as what you may bring into the United Kingdom from abroad, contact HM Customs and Excise (New King's Beam House, 22 Upper Ground, London SE1 9PJ, tel. 071/620–1313).

Traveling with Cameras, Camcorders, and Laptops

Film and Cameras If your camera is new or you haven't used it for a while, shoot and develop a few rolls of film before leaving home. Pack some lens tissue and an extra battery for your built-in light meter, and invest in an inexpensive skylight filter, to both protect your lens and provide some definition in hazy shots. Store film in a cool, dry place—never in the car's glove compartment or on the shelf under the rear window.

Films above ISO 400 are more sensitive to damage from airport security X-rays than others; very high speed films—ISO 1,000 and above—are exceedingly vulnerable. To protect your film, don't put it in checked luggage; carry it with you in a plastic bag and ask for a hand inspection. Such requests are honored at American airports but may be subject to the whims of the inspector abroad. Don't depend on a lead-lined bag to protect film in checked luggage—the airline may very well turn up the dosage of radiation to see what you've got in there. Airport metal detectors do not harm film, although you'll set off the alarm if you walk through one with a roll in your pocket. Call the Kodak Information Center (tel. 800/242–2424) for details.

Camcorders Before your trip, put new or long-unused camcorders through their paces and practice panning and zooming. Invest in a skylight filter to protect the lens, and check the lithium battery that lights up the LCD (liquid crystal display) modes. As for the rechargeable nickel-cadmium batteries that are the camera's power source, take along an extra pair so that while you're using your camcorder you'll have one battery ready and another recharging. Most new camcorders are equipped with the battery (which generally slides or clicks onto the camera body); to recharge it, with what's known as a universal or worldwide AC adapter charger (or multivoltage converter) that can be used whether the voltage is 110 or 220, all that's needed is the appropriate plug.

Videotape Unlike still-camera film, videotape is not damaged by X-rays. However, it may well be harmed by the magnetic field of a walk-through metal detector. Airport security personnel may want you to turn the camcorder on to prove that it is what you say it is, so make sure the battery is charged when you arrive at the airport. Note that although the United States, Canada, Japan, Korea, Taiwan, and other countries operate on the National Television System Committee video standard (NTSC), Russia and Ukraine use PAL/SECAM technology. So you will not be able to view your tapes through the local TV set or view movies bought there in your home VCR. Blank tapes bought abroad can be used for NTSC camcorder taping, however—although you'll probably find that they cost more there and wish you'd brought an adequate supply along.

Laptops Security X-rays do not generally harm hard-disk or floppy-disk storage though recently a number of travelers have claimed that the X-ray machine at the St. Petersburg airport wiped out the hard drive on their computers. Most airlines allow you to use your laptop aloft but request that you turn it off during takeoff and landing in order not to interfere with navigation equipment. Make sure the battery is charged when you arrive at the airport, because you may be asked to turn on the computer at security checkpoints to prove that it is what it appears to be. If you're a heavy computer user, consider traveling with a backup battery. For international travel, register your laptop with U.S. Customs as you leave the country, providing it's manufactured abroad (U.S.-origin items cannot be registered at U.S. Customs); when you do so, you'll get a certificate, good for as long as you own the item, containing your name and address, a description of the laptop, and its serial number, that will quash any questions that may arise on your return. If your laptop is U.S.-made, call the consulate of the country you'll be visiting to find out whether it should be registered with customs in that country upon arrival. Some travelers do this as a matter of course and ask customs officers to sign a document that specifies the total configuration of the system, computer and peripherals, and its value. In addition, before leaving home, find out about repair facilities at your destination, and don't forget any transformer or adapter plug you may need (*see* Electricity, *above*).

Language

Russian and Ukrainian are closely related East Slavic languages. Russian is still spoken widely in Ukraine, although its use has become a controversial political issue. With the rise of Ukrainian nationalism, Russian street signs are being replaced and public announcements are now recorded in Ukrainian. But if you speak Russian, you will have no problem getting by in Kiev. Both languages use the Cyrillic alphabet, which makes them particularly intimidating for English-speakers. If you make an effort to learn the Russian alphabet, you will be able to decipher many words; with just a rudimentary knowledge of the alphabet you will be able to navigate the streets and subways on your own. You may want to learn a few basic words in both languages, but don't expect to become conversant overnight. Hotel staff almost always speak good English, and the many restaurants and shops catering to foreigners are also staffed with English-speakers. Outside these places a good grasp of English is uncommon, though most people know at least a few words and phrases since they all took English in grade school. German is the second most common language in both countries.

Staying Healthy

The Russian and Ukrainian medical systems are far below world standards. Anyone visiting these countries runs the risk of encountering the horrors of their medical facilities, and individuals in frail health and those who suffer from a chronic medical condition should take this risk into careful consideration. You may want to purchase traveler's health insurance, which would cover medical evacuation. Sometimes even minor conditions cannot be treated adequately in-country due to the severe and chronic shortage of basic medicines and medical equipment.

These warnings aside, as long as you don't get sick, a visit to Russia or Ukraine poses no special health risk. The U.S. government affirms that the fallout from the 1986 Chernobyl nuclear accident no longer poses any risk to either short- or long-term visitors to Kiev. In all three cities most residents boil their drinking water, and visitors would be wise to do the same. The water supply in St. Petersburg is thought to contain an intestinal parasite called Giardia Lamblia, which causes diarrhea, stomach cramps, and nausea. The gestation period is two-three weeks, so that symptoms usually arise after the traveler has already returned home. The condition is easily treatable, but be sure to let your doctor know that you may have been exposed to this parasite. You should drink only boiled or bottled water in St. Petersburg. Avoid ice-cubes and use bottled water to brush your teeth. In Moscow and St. Petersburg imported, bottled water is freely available in hard-currency shops, but this is not always true in Kiev. You may want to consider bringing a small supply with you. Hotel floor attendants always have a samovar in their offices and will provide boiled water if asked. Food poisoning is common in Russia and Ukraine. Be wary of dairy products and ice cream that may not be fresh. The pirozhki (meat and cabbage-filled pies) sold everywhere on the streets are cheap and tasty, but they can give you a nasty stomach ache.

Finding a Doctor The **International Association for Medical Assistance to Travellers** (IAMAT, 417 Center St., Lewiston, NY 14092, tel. 716/754–4883; 40 Regal Rd., Guelph, Ontario N1K 1B5; 57 Voirets, 1212 Grand-Lancy, Geneva, Switzerland) publishes a worldwide directory of English-speaking physicians whose qualifications meet IAMAT standards and who have agreed to treat members for a set fee. Membership is free.

Assistance Companies Pretrip medical referrals, emergency evacuation or repatriation, 24-hour telephone hot lines for medical consultation, dispatch of medical personnel, relay of medical records, up-front cash for emergencies, and other personal and legal assistance are among the services provided by several membership organizations specializing in medical assistance to travelers. Among them are **International SOS Assistance** (Box 11568, Philadelphia, PA 19116, tel. 215/ 244–1500 or 800/523–8930; Box 466, Pl. Bonaventure, Montréal, Qué. H5A 1C1, tel. 514/874–7674 or 800/363– 0263), **Near Services** (450 Prairie Ave., Suite 101, Calumet City, IL 60409, tel. 708/868–6700 or 800/654–6700), and **Travel Assistance International** (1133 15th St. NW, Suite 400, Washington, DC 20005, tel. 202/331–1609 or 800/821– 2828), part of Europ Assistance Worldwide Services, Inc. Because these companies will also sell you death-and-dismemberment, trip-cancellation, and other insurance coverage, there is some overlap with the travel-insurance policies discussed below, which may include the services of an assistance company among the insurance options or reimburse travelers for such services without providing them.

Insurance

U.S. Residents Most tour operators, travel agents, and insurance agents sell specialized health-and-accident, flight, trip-cancellation, and luggage insurance as well as comprehensive policies with some or all of these features. But before you make any purchase, review your existing health and homeowner policies to find out whether they cover expenses incurred while traveling.

Health-and-Accident Insurance Supplemental health-and-accident insurance for travelers is usually a part of comprehensive policies. Specific policy provisions vary, but they tend to address three general areas, beginning with reimbursement for medical expenses caused by illness or an accident during a trip. Such policies may reimburse anywhere from $1,000 to $150,000 worth of medical expenses; dental benefits may also be included. A second common feature is the personal-accident, or death-and-dismemberment, provision, which pays a lump sum to your beneficiaries if you die or to you if you lose one or both limbs or your eyesight. This is similar to the flight insurance described below, although it is not necessarily limited to accidents involving airplanes or even other "common carriers" (buses, trains, and ships) and can be in effect 24 hours a day. The lump sum awarded can range from $15,000 to $500,000. A third area generally addressed by these policies is medical assistance (referrals, evacuation, or repatriation and other services). Some policies reimburse travelers for the cost of such services; others may automatically enroll you as a member of a particular medical-assistance company.

Flight Insurance This insurance, often bought as a last-minute impulse at the airport, pays a lump sum to a beneficiary when a plane crashes and the insured dies (and sometimes to a surviving passenger who loses eyesight or a limb); thus it supplements the airlines' own coverage as described in the limits-of-liability paragraphs on your ticket (up to $75,000 on international flights, $20,000 on domestic ones—and that is generally subject to litigation). Charging an airline ticket to a major credit card often automatically signs you up for flight insurance; in this case, the coverage may also embrace travel by bus, train, and ship.

Baggage Insurance In the event of loss, damage, or theft on international flights, airlines limit their liability to $20 per kilogram for checked baggage (roughly about $640 per 70-pound bag) and $400 per passenger for unchecked baggage. On domestic flights, the ceiling is $1,250 per passenger. Excess-valuation insurance can be bought directly from the airline at check-in but leaves your bags vulnerable on the ground.

Trip Insurance There are two sides to this coin. **Trip-cancellation-and-interruption insurance** protects you in the event you are unable to undertake or complete your trip. **Default** or **bankruptcy insurance** protects you against a supplier's failure to deliver. Consider the former if your airline ticket, cruise, or package tour does not allow changes or cancellations. The amount of coverage to buy should equal the cost of your trip should you, a traveling companion, or a family member get sick, forcing you to stay home, plus the nondiscounted one-way airline ticket you would need to buy if you had to return home early. Read the fine print carefully; pay attention to sections defining "family member" and "preexisting medical conditions." A characteristic quirk of default policies is that they often do not cover default by travel agencies or default by a tour operator, airline, or cruise line if you bought your tour and the coverage directly from the firm in question. To reduce your need for default insurance, give preference to tours packaged by members of the United States Tour Operators Association (USTOA), which maintains a fund to reimburse clients in the event of member defaults. Even better, pay for travel arrangements with a major credit card so that you can refuse to pay the bill if services have not been rendered—and let the card company fight your battles.

Comprehensive Policies Companies supplying comprehensive policies with some or all of the above features include **Access America, Inc.,** underwritten by BCS Insurance Company (Box 11188, Richmond, VA 23230, tel. 800/284–8300); **Carefree Travel Insurance,** underwritten by The Hartford (Box 310, 120 Mineola Blvd., Mineola, NY 11501, tel. 516/294–0220 or 800/323–3149); **Tele-Trip** (Mutual of Omaha Plaza, Box 31762, Omaha, NE 68131, tel. 800/228–9792), a subsidiary of Mutual of Omaha; **The Travelers Companies** (1 Tower Sq., Hartford, CT 06183, tel. 203/277–0111 or 800/243–3174); **Travel Guard International,** underwritten by Transamerica Occidental Life Companies (1145 Clark St., Stevens Point, WI 54481, tel. 715/345–0505 or 800/782–5151); and **Wallach and Company, Inc.** (107 W. Federal St., Box 480, Middleburg, VA 22117, tel. 703/687–3166 or 800/237–6615), underwritten by Lloyds of London. These companies may also offer the above types of insurance separately.

U.K. Residents Most tour operators, travel agents, and insurance agents sell specialized policies covering accident, medical expenses, personal liability, trip cancellation, and loss or theft of personal property. Some policies include coverage for delayed departure and legal expenses, accidents, or motoring abroad. You can also purchase an annual travel-insurance policy valid for every trip you make during the year in which it's purchased (usually only trips of less than 90 days). Before you leave, make sure you will be covered if you have a preexisting medical condition or are pregnant; your insurers may not pay for routine or continuing treatment, or may require a note from your doctor certifying your fitness to travel.

For advice by phone or for a free booklet, "Holiday Insurance," that sets out what to expect from a holiday-insurance policy and gives price guidelines, contact the **Association of British Insurers** (51 Gresham St., London EC2V 7HQ, tel. 071/600–3333; 30 Gordon St., Glasgow G1 3PU, tel. 041/226–3905; Scottish Provincial Bldg., Donegall Sq. W, Belfast BT1 6JE, tel. 0232/249176; call for other locations).

Car Rentals

Some major car-rental companies are represented in Moscow, including **Avis** (tel. 800/331–1084; in Canada, 800/879–2847), **Hertz** (tel. 800/654–3001; in Canada, 800/263–0600), and **National** (tel. 800/227–3876), known internationally as InterRent and Europcar. National also rents in St. Petersburg. In cities, unlimited-mileage rates range from about $79 per day for an economy car to $129 for a midsize car; weekly unlimited-mileage rates range from $336 to $847.

This does not include tax, which in Moscow is 14%–20%, depending on the rental agency.

Requirements An International Driver's Permit, available from the American or Canadian Automobile Association, is highly recommended.

Extra Charges Picking up the car in one city or country and leaving it in another may entail drop-off charges or one-way service fees, which can be substantial. The cost of a collision or loss-damage waiver (*see below*) can also be high. Automatic transmissions and air-conditioning are not universally available abroad; ask for them when you book if you want them, and check the cost before you commit yourself to the rental.

Cutting Costs If you know you will want a car for more than a day or two, you can save by planning ahead. Major international companies have programs that discount their standard rates by 15%–30% if you make the reservation before departure (anywhere from 2 to 14 days), rent for a minimum number of days (typically 3 or 4), and prepay the rental. Ask about these advance-purchase schemes when you call for information. Fares that come as part of fly/drive or other packages, even those as bare-bones as the rental plus an airline ticket (*see* Tours and Packages, *above*), may offer even more economical rentals.

Other sources of savings are the companies that operate as wholesalers—companies that do not own their own fleets but rent in bulk from those that do and offer advantageous rates to their customers. Rentals through such companies must be arranged and paid for before you leave the United States. Among them is **Auto Europe** (Box 1097, Camden, ME 04843, tel. 207/236–8235 or 800/223–5555; in Canada, 800/458–9503). Always ask whether the prices are guaranteed in U.S. dollars or foreign currency and if unlimited mileage is available. Find out about any required deposits, cancellation penalties, and drop-off charges, and confirm the cost of the collision-damage waiver.

One last tip: Remember to fill the tank when you return the vehicle to avoid being charged for refueling at what you'll swear is the most expensive pump in town.

Insurance and Collision-Damage Waiver The standard rental contract includes liability coverage (for damage to public property, injury to pedestrians, etc.) and coverage for the car against fire, theft (not included in certain countries), and collision-damage with a deductible—most commonly $2,000–$3,000, occasionally more. In the case of an accident, you are responsible for the deductible amount unless you've purchased the collision-damage waiver (CDW), which costs an average of $12 a day, although this varies depending on what kind of vehicle you've rented, where, and from whom.

Because this adds up quickly, you may be inclined to say "no thanks"—and that's certainly your prerogative, although the rental agent may not tell you so. Planning ahead will help you make the right decision. By all means, find out if your own insurance covers damage to a rental car while traveling (not simply a car to drive when yours is in for repairs). And check to see whether charging car rentals to any of your credit cards will get you a CDW at no charge. Before you decline, note that deductibles are occasionally so high that totaling a car would make you responsible for its full value.

Student and Youth Travel

Travel Agencies The foremost U.S. student travel agency is **Council Travel,** a subsidiary of the nonprofit Council on International Educational Exchange. It specializes in low-cost travel arrangements, is the exclusive U.S. agent for several discount cards, and, with its sister CIEE subsidiary, **Council Charter,** is a source of airfare bargains. The Council Charter brochure and CIEE's twice-yearly *Student Travels* magazine, which details its programs, are available at the Council Travel office at CIEE headquarters (205 E. 42nd Street, New York, NY 10017, tel. 212/661–1450) and at 37 branches in college towns nationwide (free in person, $1 by mail). The **Educational Travel Center** (ETC, 438 N. Francis St., Madison, WI 53703, tel. 608/256–5551) also offers low-cost rail passes, domestic and international airline tickets (mostly for flights departing from Chicago), and other budgetwise travel arrangements. Other travel agencies catering to students include **Travel Management International** (TMI, 18 Prescott St., Suite 4, Cambridge, MA 02138, tel. 617/661–8187) and **Travel Cuts** (187 College St., Toronto, Ont. M5T 1P7, tel. 416/979–2406).

Discount Cards For discounts on transportation and on museum and attractions admissions, buy the **International Student Identity Card** (ISIC) if you're a bona fide student or the **International Youth Card** (IYC) if you're under age 26. In the United States the ISIC and the IYC cards cost $15 each and include basic travel-accident and sickness coverage. Apply to **CIEE** (*see* address, *above*, tel. 212/661–1414; application is in *Student Travels*). In Canada the cards are available for $15 each from **Travel Cuts** (*see above*). In the United Kingdom they cost £5 and £4, respectively, at student unions and student travel companies, including Council Travel's London office (28A Poland St., London W1V 3DB, tel. 071/437–7767).

Hosteling An **International Youth Hostel Federation** (IYHF) membership card is the key to more than 5,300 hostel locations in 59 countries; the sex-segregated, dormitory-style sleeping quarters, including some for families, go for $7–$20 a night per person. Membership is available in the United States through **American Youth Hostels** (AYH, 733 15th St. NW,

Washington, DC 20005, tel. 202/783–6161), the American link in the worldwide chain, and costs $25 for adults 18–54, $10 for those under 18, $15 for those 55 and over, and $35 for families. Volume 1 of the two-volume *Guide to Budget Accommodation* lists hostels in Europe and the Mediterranean ($13.95, including postage). IYHF membership is available in Canada through the **Canadian Hostelling Association** (CHA, 1600 James Naismith Dr., Suite 608, Gloucester, Ont. K1B 5N4, tel. 613/748–5638) for $26.75 and in the United Kingdom through the **Youth Hostel Association of England and Wales** (Trevelyan House, 8 St. Stephen's Hill, St. Albans, Herts. AL1 2DY, tel. 0727/55215) for £9.

Traveling with Children

Tour Operators **GrandTravel** (6900 Wisconsin Ave., Suite 706, Chevy Chase, MD 20815, tel. 301/986–0790 or 800/247–7651) offers international and domestic tours for grandparents traveling with their grandchildren. The catalogue, as charmingly written and illustrated as a children's book, positively invites armchair traveling with lap-sitters aboard. **Families Welcome!** (21 W. Colony Pl., Suite 140, Durham, NC 27705, tel. 919/489–2555 or 800/326–0724) packages and sells family tours to Europe. **Rascals in Paradise** (650 5th St., Suite 505, San Francisco, CA 94107, tel. 415/978–9800 or 800/872–7225) specializes in programs for families.

Getting There On international flights, the fare for infants under 2 not oc-
Airfares cupying a seat is generally 10% of the accompanying adult's fare; children ages 2–11 usually pay half to two-thirds of the adult fare. On domestic flights, children under 2 not occupying a seat travel free, and older children currently travel on the "lowest applicable" adult fare.

Baggage In general, infants paying 10% of the adult fare are allowed one carry-on bag, not to exceed 70 pounds or 45 inches (length + width + height). The adult baggage allowance applies for children paying half or more of the adult fare. Check with the airline for particulars, especially regarding flights between two foreign destinations, where allowances for infants may be less generous than those above.

Safety Seats The FAA recommends the use of safety seats aloft and details approved models in the free leaflet **"Child/Infant Safety Seats Recommended for Use in Aircraft"** (available from the Federal Aviation Administration, APA–200, 800 Independence Ave. SW, Washington, DC 20591, tel. 202/267–3479). Airline policy varies. U.S. carriers must allow FAA-approved models, but because these seats are strapped into a regular passenger seat, they may require that parents buy a ticket even for an infant under 2 who would otherwise ride free. Foreign carriers may not allow infant seats, may charge the child's rather than the infant's fare for their use, or may require you to hold your baby during takeoff and landing, thus defeating the seat's purpose.

Facilities Aloft Airlines do provide other facilities and services for children, such as children's meals and freestanding bassinets (to those sitting in seats on the bulkhead, where there's enough legroom to accommodate them). Make your request when reserving. The annual February/March issue of *Family Travel Times* gives details of the children's services of dozens of airlines ($10; *see above*). "Kids and Teens in Flight" (free from the U.S. Department of Transportation, tel. 202/366–2220) offers tips for children flying alone.

Publications *Family Travel Times,* published 10 times a year by **Travel** *Newsletter* **with Your Children** (TWYCH, 45 W. 18th St., 7th Floor Tower, New York, NY 10011, tel. 212/206–0688; annual subscription $55), covers destinations, types of vacations, and modes of travel.

Books *Great Vacations with Your Kids,* by Dorothy Jordon and Marjorie Cohen ($13; Penguin USA, 120 Woodbine St., Bergenfield, NJ 07621, tel. 800/253–6476) and *Traveling with Children—And Enjoying It,* by Arlene K. Butler ($11.95 plus $3 shipping per book; Globe Pequot Press, Box 833, Old Saybrook, CT 06475, tel. 800/243–0495; in CT, 800/962–0973) help plan your trip with children, from toddlers to teens. *Innocents Abroad: Traveling with Kids in Europe,* by Valerie Wolf Deutsch and Laura Sutherland ($15.95 or $4.95 paperback, Penguin USA, *see above*), covers child- and teen-friendly activities, food, and transportation.

Hints for Travelers with Disabilities

Provisions for disabled travelers in Russia and Ukraine are extremely limited. Traveling with a nondisabled companion is probably the best solution. Some of the new, foreign-built hotels in Moscow offer wheelchair-accessible rooms, but beyond that special facilities at public buildings in all three cities are rare. Public transportation is especially difficult for the disabled traveler to maneuver.

Organizations Several organizations provide travel information for people *In the United* with disabilities, usually for a membership fee, and some *States* publish newsletters and bulletins. Among them are the **Information Center for Individuals with Disabilities** (Fort Point Pl., 27–43 Wormwood St., Boston, MA 02210, tel. 617/727–5540 or 800/462–5015 in MA between 11 and 4, or leave message; TDD/TTY tel. 617/345–9743); **Mobility International USA** (Box 3551, Eugene, OR 97403, voice and TDD tel. 503/343–1284), the U.S. branch of an international organization based in Britain (*see below*) and present in 30 countries; **MossRehab Hospital Travel Information Service** (1200 W. Tabor Rd., Philadelphia, PA 19141, tel. 215/456–9603, TDD tel. 215/456–9602); the **Society for the Advancement of Travel for the Handicapped** (SATH, 347 5th Ave.,

Suite 610, New York, NY 10016, tel. 212/447–7284, fax 212/
725–8253); the **Travel Industry and Disabled Exchange**
(TIDE, 5435 Donna Ave., Tarzana, CA 91356, tel. 818/368–
5648); and **Travelin' Talk** (Box 3534, Clarksville, TN 37043,
tel. 615/552–6670).

In the Main information sources include the **Royal Association for**
United Kingdom **Disability and Rehabilitation** (RADAR, 25 Mortimer St.,
London W1N 8AB, tel. 071/637–5400), which publishes
travel information for the disabled in Britain, and **Mobility
International** (228 Borough High St., London SE1 1JX, tel.
071/403–5688), the headquarters of an international membership organization that serves as a clearinghouse of travel information for people with disabilities.

Travel Agencies **Directions Unlimited** (720 N. Bedford Rd., Bedford Hills,
and Tour NY 10507, tel. 914/241–1700), a travel agency, has exper-
Operators tise in tours and cruises for the disabled. **Evergreen Travel
Service** (4114 198th St. SW, Suite 13, Lynnwood, WA 98036,
tel. 206/776–1184 or 800/435–2288) operates Wings on
Wheels Tours for those in wheelchairs, White Cane Tours
for the blind, tours for the deaf, and makes group and independent arrangements for travelers with any disability.
Flying Wheels Travel (143 W. Bridge St., Box 382,
Owatonna, MN 55060, tel. 800/535–6790; in MN, 800/722–
9351), a tour operator and travel agency, arranges international tours, cruises, and independent travel itineraries for
people with mobility disabilities. **Nautilus,** at the same address as TIDE (*see above*), packages tours for the disabled
internationally.

Publications In addition to the fact sheets, newsletters, and books mentioned above there are several free publications available
from the Consumer Information Center (Pueblo, CO
81009): "New Horizons for the Air Traveler with a Disability," a U.S. Department of Transportation booklet describ-
ing changes resulting from the 1986 Air Carrier Access Act
and those still to come from the 1990 Americans with Disabilities Act (include Department 608Y in the address); and
the Airport Operators Council's *Access Travel: Airports*
(Dept. 5804), which describes facilities and services for the
disabled at more than 500 airports worldwide.

Twin Peaks Press (Box 129, Vancouver, WA 98666, tel. 206/
694–2462 or 800/637–2256) publishes the *Directory of Travel Agencies for the Disabled* ($19.95), listing more than 370
agencies worldwide; *Travel for the Disabled* ($19.95), list-
ing some 500 access guides and accessible places worldwide; the *Directory of Accessible Van Rentals* ($9.95) for
campers and RV travelers worldwide; and *Wheelchair Vag-
abond* ($14.95), a collection of personal travel tips. Add $2
per book for shipping.

Hints for Older Travelers

Elderly travelers should consider the health risks involved in visiting Russia and Ukraine (*see* Staying Healthy, *above*).

Organizations The **American Association of Retired Persons** (AARP, 601 E St. NW, Washington, DC 20049, tel. 202/434–2277) provides independent travelers with the Purchase Privilege Program, which offers discounts on hotels, car rentals, and sightseeing, and arranges group tours, cruises, and apartment living through AARP Travel Experience from American Express (400 Pinnacle Way, Suite 450, Norcross, GA 30071, tel. 800/927–0111); these can be booked through travel agents, except for the cruises, which must be booked directly (tel. 800/745–4567). AARP membership is open to those 50 years of age and older; annual dues are $8 per person or couple.

Two other membership organizations offer discounts on lodgings, car rentals, and other travel products, along with such nontravel perks as magazines and newsletters. The **National Council of Senior Citizens** (1331 F St. NW, Washington, DC 20004, tel. 202/347–8800) is a nonprofit advocacy group with some 5,000 local clubs across the United States; membership costs $12 per person or couple annually. **Mature Outlook** (6001 N. Clark St., Chicago, IL 60660, tel. 800/336–6330), a Sears Roebuck & Co. subsidiary with 800,000 members, charges $9.95 for an annual membership.

Note: When using any senior-citizen identification card for reduced hotel rates, mention it when booking, not when checking out. At restaurants, show your card before you're seated; discounts may be limited to certain menus, days, or hours. If you are renting a car, ask about promotional rates that might improve on your senior-citizen discount.

Educational Travel **Elderhostel** (75 Federal St., 3rd floor, Boston, MA 02110, tel. 617/426–7788) is a nonprofit organization that has offered inexpensive study programs for people ages 60 and older since 1975. Programs take place at more than 1,800 educational institutions in the United States, Canada, and 45 countries overseas, and courses cover everything from marine science to Greek myths and cowboy poetry. Participants generally attend lectures in the morning and spend the afternoon sightseeing or on field trips; they live in dorms on the host campuses. Fees for two- to three-week international trips—including room, board, and transportation from the United States—range from $1,800 to $4,500.

Interhostel (University of New Hampshire, 6 Garrison Ave., Durham, NH 03824, tel. 800/733–9753), a slightly younger enterprise than Elderhostel, caters to a slightly younger clientele—that is, 50 and older—and runs programs overseas in some 25 countries. But the idea is similar: Lectures and field trips mix with sightseeing, and participants stay in dormitories at cooperating educational institutions or in modest hotels. Programs are usually two weeks in length and cost \$1,500–\$2,100, not including airfare from the United States.

Tour Operators **Saga International Holidays** (222 Berkeley St., Boston, MA 02116, tel. 800/343–0273), which specializes in group travel for people over 60, offers a selection of variously priced tours and cruises covering five continents. If you want to take your grandchildren, look into **GrandTravel** (*see* Traveling with Children, *above*).

Further Reading

Your trip to Russia and Ukraine will be greatly enhanced if you acquaint yourself with the long and interconnected histories of these two countries. Peter Neville's *A Traveller's History of Russia and the USSR* is an excellent source of historical information for the tourist. If you want more in-depth coverage, read Nicolas Riasanovsky's *A History of Russia*. Robert Massie's book *Peter the Great* is especially recommended for those traveling to St. Petersburg; it is an excellent read and is full of tantalizing historical information. Vasily Grossman's historical novel *Life and Fate* follows the lives of various people during the turbulent years of World War II. Though long, the book is a real page-turner. It was suppressed by the Soviet authorities for decades and Grossman, a war correspondent, died in 1964 thinking the last copy of his book had been destoyed by the KGB.

Arriving and Departing

From North America by Plane

Flights are either nonstop, direct, or connecting. A **nonstop** flight requires no change of plane and makes no stops. A **direct** flight stops at least once and can involve a change of plane, although the flight number remains the same; if the first leg is late, the second waits. This is not the case with a **connecting** flight, which involves a different plane and a different flight number.

Airports and Airlines Airlines serving Russian and Ukraine from the United States are **Aeroflot** (630 5th Avenue, New York, NY 10111, tel. 212/332–1050 or 800/995–5555), **Air France** (tel. 800/237–2747), **British Air** (tel. 800/247–9297), **Delta** (tel. 800/221–1212), **Finnair** (tel. 800/950–5000), **KLM** (tel. 800/777–5553), **Lufthansa** (tel. 800/645–3880), and **SAS** (tel. 800/221–2350).

Flying Time The flying time to Moscow from New York is 8½ hours; from Chicago, 10–11 hours; from Los Angeles, 12–13 hours.

Cutting Flight Costs The Sunday travel section of most newspapers is a good source of deals. When booking, particularly through an unfamiliar company, call the Better Business Bureau to find out whether any complaints have been registered against the company, pay with a credit card if you can, and consider trip-cancellation and default insurance (*see* Insurance, *above*).

Promotional Airfares All the less expensive fares, called promotional or discount fares, are round-trip and involve restrictions. The exact nature of the restrictions depends on the airline, the route, and the season and on whether travel is domestic or international, but generally you must buy the ticket—commonly called an APEX (advance-purchase excursion) when it's for international travel—in advance (7, 14, or 21 days are usual). You must also respect certain minimum- and maximum-stay requirements (for instance, over a Saturday night or at least 7 and no more than 30, 45, or 90 days), and you must be willing to pay penalties for changes. Airlines generally allow some changes for a fee. But the cheaper the fare, the more likely it is that the ticket is nonrefundable; it would take a death in the family for the airline to give you any of your money back if you had to cancel. The cheapest fares are also subject to availability; because only a certain percentage of the plane's total seats will be sold at that price, they may go quickly.

Consolidators Consolidators or bulk-fare operators—also known as bucket shops—buy blocks of seats on scheduled flights that airlines anticipate they won't be able to sell. They pay wholesale prices, add a markup, and resell the seats to travel agents or directly to the public at prices that still undercut the airline's promotional or discount fares. You pay more than you would on a charter but ordinarily less than for an APEX ticket, and, even when there is not much of a price difference, the ticket usually comes without the advance-purchase restriction. Moreover, although tickets are marked nonrefundable so you can't turn them in to the airline for a full-fare refund, some consolidators sometimes give you your money back. Carefully read the fine print detailing penalties for changes and cancellations. If you doubt the reliability of a company, call the airline once you've made your booking and confirm that you do, indeed, have a reservation on the flight.

The biggest U.S. consolidator, C.L. Thomson Express, sells only to travel agents. Well-established consolidators selling to the public include **UniTravel** (Box 12485, St. Louis, MO 63132, tel. 314/569–0900 or 800/325–2222); **Council Charter** (205 E. 42nd St., New York, NY 10017, tel. 212/661–0311 or 800/800–8222), a division of the Council on International Educational Exchange and a longtime charter operator now functioning more as a consolidator; and **Travac** (989 6th Ave., New York, NY 10018, tel. 212/563–3303 or 800/872–8800), also a former charterer.

Charter Flights Charters usually have the lowest fares and the most restrictions. Departures are limited and seldom on time, and you can lose all or most of your money if you cancel. (Generally, the closer to departure you cancel, the more you lose, although you may be charged only a small fee if you supply a substitute passenger.) The charterer, on the other hand, may legally cancel the flight for any reason up to 10 days before departure; within 10 days of departure, the flight may be canceled only if it becomes physically impossible to operate the plane. The charterer may also revise the itinerary or increase the price after you have bought the ticket, but if the new arrangement constitutes a "major change," you have the right to a refund. Before buying a charter ticket, read the fine print for the company's refund policy and details on major changes. Money for charter flights is usually paid into a bank escrow account, the name of which should be on the contract. If you don't pay by credit card, make your check payable to the escrow account (unless you're dealing with a travel agent, in which case, his or her check should be payable to the escrow account). The Department of Transportation's Consumer Affairs Office (I–25, Washington, DC 20590, tel. 202/366–2220) can answer questions on charters and send you its "Plane Talk: Public Charter Flights" information sheet.

Charter operators may offer flights alone or with ground arrangements that constitute a charter package. Well-established charter operators include **Council Charter** (205 E. 42nd St., New York, NY 10017, tel. 212/661–0311 or 800/800–8222), now largely a consolidator, despite its name, and **Travel Charter** (1120 E. Long Lake Rd., Troy, MI 48098, tel. 313/528–3500 or 800/521–5267), with Midwestern departures. **DER Tours** (Box 1606, Des Plains, IL 60017, tel. 800/782–2424), a charterer and consolidator, sells through travel agents.

Discount Travel Clubs Travel clubs offer their members unsold space on airplanes, cruise ships, and package tours at nearly the last minute and at well below the original cost. Suppliers thus receive some revenue for their "leftovers," and members get a bargain. Membership generally includes a regular bulletin or access to a toll-free telephone hot line giving details of available trips departing anywhere from three or four days to several months in the future. Packages tend to be more common than flights alone, so if airfares are your only interest, read the literature before joining. Reductions on hotels are also available. Clubs include **Discount Travel International** (114 Forrest Ave., Suite 203, Narberth, PA 19072, tel. 215/668–7184; $45 annually, single or family), **Moment's Notice** (425 Madison Ave., New York, NY 10017, tel. 212/486–0503; $45 annually, single or family), **Travelers Advantage** (CUC Travel Service, 49 Music Sq. W, Nashville, TN 37203, tel. 800/548–1116; $49 annually, single or family), and **Worldwide Discount Travel Club** (1674 Meridian Ave., Miami Beach, FL 33139, tel. 305/534–2082; $50 annually for family, $40 single).

Enjoying the Flight Fly at night if you're able to sleep on a plane. Because the air aloft is dry, drink plenty of beverages while on board; remember that drinking alcohol contributes to jet lag, as do heavy meals. Sleepers usually prefer window seats to curl up against; restless passengers ask to be on the aisle. Bulkhead seats, in the front row of each cabin, have more legroom, but since there's no seat ahead, trays attach awkwardly to the arms of your seat, and you must stow all possessions overhead. Bulkhead seats are usually reserved for the disabled, the elderly, and those who are traveling with babies.

Smoking Since February 1990, smoking has been banned on all domestic flights of less than six hours' duration; the ban also applies to domestic segments of international flights aboard U.S. and foreign carriers. On U.S. carriers flying to Russia and other destinations abroad, a seat in a no-smoking section must be provided for every passenger who requests one, and the section must be enlarged to accommodate such passengers if necessary as long as they have complied with the airline's deadline for check-in and seat assignment. If smoking bothers you, request a seat far from the smoking section.

Foreign airlines are exempt from these rules but do provide no-smoking sections, and some nations, including Canada as of July 1, 1993, have gone as far as to ban smoking on all domestic flights; other countries may ban smoking on flights of less than a specified duration. The International Civil Aviation Organization has set July 1, 1996, as the date to ban smoking aboard airlines worldwide, but the body has no power to enforce its decisions.

Staying in Russia and Ukraine

Getting Around

By Plane The airline industry in the former Soviet Union is in a state of flux bordering on chaos. Aeroflot, once the Soviet Union's only airline, is still the leading carrier within Russia and the CIS, but much of its fleet has been nationalized by the various republics. Russia has inherited Aeroflot, while the new republican airlines sport such names as Air Ukraine and Air Uzbekistan. They all offer the same outdated aircraft and abominable service for which Aeroflot is famous.

Since the collapse of the Soviet Union, many routes have been abandoned, smaller airports have been closed permanently, and the scheduled flights that remain are often canceled due to fuel shortages. Because of unpredictable service, many tour operators are now chartering flights for their groups. Seasoned business travelers frequently choose to fly circuitous routes on international carriers (i.e., Moscow–Helsinki–Kiev), which often proves faster and certainly more reliable than flying direct on Aeroflot.

If you are flying as an independent traveler within the CIS, purchase your ticket in hard currency before you leave home. Foreigners are not allowed to fly on tickets purchased in rubles; hard-currency tickets are available in-country, but purchasing one is often a long and frustrating endeavor. Be forewarned that delays and outright cancellations are common, and you should reconfirm your booking in person as soon as you arrive in the country. On the day of your departure, get to the airport early to avoid being bumped. Bring some snacks and beverages with you—after a meal on Aeroflot, Western airline food will seem gourmet. On flights shorter than four hours the only refreshment served is vile-tasting mineral water. Planes are usually boarded with no regard for assigned seats; passengers either take a bus or walk en masse across the runway to their waiting plane and then push and shove their way aboard. If you are traveling with a group of foreign tourists, you may be granted the courtesy of boarding ahead of the Russian passengers. If you are traveling independently, it is likely that you will be completely ignored and left to your own defenses. If you encounter any difficulties, assert your rights and make it clear to everyone that you paid for your ticket in hard currency.

The rules regulating carry-on luggage are strict but often disregarded. Pack as much as you can in your carry-on, including all of your valuables, since checked luggage is frequently lost and/or pilfered. Many airports have a special section set aside for foreign travelers, a holdover from the days when foreigners received preferential treatment by Soviet authorities. These sections are usually more comfortable and often have a hard-currency shop or café where you can buy snacks and refreshments.

By Train Train travel is by far the most convenient and reliable mode of transportation in Russia and Ukraine. Remarkably, most trains leave exactly on time; there is a broadcast warning five minutes before departure, but no whistle or "all aboard!" call, so be careful not to be left behind. There are four classes. The highest class, "deluxe," is usually only available on trains traveling international routes. The deluxe class offers two-berth compartments with soft seats and private washrooms; the other classes have washrooms at the end of the cars. The first-class service is called "soft-seat," with spring-cushioned berths; there are two berths in each compartment. There is no segregation of the sexes and no matter what class of service you choose, chances are good that you will find yourself sharing a compartment with someone of the opposite sex. The second, or "hard-seat," class has a cushion on wooden berths, with four berths to a compartment. The third class—wooden berths without compartments—is rarely sold to foreigners unless specifically requested. Most compartments have a small table, limited room for baggage (including under the seats) and a radio that can be turned down, but not off. In soft class there is also a table lamp. The price of the ticket may or may not include use of bedding; sometimes this fee (which increases daily with the inflation rate) is collected by the conductor.

All the cars are also equipped with samovars. Back in the days of communism, the conductor would offer tea to passengers before bedtime. These days the train is often out of tea and sometimes even out of water, so bring your own snacks and beverages. Most conductors run their own small businesses selling champagne and caviar, so don't be surprised if you're approached with such an offer. The communal bathrooms located at both ends of each car are notoriously dirty, so bring premoistened cleansing tissues for washing up and water for brushing your teeth. Definitely pack toilet paper. Also be sure to pack a heavy sweater. The cars are often overheated and toasty warm, but sometimes they are not heated at all, so in winter it can get very cold.

There are numerous day and overnight trains between St. Petersburg and Moscow and between Moscow and Kiev. There is also train service between Kiev and St. Petersburg, but the trip is a long one (over 30 hours). The past few years have witnessed increased crime on the overnight trains; the safest option for travel between Moscow and St. Petersburg is the high-speed day-train *Avrora*, which makes the trip in just under six hours. If you are traveling alone on an overnight train, you should take extra security precautions. The doors to the compartments can be locked, but the locks can be picked, so you might consider bringing a bicycle chain. You may also want to buy out the entire compartment so as not to risk your luck with unknown compartment-mates.

Train travel in Russia may be primitive by Western standards, but it offers an unrivaled opportunity to glimpse the quaint Russian countryside, which is dotted in places with colorful wooden cottages. If you are traveling by overnight train, be sure to set your alarm and get up an hour or so before arrival so that you can watch at close hand the peasants going about their morning rounds in the rural areas just outside the cities.

Purchasing a domestic train ticket outside the CIS can be difficult, but tickets are easily purchased within the country. Tickets go on sale 10 days prior to departure. As of fall 1993, train tickets sold to foreigners for travel within Russia must be paid for with foreign currency. This is now being strictly enforced. A one-way ticket between Moscow and St. Petersburg on an overnight train now costs just under $25.

By Car Traveling by car in the former Soviet Union is only for those who prefer a challenging adventure over comfort and safety. Even the main highways are potholed and in poor condition. Repair stations are few and far between, and there is a severe shortage of gasoline. In addition, you should not underestimate the risk of crime; highway robbery and car theft are on the rise, and foreign drivers are number-one targets. Russian drivers routinely remove their window blades, side mirrors, and anything else removable when parking their car for the evening, since theft of these items is common. Also, you should never leave anything of value inside your car.

Requirements Tourists driving in Russia or Ukraine will need an international driver's license and an international certificate of registration of the car in the country of departure. You will also need a certificate of obligation promising to take the car out of the country, to be registered with customs at the point of entry.

Rules of the Road Driving regulations are strict, but they are often broken by local drivers; a good rule of thumb is to drive defensively. Traffic keeps to the right. The speed limit on highways is 90 kph (56 mph); in towns and populated areas it is 60 kph (37 mph), although on the wide streets of Moscow few people observe this rule. You can proceed at traffic lights only when the light is green—this includes left and right turns. You must wait for a signal—an arrow—permitting the turn, and give way to pedestrians crossing. Wearing front seatbelts is compulsory; driving while intoxicated carries very heavy fines, including imprisonment. Do not consume any alcohol at all if you plan to drive. You should also keep your car clean—drivers can be fined for having a dirty car.

Insurance Insurance is required of foreign motorists. As many foreign insurance companies are unwilling to insure cars touring Russia and Ukraine, or will charge very high premiums, you may wish to insure with the Russian firm **Ingosstrakh** (12 Pyatniskaya ulitsa, Moscow, tel. 095/231–1677, fax 095/230–2518, telex 411144).

Police Traffic control in Russia and Ukraine is exercised by traffic inspectors (GAI) who are stationed at permanent posts; they also patrol in cars and on motorcycles. They may stop you for no apparent reason other than simply to check your documentation. Information on rules and road conditions can be obtained from them; they will also supply directions to motels, campsites, restaurants, and filling and service stations.

Gasoline and Repairs The gasoline shortage in Russia, and especially in Ukraine, is severe. You should fill up at every opportunity. In rubles, gasoline is very inexpensive, but you will have to wait in long lines; often drivers line up hours before an expected delivery of gasoline. In all three cities you can find foreign-currency gasoline stations, where lines are much shorter, but even these are not immune to the local shortages. It's also difficult to find unleaded gasoline. Finally, since repair stations are few and poorly stocked, tourists are advised to bring a complete set of tools, a towing cable, a pressure gauge, a pump, a spare wheel, a repair outfit for tubeless tires, a good jack and one or two tire levers, gasoline can, a spare fan belt, spare window-screen blades, and spark plugs. You should also have a set of lamp bulbs and fuses, a set of contact-breaker points for the ignition distributor, a spare condenser, a box of tire valve interiors, and a roll of insulating tape.

Telephones

Local Calls At present, most coin-operated telephones in Moscow take the new one-ruble coin (as opposed to the old Soviet version) or special tokens. (The tokens, available at kiosks, currently cost about 10 rubles, but the price is likely to rise.) A sign above the telephone indicates whether it takes coins (*monety*) or tokens (*zhetony*). In St. Petersburg, public telephones take subway tokens. In both cities, however, you may still find public phones that operate on 15-kopeck coins; these coins are no longer in general circulation, but are sometimes found on sale at kiosks. In Ukraine, where rubles in general are no longer in circulation, public telephones work without any coin at all. This situation is likely to change, however, as soon as the Ukrainian government introduces a bona fide Ukrainian currency complete with metal coins.

International Calls Most hotels offer satellite telephone booths where for several dollars a minute you can make an international call in a matter of seconds. If you want to economize, you can visit the main post office and order a call for rubles (sometimes there is a wait of up to 3 days). The per-minute rate increases frequently to keep pace with inflation but in recent years has never exceeded more than a dollar a minute. From your hotel room or from a private residence, you can dial direct. To place your call, dial 8, wait for the dial tone, then dial the country code (for the United States, 101) followed by the number you are trying to reach. In the new joint-venture hotels, rooms are often equipped with international, direct-dial (via satellite) telephones, but beware that the rates are hefty.

Mail

Postal Rates Postal rates increase at nearly the same rapid pace as inflation, but again the advantageous exchange rate vis-à-vis the dollar keeps rates low for foreigners. You can buy international envelopes and postcards at post-offices and in hotel-lobby kiosks. Beware that the postal system in the former Soviet Union is notoriously inefficient and mail is often lost. DHL and Federal Express have offices in Moscow and St. Petersburg if you need to send something important back home. Postcards generally have a better chance of reaching their destination than letters.

Receiving Mail Mail from outside the CIS takes approximately four weeks to arrive, sometimes longer, and sometimes it never arrives at all. If you absolutely must receive something from home during your trip, consider using an express-mail service, such as DHL or Federal Express.

Tipping

In the postcommunist era, tipping is rapidly becoming an accepted practice, so when in doubt, tip. Cloak-room attendants, waiters, porters and taxi drivers will all expect a tip, preferably in foreign currency. Add an extra 10% to 15% to a restaurant bill or taxi fare. Some restaurants are now adding a service charge to the bill automatically, so double-check before you leave a big tip. If you're paying by credit card, leave the tip in cash—the waiter will never see it if you add it to the credit-card charge.

Opening and Closing Times

State banks are usually open 9:30–1, and the many new private banks are normally open 10–6. Private exchange offices and those in hotels are usually open 9–6 daily, with an hour break for lunch between 1 and 3 PM. Museums keep varying hours; many are closed on Mondays and Tuesdays. Last entry is usually an hour before closing time, and museums often close an hour earlier the day before their closed day. Stores likewise keep varying hours, with grocery stores normally opening at 8 or 9 AM and department stores opening at 11 AM. Closing times also vary; stores are rarely open past 8 or 9 PM. Many shops are closed on Sundays, and almost every store closes for an hour at lunchtime between 1 and 3 PM. Restaurants usually open around noon and often close by midnight, although many are staying open later these days. Many restaurants, especially those that are state-run, close for a "dinner" break somewhere between 4 and 6 PM.

Public Holidays

January 1 and 2, January 7 (Russian Orthodox Christmas), February 23 (Soviet Army Day), March 8 (International Women's Day), May 1 (Formerly International Labor Day, which in recent years has turned into a celebration of spring), May 9 (Victory Day), June 12 (Russian Independence Day), November 7 and 8 (Anniversary of the Bolshevik Revolution, which may or may not continue to be observed).

Shopping

The shopping scene in the former Soviet Union has exploded in recent years, and you may come away with the impression that the entire place is just one big flea market. Shopping opportunities abound, but Russia and Ukraine are far from being a shopper's paradise; the goods for sale in the makeshift kiosks crowding the city streets and subways are often of little interest to the tourist. You'll find the best buys and higher quality goods in art salons, souvenir shops and hard-currency stores. The last is a special type of store catering to the Russian nouveau riche and the growing foreign community; such stores do not accept rubles or Ukrainian coupons but only foreign, or "hard," currency. The foreign tourist may find these stores a boon, as they stock imported goods and hard-to-find Russian products.

The hard-currency stores are mostly self-service, but in large department and grocery stores you may have to line up three times to make a purchase—first at the counter to pick out what you want and collect a ticket for the item, then at the cashier's to pay and get the ticket stamped, and then again at the counter to collect your purchase. In Russia the most popular souvenir is the matryoshka, a set of wooden nesting dolls that come in various shapes and sizes; "political" Matryoshkas with portraits of Soviet, Russian, and even American political leaders are particularly popular. Other gift items to look for are colorful scarves, silver-gilt and enamelware, amber, khokhloma (lacquered wood), clay figurines from Kymkovo, and black lacquered, papier-mâché boxes, commonly referred to as Palekh boxes, after the town in which the art form originated. Genuine Palekh boxes are very expensive, and the ones that are sold on the streets at greatly reduced prices are mostly imitations made of wood instead of papier-mâché. Samovars and fur hats are also popular with foreign tourists, but if you buy these items for rubles, you may have to pay an export fee at the border. The blue-and-white porcelain from the town of Gzhel is another good buy, but again be wary of imitations sold on the streets. St. Petersburg's famous porcelain factory produces beautiful, brightly painted cups and saucers that can still be found in ruble stores at very reasonable prices. Russian watches (Raketa brand and military watches) are also fun buys. Music-lovers should check out the "Melodiya" record shops; recordings of great Russian artists made in the Soviet era are now being rereleased on compact discs, which are often available at very reasonable prices.

Sports and Outdoor Activities

Skiing and hunting packages to Moscow and St. Petersburg are available, some through Intour Service. Cross-country skiing is a particularly popular sport in Russia and

Ukraine, and all three cities have acres of wooded parkland perfect for cross-country skiing. Outdoor skating rinks also abound, and there are downhill skiing facilities just outside of Moscow. Rentals of skis and skates are only available sporadically, so you should bring your own equipment or make prior arrangements for rentals. If you plan to go hunting, you may bring your own hunting gun provided you carry a voucher issued by an accredited travel agent attesting to the fact that you intend to hunt. All sporting rifles must be presented for customs inspection and the serial numbers declared on the customs form.

Dining

The dining scene in all three cities has changed dramatically in the past few years. In terms of sheer number and types of restaurants, Moscow is far ahead of St. Petersburg and Kiev, but in all three cities you'll find a variety of cuisines and price ranges.

If you are traveling on an organized tour, you can expect your hotel meals to be hearty and ample but far from gourmet. Breakfast is often a familiar omelet or fried eggs, but don't be surprised if the meal includes cabbage salad, fish, or hot dogs (served with cold peas), which are all standard breakfast fare. If you depend on coffee to wake you up in the morning, bring a small jar of instant coffee with you; sometimes only tea is available in the morning and sometimes hotel restaurants use "coffee-flavored drink" instead of genuine coffee. The main meal of the day is served in mid afternoon and usually consists of a starter, soup, and a main course. Supper is traditionally a lighter meal, with just an appetizer and a main course. The main course will be either meat or fish; the fish you are most likely to be served are sturgeon, halibut, or herring. A favorite meat dish is beef Stroganoff, beef stewed in sour cream and served with mushrooms and fried potatoes. The soup is likely to be borscht, a beetroot soup, or *shchi*, cabbage soup. Other national dishes include piroshki, fried rolls filled with cabbage or meat, and blini, small, light pancakes rolled and filled with caviar, fish, melted butter, jam, or sour cream.

In Ukraine, you may be lucky enough to be served a well-cooked Chicken Kiev—fried chicken breast filled with melted butter that shoots forth when you pierce the chicken with your fork. Another Ukrainian specialty is *vareniky*, sweet dumplings filled with fruit or cheese.

When you tire of the traditional hotel cuisine, you can explore the many new private restaurants and joint-venture establishments that have recently opened in all three cities. Keep in mind that a restaurant meal requires advanced planning; even if the restaurant is half-empty, you may be refused a table if you don't have a reservation. Set aside an entire evening for your restaurant meal; Russians and

Ukrainians consider dining out to be a form of entertainment, and table turnover is virtually an unknown concept.

The two most typical drinks in both countries are tea and vodka. Tea is usually served black in a tall glass with metal holders. You may be given a small dish of fruit jam to mix in by the spoonful instead of sugar. Vodka is often flavored and colored with herbs and spices. *Limonnaya*, lemon-flavored vodka, is particularly popular with American tourists, as is *Pertsovka*, pepper-flavored vodka. Other varieties include *starka* (a dark, smooth "old" vodka), *pshenichnaya* (made from wheat), *ryabinovka*, in which ashberries have been steeped, and *tminaya* (caraway-flavored vodka). Be wary of the *krepkaya* vodka, which at 110 proof is the strongest variety. In Ukraine, try *khorilka s pertsem* (with hot peppers).

Drinks are normally ordered by grams (100 or 200) or by the bottle. An average bottle holds about three-quarters of a liter. In foreign-run establishments you will often find an impressive wine list with imported wine and foreign liquors, but the state-run restaurants and smaller cooperatives usually have only vodka and wine available. Georgian wine is excellent, although supplies have become limited (distribution has been disrupted by the ongoing ethnic strife in that country).

Getting a quick snack on the go is not an easy feat in any of the cities and is particularly difficult in Kiev. State-run cafés and *stolovayas* (cafeterias) abound, but the quality of the food and service often leaves a lot to be desired. If you're sightseeing on your own, you'd be smart to plan your day around the place where you'll have lunch. If you find yourself suddenly suffering from hunger pangs in the middle of the day, you can always stop by a *khleb* store (bakery). Russia and Ukraine are famous for their delicious bread, which makes an inexpensive and filling snack.

Lodging

Detailed information about the hotels available in each city can be found in the chapter on each individual city. In most instances you can book reservations (and request visa support for your Russian visa) directly with the hotel (in the past, all hotel reservations had to be made through Intourist, the official state tourist agency of the Soviet Union). But it is difficult to communicate with the CIS. In addition to the language barrier, placing a call to Russia or Ukraine can be extremely time-consuming. International telephone lines are often overloaded and once you get through, you may find that no one answers the phone. You will probably have an easier time making hotel reservations through a travel agent. Easiest of all, and by far the least expensive route, is to book a spot with an organized tour.

Until the early 1990s, hotels catering to foreign tourists were controlled by Intourist and Sputnik, a branch of the Komsomol specializing in youth tourism. Most of the hotels built and owned by Intourist and Sputnik are now operating as independent establishments, but capitalism is catching on slowly, and service and accommodations have improved only slightly. If you are traveling with an organized tour, you will probably land in one of the old Intourist hotels, most of which are bleak, modern high rises. Accommodations at these hotels are adequate but far from luxurious. Standard items found in most Western hotels, such as soap, shampoo, and even sink stoppers, are rarely provided. Rooms usually come with telephone and televisions, but don't expect room service or in-room movies. The hot-water supply may be interrupted, a problem that occurs most frequently in summer. Many hotels still have key attendants on each floor to whom you are supposed to relinquish your room key every time you leave the hotel. Since only one key is given out for a double room, you may find this a convenient system. But the key attendant often leaves the key unattended (in an open box on the desk in front of the stairwell), so if you can coordinate your schedule with your roommate, you're better off "attending" to the key yourself. The key attendants—usually rather stern elderly women—can be quite friendly and helpful, however. They can provide extra blankets or help get a leaky faucet fixed. They almost always have a samovar in their office and will provide hot water for tea or coffee.

Hostels Accommodations at Sputnik hotels, the Soviet Union's answer to youth hostels, vary tremendously but are often just as good as the more expensive Intourist hotels. Rooms are usually doubles or triples with only the basic necessities provided (bath and bed but little else). Sputnik hotels are most commonly found on the city outskirts.

Home Stays Visa restrictions make it virtually impossible for Western tourists to make their own arrangements to stay in a private home. In order to obtain a Russian visa, you must first have a confirmed hotel reservation or an official invitation from a Russian organization. But if you're interested in a more native experience, home-stay options are now available as part of package tours. If you opt for a home stay, ask lots of questions. How are the families chosen and screened? What are the living conditions? Will you have your own room? Do your hosts speak English? If you book a tour through a travel agency, the Russian visa should be included as part of the package.

Credit Cards

The following abbreviations have been used: AE, American Express; D, Discover; DC, Diners Club; MC, MasterCard; V, Visa.

2 Moscow

By Juliette
Shapland, with
contributions from
Katherine Semler
and Sam Lardner

It is difficult for Westerners to comprehend what an important place Moscow holds in the Russian imagination as a symbol of spiritual and political power. Through much of its history the city was known as Holy Moscow and was regarded by Russians as a place of pilgrimage not unlike Jerusalem, Mecca, or Rome. Founded more than 850 years ago as the center of one of several competing minor principalities, Moscow eventually emerged as the center of a unified Russian state in the 15th century. One hundred years later it had grown into the capital of a strong and prosperous state, one of the largest in the world. Although civil war and Polish invasion ravaged the city in the early 17th century, a new era of stability and development began with the establishment of the Romanov dynasty in 1613.

The true test for Moscow came under Peter the Great. Greatly influenced by his exposure to the West, Peter deliberately turned his back on the old traditions of Moscow, establishing his own new capital—St. Petersburg—on the shores of the Baltic Sea. Yet Western-looking St. Petersburg never replaced Moscow as the heart and soul of the Russian nation. Moscow continued to thrive as an economic and cultural center, despite its demotion. More than 200 years later, within a year of the Bolshevik revolution in 1917, the young Soviet government restored Moscow's status as the nation's capital. In a move just as deliberate as Peter the Great's, the new communist rulers transferred their government back to the Russian heartland, away from the besieged frontier and away from Russia's imperial past.

Moscow thus became the political and ideological center of the vast Soviet empire. And even though that empire has now crumbled, the city retains its importance as a political, industrial, and cultural capital. The ancient Russian predilection for central authority was strengthened under the Soviet regime, and Moscow was reaffirmed as the locus of that authority. No one today challenges Moscow's status as capital of Russia or as the effective if not official center of that loosely defined political formation known as the Commonwealth of Independent States. With a population of more than 9 million, Moscow is Russia's largest city and the most popular place of residence in the country. It is still home to the country's most renowned theaters, film studios, and cultural institutions. It is still the country's most important transportation hub (even today most flights to the former Soviet republics are routed through Moscow's airports). And it is still the locus of the continuing power struggles in the Russian government.

During the Soviet years, when all things foreign were regarded with deep suspicion, Moscow was the embodiment of the extreme isolationism of the Russian communist regime. Sweeping political changes in the past few years have dramatically changed attitudes toward outsiders. Desperate to salvage its failing economy, the Russian government is actively pursuing foreign investments and is even turning to foreign governments for economic assistance and advice.

Nowhere in Russia are the dramatic contrasts of this new era more evident than in Moscow. Pedestals that formerly supported Soviet heroes stand empty on street corners and plazas, waiting for new heroes to step up or for old ones to be reinstated. Numerous churches destroyed, abandoned, or closed in the Soviet era are now being lovingly refurbished or rebuilt. Neon advertisements shine from the rooftops of Stalinist-era socialist-realist buildings. Gleaming new hotels built by Western firms stand next to dilapidated buildings hidden behind rickety scaffolding. The city's streets and squares bustle with activity. Soviet consumers have abandoned the old state department stores for endless rows of makeshift wood kiosks on the streets, which offer an eclectic array of products that were unavailable during the Soviet years. Some sections of the city have been transformed into virtual 24-hour flea markets. This lively street life vividly reflects the commotion and excitement (as well as the pain and trauma) involved in the ongoing struggle to move from a system of centralized control and five-year plans to democracy and a more fluid free-market system.

Essential Information

Important Addresses and Numbers

Tourist Information
Moscow does not have a tourist information center. To fill the void, the service bureaus of all the major hotels offer their guests (and anyone else willing to pay their fees) a wide variety of tourist services, including help in booking group or individual excursions, making a restaurant reservation, or purchasing theater or ballet tickets. For the latest on what's happening in Moscow, there are two English-language newspapers—*Moscow Times* and *Moscow Tribune.* The quarterly magazine *Moscow Guide* is also an excellent source of information on restaurants, art galleries, and museum exhibits.

Embassies
United States (19/23 Novinsky Bulvar, tel. 095/252–2451 or 095/252–2459), **Canada** (23 Starokonyushenny Pereulok, tel. 095/241–5882 or 095/241–5070), and **United Kingdom** (14 Naberezhnaya Morisa Toreza, tel. 095/231–8511).

There is often a long line of visa applicants snaking around the entrance to the U.S. embassy. If you need to visit the embassy, be aware that you do not need to stand in this line; just walk to the front and show the guard your passport, and he will let you by.

Emergencies
Police (tel. 02), **ambulance** (tel. 03). You will probably want to ask the assistance of a hotel staff member before trying

to place an emergency call, since few telephone operators speak English.

Hospitals and Clinics With any luck, you won't ever have to experience the horrors of the Russian medical system. It is plagued by a lack of medicines, low hygiene standards, and shortages of disposable needles and basic medical equipment. If you are simply feeling under the weather and the situation is not urgent, you may be best off not contacting a doctor at all. If you think you are seriously ill, try to contact one of the following Western establishments now open in Moscow. They all require payment in hard currency.

The American Medical Service (3 Shmitovsky Proyezd, tel. 095/256–8212 or 095/256–8378) provides a full range of diagnostic services and has a pharmacy with Western medicines. It has a doctor on call 24 hours a day and can help arrange evacuation out of the country. **The European Medical Center** (3 Gruzinsky Pereulok, tel. 095/253–0703) has French-speaking staff and also provides 24-hour emergency service. **The Sana Medical Center** (65 Nizhnaya Pervomaiskaya, tel. 095/464–1254 or 095/464–2563) is a French-Russian joint venture offering a wide range of medical services, by appointment only. It is open weekdays 10–5.

Foreign tourists are usually hospitalized in the **Botkin Hospital** (5 Vtoroi Botkinsky Proyezd, tel. 095/945–0033).

Dentists Russian dental facilities are as grim as other medical facilities, so be sure to complete any pending dental work at home prior to your departure. In an emergency, you are probably best off contacting one of the new foreign joint ventures. The **American Medical Service** (*see above*) also provides dental care. **Medical Interline** (3 ul. Tverskaya, room 2030, tel. 095/203–9533 or 095/203–8631), a Russian-Swiss joint venture located in the Intourist Hotel, has a multilingual staff and Western dental equipment.

Where to Change Money All the major hotels have exchange bureaus where you can change your dollars for rubles. In addition, you will find unofficial, fly-by-night exchange bureaus all over the city, but these are best avoided, since your chances of getting shortchanged are high. It is becoming increasingly difficult to exchange traveler's checks for rubles, and almost impossible to cash them for dollars. At press time (fall 1993), the **Dialog Bank** in the Slavyanskaya Hotel (2 Berezhkovskaya Naberezhnaya, first floor, tel. 095/941–8434) was still accepting traveler's checks for rubles. The **American Express Office** (*see* Travel Agencies, *below*) will cash American Express traveler's checks for rubles and, if it has cash available, for dollars. You can also obtain dollars by writing the office a personal check and having the exchange charged to your American Express card.

English-Language Bookstores Moscow's newest English-language bookstore is **Zwemmers** (18 Kuznetsky Most). Russia's largest bookstore, **Dom**

Knigi (The Book House, 26 Novy Arbat, tel. 095/290–4507), has an English-language section, but lately the selection has been better on the front-door steps, where individual sellers spread out their wares. The bookstore on the first floor of the **Kosmos Hotel** (150 Prospekt Mira) has a good selection of maps, postcards, and English-language guide-books to Moscow and the surrounding region.

You can pick up copies of the newspapers *Moscow Times* and *Moscow Tribune* as well as the quarterly *Moscow Guide* in just about any hard-currency store.

Late-Night Pharmacies are generally open only until 8 or 9 PM, and most
Pharmacies do not carry Western-brand medicines. For prescription re-fills, you'll have the best luck contacting one of the foreign joint-venture pharmacies. The **American Medical Service** (*see above*) has a well-stocked pharmacy and a doctor on call 24 hours a day. You could also try **Unipharm** (13 Skatertny Pereulok, tel. 095/202–5071) or the conveniently located **Farmakon** (4 ul. Tverskaya, tel. 095/292–0843).

Travel Agencies **American Express** (21-A Sadovaya-Kudrinskaya, tel. 095/254–4305 or 095/254–4495; open weekdays 10–1 and 2–5) offers assistance in making international travel arrange-ments. It will also replace your lost traveler's checks and credit cards, or issue you a cash advance against your credit card, provided you can write a personal check. The office recently installed an ATM machine for its card holders; there is a 5% commission on its use.

Barry Martin Travel (Mezhdunarodnaya Hotel, room 940, tel. 095/253–2940) provides assistance to both international and domestic travelers. For domestic itineraries only, there is always **IntourService** (4 ul. Belinskovo, tel. 095/203–8954 or 095/202–9975), a successor to Intourist, the tourist agency that monopolized the entire tourist industry in the former Soviet Union. IntourService provides many of the same services that Intourist did, primarily helping for-eigners book hotel accommodations and obtain train and plane tickets.

Arriving and Departing by Plane

Airports and As the single most important transportation hub in the
Airlines CIS, Moscow has several airports. Most international flights arrive at **Sheremetyevo II** (tel. 095/578–9101), which currently handles an estimated 15,000 passengers daily. One of the most modern in Russia, Sheremetyevo II was built in 1979, when there was much less international traf-fic; these days it is just barely coping with the current traf-fic. Expect long lines at customs and at the baggage carousel. When you walk through the single exit out of cus-toms, you will be greeted by mobs of Russians awaiting ar-riving passengers and eager gypsy cab drivers shouting *"Taksi! Taksi!"*

In addition to its international airport, the city has four domestic terminals. **Sheremetyevo I** (tel. 095/578–5973 or 095/507–5614), some 30 kilometers (19 miles) northwest of the city center, services domestic flights to St. Petersburg and the former Baltic republics (Estonia, Latvia, and Lithuania). **Domodedovo** (tel. 095/234–8656 or 095/234–8655), one of the largest airports in the world, is located some 48 kilometers (30 miles) southeast of Moscow; flights depart from here to the republics of Central Asia. **Vnukovo** (tel. 095/436–2967), 29 kilometers (18 miles) southwest of the city center, services flights to Georgia, the southern republics, and Ukraine. **Bykovo**, the smallest of the domestic terminals, generally handles flights within Russia and some flights to Ukraine. Be sure to find out from your travel agent which airport your flight is supposed to leave from. Also be aware that domestic flights have been drastically cut back in the past few years and the above information is likely to change.

If you are departing from Domodedovo or Vnukovo airport, look for the special lounges set aside for foreign tourists; they are much more comfortable than the general waiting area.

For general information on arriving international flights, call 095/578–7518 or 095/578–7816. These lines are often busy; if possible, call the airline. For information on domestic Aeroflot flights, call 095/155–0922. Calling the airports directly is usually a complete waste of time; the line is almost always busy, and even if it's not, no one answers.

Aeroflot (tel. 095/155–0922 or 095/238–7786) operates flights from Moscow to just about every capital of Europe, as well as to Canada and the United States. Among the international airlines with offices in Moscow are **Air France** (tel. 095/237–2325 or 095/237–3344), **British Air** (tel. 095/253–2492), **Delta** (tel. 095/253–2658 or 095/253–9871), **Finnair** (tel. 095/292–8788 or 095/292–3337), **KLM** (tel. 095/253–2150 or 095/253–2151), **Lufthansa** (tel. 095/975–2501), and **SAS** (tel. 095/925–4747).

Between the Airport and Downtown You would be wise to make advance arrangements for your transfer from the airport. There are plenty of taxi cabs available (many of them gypsy cabs), but stories are rampant of foreign tourists being swindled (or worse) by taxi drivers. Most hotels will provide airport transfers (for an additional fee) upon request. All of the airports are serviced by municipal buses operating out of the **City Airport Terminal** (*Aerovokzal*) at 37 Leningradsky Prospect, near the Aeroport subway station. Service is unreliable and inconvenient, especially if you have any luggage, but very inexpensive. The schedule is slightly erratic, but theoretically a bus departs from Sheremetyevo II (International) Airport every two hours or so; service to Domodedovo and Vnukovo domestic airports is more frequent.

Arriving and Departing by Car, Train, and Boat

By Car You can reach Moscow from Finland and St. Petersburg by taking the Helsinki–St. Petersburg Highway (*shosse*) through Vyborg and St. Petersburg and continuing from there on the Moscow–St. Petersburg Highway. Be aware that driving in Russia is invariably more of a hassle than a pleasure. Gas shortages are frequent, repair shops are rare, and roads are very poorly maintained. In addition, you face the risk of car theft, a crime that is on the rise.

By Train Moscow is also the hub of the country's railway system, and the city's nine railway stations handle some 400 million passengers annually. There are several trains daily to St. Petersburg, and overnight service is available to Helsinki. All the major train stations have a connecting subway stop, so they are easily reached by public transportation. The most important stations are: **Belorussky Vokzal** (Belorussian Station), for trains to Belorussia, Lithuania, Poland, Germany, and France; **Kazansky Vokzal** (Kazan Station), for points south, Central Asia, and Siberia; **Kievsky Vokzal** (Kiev Station), for Kiev and western Ukraine, Moldavia, Slovakia, the Czech Republic, and Hungary; **Kursky Vokzal** (Kursk Station), for eastern Ukraine, the Crimea, and southern Russia; **Leningradsky Vokzal** (Leningrad Station), for St. Petersburg, northern Russia, Estonia, and Finland; **Paveletsky Vokzal** (Pavelets Station), for eastern Ukraine and points south; **Rizhksy Vokzal** (Riga Station), for Latvia; **Yaroslavsky Vokzal** (Yaroslav Station) for points east, including Mongolia and China. The Trans-Siberian Express departs from the Yaroslavsky Vokzal every day at 2.

The past few years have witnessed increased crime on the most heavily traveled routes, and as a result many travelers to St. Petersburg now prefer the high-speed, day-train *Avrora*, which makes the trip in just under six hours. Of the numerous overnight trains, the most popular is the *Krasnaya Strela* (*Red Arrow*), which leaves Moscow at 11:55 PM and arrives the next day in St. Petersburg at 8:25 AM. Overnight trains are considered more dangerous than day trains, and if you are traveling alone, you should take added precautions. Experienced travelers in Russia bring their own lock and buy out the entire compartment so as not to risk their luck with unknown compartment mates.

For information on train arrival and departure schedules, call 095/266-9000 or 095/266–9999. Tourists must travel on a special, higher-priced ticket for foreigners. You can purchase it at the railway station on the day of departure (up to 24 hours in advance) or at the special ticket office for foreigners at 6 ulitsa Griboyedova (subway station: Chistyie Prudy). Tickets may be purchased up to 10 days in advance; bring your passport.

By Boat Moscow has two river ports: the Northern River Terminal (Severny Rechnoy Vokzal, 51 Leningradskoye Shosse, tel. 095/457–4050) and the Southern River Terminal (Yuzhny Rechnoy Vokzal, Andropov Prospect, tel. 095/118–7955). International cruise lines offering tours to Russia usually disembark in St. Petersburg and continue from there by land. It is possible, however, to book a two-way cruise from Moscow along the Moscow-Volga canal, which makes for a pleasant way to see the ancient cities of the Golden Ring. Some 129 kilometers (80 miles) long, the Moscow-Volga canal links the Russian capital with the Caspian Sea, the Black Sea, the White Sea, and the Azov Sea. The Moscow port for long-distance passengers is the **Rechnoy Vokzal** (northern port) on the Khimki reservoir.

Getting Around

If you look at a map of Moscow, you will see that the city consists of a series of distinct circles with the Kremlin and Red Square at its center. The most famous and important sites are clustered within the first circle, which was once enclosed by the fortification walls of Kitai Gorod, the city's oldest settlement outside the Kremlin. This area can be easily covered on foot. Beyond that, the sights are more spread out and are best reached by subway. To get a sense of the city's geographic layout, you might consider hiring a car for a few hours and traveling around the main roads encircling the city—the Boulevard and Garden Rings. The walking tours below begin at the city center and follow the historic routes that radiate out from the Kremlin.

By Subway The Moscow subway (in Russian, *metro*) ranks among the world's finest public transportation systems. Opened in 1935, the system's earliest stations—in the city center and along the circle line—were built as public palaces and are decorated with chandeliers, sculptures, stained-glass windows, and beautiful mosaics. With more than 200 kilometers (124 miles) of track, the Moscow subway carries an estimated 8 million passengers daily. Even in today's hard economic times, the system continues to run efficiently, with trains leaving the stations every 50 seconds during rush hour. It leaves New Yorkers green with envy.

The subway is easy to use and incredibly inexpensive. Stations are marked with a large illuminated "M" sign and are open daily 5:30 AM–1 AM. The fare is the same regardless of distance traveled. You purchase a subway token (available at all stations) and insert it into the slot at the turnstile upon entering. Stations are built deep underground (during World War II they doubled as bomb shelters); the escalators run fast, so watch your step. If you use the subway during rush hour (4–6 PM), be prepared for a lot of pushing and shoving.

Pocket maps of the system are available in newspaper kiosks or from individual vendors at subway stations. Plan your

Moscow Metro

Rechnoi Vokzal
Otradnoye
Medvedkovo
Ulitsa Podbelskovo

Vodny Stadion
Vladkino
Babushkinskaya
Voikovskaya
Petrovsko-Razumovskaya
Sviblovo
Sokol
Botanichesky Sad
Cherkizovskaya
Preobrazhenskaya Ploshchad
Aeroport
Timiryazevskaya
VDNKh
Dynamo
Dmitrovskaya
Alekseevskaya
Sokolniki
Rizhskaya
Krasnoselskaya

Planernaya
Skhodnenskaya
Tushinskaya
Shchukinskaya
Savyolovskaya
Oktyabrskoye Polye
Polezhayevskaya

Begovaya
Mendeleyevskaya
Shcholkovskaya
Ulitsa 1905 Goda
Belorusskaya
Novoslobodskaya
Prospekt Mira
Pervomaiskaya
Molodyozhnaya
Izmailovskaya

Kuntsevskaya
Barrikadnaya
Tsvetnoi Bulvar
Sukharevskaya
Komsomolskaya
Izmailovsky Park
Pionerskaya
Krasnopresnenskaya
Semyonovskaya

Filyovsky Park
Turgenevskaya
Krasniye Vorota
Elektrozavodskaya
Bagrationovskaya
Chistye Prudy
Fili
Mayakovskaya
Baumanskaya
Kutuzovskaya
Pushkin-skaya
Liubyanka
Studencheskaya
Novogireyevo

Kievskaya
Tverskaya
Chekovskaya
Kurskaya
Kuznetsky Most
Perovo
Smolenskaya
Shosseh Entuziastov
Arbatskaya
Aviamotornaya
Smolenskaya
Okhotny Ryad
Kitai Gorod
Teatralnaya
Ploshchad Revolyutsii
Ploshchad Ilyicha
Aleksandrovsky Sad
Vorovitskaya
Biblioteka Imeni Lenina
Arbatskaya
Tretyakovskaya
Marksistskaya
Kropotkinskaya
Novokuznetskaya
Taganskaya
Park Kultury
Polyanka

Frunzenskaya
Sportivnaya
Paveletskaya
Proletarskaya
Volgogradsky Prospekt
Leninskiye Gori
Oktyabrskaya
Dobryninskaya
Universitet
Serpukhovskaya
Avtozavodskaya
Prospekt Vernadskogo
Kolomenskaya
Tekstilshchiki
Yugo-Zapadnaya
Kuzminki

Tuzhnaya
Kashirskaya
Nagatinskaya
Ryazansky Prospekt
Shabolovskaya
Nagornaya
Leninsky Prospekt
Nakhimovksy Prospekt
Vykhino
Akademicheskaya
Profsoyuznaya
Noviye Cheryomushki
Kantemirovskaya
Kaluzhskaya
Kakhovskaya
Belyayevo
Lenino
Konkovo
Sevastopolskaya
Orekhovo

Varshavskaya
Tyoply Stan
Chertanovskaya
Domodedovskaya
Yuzhnaya
Prazhskaya
Krasnogvardeiskaya

route beforehand and have your destination written down in Russian and its English transliteration to help you spot the station. Each station is announced over the train's public address system as you approach it, and the name of the next one is given before the train moves off. Reminders of interchanges and transfers are also given.

If you want to avoid the long lines for subway tokens, you can purchase a pass (*yediny bilyet*) that is valid for all modes of public transportation. Metro passes are on sale at the same counters as the subway tokens. They are inexpensive and well worth the added convenience.

By Bus, Tram, and Trolley Buses, trams, and trolleys operate on the honor system. Upon boarding, you validate your ticket by canceling it with one of the machines attached to a wall of the vehicle. The buses and trolleys are almost always overcrowded, and chances are good that you won't be able to reach the canceling machine. Ask the person next to you to pass your ticket along; the canceled ticket will make its way back to you.

You can purchase strips of tickets at subway stops and at kiosks throughout the city, or from the bus driver after you have boarded (although often the driver will be out of tickets). The ticket is valid for one ride only; if you change buses you must pay another fare. Buses, trams, and trolleys operate from 5:30 AM to 1 AM, although service in the late-evening hours and on Sunday tends to be unreliable.

By Taxi Foreign tourists should exercise caution when using taxicabs. It is advised not to get into a car with more than one person in it, and you are best off ordering a cab by phone or through your hotel's service bureau. In today's strained economy, foreign tourists are crime targets. Gypsy cabs are common and often cruise the larger hotels and hard-currency restaurants in search of innocent foreigners. If you speak Russian, you can order a cab by telephone. For bookings one to seven days in advance, call 095/227–0000 or 095/227–0040; for same-day bookings, call 095/927–0000 or 095/927–2108. There is sometimes a delay of several hours, but usually the cab arrives within the hour. If you order a cab in this way, you pay the official state fare in rubles (which is very reasonable when calculated in dollars), plus a fee for the reservation. Drivers will appreciate and expect a tip of at least 20%. If you hail a cab on the street, expect to pay in dollars; fares for foreigners generally begin at $5.

By Car There are numerous car rental agencies in Moscow, including **Hertz** (tel. 095/434–5332 or 095/578–7532) and **Avis** (tel. 095/578–5646). You can rent a car with a driver from **IntourService** (tel. 095/203–1487 or 095/203–1497) for $12–$20 hour, depending on the make of the car. The Japanese-Russian joint-venture company **InNis** (tel. 095/927–1187) also offers chauffeur service, starting at $16 an hour.

Guided Tours

Every major hotel maintains a tourist bureau through which individual and group tours to Moscow's main tourist sights can be booked. In addition, there are numerous private agencies: **IntourService** (*see* Travel Agencies, *above*) offers a bus tour of the city for $10 and a walking tour of the Kremlin grounds for $15. **Apex Travel World** in the Radisson Slavyanskaya Hotel (tel. 095/941–8306 or 095/941–8426) is another major tourist agency offering excursions in and around Moscow. For more unusual destinations, try the newly formed joint-stock company **ARKA** (42 Bolshaya Ordynka, tel. 095/233–2110 or 095/233–0625). In addition to the standard tours, it offers guided excursions to such places as Lubyanka (KGB headquarters) and Stalin's dacha in Kunstevo.

Exploring Moscow

Highlights for First-Time Visitors

Armory Palace (*see* Tour 1)
Diamond Fund (*see* Tour 1)
Kitai Gorod (*see* Tour 2)
Kremlin (*see* Tour 1)
Novodevichy Monastery (*see* Tour 8)
Kolomenskoye (*see* Off the Beaten Track)
Pushkin Museum of Fine Arts (*see* Tour 6)
St. Basil's Cathedral and Red Square (*see* Tour 2)
Tretyakov Art Gallery (*see* Tour 7)
Zagorsk (*see* Excursions)

Tour 1: The Kremlin and Red Square

Numbers in the margin correspond to points of interest on the Kremlin and Moscow maps.

The logical place to begin your exploration of Moscow is at its heart, the **Kremlin,** situated at the very center of the city, atop Borovitsky (Pine Grove) Hill. The first wooden structure was erected on this site sometime in the 12th century. As Moscow grew, it followed the traditional pattern of Russian cities, developing in concentric circles around the elevated fortress at its center (the Russian word *kreml* means citadel or fortress). After Moscow emerged as the center of a vast empire in the late 15th century, the Kremlin came to symbolize the mystery and power of Russia. In the 20th century the Kremlin became synonymous with the Soviet government, and "Kremlinologists," Western specialists who studied the movements of the politicians in and around the fortress, made careers out of trying to decipher Soviet Russian policies. Much has changed in the last decade, as the former Soviet Union has unraveled. But despite

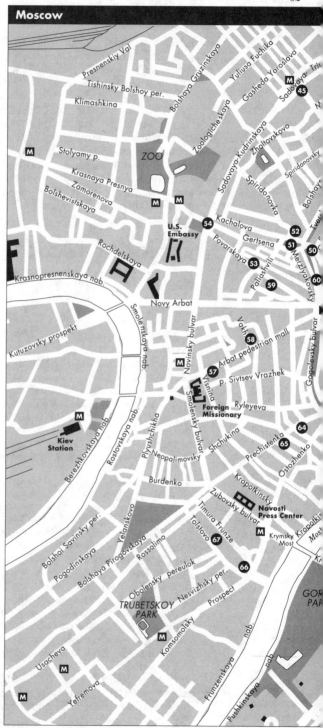

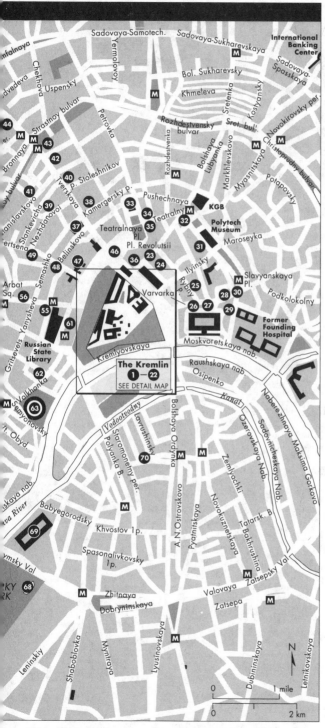

Kremlin

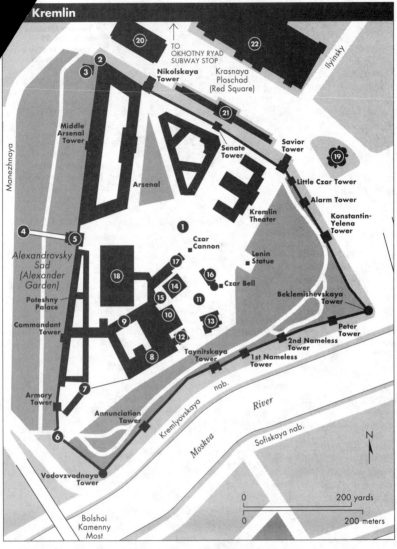

TO OKHOTNY RYAD SUBWAY STOP

Ilyinsky

Nikolskaya Tower

Krasnaya Ploschad (Red Square)

Manezhnaya

Middle Arsenal Tower

Senate Tower

Savior Tower

Arsenal

Little Czar Tower

Alarm Tower

Kremlin Theater

Konstantin-Yelena Tower

Czar Cannon

Lenin Statue

Alexandrovsky Sad (Alexander Garden)

Czar Bell

Beklemishevskaya Tower

Poteshny Palace

Commandant Tower

Peter Tower

2nd Nameless Tower

Taynitskaya Tower

1st Nameless Tower

Armory Tower

nab.

Kremlyovskaya

River

Annunciation Tower

Sofiskaya nab.

Moskva

N

Vodovzvodnaya Tower

Bolshoi Kamenny Most

| 0 | 200 yards |
| 0 | 200 meters |

Arkhangelsky Sobor, **13**

Blagoveshchensky Sobor, **12**

Bolshoi Kremlyovsky Dvorets, **8**

Borovitsky Tower, **6**

Cathedral Square, **11**

Dvorets Syezdov, **18**

GUM, **22**

Istorichesky Muzey, **20**

Kremlin, **1**

Kolokolnya Ivan Veliky, **16**

Kutafya Tower, **4**

Mavzolei Lenina, **21**

Oruzheynaya Palata, **7**

St. Basil's Cathedral, **19**

Sobakina Tower, **2**

Sobor Dvenadtsati Apostolov, **17**

Terem, **9**

Tomb of the Unknown Soldier, **3**

Troitskaya Bashnya, **5**

Tserkov Rispolozheniya, **15**

Uspensky Sobor, **14**

all the dramatic changes, the Kremlin remains mysteriously alluring. You'll find many signs of the old—and new— Russian enigma as you tour the ancient Kremlin grounds, where, before the black-suited men of the Bolshevik Revolution took over, czars were crowned and buried.

You can buy tickets for the Kremlin grounds and cathedrals for rubles at the kiosk in the **Aleksandrovsky Sad** (Alexander Garden) outside the Kremlin walls. There is a two-tiered price system; foreigners pay slightly more than Russians, but the cost is still insignificant. For entrance to the Armory and Diamond Fund, however, foreigners must pay in hard currency, a rule that is strictly enforced. There are four tours daily, at 10, noon, 2:30, and 4:30. Join the line that forms outside the Armory entrance about 15 minutes before the tour; you can buy a ticket ($10) inside just before the tour begins. You may want to consider a tour of the Kremlin grounds that includes the Armory, available from IntourService for approximately $22. The Kremlin grounds and Cathedrals are open every day 10–6 except Thursday. The Armory and Diamond Fund are also closed on Thursday.

The tour starts at the **Okhotny Ryad** (Hunter's Row) subway stop. When you emerge from the subway, you will find yourself on the opposite side of Manezhnaya Square from the Kremlin and Red Square. The first thing you see is the red-brick **History Museum** (*see* Tour 2) and, to its right, the Kremlin's battlemented walls. In some places 65 feet high and 10 to 20 feet thick, they have stood in their present form practically unchanged since the end of the 15th century. Follow the underpass running below Manezhnaya Square to the northernmost point of the Kremlin, the so-called ❷ **Sobakina Tower** (to your far right as you emerge from the underpass, on the other side of the History Museum). The Sobakina Tower, more than 180 feet high, was an important part of the Kremlin's defenses. Its thick walls concealed a secret well, which was of vital importance during times of siege.

Adjacent to the Sobakina Tower is a monumental, wrought-iron gate marking the entrance to the **Alexandrovsky Sad.** Laid out in the 19th century by the Russian architect Osip Bove, the garden stretches along the northwest wall of the Kremlin, where the Neglinnaya River once flowed. The river now runs beneath the garden, through an underground pipe. Just beyond the garden entrance, situated to your left ❸ against the Kremlin wall, is the **Tomb of the Unknown Soldier.** It was dedicated on May 9, 1967, the 22nd anniversary of the Russian victory over Germany. The body resting under the red granite slab is that of an unidentified Soviet soldier, one of those who, in the autumn of 1941, stopped the German attack at the village of Kryukovo, just outside Moscow. To the right of the grave there are six urns holding soil from the six "heroic cities" that so stubbornly resisted the

German onslaught: Odessa, Sevastopol, Volgograd (Stalingrad), Kiev, Brest, and Leningrad (St. Petersburg). The gray obelisk just beyond the Tomb of the Unknown Soldiers was erected in 1918 to commemorate the Marxist theoreticians who contributed to the Bolshevik Revolution. It was created out of an obelisk put up three years earlier, in honor of the 300th anniversary of the Romanov Dynasty. The arched "ruins" along the Kremlin wall, opposite the Obelisk, were designed by Osip Bove when he created the park. In the 19th century it was fashionable to include authentic-looking ruins in a landscaped park.

Looking up from the garden to the Kremlin walls, you see a large yellow building, the Arsenal. Begun in 1701 by Peter the Great, it was finished only at the end of the 18th century; its present form dates from the early 19th century, when it was reconstructed by Bove (the same architect who designed the Alexander Garden), after it was partially destroyed in the 1812 fire. The simple yet impressive two-floored building was originally commissioned by Peter the Great as a weapons arsenal; today it houses government offices.

Continuing along the garden's path, you reach a double bastion lined by a stone bridge on nine pillars. The white, outer bastion defended the approach to the bridge, which once functioned as a drawbridge over the Neglinnaya River. The ❹ outer tower is called **Kutafya,** which in Old Slavonic means "clumsy" or "confused," so called because it differs so in shape and size from the other towers of the Kremlin. The ❺ Kutafya Tower leads to the massive **Troitskaya Bashnya** (Trinity Tower), the tallest in the Kremlin wall. It rises 240 feet above the garden. Its deep, subterranean chambers were once used as prison cells. It is said that Napoleon lost his hat when he entered the Kremlin through this gate in 1812.

Continue through the garden by walking under the archway of the bridge. Here, on the left-hand side of the garden's pathway, you will find the kiosk where you purchase tickets to the Kremlin grounds and cathedrals. Tell the clerk that you want *"fsye bilyeti"* (all tickets). You can not buy tickets to the cathedrals once you have entered the Kremlin grounds, so be sure you get all the tickets you need now to save yourself the trip back. Beware of scalpers who will offer you tickets to the Armory at reduced prices; the tickets they sell are usually invalid for foreigners. Continue through the garden to its end at the western corner of the Kremlin. To your left a path leads up a steep incline to the ❻ pyramid-shaped **Borovitsky Tower,** the main entrance to the Kremlin. It rises to more than 50 meters (150 feet). At its foot a gate pierces its thick walls, and you can still see the slits for the chains of the former drawbridge. Black Volgas carrying government employees to work go whizzing through the vehicular entrance. Uniformed security guards stand at the separate pedestrian entrance, which opens promptly at 10 AM every day except Thursday.

The yellow building to your immediate left as you enter the Kremlin houses the **Oruzheynaya Palata** (Armory Palace), the oldest and richest museum in the Kremlin. It was originally founded in 1806 as the Imperial Court Museum, which was created out of three royal treasuries: the Court Treasury, where the regalia of the czars and ambassadorial gifts were kept; the Stable Treasury, which contained the royal harnesses and carriages used by the czars during state ceremonies; and the Armory, a collection of arms, armor, and other valuable objects gathered from the country's chief armories and storehouses. The Imperial Court Museum was moved to the present building in 1851. It was further enhanced and expanded after the Bolshevik Revolution with valuables confiscated and nationalized from wealthy noble families as well as from the Patriarchal Sacristy of the Moscow Kremlin. It now contains some 4,000 exhibits dating from the 12th century to 1917, including a rare collection of 17th-century silver. The museum tour begins on the second floor, which may cause some confusion if you visit the Armory on your own. Halls VI–IX are on the first floor, and Halls I–V are on the second floor.

Halls I and II display works of goldsmiths and silversmiths of the 12th through 19th centuries. Hall II contains a collection of 18th- to 20th-century jewelry. One of the most astounding exhibits is the collection of Fabergé eggs on display in Hall II (case 23). Among them is a silver egg whose surface is engraved with a map of the Trans-Siberian Railroad. The "surprise" inside the egg, which is also on display, was a golden clockwork model of a train with a platinum engine, windows of crystal, and a headlight made of a tiny ruby.

Hall III contains Oriental and Western European arms and armor, including heavy Western European suits of armor of the 15th to 17th century, pistols, and firearms.

Hall IV has a large collection of Russian arms and armor from the 12th to early 19th century, with a striking display of helmets. The earliest helmet here dates from the 13th century and is ascribed to Prince Yaroslav, father of Alexander Nevsky. Here, too, you will find the helmet of Prince Ivan, the son of Ivan the Terrible. The prince was killed by his father at the age of 28, an accidental victim of the czar's unpredictable rage. The tragic event has been memorialized in a famous painting by Ilya Repin (now in the Tretyakov Gallery; *see* Tour 7, *below*) showing the frightened czar holding his mortally wounded son. Russian chainmail, battle axes, maces, harquebuses, ceremonial armor, and Russian and Oriental sabers are also in this hall. A highlight of the collection is the large Greek quiver belonging to Czar Alexei, his Oriental saber, and a heavy golden mace presented to him by the Persian Shah Abbas. Among the sabers on display here are those of Kuzma Minin and Dmitry Pozharsky, the national heroes who led the battle to oust the Polish forces from Moscow during the Time of Troubles in the early 17th century. Later you will see their statue on Red Square.

Hall V is filled with foreign gold and silver objects, mostly ambassadorial presents to the czars. History buffs will be interested in the "Olympic Service" of china presented to Alexander I by Napoleon after the signing of the Treaty of Tilsit in 1807.

Hall VI has vestments of silk, velvet, and brocade, embroidered with gold and encrusted with jewels and pearls. They were once worn by the czars, patriarchs, and metropolitans.

Hall VII contains the regalia and the imperial thrones. The oldest throne, veneered with carved ivory, belonged to Ivan the Terrible. The throne of the first years of Peter the Great's reign, when he shared power with his older brother Ivan, has two seats in front and one hidden in the back. The boys' older sister Sophia, who ruled as regent from 1682 to 1689, sat in the back, prompting the young boys to give the right answers to the queries of ambassadors and others. Another throne, covered with thin plates of gold and studded with more than 2,000 precious stones and pearls, was presented to Czar Boris Godunov by Shah Abbas of Persia. The throne of Czar Alexei, also from Persia, is decorated with 876 diamonds and 1,223 other stones. Among the crowns, the oldest is the sable-trimmed Cap of Monomakh, which dates to the 13th century. Ukraine is now asking for it back, since it originally belonged to the Kievan prince Vladimir Monomakh. It was a gift to the prince from his grandfather, the Byzantine emperor, and is revered as a symbol of the transfer of religious power from Byzantium to Russia. Also on display in this section are several coronation dresses, including the one Catherine the Great wore at her coronation in 1762.

Hall VIII contains dress harnesses of the 16th through 18th centuries. On display are Russian saddles, including one used by Ivan the Terrible, and other items once belonging to the Moscow Kremlin Equestrian Department.

Hall IX has a marvelous collection of court carriages. The oldest one came from England and is believed to have been presented to Czar Boris Godunov by King James I. Here you will find the Winter Coach that carried Elizabeth Petrovna from St. Petersburg to Moscow for her coronation. Catherine the Great's French carriage, painted by François Boucher, is arguably the most attractive of the collection.

The **Almazny Fond** (Diamond Fund) is located in the same building as the Armory. Admission is by a separate ticket ($16) available at the entrance to the vaulted chambers, or through an IntourService tour ($25). The tour is recommended, if only because there are no signs, in any language, explaining the displays. This amazing collection of diamonds, jewelry, and precious minerals was established in 1922 by the young Soviet government. The items on display date from the 18th century to the present. Highlights of the collection are the Orlov Diamond, a present from Count Orlov to his mistress, Catherine the Great; and the Shah Diamond, which was given to Czar Nicholas I by the Shah of Persia as a sign of condolence after the assassination of Alexander Griboyedov, the Russian ambassador to Persia and a well-known poet.

As you exit the armory, you will see a courtyard to your left, closed off by a wrought-iron railing. The building on the right-hand side of the courtyard, adjoining the armory, ❽ is the **Bolshoi Kremlyovsky Dvorets** (Grand Kremlin Palace). It actually consists of a group of buildings. The main section is the newest, built between 1838 and 1849. Its 375-foot-long facade faces south, overlooking the Moskva River. This was for centuries the site of the palace of the grand dukes and czars, but the immediate predecessor of the present building was badly damaged in the 1812 conflagration. Today it is the seat of the Russian parliament and receives visiting foreign heads of state. It is not open to the general public, and even members of the press have trouble obtaining permission to enter. Nevertheless, tours have been arranged in the past; all it takes is a contact in the Russian government.

The other buildings of the Grand Kremlin Palace include ❾ the **Terem,** one of the oldest parts of the Kremlin, where the czarina would receive her visitors, and the 15th-century ❿ **Granovitaya Palata** (Palace of Facets). Both of these buildings are also closed to the public, but a portion of the Granovitaya Palata's facade, whose diamond-shaped stone facings lend it its name, is visible from the Square of Cathedrals, our next stop in the Kremlin.

Continue up the path past the Grand Kremlin Palace. A few steps bring you to the ancient center of the Kremlin, ⓫ **Cathedral Square.** The paved square is framed by three large cathedrals in the old Russian style, the imposing Ivan Bell Tower, and the Granovitaya Palata. All of the cathedrals here are open to the public as museums.

To your immediate left as you enter the square is the ⓬ **Blagoveshchensky Sobor** (Annunciation Cathedral), which was the private chapel of the royal family. This remarkable monument of Russian architecture links three centuries of art and religion. Its foundations were laid in the 14th century, and in the 15th century a triangular brick church in the early Moscow style was erected on this site. Partially destroyed by fire, it was rebuilt during the reign of Ivan the Terrible, when six new gilded cupolas were added. Czar Ivan would enter the church by the porch entrance on the southeast side, which was built especially for him. He was married three times too many (for a total of six wives) for the rules of the Orthodox religion and was therefore not allowed to enter the church by the main entrance. The interior is decorated by brilliant frescoes painted in 1508 by the Russian artist Feodosy. The polished tiles of agate jasper covering the floor were a gift from the Shah of Persia. Most striking of all is the chapel's iconostasis. The fine icons of the second and third tiers were painted by some of Russia's greatest masters—Andrei Rublyov, Theophanes the Greek, and Prokhor of Gorodets.

Standing opposite the Annunication Cathedral, to your right as you enter the square, is the **Arkhangelsky Sobor** (Cathedral of the Archangel). This five-domed cathedral was commissioned by Ivan III (also known as Ivan the Great), whose reign witnessed much new construction in Moscow and in the Kremlin in particular. The cathedral was built in 1505–09 to replace an earlier church of the same name. The architect was the Italian Aleviso Novi, who came to Moscow at the invitation of Ivan III. You will notice distinct elements of the Italian Renaissance in the cathedral's ornate decoration, particularly in the scallop-shaped gables on its facade. Until 1712, when the Russian capital was moved to St. Petersburg, the cathedral was the burial place of the Russian princes and czars. Inside you will find 46 tombs, including that of Ivan Kalita (Ivan Moneybags), who was buried in the earlier cathedral in 1340. Ivan Moneybags, who earned his nickname because he was so good at collecting tribute, was the first Russian ruler to claim the title of grand prince. The tomb of Ivan the Terrible is hidden behind the altar; that of his young son Dmitry is under the stone canopy to your right as you enter the cathedral. Dmitry's death at the age of seven is one of the many unsolved mysteries in Russian history. He was the last descendent of Ivan the Terrible, and many believe he was murdered, since he posed a threat to the ill-fated Boris Godunov (who at the time ruled as regent). A government commission set up to investigate Dmitry's death concluded that he was playing with a knife and "accidentally" slit his own throat. The only czar to be buried here after 1712 was Peter II (Peter the Great's grandson), who died of smallpox while visiting Moscow in 1730.

The walls and pillars of the cathedral are covered in frescoes that tell the story of ancient Russian history. The original frescoes, painted right after the church was built, were repainted in the 17th century by a team of more than 50 leading artists from several Russian towns. Restoration work in the 1950s uncovered some of the original medieval frescoes, fragments of which can be seen in the altar area. The pillars are decorated with figures of warriors; Byzantine emperors; the early princes of Kievan Rus, Vladimir, and Novgorod; as well as the princes of Moscow, including Vasily III, the son of Ivan the Great. The frescoes on the walls depict religious scenes, including the deeds of Archangel Michael. The carved Baroque iconostasis is 13 meters (43 feet) high and dates from the 19th century. The icons themselves are mostly 17th-century, although the revered icon of Archangel Michael is believed to date back to the 14th century.

The dominating structure of Cathedral Square is the massive **Uspensky Sobor** (Assumption Cathedral), bordering the north side (to your right as you exit the Cathedral of the Archangel). One of the oldest edifices of the Kremlin, it was designed after the Uspensky Sobor of Vladimir. It was built in 1475–79 by the Italian architect Aristotle Fiorovanti, who had spent many years in Russia studying traditional Russian architecture. Topped by five gilded domes, it is both austere and solemn. The ceremonial entrance faces Cathedral Square; the visitor's entrance is on the west side (to the left). After visiting the Archangel and Annunciation cathedrals, you will be struck by the spacious interior here, unusual for a medieval church. Light pours in through two rows of narrow windows. The cathedral contains rare ancient paintings, including the icon of the Virgin of Vladimir (the work of an 11th-century Byzantine artist), the 12th-century icon of St. George, and the 14th-century Trinity. The carved throne in the right-hand corner belonged to Ivan the Terrible, and the gilded wood throne to the far left was the seat of the czarina. Between the two is the patriarch's throne. Until the 1917 revolution, Uspensky Sobor was Russia's principal church. This is where the crowning ceremonies of the czars took place, a tradition that continued even after the capital was transferred to St. Petersburg. Patriarchs and metropolitans were enthroned and buried here. After the revolution the church was turned into a museum, but in 1989 religious services were resumed here on major church holidays.

To the left of Uspensky Sobor is the smaller, single-domed **Tserkov Rizpolozheniya** (Church of the Deposition of the Virgin's Robe). It was built in 1484–86 by masters from Pskov. Once the private church of the Moscow patriarch, it was rebuilt several times and restored to its 15th-century appearance by Soviet experts in the 1950s. The building boasts brilliant frescoes dating from the mid-17th century covering all of its walls, pillars, and vaults. Its most precious treasure is the iconostasis by Nazary Istomin. On display inside the church is an exhibit of ancient Russian wooden sculpture from the Kremlin collection.

Cross the square to the eastern side, which is bordered by the **Kolokolnya Ivan Veliky** (Ivan the Great Bell Tower), the tallest building in the Kremlin. The octagonal main tower is 263 feet high—3 feet higher than the Hotel Rossia (on the opposite side of Red Square), in accordance with the tradition established by Boris Godunov that the bell tower remain the tallest building in Moscow. The first bell tower was erected on this site in 1329. It was replaced in the early 16th century, during the reign of Ivan the Great (hence the bell tower's name). But it was during the reign of Boris Godunov that the tower received its present appearance. In 1600, the main tower was rebuilt, crowned by an onion-shaped dome, and covered with gilded copper. For many years it served as a watchtower; Moscow and its environs could be observed within a radius of 32 kilometers (20 miles). Altogether, the towers have 52 bells, the largest weighing 70 tons. The annex of the bell tower is used for temporary exhibits of items from the Kremlin collection. Tickets for the exhibit are purchased at the entrance; foreigners are charged in hard currency ($10).

Leave Cathedral Square by walking through the open space to the left of the bell tower. You will come out to the road where vehicular traffic passes; across the road are the working buildings of the Russian government. They are off-limits to the public, and uniformed policemen blow whistles at anyone who dares to walk in their direction. To your immediate left is the huge Czar Cannon. It has the largest caliber of any gun in the world, but it has never fired a single shot. Cast in bronze in 1586 by Andrei Chokhov, it weighs 40 tons and is 17½ feet long. Its present carriage was cast in 1835, purely for display purposes.

Not far from the world's largest cannon is the world's largest bell. Like the cannon that was never shot, the Czar Bell was never rung. It is mounted on a stone pedestal at the foot of the Ivan the Great Bell Tower (on the opposite side, to your right). Commissioned in the 1730s, the bell was damaged when it was still in its cast. It weighs more than 200 tons and is 20 feet high. The bas-reliefs on the outside show Czar Alexei Mikhailovich and Czarina Anna Ivanovna.

Follow the path along the road leading to your left out of the Kremlin. The last of the buildings open to the public is the **⑰ Sobor Dvenadtsati Apostolov** (Cathedral of the Twelve Apostles) and the **Patriarshy Dvorets** (Patriarch's Residence), situated to the north of the Assumption Cathedral. The church was built in 1655–56 by Patriarch Nikon, who used it as his private church. Since 1963 the buildings have housed the Museum of 17th-century Applied Art. The exhibits were taken from the surplus of the State Armory Museum and include books, items of tableware, clothing, and household linen.

Return to the road, bear left and return to the Kutafya Tower. As you exit, you will notice a rectangular structure of glass and aluminum on your left looking horribly out of **⑱** place. This is the **Dvorets Syezdov** (Palace of Congresses), built in 1962 to accommodate meetings of Communist Party delegates from across the Soviet Union. Today it is affiliated with the Bolshoi Theater and is used exclusively for concerts and ballets.

Turn right after passing through the Kutafya Tower and walk back down to the Alexander Garden. Retrace your steps through the garden past the Tomb of the Unknown Soldier. Turn right once again, following the wall of the Kremlin. World-famous for grand military parades during the Soviet era, **Krasnaya Ploshchad** (Red Square) was originally called the Torg, the Slavonic word for marketplace. Today Red Square is often the site of demonstrations by die-hard communists, and when the Russian Parliament is in session, the square is closed as a security precaution. Do not despair, however, for the square is often open at night. Try returning at 9 or 10 PM for the changing of the guard (every hour, on the hour, 24 hours a day); the square is even more impressive when the red stars of the Kremlin towers light up the night and the entire area is illuminated by floodlights. You may think that Red Square has something to do with communism or the Bolshevik Revolution. In fact, however, the name dates back to the 17th century. The adjective *krasny* originally meant "beautiful," but over the centuries the meaning of the word changed to "red," hence the square's present name.

As you climb the slight incline leading up to Red Square, ⓳ the multicolored onion domes of **St. Basil's Cathedral** slowly come into view. Although it is popularly known as St. Basil's Cathedral, its proper name is the **Pokrovsky Sobor** (Church of the Intercession). It was commissioned by Ivan the Terrible to celebrate his conquest of the Tatar city of Kazan on October 1, 1552, the day of the feast of the Intercession. The central chapel, which rises 33 meters (107 feet), is surrounded by eight towerlike chapels linked by an elevated gallery. Each of the chapels is topped by an onion dome carved with its own distinct pattern and dedicated to a saint on whose day the Russian army won battles against the Tatars. The cathedral was built between 1555 and 1560 on the site of an earlier Trinity Church where the Holy Fool Vasily (Basil) had been buried in 1552. Basil was an adversary of the czar, publicly reprimanding Ivan the Terrible for his cruel and bloodthirsty ways. He was protected from the czar by his status as a Holy Fool, for he was considered by the Church to be an emissary of God. Ironically, Ivan the Terrible's greatest creation came to be known by the name of his greatest adversary. In 1558 an additional chapel was built in the northeast corner over Basil's remains, and from that time on the cathedral has been called St. Basil's.

Very little is known about the architect who built the cathedral. It may have been the work of two men—Barma and Postnik—but now it seems more likely that there was just one architect, Postnik Yakovlyev, who went by the nickname Barma. Legend has it that upon completion of the cathedral, the mad czar had the architect blinded to ensure he would never create such a masterpiece again.

After the Bolshevik Revolution, the cathedral was closed and in 1929 turned into a museum dedicated to the Russian conquest of Kazan. Although services are now occasionally held here on church holidays, the museum is still open. The antechamber contains displays outlining the various stages of the Russian conquest of Kazan as well as examples of 16th-century Russian and Tatar weaponry. Another section details the history of the cathedral's construction, with displays of the building materials used. After viewing the museum exhibits, you are free to wander through the cathedral's many chapels. Compared to the exotic exterior, the dark and simple interiors are a disappointment. The brick walls are decorated with faded flower frescoes. The most interesting is the main chapel, which contains a 19th-century Baroque iconostasis. *Red Sq., tel. 095/298–3304. Open Wed.–Mon. 11–3:30. Admission: $3. Closed 1st Mon. of month.*

The statue just outside St. Basil's originally stood in the center of the square. It depicts Kuzma Minin, a Nizhni-Novgorod butcher, and Prince Dmitry Pozharsky, who liberated Moscow in October 1612 from Polish-Lithuanian occupation. The work of Ivan Martos, it was erected in 1818, paid for by public subscription.

The strange, round, white-stone platform in front of the cathedral is the so-called **Lobnoye Mesto**. Its literal translation is "place of the forehead," but it has come to mean "execution site," for it was right next to the platform that public executions were carried out. The platform was built in 1534 and was used by the czars as a podium for public speeches. Imperial *ukazy* (decrees) were proclaimed from here, and when the heir apparent reached the age of 16, he was presented to the people from this platform.

Opposite St. Basil's, at the north end of Red Square, stands ❷⓪ the redbrick **Istorichesky Muzey** (History Museum), built in 1874–83 in the pseudo-Russian style, which combined a variety of architectural styles. You may remember the building's twin towers from watching Soviet military parades on television. Against the backdrop of the towers' pointed spires, the tanks and missiles rolling through Red Square seemed to acquire even more potency. The museum was closed in 1986 for restoration work, and no date has been set yet for its reopening. Before it closed, its extensive archaeological and historical materials outlined the development of Russia as well as that of the peoples of the former Soviet Union. In typical Soviet fashion, the exhibits focused on the growing political unrest in prerevolutionary Russia, which culminated (naturally, according to Marx) in the Bolshevik Revolution. Much has changed since 1986, and when it finally opens again, the museum's exhibits may be altered to reflect the new political order in Russia today. The museum also contains a rich collection of Russian arms and weaponry. *1/2 Red Sq., tel. 095/228–8452. Closed for restoration.*

On the west side of the square, running along the Kremlin wall, is the **Mavzolei Lenina** (Lenin Mausoleum). Inside, Lenin's embalmed body lies in state. Except for a brief interval during World War II, when his body was evacuated to the Urals, Lenin has been on view here since his death in 1924. Whether it is really Lenin or a wax look-alike is probably one of those Russian mysteries that will go down in history unanswered. After Stalin's death in 1953, his embalmed body was placed next to Lenin's, and the site became known as the Stalin-Lenin Mausoleum. When Stalin was later discredited in the Khrushchev era, his body was moved to the burial grounds outside the mausoleum, along the Kremlin wall. The pyramid-shaped mausoleum is made of red, black, and gray granite, with a strip of black granite near the top level symbolizing a belt of mourning. It was from the balcony of the mausoleum that Soviet leaders watched parades. Designed by the architect Alexei Shchusev, the modern structure conforms with the ancient architectural ensemble of Red Square.

You can join the throngs of people lining up for a glimpse of the embalmed Soviet leader on Tuesday, Wednesday, Thursday, and Saturday from 10 to 1, and on Sunday from 10 to 2. Although Lenin's popularity has dropped significantly in the past few years, the lines to see his body are still very long. Foreign tourists are often allowed to jump the line. The place to go is the corner of the History Museum on Red Square, opposite the entrance to the Alexander Garden. Show your passport or hotel card to the guard, and he may let you pass. A visit to the mausoleum is a serious affair. The surrounding area is cordoned off during visiting hours, and all those entering are screened by uniformed policemen. It is forbidden to carry a camera or any large bag inside (you can check your belongings at the coat-check at the History Museum). Inside is cold and dark. It's considered disrespectful to put your hands inside your pockets while paying your respects (the same applies when you visit an Orthodox church), and the guards have been known to reprimand people for unbuttoned collars or sweaters. The line moves quickly, and before you know it you are ushered out of the mausoleum to the special place where such discredited leaders as Stalin, Zhdanov, Dzerzhinsky, Brezhnev, Chernenko, and Andropov are buried. The American journalist John Reed is also buried here, alongside the Kremlin wall. Urns set inside the Kremlin wall contain ashes of the Soviet writer Maxim Gorky; Sergei Kirov, the Leningrad Party leader whose assassination in 1934 sparked the great purges; the first Soviet cosmonaut, Yuri Gagarin; and other Soviet eminences.

The hourly changing of the guard outside Lenin's tomb is a memorable event. At three minutes before the hour, two soldiers and a corporal march out from the Kremlin's Savior Gate in a swinging, goose-step gait. The soldiers change places exactly 15 seconds before the hour, and the change is completed just as the Kremlin bells begin to ring. If you visit in winter, you will then see what is meant by Mother Russia caring for her children. Before the corporal leaves the soldiers standing at rigid attention in front of the entrance to the tomb, he stops and, in a most unmilitary gesture, turns up their coat collars against the bitter arctic winds that sweep across the Red Square. Then, in a most formal military manner, the corporal and the two relieved guards march off again to the Kremlin, using that same swinging gait.

㉒ Red Square is bordered on the east side by the long facade of **GUM** (pronounced "goom"), short for *Gosudarstvenny Universalny Magazin* or State Department Store. Formerly called the Upper Trading Rows, it was built in 1889–93 on the site where rows of trading stalls once stood. Three long passages with three stories of shops run the length of the building. Each passage is covered with a glass roof, and there are balconies and bridges on the second and third tiers. Another series of passages runs perpendicular to the three main lines, creating a mazelike mall. The numerous shops range from state-run kiosks selling Soviet stamps to recently opened foreign-run ventures, such as Benetton and Stockman's. *3 Krasnaya Ploshchad. Open Mon.–Sat. 8–8, Sun. 10–6.*

Tour 2: Kitai Gorod

This tour explores the twisting and winding streets of **Kitai Gorod**, the oldest section of Moscow outside the Kremlin. The literal translation of Kitai Gorod is Chinatown, but there has never been a Chinese settlement here. The origin of the word *kitai* is disputed; it may come from the Tatar word for fortress, but most likely it derives from the Russian word *kita*, in reference to the bundles of twigs that were used to reinforce the earthen wall that once surrounded the area.

Kitai Gorod begins where Red Square ends. A good starting point for your tour is Nikolskaya ulitsa, which begins at the corner opposite the Historical Museum and runs along the north side of GUM. Settlement of this area began in the 12th century, around the same time that the fortified city of Moscow was founded on Borovitsky Hill (the site of the present-day Kremlin). By the 14th century Kitai Gorod was a thriving trade district, full of shops and markets. At that time it was surrounded by earthen ramparts, which were replaced in the 16th century by a fortified wall. Remnants of that wall remain, and we will pass them later. As the city grew, so did Kitai Gorod. At the time of the Bolshevik Revolution it was the city's most important financial and commercial district, with major banks, warehouses, and trading companies concentrated here.

Time Out Before you begin your tour of Kitai Gorod, you may want to take a break at the **Ogni Moskvy** (Lights of Moscow) café on the top floor of the Moskva Hotel (the concrete structure dominating Manezhnaya Square). It can be a trick to find. Enter the hotel by the side entrance across from the Lenin Museum, and take the elevator to the 15th floor. To reach the café, you will need to walk the length of the balcony overlooking Manezhnaya Square. From here you get a bird's-eye view of the Kremlin to the south. To the north, a panoramic view of the entire city of Moscow opens up. On a clear day you can see all the way to Sparrow Hills, topped by the wedding-cake skyscraper of Moscow University. The food is only average, but with views like these, you won't care. *7 Okhotny Ryad. Open daily for lunch 11 AM–4 PM.*

Named after the Kremlin's Nikolskaya Gate Tower, Nikolskaya ulitsa is one of the oldest streets in Moscow. For three centuries the corner with Red Square, between the History Museum and GUM, was marked by the **Kazansky Sobor** (Cathedral of Our Lady of Kazan). It was built in 1633–36 to commemorate Russia's liberation from Polish occupation during the Time of Troubles. The cathedral was purposely blown up in 1936 and is now being rebuilt (cupolas are now visible above the barricades). An icon of Our Lady of Kazan, covered by a wooden pavilion, stands just outside the construction site. Make your way through the teeming crowds of shoppers on Nikolskaya ulitsa to No. 7 (on the left-hand side as you walk away from Red Square), the former Slavonic-Greco-Latin Academy. It was opened in the **Zaikonospassky (Behind-the-Icons) Monastery** in 1687 and was Russia's first institution of higher learning. The monastery itself was founded at the beginning of the 17th century by Boris Godunov. Hidden inside the courtyard between buildings No. 7 and No. 8 is the monastery's surviving cathedral, built in 1717–42 in the style of Moscow Baroque.

Farther down the street, also on the left-hand side, is a brightly painted white-and-green building with an elaborate facade (No. 15). The building was erected in 1810–14 on the site of the 16th-century Pechatny Dvor (Printing Yard), where Russia's first printed book was assembled in 1553. The white-stone facade is covered with intricate carvings. Look for the lion and unicorn, the coat-of-arms of the Royal Printing Yard. Today the building is home to the Moscow Institute of Historical Records.

Turn right onto **Ilinsky Proyezd** (Ilinsky Passage), which begins just past the building of the old Printing Yard. In the courtyard half-way down the block, opposite the entrance to the subway, is the **Bogoyavlensky Sobor** (Cathedral of the Epiphany Monastery), founded by Prince Danil of Moscow in the 13th century. The church is much newer than the monastery it was built to serve, erected only in the late 17th century. It is missing its steeple, which gives it the sad look of a tree stub. It is now under reconstruction.

Continuing down the street, Ilinsky Passage intersects with Ilinskaya ulitsa. Before the 1917 revolution, this was Moscow's Wall Street. The street is lined with the impressive facades of former banks. On the left-hand corner is the former Ryabushinsky Bank. This art-nouveau masterpiece was designed by Fyodor Shekhtel at the turn of the century for the rich merchant Ryabushinsky. The pale-orange building on the opposite side of the street is the former Birzha (Stock Exchange). Built in the classical style at the end of the 19th century, it now houses Russia's Chamber of Commerce and Industry. As you cross the street, look to your right; Illinskaya ulitsa leads directly to the Kremlin's Savior Gate Tower. As you cross the street, watch out for black Volgas whizzing by—this is the favored route to the office of Yeltsin and his colleagues.

Continuing straight, you enter Rybny Pereulok (Fish Lane), which begins across the intersection from Ilinsky Passage. The entire block of Fish Lane is taken up by the twin buildings of the **Gostinny Dvor** (Merchant Arcade). To your right is the Old Merchant Arcade, originally built by the Italian architect Quarenghi in 1791–1805; to your left is the New Merchant Arcade, built in 1838–40 on the site of the old fish market.

Walk the length of the buildings, and you come out onto **Varvarka ulitsa** (Barbara Street), one of Moscow's oldest streets. The opposite side of the street is lined with quaint old churches and buildings, but the first thing you notice is the gray bulk of the massive Rossia Hotel, located just beyond Varvarka Street and dominating the area. With accommodation for 6,000, the Rossia is one of Europe's largest hotels. Russians often joke that the Soviets chose this site for the hotel because foreign tourists wouldn't ever have to leave their room: Varvarka Street, with its rich mixture of architecture was all they would ever need to see.

The street takes its name from the **Tserkov Velikomuchenitsy Varvary** (St. Barbara's Church), located at the far corner, to your right. Next to it stands the English House, a white-stone building with a steep shingled roof and narrow windows. Built in the mid-16th century, it became known as the English House because Ivan the Terrible—wanting to encourage foreign trade—presented it to English merchants trading in Moscow. Next comes the white-stone **Tserkov Maksima Blazhennovo** (Church of St. Maxim the Blessed), built in 1698 on the site where the Holy Fool Maxim was buried. Today it contains a folk-art exhibit of wood carvings, embroidery, and other handicrafts. All the art work is for sale. *Tel. 095/298–1312. Open daily 11–6.*

The pointed bell tower situated just before the ramp leading to the Rossia hotel was once attached to the red brick Znamensky Cathedral on the other side of the ramp; it is set back from the street, with its foundation on the slope be-

㉗ low. The **Znamensky Sobor** (Cathedral of the Sign) was part
of the monastery of the same name, built on the estate of
the Romanovs in the 16th century, right after the establishment of the Romanov dynasty. After the death of the last
heir to Ivan the Terrible, a dark period set in, marked by
internal strife and foreign intervention. That period, commonly known as the Time of Troubles, ended in 1613, when
the Boyar Council elected the young Mikhail Romanov czar.
It is believed that Mikhail Romanov was born in the house
at No. 10. Today the mansion houses a lovely museum called
㉘ the **Palace of the 16th and 17th centuries in Zaryadye.** The
museum, which reopened in 1991 after extensive renovations, is devoted to the *boyar* (nobleman) lifestyle of the
16th and 17th centuries. The rooms are furnished to show
how the boyars lived, with period clothing, furniture, and
household items on display. During the week, the museum
is generally open only to groups with advance reservations,
but if you ask, you may be allowed to join a group. On Sunday the museum is open to the general public. Once again,
tourists can visit only in groups, but after a short wait,
enough people will gather to form a tour. *10 ul. Varvarka,
tel. 095/298-3706. Open Mon., Thurs.–Sun. 10–5; Wed.
11–6.*

Before leaving Varvarka Street, take note of the blue
㉙ **Tserkov Georgiya na Pskovskoy Gorke** (Church of St.
George on Pskov Hill) at No. 12. The five-domed church,
built in 1657, stands right next to the Romanov Mansion. If
you walk down the path to the left of the church (leading to
the Rossia Hotel) you can glimpse a remnant of the 16th-
century brick fortification wall mentioned earlier. It stands
to your left, opposite the hotel's eastern facade. Return
now to Varvarka Street, and climb the narrow Ipatevsky
Pereulok, on the right-hand side of the street as you face
the Kremlin. At the top of the incline you will find one of
Moscow's best-preserved 17th-century churches, the
㉚ **Tserkov Troitsy v Nikitnikach** (Church of the Trinity in
Nikitniki). It is a lovely redbrick creation that mixes Baroque decoration with the principles of ancient Russian
church architecture. Painted with white trim and topped
by five green cupolas, the church was built in 1635–53 for
the merchant Grigory Nikitnikov. The private chapel on
the south side was the family vault. The murals and iconostasis were the work of Simon Ushakov, a famous icon painter whose workshop was located nearby, in the brick
building across the courtyard. The church is open as a museum of 17th-century architecture. *3 Nikitnikov Pereulok,
tel. 095/298-5018. Open Fri.–Mon. 10–5; Wed., Thurs.
noon–6.*

As you exit the church, turn left and walk down to the end of
the lane. You come out onto **Novaya Ploshchad** (New
Square), which is more like a boulevard than a square. To
your right, at the bottom of the hill, **Slavyanskaya
Ploshchad** (Slavyansky Square) opens up. Until only re-

cently known as Ploshchad Nogina, the area was almost completely rebuilt during the Soviet era. A survivor of the reconstruction was the redbrick church at the bottom of the hill, the Church of All-Saints in Kulishki. This is also an example of 17th-century church architecture, but it has not been as well maintained as the Trinity Church. It was recently returned to the Orthodox Church and is now open for services (10 AM and 5 PM).

In the park dividing Novaya Ploshchad stands the Plevna Memorial, an octagonal, towerlike monument commemorating the Russian soldiers who fell in the Battle of Plevna in the Russo-Turkish War (1878). The monument was erected in 1887.

Walking up the hill (left as you leave Nikitnikov Pereulok), **③①** you reach the **Museum of the History of Moscow,** housed in the former **Church of St. John the Baptist** (1825). The museum was founded in 1896 and provides an outline of Moscow's architectural history, showing the various stages of development through paintings and artifacts. It is a small museum, and it is worth stopping in for a view of the Moscow you have been trying to imagine as you explore the city's oldest parts. *12 Novaya Ploshchad, tel. 095/924–8490. Open Tues., Thurs., weekends 10–6; Wed., Fri. noon–8. Closed last day of month.*

On the opposite side of the street is the **Polytechnical Museum**. The building takes up the entire block. The museum was opened in 1872 (it was originally called the Museum of Applied Knowledge) and today houses exhibits devoted to Soviet achievements in science and technology. *3/4 Novaya Ploshchad, tel. 095/923–0756. Open Tues.–Sun. 10–6. Closed last Thurs. of month.*

A short distance from the Polytechnical Museum, Novaya **③②** Ploshchad intersects with the circular **Lubyanskaya Ploshchad,** which was recently returned to its prerevolutionary name. In 1926 it had been renamed Dzerzhinsky Square, in honor of Felix Dzerzhinsky, a Soviet revolutionary and founder of the CHEKA, the KGB's forerunner. His statue once stood in the center of the square, but was toppled in the aftermath of the failed August 1991 coup. The large yellow building facing the square, with bars on the ground-floor windows, is the notorious Lubyanka Prison and KGB headquarters.

The department store on the west side of the square is **Detsky Mir** (Children's World), which used to specialize exclusively in toys and clothing for children. With the new economic reform legislation, the strict rules governing merchandise and trade have been broken. As a result you can find just about anything in Detsky Mir today—anything but children's merchandise, that is!

Bearing left, walk around Lubyanka Square to the west side, where it converges with the broad street of **Teatralny**

Proyezd (Theater Passage). In a side street to your right stands the recently refurbished Savoy Hotel (3 ul. Rozhdestvenka), built in connection with the celebrations honoring 300 years of the Romanov Dynasty. On the left-hand side of the street is a statue of Ivan Fyodorov, the printer who produced Russia's first book at the Old Printing House we passed earlier on Nikolskaya Street. The arched gateway just beyond the statue links Teatralny Proyezd with Nikolskaya ulitsa in Kitai Gorod. Theater Passage leads into Theater Square, where three of Moscow's most important theaters are located.

In the center of the square stands a statue of Karl Marx, carved on the spot from a 200-ton block of granite and un-
㉝ veiled in 1964. Opposite stands the **Bolshoi (Big) Theater,** the oldest in Moscow. Formerly known as the Great Imperial Theater, it was completely rebuilt after a fire in 1854 and now seats 2,155 people. Its ballet company is world-famous. The building is remarkable architecturally, with its monumental colonnade topped by a quadriga of bronze horses, and its crimson-and-gold interior. *Teatralnaya Ploshchad, tel. 095/292–9986.*

The Bolshoi Theater is bordered by two more theaters. To the left, on the corner farthest away from you, is the **Central Children's Theater.** To the right is the **Maly (Little) The-**
㉞ **ater,** with the statue of the Russian satirist Alexander Ostrovsky in front of it. The Maly, formerly known as the Little Imperial Theater, is famous for its staging of Russian classics, especially those of Ostrovsky. Opened in 1824, it was once called by Gorky "the Russian people's university." *1/6 Teatralnaya Ploshchad, tel. 095/923–2621.*

Taking up the block on the southeast corner, to your left as
㉟ you enter Theater Square, is the **Metropol Hotel.** It was reconstructed in the late 1980s and its brilliant art-nouveau facade has been restored to its original appearance. Like the Savoy, it was built in the early 20th century in preparation for the anniversary celebrations commemorating 300 years of the Romanov dynasty. It has been the venue of many a historical speech, and for a time the Central Committee of the Russian Soviet Federal Republic met here under its first chairman, Yakov Sverdlov. Until 1990, Theater Square was named Sverdlov Square, in his honor.

Time Out The small lobby bar at the Savoy Hotel (3 ul. Rozhdestvenka) is a favorite spot with Moscow's foreign community. Join them in its gilded interiors for a spicy-hot bowl of French onion soup or a club sandwich. The hotel also has a famous—and very expensive—restaurant. The bar menu, while by no means cheap, is more reasonably priced. The service is professional, and it's a great place to take a break after fighting the crowds of downtown Moscow.

Turn left at the corner and walk by the hotel's main entrance. The fragmented brick wall just behind the small park to your right is the other surviving remnant of the 16th-century fortification wall that once surrounded Kitai Gorod. The passageway between the arcaded house behind it leads to Nikolskaya Street. Walk past the park, and you will soon reach the Teatralnaya subway station. If you are not entirely exhausted, you may want to make one last stop at the Lenin Museum, which is located in the redbrick building on the corner, just a few steps from the entrance to the subway.

36 The **Tsentralny Muzey V. I. Lenina** (Central Lenin Museum) is located in the building of the former Moscow Duma. Although Lenin's revolution has been almost completely discredited, the museum is still open and free of charge to the public. Until 1991, the museum was supported by the Soviet government, but today it is desperately seeking donations from the public to keep its doors open. The museum's 22 halls contain several thousand exhibits, covering virtually every moment in the revolutionary leader's political career. Among the exhibits are Lenin's personal belongings—his desk (with secret drawers), a coat with bullet holes (the one he was wearing during an attempted assassination), and his car. Newsreels of him (from 1917 to 1924) are shown every 20 minutes in Hall 22. If time permits, the museum is worth a visit, especially for those tourists who did not visit the Soviet Union in the days of communism. It offers a now rare glimpse into the Soviet past and its all-encompassing propaganda. *Ploshchad Revolutsii 2, tel. 095/925–4808. Open Tues.–Sun. 9:30–6. Closed last day of month.*

Tour 3: Up Tverskaya Ulitsa

Tverskaya Street is a Russian rendition of New York's Fifth Avenue. As the main shopping artery, it attracts out-of-towners searching hungrily for a good buy, as well as the foreign investor looking for a lucrative place to set up shop. The street is lined with massive apartment buildings whose ground floors house some of the city's best and biggest stores. In recent years, many of the old state-run enterprises have been ousted, much to the chagrin of Muscovites, and replaced with neon-lit cooperatives and foreign ventures dealing in foreign currency and very high prices. On the sidewalks outside, individuals sell the widest assortment of goods imaginable—from vodka to cheese to Polish shampoo. Their numbers increase at dusk, when the whole street acquires the ambience of an Eastern bazaar. If you think the goods for sale look as if they have been pulled out of a closet, you are probably close to the truth. For years, back when prices were subsidized by the state and goods were scarce, people would buy far more than they actually needed, in anticipation of the rainy day everyone knew was coming. Finally that rainy day has arrived, and the goods are making their way back to the market. The tourist probably won't find much worth purchasing. Any Russian will tell you to stay away from the vodka and caviar—stories are constantly circulating about contamination from such goods sold on the streets.

There are several metro stops along Tverskaya ulitsa; we will start at the bottom of the street, at the Okhotny Ryad (Hunter's Row) station. When you emerge, Red Square is behind you; to your left stands the fading skyscraper of the Intourist Hotel. The street was given its present form in the mid '30s, during the first plan of reconstruction, though it had been an important route for centuries—the line of the road that led from the Kremlin to the ancient town of Tver. Later that road was extended all the way to the new capital on the Baltic Sea, St. Petersburg. From 1932 to 1990 Tverskaya was known as Gorky Street, in honor of the writer Maxim Gorky, the father of Soviet socialist realism. In 1990, the first section of the street, leading from the heart of town to Triumfalnaya Square, was given back its prerevolutionary name. The renaming was completed a year later, when the second section, ending at the Belorussian Railway Station, was also returned to its old name—Tverskaya Yamskaya. Until the rebuilding in the 1930s, Tverskaya Street was narrow and twisting, lined in places with wooden houses. Today it is a broad, busy avenue, a tribute to the grandiose reconstruction projects of the Stalinist era.

Walking up the left-hand side of the street, you pass, at No. 5, a short building with an arched entrance. This is the **Yermolova Theater**, founded in 1937 and named after a famous Russian actress. One short block farther, on the same ❸❼ side of the street, you come to the **Central Telegraph Office,** whose striking semicircular entrance is adorned with a large, illuminated, and constantly revolving globe. Inside, you can buy stamps, send a fax home, or even make a phone call abroad.

On the opposite side of the avenue, **Kamergersky Pereulok** (formerly Khudozhestvenny Proyezd, or Arts Lane) leads off to the right. The small green building on the left-hand ❸❽ side of this street houses the **Moscow Art Theater** (MKhAT), famous for its productions of the Russian classics, especially those of Chekhov. Founded in 1898 by the celebrated actor and director Konstantin Stanislavsky (1863–1938) and Vladimir Nemirovich-Danchenko (1858–1943), the theater staged the first productions of Chekhov's and Gorky's plays. It was here that Stanislavsky developed his theories into the "Stanislavsky Method," based on the realistic traditions of the Russian theater. After the successful production of Chekhov's *Seagull* (the first rendition bombed in St. Petersburg), they chose this bird as their emblem. (An affiliated, modern Moscow Art Theater with a seating capacity of 2,000 was opened in 1972 on Tverskoy Boulevard, near

Stanislavsky's home). *Kammergersky Pereulok 3, tel. 095/299-8760 or 095/290-5128.*

As you continue up Tverskaya on the left-hand side of the street, the next block is taken up by two large apartment buildings whose lower facade is lined with granite. They were built right after the war, in 1947–50. There is a great story of revenge behind the granite facade. The granite was supposed to have been used to build a Nazi victory monument—it had been brought to Moscow by Nazi troops at the height of the Siege of Moscow, when a German victory seemed imminent.

If you want to take a break from the hustle and bustle of Tverskaya, wander down ulitsa Nezhdanovoi, a side street to the left. You enter the street through the arched passageway of building No. 11. At the end of the block, you
39 come upon the pretty **Tserkov Vozkresseniya** (Church of the Resurrection), one of the few lucky churches to have stayed open throughout the years of Soviet rule. As a survivor, the church was the recipient of many priceless icons from less fortunate churches destroyed or closed by the Soviets. Services are still held here daily. *Yeliseyevsky Pereulok, tel. 095/229-6616.*

Return to Tverskaya ulitsa. Another short stretch brings
40 you to the small **Sovietskaya Ploshchad** (Soviet Square), stubbornly clinging to its old name. In the small park to your right stands a statue of Prince Yuri Dolgoruky, the founder of Moscow in 1147. The equestrian statue was erected in 1954, shortly after the celebrations marking Moscow's 800th anniversary. The handsome red building on the opposite side of the street is the Moscow City Council (Mossoviet). It was built at the end of the 18th century by Matvey Kazakov for the Moscow governor-general. During the reconstruction of Tverskaya Street in the 1930s, the building was actually moved back 14 meters in order to widen the street. The top two stories—a mirror image of the mansion's original two stories—were also added at that time.

Time Out Of all the foreign-run joint ventures in Moscow, **Pizza Hut** takes the prize for having most successfully re-created the atmosphere of a Western franchise. Step inside and in an instant you are back on the other side of the ocean. The decor is amazing, if only because it is just like that of any other Pizza Hut. The pizza is good, but the salad bar is a disappointment—lots of coleslaw but no lettuce. Service is swift and pleasant. This is the perfect place for a quick snack and a well-earned break from Russian reality. *Ul. Tverskaya 12, tel. 095/243-1727. Hard currency only; cash or credit cards.*

Farther up the street, again on the left-hand side, you pass ulitsa Stanislavskovo, named for the theater director

Konstantin Stanislavsky, whose Moscow Art Theater we passed earlier. Stanislavsky lived for a time in the building (41) at No. 6. Close by, at No. 7, is the **Russian Folk Art Museum**, founded by a wealthy merchant and patron of the arts, Savva Morozov. Its displays a rich collection of Russian folk art dating from the 17th century to the present, including antique and modern pottery, ceramics, glassware, metalwork, wood, bone, embroideries, lace, and popular prints. *ul. Stanislavskovo 7, Open Mon., Wed., Fri.–Sun. 11–5:30; Tues., Thurs. noon–7:30.*

Of all the stores and boutiques on Tverskaya Street, you'll find the most dazzling interior in the grocery store at No. 14, just beyond Stanislavskovo but on the right-hand side of the street. The store has an official, generic title—Gastro- (42) nome No. 1—but most people still call it **Yeliseyevsky's,** after the rich merchant from St. Petersburg who owned the store before the revolution. The interior sparkles with chandeliers, stained glass, and gilded wall decorations. Unfortunately the stocks—no different from those of any other state-run grocery store—do not match the interiors.

(43) **Pushkinskaya Ploshchad** (Pushkin Square), where Moscow's first outer ring, the Bulvar (Boulevard), crosses Tverskaya ulitsa, is the site of Moscow's first McDonald's (opened here in early 1990). On sunny days the line to get in snakes around in endless circles in the small park to your left. If you are simply dying for a hamburger, don't despair, because the line moves relatively quickly. The park on the right-hand side of the street is a popular meeting place for Muscovites. A fountain stands in the center of a terraced park, which is lined with benches full of resting and waiting people. A bronze statue of Pushkin stands at the top of the park. It is the work of Alexander Opekushin and was erected by public subscription in 1880. Summer and winter, fresh flowers on the pedestal prove that the poet's admirers are still ardent and numerous.

Bordering the square to the right and left of the park are the offices of some of Russia's largest and most influential newspapers: *Izvestia (News)*, once the mouthpiece of the Soviet government and now considered a liberal newspaper; *Trud (Labor)*, the official newspaper of the trade unions and of late a conservative voice; and *Moscow News*, the newspaper that helped give *glasnost* true meaning back in the early years of *perestroika*. Its brave editor allowed articles on topics then considered extremely controversial, from Stalinist collectivization to the ethnic strife in Armenia and Azerbaijan.

The **Rossia Movie Theater,** bordering the west side of Pushkin Square, was built in 1961. It stands on the site of the former Strastnoi Monastery (Convent of the Lord's Passion), whose history dated back to the mid-17th century. It was destroyed in the grim year of 1937. All that remains of the ancient monastery is the white-stone Church of Nativity near the corner with ulitsa Chekhova (to the far left as you face the theater).

Continuing along Tverskaya ulitsa, you reach the attractive railings of the former **English Club,** once the social center of the Moscow aristocracy. It stands on the left-hand side of the street, and its entrance is flanked by two smirking lions. Built by Giliardi in 1787, the mansion was rebuilt in the classical style after the Moscow Fire of 1812. Since 1926, it has housed the Central Museum of the Revolution. Although it retains many of its former exhibits—heavily imbued with Soviet propaganda—the museum has been updated recently to reflect the changing political situation in Russia today. The permanent exhibit, located on the second floor, begins with a review of the first workers' organizations in the 19th century. The exhibits outlining the 1905 and 1917 revolutions include the horse-drawn machine-gun cart of the First Cavalry Army, the texts of the first decrees of the Soviet government on peace and land, dioramas and paintings portraying revolutionary battles, and thousands of other relics. The next rooms outline the history of Soviet rule, with extensive material devoted to Stalin's rise to power. The final exhibit is dedicated to the 1991 August coup. It features a reconstructed version of the barricades set up outside the Russian Parliamentary Building, where Yeltsin made his famous appeals to the Russian people. Explanations of the exhibits are only in Russian, but you can arrange for a guided tour in English by calling ahead. The cost is insignificant; entry to the museum itself is free of charge. You will also find interesting temporary exhibits on the first floor of the museum. *Ul. Tverskaya 21, tel. 095/ 299–6724. Open Tues.–Sat. 10–6, Sun. 10–5. Closed last Fri. of month.*

As you continue in the same direction, the next major intersection is **Triumfalnaya Ploshchad,** where the grand boulevard of Moscow, the Sadovaya (Garden) Ring, crosses Tverskaya Street. Traffic here passes through a tunnel running below Tverskaya Street; there is an underpass for pedestrians. A statue of the revolutionary poet Vladimir Mayakovsky stands in the center of the square. It is generally believed that Mayakovsky committed suicide in 1930 out of disillusionment with the revolution he had so passionately supported.

Triumfalnaya Ploshchad is a center of Moscow's cultural life. The Tchaikovsky Concert Hall stands on the corner nearest you. It was opened in 1940 and seats 1,600. The Satire Theater is right next door, on the Sadovaya Ring. On the far side of the square stands the Moskva Cinema; the popular Mossoviet Theater is also located nearby, at 16 Bolshaya Sadovaya. To your far left you see the multitiered tower of the imposing Peking Hotel. Opened in 1956 as a mark of Sino-Soviet friendship, it houses one of the city's best Chinese restaurants.

While you're here, it's worth riding the escalator down for a peek at the spectacular interior of the Mayakovskaya subway station. Its ceiling is decorated with colorful, fluorescent mosaics depicting Soviet achievements in outer space. Like many of the early subway stations, it is built very deep underground and doubled as a bomb shelter during World War II. Stalin made a famous speech here on the 24th anniversary of the Bolshevik Revolution, at the height of the Siege of Moscow.

On the north side of Triumfalnaya Ploshchad, Tverskaya ulitsa becomes **Tverskaya Yamskaya**. This last section of the street has been the object of serious reconstruction in the past few years, and there is little of historical interest along this stretch. The street ends at the Belorussky Vokzal (Belorussian Railway Station), which has two interconnecting subway stations. A statue of Maxim Gorky, erected in the 1940s, stands in a small park outside the station. It is located near the site of the former Triumphal Gates, built in the 19th century by the architect Osip Bove to commemorate the Russian victory in the war with Napoleon. The gates were demolished in a typical fit of destruction in the 1930's. Fragments can be found on the grounds of the Donskoy Monastery (*see* Off the Beaten Track, *below*). A replica of the original gates was erected in 1968 near Poklonnaya Hill, at the end of Kutuzovsky Prospect.

Tour 4: The Old Moscow of Herzen Street

Ulitsa Gertsena (Herzen Street) is one of the many old streets radiating from the Kremlin, running more or less parallel with Tverskaya Street to the northeast and New Arbat to the southwest. The street was laid out along the former road to Novgorod, an ancient town to the northwest of Moscow, and is divided into two sections. The first part is lined with 18th- and 19th-century mansions and begins at Manezhnaya Square, across from the fortification walls of the Kremlin. The second section, notable for its enchanting art-nouveau mansions, starts at Nikitskyie Vorota (Nikolai Gates) Square, where Gertsena Street intersects with the Boulevard Ring. Before the 1917 revolution, Gertsena Street was named Bolshaya Nikitskaya, after the Nikolai Gates of the former white-stone fortification wall. It was renamed in 1920 in honor of the 19th-century philosopher Alexander Herzen. Although Herzen spent a great deal of his adult life in self-imposed exile in London and Paris, he exerted a tremendous influence on Russian sociopolitical thought in the mid-19th century. He was a progressive writer and a fierce advocate of liberal reform.

46 The tour begins at **Manezhnaya Ploshchad** (Manege Square). The closest subway station is Okhotny Ryad (Hunter's Row). Take the exit that leads to the National Hotel, which stands at the corner of Manezhnaya Square and Tverskaya Street. The hotel has been under reconstruction for several years now and is currently hidden behind clunky scaffolding. Expectations are high for the upcoming unveiling—before it closed, the National was one of Moscow's finest hotels.

The building next to the National Hotel houses the offices of Intourist, the travel agency that until recently enjoyed a monopoly over the entire tourist industry of the former Soviet Union. Until 1950 the building housed the U.S. Embassy. Older city residents still fondly recall how the Americans posted here joined in the spontaneous celebrations that erupted all over the city when the end of World War II was announced. They'll tell you how the Americans kept the party going, rolling beer kegs out these doors and onto Red Square across the way.

For years Manezhnaya Square was known as "50th Anniversary of the October Revolution Square." Thankfully, that cumbersome mouthful has been abandoned. Its present (and prerevolutionary) name comes from the imperial riding school (Manege) situated in the center of the square. Built in 1817, it has an interesting design: there are no internal columns supporting its huge roof—just the four walls. After the revolution the building was used as the Kremlin garage and then, in the late '50s, was revamped into the Central Exhibition Hall, which is used primarily for temporary art exhibits. *1 Manezhnaya Ploshchad, tel. 095/202–9304.*

Bordering the opposite side of the square from the Manege and towering over it is the Moskva Hotel. Opened in 1935, it was one of the first structures erected as part of Stalin's reconstruction plan for Moscow. If you look carefully at the facade, you'll notice that the design on the west side doesn't match the design on the east side. Legend has it that Stalin was given a preliminary draft that showed two possible versions for the hotel. He was supposed to sign under the one he liked best, but instead he signed his name right across the middle. The story goes that the architects, too timid to go back to Stalin a second time, went ahead and built the hotel with its asymmetrical facade.

Continuing along the north side of the square, you come to 47 the old campus of **Moscow State University.** It is Russia's oldest university, founded in 1755 by the father of Russian science, Mikhail Lomonosov. The classical buildings here were originally designed by Matvei Kazakov, in 1786–93. They were rebuilt and embellished in the mid-19th century, after the 1812 fire. The university's new campus is situated on Sparrow Hills (formerly Lenin Hills) in the largest of the so-called Stalin Gothic skyscrapers.

Passing the university, you come to Herzen Street. Turn right, and one block up, at the corner of ulitsa Belinskovo, 48 you reach the city's **Zoological Museum.** It is always swarming with schoolchildren, who take a special delight in its huge collection of mammals, birds, amphibians, and reptiles. The museum also has a huge collection of insects (more than 1 million), and recently a collection of more than 100,000 butterflies was donated by a Moscow resident. *Ul. Gertsena 6., tel. 095/203-3569. Open Sun., Tues., Sat. 10-5; Wed., Fri. noon-7. Closed last Tues. of month.*

Just beyond the Zoological Museum, on the left-hand side of the street, is the **Tchaikovsky Conservatory**. You may have seen its magnificent concert hall on television; this is where the famous Tchaikovsky Piano Competition takes place. The conservatory was founded in 1866 and moved to its present location in 1870. Rachmaninoff, Scriabin, and Tchaikovsky number among the famous composers who have worked here. There is a statue of Tchaikovsky in the semicircular park outside the main entrance. It was designed by Vera Mukhina, a famous Soviet sculptor. You can buy tickets (at very reasonable prices) for excellent concerts of classical music in the lobby ticket office in the main building. *Ul. Gertsena 13, tel. 095/229-2183.*

Take a quick diversion off Herzen Street now, turning right onto ulitsa Stankevicha, which begins just past the conservatory. The attractive red sandstone church at No. 8 was Moscow's **Episcopalian Church**. After the revolution it was closed and turned into a recording studio, but recently the English have taken it back.

Continuing now up Herzen Street, you pass, on the left-hand side, a three-story brick house. The name MAYAKOVSKY is printed in black on a sign hanging vertically down the side. For a time known as the Theater of Revolutionary Satire, today it is famous as the **Mayakovsky Drama Theater.** *Ul. Gertsena 19, tel. 095/290-6241.*

One more block brings you to the square named **Nikitskyie Vorota**, after the gates of the white-stone fortification walls that once stood here. To your right is a modern building with square windows; this is home to TASS, once the official news agency of the Soviet Union and the mouthpiece of the Kremlin. In the park in the center of the square stands a monument to Kliment Timiryazev, a famous botanist.

The busy road in front of you, intersecting Herzen Street, is the Boulevard Ring, which forms a semicircle around the city center. It begins at the banks of the Moskva River, just south of the Kremlin, running in a northeastern direction. It curves eastward, and then south, finally reaching the river bank again after several miles, near the mouth of the Yauza River, northeast of the Kremlin. Its path follows the lines of the 16th-century white-stone fortification wall that gave Moscow the name "White City." It was a privilege to live inside its walls, one that was reserved for the court nobility and craftsmen serving the czar. The wall was torn down in 1775, on orders from Catherine the Great, and the present Boulevard Ring was built in its place. It is divided into 10 sections, each with a different name. Running along its center is a broad strip of trees and flowers, dotted with playgrounds and benches. You may want to take a break and rest on its benches.

On the other side of the boulevard, facing the square, is the classical **Tserkov Bolshovo Vozneseniya** (Church of the Great Ascension). Like Moscow University, it was designed by Matvei Kazakov and built in the 1820s. For years it stood empty and abandoned, but recently religious services were resumed here. The church is most famous for having been the site where the Russian poet Alexander Pushkin married the younger and far less intelligent Natalya Goncharova. History has judged Natalya harshly. She was probably not guilty of adultery, although she did enjoy flirting. Pushkin died outside St. Petersburg six years after their wedding, in a duel defending her honor.

Herzen Street veers sharply to the left here, so that if you continue straight across the square, you'll end up on ulitsa Kachalova. On the corner to your right is a marvelous example of Moscow Art Nouveau, the **Ryabushinsky Mansion,** built in 1901 for a wealthy banker and designed by the architect Fyodor Shektel. (If you arrived in Moscow by train, you probably noticed the fanciful Yaroslavl Railway Station, another of his masterpieces, located opposite the Leningrad Railway Station). The mansion has been wonderfully preserved, thanks in part to the fact that Maxim Gorky, the father of Soviet socialist realism, lived here from 1931 until his death in 1936. The mansion is open as the **Gorky House Museum** (the entrance is around the corner, on ulitsa Spiridonovka). Considering Gorky was a champion of the proletariat, his home was rather lavish. But in a typical twist of Soviet reality, Gorky hated the *style moderne*. The spectacular interior is replete with a twisting marble staircase and stained-glass roof. Only the first floor is open to the public, but if you speak with the friendly museum attendants (who will insist that you sign their guest book), they may let you take a peek upstairs. *Ul. Kachalova 6/2, tel. 095/290–5130. Open Thurs., weekends 10–5; Wed., Fri. noon–6. Closed last Thurs. of month.*

Follow the road behind the Cathedral of the Ascension and continue straight onto Paliashvili Street (which leads to the left off Herzen Street). The statue in the park behind the church is of Alexey Tolstoy, a relative of Leo and a well-known Soviet writer of historical novels. Walk down Paliashvili Street until you reach the busy intersection with ulitsa Povarskaya, where you should turn right. As you walk down Paliashvili you pass several side streets with names like Stolovy (Dining Room), Skaterny (Tablecloth), and Khlebny (Bread). The streets are named after the servants of the czar (the waiters, the linen makers, the baker) who lived in this area. Today the district houses many foreign embassies.

Time Out The café on the corner between Paliashvili and Herzen streets is the perfect place for a foreign tourist who doesn't speak Russian. There are no menus; the available dishes are all lined up at the main counter, and you pick which one you want by pointing—no verbal communication necessary at all. You then make yourself comfortable at a table, and after a short while a waitress will bring your meal. The café's name—Vareniki—indicates that it specializes in boiled dumplings (filled with cheese or potatoes). Unfortunately, *vareniki* are not always available, but the café serves a decent *lobio* (spicy baked butter beans) and hearty soups. *Open daily noon–6. Inexpensive.*

Ulitsa Povarskaya (Cook Street) is where the czar's cooks once lived. After the revolution the street was renamed Vorovskovo, in honor of a Soviet diplomat who was assassinated by a Russian, and it was only recently returned to its prerevolutionary name. Povarskaya Street is an important center of the Moscow artistic community, with the film actors' studio, the Gnesin Institute of Music, and the Central House of Writers all located here. Many of the old mansions have been preserved, and the street retains its prerevolutionary tranquility and charm.

The mansion at No. 25 (on the left-hand side of the street) 🜊53 houses the **Gorky Memorial Museum.** For Gorky buffs only, the museum is packed with the letters, manuscripts, and pictures of the great proletarian writer. *Ul. Povarskaya 25, tel. 095/290–5130. Open Mon., Tues., Thurs. 10–5; Wed., Fri. noon–7. Closed 1st Thurs. of month.*

Near the end of Povarskaya Street, you pass the **Central House for Writers,** which functions as an exclusive club (with one of the city's very best restaurants) for members of the Writer's Union. Next door (No. 52) is a large mansion, enclosed by a courtyard, that houses the administrative offices of the Writer's Union. It is commonly believed that Leo Tolstoy used this mansion as a model for his description of the Rostov home in *War and Peace.* A statue of Tolstoy stands in the courtyard.

Povarskaya Street comes out onto Sadovaya Street; a bit 🜊54 farther down to the right is **Ploshchad Kudrinskaya** (Kudrinsky Square). Cars race in front of you along the busy Sadovaya (Garden Ring), yet another of the circular roads encompassing Moscow. The first thing to catch your eye will be the 22-story skyscraper directly across the street, one of the seven Stalin Gothics. This one is 160 meters (525 feet) high. The ground floor is taken up by shops and a movie theater, and the rest of the building contains residential apartments. This area saw heavy fighting during the uprisings of 1905 and 1917 (until recently the plaza was named Ploshchad Vosstaniya, or Uprising Square). The Barrikadnaya (Barricade) subway station is very close

by. Cross the street and bear right down the hill; you'll see
people streaming into the station to your right.

Tour 5: The Arbat, New and Old

One of downtown Moscow's most important avenues is **Novy
Arbat** (New Arbat), linking the Kremlin through Arbat
Square with the western reaches of the Moskva River. For
almost 30 years the street was named Kalinin Prospect, in
honor of Mikhail Kalinin, an old Bolshevik whose prestige
plummeted after the 1991 August coup. The first stretch of
the former Kalinin Prospect—from the Kremlin's Trinity
Tower to Arbat Square—has been given back its prerevolutionary name of Vozdvizhenka Street. The second section,
now called New Arbat, begins where Vozdvizhenka ends, at
Arbat Square. In contrast to Vozdvizhenka, which has retained some of its prerevolutionary charm, New Arbat is a
modern thoroughfare. Once a maze of narrow streets and
alleys, the avenue was widened and modernized in the
1960s, with the goal of making it the showcase of the Soviet
capital. New Arbat is indeed a showcase of sorts, but a sad
one. This grand avenue of the former Soviet capital has
come to reflect both the malaise and the chaos of the struggling Russian economy. When you get up close, it becomes
clear that shoddy construction has resulted in the prema-
ture decay of the once modern high rises. The avenue's
broad sidewalks are now covered with makeshift plywood
kiosks selling a strange assortment of goods, from wigs to
sneakers. Individual street vendors spread out their wares
in front of the big, state-run stores lining the avenue's path.

We will start at the bottom of Vozdvizhenka and work our
way up to Arbat Square. Take the subway to either the
Arbatskaya station on the dark blue line or to Biblioteka
imeni Lenina (Lenin Library) on the red line. To confuse
matters, there is also an Arbatskaya station on the light
blue line, but that will leave you at the wrong end of Arbat
Square.

When you emerge from the subway, bear left, walking
away from the Kremlin. Vozdvizhenka, like many other
Moscow streets, has recently been the focus of massive reconstruction, and most of its prerevolutionary facades are
hidden behind scaffolding. The drawings and photographs
⑤ at the **Shchusev Architecture Museum** will give you an idea
what the area used to look like. The museum's permanent
home, an 18th-century classical mansion at ul. Vozdvizhenka 5, is closed for reconstruction. The exhibits have
been moved to a building right behind it, which can be
reached via Marx and Engels Street, the first side street to
your left. When you enter this narrow street, the first thing
to catch your eye is a white-brick, two-story building,
which in the 17th century was the court apothecary. Turn
right into the courtyard; the entrance to the museum is to
your immediate left. The permanent and temporary exhib-

its here trace the history of Russian archi̇̄
11th century to the present day. *Ul. Vozdv̇̄*
095/290–4855. Open Tues.–Sun. 10–6.

Returning to Vozdvizhenka, on the right-hand si̇̄
street you will pass Voyentorg (Military Depar̄̇̄
Store), which is also closed for reconstruction. It beca̋
popular at the height of *perestroika*, when military uni̇̄
forms would catch a high price on the black market, popular
as they were with foreign tourists. Just beyond Voyentorg,
you pass a small square that is strangely empty. A statue of
Mikhail Kalinin once stood here, but now only the pedestal
remains.

Staying on the right-hand side of the street, you are bound
to be curious about the building a bit farther up that looks
like a Moorish castle. It was built in the late 19th century by
the architect V. A. Mazyrin for the wealthy (and eccentric)
industrialist Morozov. The interior is almost an anthology
of decorative styles, ranging from imitation Tudor to classical Greek and Baroque. The building is now the so-called
56 **Friendship House,** a holdover from the Soviet days when
Russians and foreigners were supposed to meet only in officially sanctioned places.

The busy intersection just beyond the Friendship House is
Arbatskaya Ploshchad (Arbat Square), where Vozdvizhenka crosses the Boulevard Ring. To reach the other side
of the square, take the pedestrian underpass, which of late
has become a bustling marketplace. The stairs are lined
with people selling adorable kittens and puppies; their furry heads stick out from a bag or from underneath a coat. In
the underpass itself, artists set up their easels, trying to
entice passersby into getting their portraits painted. When
you emerge from the minimall of the underpass, you will be
directly in front of the Praga restaurant, a three-story classical building whose history dates back to before the revolution. To your left Arbat Street (not to be confused with New
Arbat Street), one of the oldest sections of Moscow. Just
beyond the opening to Arbat Street, in the distance to your
far left, at the start of Gogol Boulevard, stands a statue
erected in the 1950s of the 19th-century Russian writer
Nikolai Gogol.

Arbat Street is a revered place among Muscovites, who
usually refer to it simply as "the Arbat." Its history dates
back to the 16th century, when it was the quarter of court
artisans. The names of the surrounding streets still recall
their names—from Plotnikov (Carpenter) to Serebryany
(Silversmith) to Kalachny (Pastry Cook). Early in the 19th
century it became the district of the aristocracy, while a
century later it became a favorite shopping street, a role
that has recently been revived. The whole area is now under
a preservation order and has become a cobbled pedestrian
precinct with gift shops in the restored buildings. Closed to
all traffic, the Arbat attracts artists, poets, and musicians.

ld easily spend a whole day strolling the Arbat,
g through the stores and stopping for a break in its
us cafés. If you walk all the way to the opposite end,
find **Alexander Pushkin's apartment.** The poet lived
h his beautiful bride Natalya Goncharova for sever-
s in 1831, right after they were married. Experts
created the original layout of the rooms and interi-
ation, and the apartment is now open as a museum.
53 Arbat, tel. 095/241–3010. Open Wed.–Sun. 10–6.

The tour takes a right about halfway down the Arbat, onto
the narrow ulitsa Vakhtangova. The impressive building on
the right-hand corner is the **Vakhtangov Theater.** Named after Stanislavsky's pupil Evgeny Vakhtangov (1883–1922),
it is an excellent traditional theater. A few doors up ulitsa
Vakhtangova, on the left-hand side of the street, you come
to the Alexander Scriabin Museum. It is housed in the composer's last apartment, where he died of blood poisoning in
1915. There are many such dusty house-museums in Moscow, but this one is particularly charming. Visitors here are
rare, as Muscovites long ago apparently tired of their own
museums, and foreign tourist groups are not usually
brought here. The rooms are arranged and furnished just
as they were when Scriabin lived here. Downstairs there is
a concert hall where accomplished young musicians perform his music. If you want to see a concert, you should call
ahead to find out the current schedule; usually they are held
on Wednesday and Friday evenings. *Ul. Vakhtangova 11,
tel. 095/241–1901. Open Thurs., weekends 10–3; Wed., Fri.
noon–7. Closed last Fri. of month.*

As you exit the museum, turn right, backtracking slightly
to the building at No. 7. Walk through the archway and bear
right through the courtyard. There are two gems hidden
away in this run-down courtyard. The yellow mansion behind the iron gate to your right is the **Spasso House,** the residence of the American ambassador. This neoclassical
mansion was built in the early 20th century for a wealthy
merchant. What you see is actually the backside of the
building; it is much more impressive from the front. Keep
walking straight, past the Spasso House, and you will discover, to your left, the lovely **Church of the Transfiguration
on the Sands.** Built in the 17th century, it was closed after
the 1917 revolution and turned into a cartoon-production
studio. The church is famous for having featured in Vasily
Polenov's well-known canvas *Moskovski Dvornik (Moscow
Courtyard),* which is now in the Tretyakov Gallery (*see*
Tour 6). If you have seen the painting, you will be amazed
by how the surrounding area has been transformed from a
quaint, pastoral suburb into a squalid, inner-city courtyard.

Retrace your path back to Vakhtangov Street and turn left.
Follow the narrow street for approximately one block, and
you will come out onto the busy New Arbat Street. Since

the entire area was rebuilt in the
terest here, except for the shop
find something worth buying
onto New Arbat, and you wi.
Square, where the tour began.
through the crowds of shoppers and ,
out for the country's largest bookstore,
Book House), at No. 26, on the left-hand side.
glish-language section, but you'll probably find a ь
lection among the individual vendors outside the store.

Time Out The Irish-run **New Arbat Store** (19 Novy Arbat), located near
the end of the block of buildings on the right-hand side of
the street, has one of Moscow's biggest and best-stocked hard-
currency grocery stores. The hard-currency section is on
the second floor, where the selection (and the prices) match
what you might find in New York City. Attached is the
small **Shamrock Pub,** where you can get a reasonably priced
sandwich or bowl of soup (for hard currency only) in a lively
but friendly atmosphere.

---

59 Near the end of the street, at the corner with ulitsa Povarskaya, the 17th-century **Tserkov Simeona Stolpnika**
(Church of St. Simon the Stylite) stands out in stark contrast to the modern architecture dominating the area. During the reconstruction of New Arbat in the 1960s many old
churches and buildings were destroyed, but this one was
purposely left standing, as a "souvenir" of the past. For
years it housed a conservation museum, but now it has been
returned to the Orthodox Church. Nothing remains, however, of the original interiors.

60 The last stop on this tour is a visit to the **Gogol statue,** which
used to stand at the start of Gogol Boulevard. When you
reach Arbat Square, turn left up Nikitsky Boulevard. The
statue stands inside the first courtyard to your left, near
the apartment building where the writer spent the last
months of his life. This statue is very different from the
monumental one seen at the beginning of this tour, at the
beginning of Gogol Boulevard. This one captures Gogol's
sad disposition perfectly. He gazes downward, with his
long, flowing cape draped over his shoulder, protecting him
from the world. Gogol is probably best known in the West
for his satirical drama *Revizor* (*The Inspector General*),
about the unannounced visit of a government inspector to a
provincial town. Characters from this and other Gogol
works are engraved on the pedestal.

Tour 6: From the Russian State Library to the Kropotkinskaya District

This tour takes you through an old section of Moscow known
as Kropotkinskaya. It takes its name from its main street,
which was called Kropotkinskaya under the Soviets but has

now been returned to its 16th-century name of
Prechistenka. This is yet another ancient section of Moscow
whose history dates back nearly to the foundation of the
city itself. Almost none of its ancient architecture has survived, but this time the Soviets are not entirely to blame.
The area suffered badly during the 1812 conflagration of
Moscow, and most of its architecture dates to the postwar
period of reconstruction, when neoclassicism and the so-
called Moscow Empire style were in vogue. Before the revolution, the Kropotkinskaya district was the favored residence of the old nobility—the ones who got left behind
when Peter the Great revamped the government and transferred the capital to St. Petersburg. It was also the heart of
the literary and artistic community, and there were several
famous literary salons here. Prince Kropotkin, for whom
the street was named, compared it with the Saint-Germain
quarter of Paris.

The tour starts at the **Russian State Library,** better known
by its old name, the Lenin Library. It's located at the bottom of ulitsa Vodvizhenka, at the corner of ulitsa
Mokhovaya (Moss Street, where moss used for wall caulk-
ing was once sold). To reach it, take the subway to the station directly beneath the library (still called Biblioteka
imeni Lenina). The library is Russia's largest, with more
than 30 million books and manuscripts. The main facade is
adorned with bronze busts of famous writers and scientists. The portico, supported by square black pillars, is approached by a wide ceremonial staircase. Although it's a
modern building, built between 1928 and 1940, portions of
the building are under reconstruction; when the subway
beneath it was being expanded in the 1980s, the library suffered structural damage and a large crack appeared in its
foundation.

A former mansion across the street from the library houses
the Mokhovaya Branch of the **Central Revolution Museum.**
The museum used to be devoted to Mikhail Kalinin, the first
president of the Presidium of the Supreme Soviet and long a
venerated hero of the Bolshevik Revolution. Many a square
received his name during the Soviet era (the ancient town of
Tver was also renamed in his honor), but after the 1991 August coup Kalinin became a hated symbol of the old regime.
The museum was completely revamped and now houses two
small historical exhibits. The first (on the second floor) is an
exhibit of political portrait art, including such interesting
historical figures as Rasputin and Sergei Kirov (the Leningrad Party leader who was assassinated—probably on
Stalin's orders—in 1934). A highlight of the collection is
Ilya Repin's portrait of Alexander Kerensky, head of the
transitional government established after the February
1917 revolution. The exhibit on the first floor, called "70
Years of Soviet Life," covers the development of Soviet
propaganda. On display is a conglomeration of seemingly
unconnected materials, from presents given to Stalin (such

as a Chinese vase with his portrait on it and a huge *palekh* box with "40 Years of October" painted on the cover) to wire from the Salevetsky Island concentration camp. Posters glorifying the farm worker dating from the period of forced collectivization are hung near an old voting booth, emphasizing the scam behind communist elections. The objective of this strange collection of political materials is to show how Soviet reality differed from Soviet propaganda. The exhibit ends with a display on the 1991 August coup, which includes sections of the barricades set up outside the Russian Parliament Building (the "White House"). *Ul. Mokhovaya 21, tel. 095/202–0367. Open Tues.–Sun. 10–5:30. Tours in Russian may be arranged in advance, tel. 095/202–7126.*

Just beyond the Revolution Museum (turning left as you exit), you come to Borovitsky Square, where several old streets converge. To your left, ulitsa Znamenka descends toward the Borovitsky Gate of the Kremlin and then continues across the Great Stone Bridge of the Moskva River. To your right Bolshaya Polyanka leads up a steep incline. Ulitsa Volkhonka lies straight ahead, leading into the Kropotkinskaya district. On the hillock to your right, facing the Kremlin gates, is one of Moscow's most beautiful old mansions, the Pashkov House. The central building is topped by a round belvedere and flanked by two service wings. Designed by Vasily Bazhenov, one of Russia's greatest architects, the mansion was erected in 1784–86 for the wealthy Pashkov family. In the 19th century it housed the Rumyantsev collection of art and rare manuscripts. Following the 1917 revolution, this museum was closed; the art collection was transferred to the Hermitage and Pushkin museums of fine art, and the manuscripts were donated to the Lenin Library. The building, which is currently in a catastrophic state of disrepair and under reconstruction, now belongs to the Russian State Library.

Cross the square and continue straight onto ulitsa Volkhonka, which was first laid out sometime in the late 12th or early 13th century. It received its present name in the mid-18th century, in honor of Prince Volkhonksy, who lived in the mansion at No. 8. After one block you reach the **②** **Pushkin Museum of Fine Arts,** in the middle of a small park to your right. Founded by Ivan Vladimirovich Tsvetayev (1847–1913) of Moscow University, the museum was originally established as a teaching aid for art students, which explains why many of the works are copies. The present building dates from 1895 to 1912 and was first known as the Alexander III Museum. It was renamed the Pushkin Museum in 1937, on the centennial of the Russian poet's death. It is the largest museum of fine art in Russia after St. Petersburg's Hermitage, and its collection is a veritable smorgasbord of world-class art. *Ul. Volkhonka 12, tel. 095/203–7412. Open Tues.–Sun. 10–7.*

The first-floor exhibit halls contain a fine collection of ancient Egyptian art (Hall 1); Greece and Rome are well represented, though mostly by copies (Room 7). The Italian school from the 15th century (Room 5) is represented by Botticelli's *The Annunciation*, Tomaso's *The Assassination of Caesar*, Guardi's *Alexander the Great at the Body of the Persian King Darius. The Beheading of John the Baptist* by Sano Di Pietro. When you reach the Dutch School of the 17th Century (Hall 10), look for Rembrandt's *Portrait of an Old Woman*. There are some who believe that this is Rembrandt's sister-in-law. Flemish and Spanish art from the 17th century is also well represented with paintings by Murillo, Rubens, and Van Dyck (Hall 11).

On the museum's second floor you are treated to a stunning collection of Impressionist art. There are many fine canvasses by Picasso (Hall 17), including several from his "blue" period. The same hall contains a fascinating work by Henri Rousseau, *Jaguar Attacking a Horse*. French Impressionism is represented by Cézanne, Gauguin, and Matisse. There is a total of 10 works by Gauguin, mainly in Hall 18, where you also find Cézanne's *Pierrot* and *Harlequin*. The museum owns several works by Matisse (Hall 21), although often they are not all on display. In the same hall you find the poignant *Landscape at Auvers After the Rain* by Vincent van Gogh. The collection ends at Hall 23, where you find works by Degas, Renoir, and Monet, including Monet's *Rouen Cathedral at Sunset*.

Just past the Pushkin Museum, taking up the entire block between Volkhonka and the quay of the Moskva River, is **63** the **Moscow Pool,** one of the world's largest outdoor swimming pools. It is divided into several sections, for training, competition, diving, and public swimming. The pool is open all year long, even in the coldest days of winter. The water is heated, and the steam rising up above the pool keeps the swimmers protected from the bitter cold air. The pool is connected to the locker rooms by covered tunnels, and you reach it by swimming through the tunnel. The public section is open 7 AM–10 PM, and for a small fee, anyone can use the pool.

There is an amazing tale of destruction behind the building of the Moscow Pool. It occupies the site where the Cathedral of Christ Our Savior once stood. Built between 1839 and 1883 as a memorial to the Russian troops who fell in the war with Napoleon, the cathedral was the largest single structure in Moscow and dominated the city skyline. It took almost 50 years to build but only a few hours to destroy. On December 5, 1931, the cathedral was blown up. The site had been chosen for the construction of a mammoth new "Palace of Soviets," which was to replace the Kremlin as the seat of the Soviet government. Plans called for topping the 420-meter (1,378-foot) structure with a 100-meter (300-foot) statue of Lenin, who, had the plans ever materialized, would have spent more time above the clouds than in plain view. World War II delayed construction, and later the entire project was scrapped; it was discovered that the land along the embankment was too damp to support such a heavy structure. The site lay empty and abandoned until 1958, when the Moskva Pool was constructed to fill the space where the church once stood.

Time Out The restaurant at the corner of Ostozhenko and Semyonovsky Proyezd is the second restaurant opened in Moscow by an American businessman from Trenton, New Jersey. It's hard to miss the shiny neon lights on its facade—**Tren-Mos Bistro**. They call attention to themselves in this old district dominated by the elegant mansions of Moscow's bygone aristocracy. The menu features such American favorites as cheeseburgers and pizza. The prices, however, are rather un-American. *1/9 Ostozhenko, tel. 095/ 202–5722.*

Just beyond the pool, Volkhonka Street intersects with the Boulevard Ring. To your right, across the street, is the entrance to the Kropotkinskaya subway station. At this point Volkhonka Street ends, splitting into Prechistenka (to the right) and Ostozhenko (to the left). The white-stone building in the small park between the two streets is the 17th-century palace of Prince Golovin. Cross the square and walk up Prechistenka. At the corner with Krushevskaya ulitsa stands a fine yellow mansion built in the 19th century by the architect Afansey Grigoriev. Since 1961 it has
64 housed the **Pushkin Memorial Museum.** Pushkin never lived here and probably never even visited the place, so it is a rather dry museum, full of manuscripts and letters. The museum is especially interesting to students of Russian poetry. *12 Prechistenka, tel. 095/202–7998. Open Tues. (groups tours only), Fri.–Sun. 10–6; Wed., Thurs. 11–7. Closed last Fri. of month.*

Not far from the Pushkin Museum, on the opposite side of the street, is yet another Grigoriev creation housing yet an-
65 other literary museum. The **Leo Tolstoy Memorial Museum** is similar to the Pushkin Museum. It was opened at another location in 1911 and moved here in 1920. The mansion, a fine example of the Moscow Empire style, belonged to the minor poet Lopukhin, a distant relative of Tolstoy. The exhibit halls contain a rich collection of manuscripts and photographs of Tolstoy and his family, as well as pictures and paintings of Tolstoy's Moscow. Even if you don't speak Russian, you can read the writer's life story through the photographs. If you decide to visit, look for the picture of 19th-century Moscow in the second hall (on the left-hand wall). The huge cathedral taking up more than half the photograph is the Cathedral of Christ Our Savior—the one blown up and eventually replaced by the Moskva swimming pool. *11 Prechistenka, tel. 095/202–3091. Open Tues.–Sun. 11–5:30. Closed last Fri. of month.*

If you are feeling energetic and want to see more of the area's mansions, you can continue walking straight along Prechistenka ulitsa. No. 17, on the left-hand side, belonged to the poet Denis Davidov; and a bit farther, at No. 19, you find the former mansion of Prince Dolgoruky (the building is presently under reconstruction). No. 21 now houses the Russian Academy of Arts. The mansion originally belonged to Count Potemkin and then later to the wealthy merchant Savva Morozov, whose private art collection was one of the largest in Moscow (you can see it in the Pushkin Fine Arts Museum we passed earlier).

We will now begin making our way back toward the Kropotkinskaya subway. After you exit the Tolstoy museum, turn left onto Lopukhinsky Pereulok, and walk one block to Ostozhenko, which runs parallel to Prechistenka. In the distance to your right, you can see the remnants of the **Zachatievsky Monastery** (Convent of the Conception). Founded in 1360 by the metropolitan Alexei, this is the oldest structure in the district, although nothing remains of the original buildings. Only the 17th-century redbrick Gate Church survives, and even that is in catastrophic condition.

Turn left now onto Ostozhenko, walk one block, and then turn right onto Vtoraya (2nd) Obydennaya. Soon you come to the pretty St. Prophet Eliah Church, built in one day in 1702. Turn left and at the end of this short street you come out onto Semyonovsky Proyezd (the Moskva swimming pool is across the street). At the bottom of the street, facing the Moskva River, is one of the finest examples of Moscow Art Nouveau. The facade of the steep-roofed building is covered in colorful mosaics. Known as the **Pertsov House,** it was built in 1905–07 by the architects Schnaubert and Zhukov. To reach the subway again, walk back up Semyonovsky Proyezd, away from the Moskva River.

Tour 7: Gorky Park Area

This tour takes you to sites around Gorky Park and then, via subway, to Moscow's greatest art museum, the Tretyakov Gallery. Gorky Park, made famous by Martin Cruz Smith's novel of the same name, is situated along the banks of the Moskva River, between two major subway stops—the Oktyabrskaya station on the orange and circle lines and the Park Kultury station on the red and circle lines. The tour begins at the Park Kultury stop, but if your only destination is Gorky Park, the Oktyabrskaya station is closer.

Turn right upon leaving the Park Kultury subway station (you want the Zubovsky street exit) and walk along Komsomolsky Prospect one long block. At the corner with ulitsa Lva Tolstovo (Leo Tolstoy Street) stands the striking ❻❻ **Tserkov Nikoly v Khamovnikakh** (Church of St. Nicholas of the Weavers). The church remained open throughout the years of Soviet rule and is wonderfully preserved. The elegant, tent-roofed bell tower is particularly impressive. The church was built in 1679–82 and is topped by five onion-shaped gilded domes. The orange and green trim against the background of its perfectly white facade makes it look like a frosted gingerbread house. The design was actually meant to re-create a colorful piece of woven cloth; the church was commissioned by the weavers who settled in considerable numbers in this quarter in the 17th century. Morning and evening services are held here daily. The entrance to the church is through the courtyard, off Leo Tolstoy Street.

⑥ The next stop is the **Leo Tolstoy House Museum,** where Russia's great novelist spent his winters. As you walk up the street named in his honor, you pass, on the right-hand side, a rectangular, white-stone building with a steep wood-shingled roof. It dates from the 17th century, when it housed the Weaver's Guild. Tolstoy's estate is a bit farther up the street, on the left-hand side, situated behind a long fence. Tickets to the museum are sold in the kiosk at the entranceway. There are signs in English explaining the various rooms, but you might want to consider a guided excursion (which must be booked in advance). The enthusiastic guides give a delightful tour, taking you into every corner of the old house. They'll tell you the story behind every item on display, from the family's dining service to the paintings on the walls, many of which were painted by Tolstoy's daughter. *21 ul. Lva Tolstovo, tel. 095/246–9444.*

Tolstoy (1828–1910) bought the house in 1882 and spent his winters here with his family until 1901 (he preferred his country estate in Yasnaya Polyana in the summer). Sixteen of the original rooms have been preserved as they were when Tolstoy lived here. The years here were not particularly happy ones. By this time Tolstoy had already reached his "religious conversion," which prompted him to disown his earlier great novels, including *War and Peace* and *Anna Karenina.* His religious conversion sparked a feud among his own family members, and the guide will tell you how it manifested itself even at the dining table: Tolstoy's wife, Sofia Andreevna, would sit at one end with the sons, while the writer would sit with his daughters at the opposite end. In addition to housing the dining room, the ground floor contains the daughters' bedrooms and the nursery, where Tolstoy's seven-year-old son died of scarlet fever in 1895, a tragedy that haunted Tolstoy for the rest of his life. Upstairs, you find Tolstoy's study, where he wrote his last novel, *Resurrection,* and received guests. The grand piano here was played by such greats as Rachmaninoff and Rimsky-Korsakov.

Retrace your steps to the Park Kultury subway stop. When you reach the corner with busy Zubovsky Bulvar, turn right and follow the path across the **Krymsky Most** (Crimea

Bridge). The bridge spans the Moskva River, and in nice weather it offers a fine vantage point for the riverbanks. If you prefer, you can take Trolley Bus 10 or B (the stop is on Zubovsky Bulvar, right in front of the subway entrance) one stop; it will drop you off directly in front of the main entrance to Gorky Park.

Time Out If you are feeling adventurous, check out **Guriya** (7 Komsomolsky Prospect, open 10–8), a popular and inexpensive Georgian café hidden behind the high rises across the street from the Church of St. Nicholas. A heavy cloud of cigarette smoke hangs in the air, and the floors are covered in mud, but it is always packed with Georgians, who come here for the *pkhali* (fried eggplant in walnut sauce) and *lavash* (flat bread baked in an earthen oven). An English-language menu is available. The café is in the courtyard behind building No. 7.

68 Muscovites usually refer to **Gorky Park** as Park Kultury (Park of Culture); its official title is actually the Central Park of Culture and Leisure named for Maxim Gorky. The park was founded in 1928 and covers an area of 110 hectares (275 acres). It is definitely the city's most popular park, and in the summer, especially on weekends, it is full of children and adults alike enjoying its many attractions. The park's green expanse is dominated by a giant Ferris wheel; if you're brave enough to ride it, you'll be rewarded with great views of the city. Stretching along the riverside, the park includes the Neskuchny Sad (Happy Garden) and the Zelyony Theater (Green Theater), an open-air theater with seating for 10,000. The park has a boating pond, a fairground, sports grounds, a rock club, and numerous stand-up cafés. In summer boats leave from the pier for excursions along the Moskva River, and in winter the ponds transform into skating rinks. *9 Krymsky Val. Open summer, daily 9–noon; winter, daily 10–10.*

Directly across the street from the entrance to Gorky Park **69** is the **House of Artists,** a huge, modern building that also houses a branch of the Tretyakov Gallery. The entrance facing the street leads to the exhibit halls of the Artists' Union, where union members display their work. Despite the unpromising proletariat sculptures in the park outside, the work here is generally interesting, some of it very good, and most of it for sale. The extensive exhibit halls are spread out among three floors. There are also numerous kiosks and counters selling arts-and-crafts items that may be of interest to the tourist. You'll find the best selection of postcards and art books here as well, for sale at very reasonable prices. *10 Krymsky Val, tel. 095/238–9843. Open Tues.–Sun. 11–9.*

Time Out Juice, coffee, and light snacks are available in the café on the ground floor of the House of Artists. It's stand-up only, but you can mingle with union members and hear the latest on trends in contemporary Russian art.

If you're looking for the New Branch of the Tretyakov Art Gallery, go around to the side entrance. This branch was opened after the original Tretyakov Gallery was closed for restoration work in 1986. Here the museum displays its collection of 20th-century art, which includes examples of socialist realism, political portrait art, as well as works that were once considered inappropriate and outlawed by the Soviet regime. In the garden out back there is an extremely interesting collection of recently toppled statues. Here you will find the remains of monuments to such disgraced leaders as Lenin, Kalinin, and Sverdlov. Felix Dzerzhinksy (founder of the CHEKA) lies on his side; he once stood proudly outside his former office on Lubyanka Square, opposite KGB headquarters. *11 Krymsky Val (side entrance, on the right), tel. 095/230–1116 or 095/230–7788. Open Tues.–Sun. 10–7.*

The final destination on this tour is the main branch of the
70 Tretyakov Art Gallery, the country's largest and most important depository of Russian art. It is only one stop away on the subway. Walk up the incline to the left of Gorky Park (as you face the entrance) and take the orange line (not the circle line) to the Tretyakovskaya station. Bear left at every turn as you exit the subway, and you will emerge near Ordynsky Pereulok (which is again to your left). The museum is located one block away. *Lavrushinsky Pereulok 12, tel. 095/231–1362; tours, 095/238–2054. Open Tues.–Sun. 10–7.*

The original building of the Tretyakov Gallery is a work of art itself. It was designed by the Russian artist Victor Vasnetsov and built in the fanciful style of early Russian Art Nouveau. Unfortunately, you can glimpse the building—a shell of its former self—only through the construction workers' barricades. It was closed in 1986 for major reconstruction; the project has been plagued by a series of miscalculations, and the work is still far from complete. The museum staff is hesitant even to name a tentative date; it might possibly reopen again by the summer of 1994.

A portion of the museum's vast collection is on display in a new exhibition building right next door to the original one (not to be confused with the "New Branch" on Krymsky Val). The collection was started in 1856 by the wealthy brothers Pavel and Sergei Tretyakov, who donated it to the city of Moscow in 1892. The collection was further enhanced following the Bolshevik Revolution, when the Soviet government confiscated and nationalized numerous private art collections. Its holdings of paintings, ancient Russian art, sculptures, drawings, and engravings number more than 100,000; the new exhibit hall has room to display only 250–

300 items. Since space is scarce, the exhibit changes periodically, with the works on view rotated in and out of storage.

The new building is divided into three sections. A tape-recorded tour is available for each. The recording quality is poor, but the cost is insignificant. There are few other explanations in English, so you may be lost without it. The first section is devoted to ancient Russian art. The icons on display date from the 11th to 17th century; many were transferred here from the Kremlin churches in the 1930s. The highlights of the collection are the icons by Dionysius, Feofan Grek, Andrei Rublyov, and Danil Chorny, masters of the art of icon painting in the late 14th and early 15th centuries. Here you will find Rublyov's celebrated *Holy Trinity*, originally painted for the Trinity Cathedral of the Trinity–St. Sergius Monastery (Sergiyev Posad or Zagorsk). The collection of 17th-century icons includes works by Simon Ushakov.

The second section of the new exhibit hall is devoted to Russian art from the 18th through 19th centuries. Only a very small portion of the museum's fine collection is on display here, and lovers of Russian art will be sorely disappointed by what's missing. The exhibit in this section tends to change more frequently.

The last section consists of just one small room where masterpieces of the early 20th century are displayed. These include Kuzma Petrov-Vodkin's brilliant *Swimming the Red Horse*, two works by Kandinsky, and two by Malevich.

Tour 8: Novodevichy Convent and Cemetery

Novodevichy Monastyr (New Maiden's Convent) is one of Moscow's finest and best-preserved ensembles of 16th- and 17th-century Russian architecture. There is much to see here. The monastery is interesting not only for its impressive cathedral and charming churches but also for the dramatic chapters of Russian history that have been played out within its walls. It stands in a wooded section bordering a small pond, making this a particularly pleasant place for an afternoon stroll. Although it is no longer a functioning convent, one of its churches is open for services. After the Bolshevik Revolution, the convent was made part of the History Museum. Its exhibits boast rare and ancient Russian paintings, both ecclesiastical and secular, woodwork and ceramics, and fabrics and embroidery. There is also a large collection of illuminated and illustrated books, decorated with gold, silver, and jewels. Attached to the monastery is a fascinating cemetery where some of Russia's greatest literary, military, and political figures are buried. *1 Novodevichy Proyezd, tel. 095/246–8526. Open Wed.–Mon. 10–5. Closed last Mon. of month.*

To reach the monastery, take the subway to the Sportivnaya station. Leave the subway via the stadium exit, and then follow the road to your right. It will lead you through a small park and eventually to the southeast corner of the monastery. When you come out onto Luzhnetsky Proyezd, you will see the monastery's whitewashed walls to your right. Turning right, walk up the street; the main entrance is at the other end, off Bolshaya Pirogovskaya Street. The green-colored gates directly across from you as you enter the street mark the entrance to the cemetery, where we will return later.

Enclosed by a crenelated wall with 12 colorful battle towers, the monastery consists of several groups of buildings. It was founded in 1524 by Czar Vasily III to commemorate Moscow's capture of Smolensk and was intended to serve not only as a religious institution but also as a defense fortification. Its location is significant, as it stands on the road to Smolensk and Lithuania. Having been founded by the czar, it enjoyed an elevated position among the many monasteries and convents of Moscow and became a convent primarily for ladies of noble birth. Little remains of the original structure. The monastery suffered severely during the Time of Troubles, a period of internal strife and foreign intervention that began in approximately 1598 and lasted until 1613, when the first Romanov was elected to the throne. Its present appearance owes much to the 17th century, when the monastery was significantly rebuilt and enhanced.

Among the first of the famous women to take the veil here was Irina, wife of the feebleminded Czar Fyodor and the sister of Boris Godunov. Opera fans may remember the story of Boris Godunov, the subject of a well-known work by Mussorgsky. Godunov was a powerful nobleman who exerted much influence over the czar. When Fedor died, Godunov was the logical successor to the throne, but rather than proclaim himself czar, he followed his sister to Novodevichy. Biding his time, Godunov waited until the clergy and townspeople begged him to become czar. His election took place here, inside the Cathedral of Smolensk. His rule was an ill-fated one, touching off the Time of Troubles.

In the next century, Novodevichy became the residence of yet another royal, Sophia, the half-sister of Peter the Great. She ruled as regent from 1682 through 1689 and was responsible for much new construction at the monastery. The power-hungry Sophia was later deposed by her half brother Peter, who kept her prisoner inside the Novodevichy. Even that was not enough to restrain the ambitious Sophia, and from her cell at the convent she organized a revolt of the *streltsy* (Russian militia). The revolt was summarily put down, and to punish Sophia, Peter had the bodies of the dead *streltsy* hung up along the walls of the convent and outside Sophia's window. Despite his greatness, Peter had a weakness for the grotesque, especially when it came to punishing his enemies. He left the decaying bodies hanging in the monastery for more than a year. Yet another of the convent's "inmates" was Yevdokiya, Peter's first wife. Peter considered her a pest and rid himself of her by sending Yevdokyia to a convent in faraway Suzdal. She outlived him, though, and eventually returned to Moscow. She spent her final years at Novodevichy, where she is buried.

You enter the convent through the arched passageway topped by the **Preobrazhenskaya Tserkov** (Gate Church of the Transfiguration), widely considered one of the best examples of Moscow Baroque. To your left as you enter is the ticket booth, where tickets are sold to the various exhibits housed in the monastery. The building to your right is the Lophukin House, where Yevdokyia lived from 1727 to 1731. Sophia's prison, now a guardhouse, is situated to your far right, in a corner of the northern wall.

The dominating structure inside the monastery is the huge five-domed **Sobor Smolenskoy Bogomateri** (Cathedral of the Virgin of Smolensk), dedicated in 1525 and built by Alexei Fryazin. It may remind you of the Kremlin's Assumption Cathedral, after which it was closely modeled. Inside, there is a spectacular iconostasis with 84 wooden columns and icons dating from the 16th and 17th centuries. Simon Ushakov, a leader in 17th-century icon art, was among the outstanding Moscow artists who participated in the creation of the icons. Yet another historical tale connected to the monastery tells how the cathedral was slated for destruction during the War of 1812. Napoleon had ordered the cathedral dynamited, but a brave nun managed to extinguish the fuse just in time and the cathedral was spared.

To the right of the cathedral is the **Uspenskaya Tserkov** (Church of the Assumption) and **Refectory,** originally built in 1687 and then rebuilt after a fire in 1796. It was here that the blue-blooded nuns would have their meals.

If a monastery can have a symbol other than an icon, then Novodevichy's would be the ornate belfry towering above its eastern wall. It rises 71 meters (236 feet) and consists of six ornately decorated tiers. The structure is topped by a gilded dome that can be seen from miles away.

Time Out **U Pirosmani,** a restaurant specializing in the spicy cuisine of the former Soviet republic of Georgia, is situated across the pond from the monastery. On weekdays, it is almost always possible to get a table without a reservation. If you are visiting on a weekend, you may want to book ahead. *4 Novodevichy Proyezd, tel. 095/247-1926. Food bill paid in rubles, alcohol in dollars. AE.*

Leaving the monastery, retrace your steps, walking back down Luzhnetsky Proyezd. The entrance to the **Novodevichy Kladbishche** (cemetery) is marked by a pair of

green gates. Unless you have r'
have to buy tickets to enter; tj
wooden kiosk directly across t'
an excursion in English fron.
reau, which we highly recommenu ˎ
contains a fascinating collection of meı.
difficult for non-Russian speakers to identiı,
You may wonder how a cemetery could be controveᵣˍ
this one was. For more than a generation the Novodevıᵤˍ
Cemetery was closed to the general public, in large part because the controversial Nikita Khrushchev is buried here.
Thanks to *glasnost*, the cemetery was opened in 1987, and
now anyone is welcome to enjoy its treasures. *Luzhnetsky
Proyezd, tel. 095/246–6614. Open daily 10–5.*

Khrushchev's grave is near the back of the cemetery, at the
end of a long tree-lined walkway. If you can't find it, any of
the babushki will point out the way. They will usually reflect their opinion of him in the way they gesture, for they
almost certainly will not speak English. The memorial consists of a stark black-and-white slab, with a curvilinear border marking the separation. The contrast of black and
white symbolizes the contradictions of his reign. It caused a
great furor of objection among the Soviet hierarchy when it
was unveiled. The memorial was designed by the artist
Ernest Neizvestny, himself a controversial figure. In the
1960s Khrushchev visited an exhibit of contemporary art
that included some of Neizvestny's works. Khrushchev dis-
missed Neizvestny's contributions as "filth," to which the
artist replied, "In front of my work, I am the Premier."
Considering the times, it was a brave thing to say to the
leader of the Soviet Union. Neizvestny eventually joined
the ranks of the great emigré artists.

Many of those buried in the cemetery were war casualties in
1941 and 1942. The memorials often include a lifelike portrayal of the person being remembered or convey a scene in
that person's life. Flowers and photographs of the dead are
at almost all the graves. Among the memorials you might
want to look for are those to the composers Prokofiev and
Scriabin and the writers Chekhov, Gogol, and Mayakovsky. Chekhov's grave is decorated with the trademark
seagull of the Moscow Art Theater, the first to successfully
produce his plays. Along the right-hand wall (the southwest wall of the monastery) you will find a memorial of a
crash of a huge Soviet aircraft where all the crew members
are interred. The grave of Stalin's wife, Nadezhda
Aliluyeva, is marked by a simple tombstone with a bust of
this poor woman. She supposedly committed suicide, although many hold Stalin responsible for her death. Theodore Chaliapin, the opera singer who was stripped of his
Soviet citizenship while on tour in France in the 1920s, is
also buried here. His remains were transferred here in
1984. His grave is marked by a marvelous lifelike represen-

tation of him that conveys the fervor and passion that characterized his singing.

Tour 9: The Monasteries of Southeast Moscow

This tour will take you to three ancient monasteries located along the banks of the Yauza River, in the southeast section of Moscow. Their history dates back to Moscow's earliest days, when it was the center of a fledgling principality and constantly under threat of enemy attack. A series of monasteries was built across the river from the Kremlin to form a ring of defense fortifications. Two of the monasteries on this tour were once part of that fortification ring. This former suburban area did not fare well as the city grew. Beginning in the 19th century, factories were built along the banks of the river, including the famous Hammer and Sickle metallurgical plant. Today this is one of Moscow's bleaker sections, marked by busy highways, monolithic residential high rises, and factories. But in their midst you find the quaint monasteries of Moscow's past, not always in the best condition, but nevertheless lasting reminders of Moscow's origins.

The tour begins at **Novospassky Monastery** (New Savior Convent), which you can reach by taking the subway to the Proletarskaya station. If you bear left at every turn as you exit the subway, you will emerge on Tretoye (Third) Krutitskoye highway, just before it intersects with Sarinsky Proyezd. As you head in the direction of the river, the yellow belfry of the monastery gate church will appear above the new construction, in the distance to your right (southwest). When you reach the intersection, use the underground passageway to cross to the other side. It is just a short walk from here up a slight incline to the monastery's entrance.

The monastery was built in 1462, but its history dates back to the 13th century. It was originally founded inside the Kremlin, and it is called the "New" Monastery because of its new site on the banks of the Yauza River. Its transfer was ordered by Ivan III, who wanted to free up space in the Kremlin for new construction. Often called Ivan the Great, Ivan III was the first Russian leader to categorically (and successfully) renounce Russia's allegiance to the khan of the Golden Horde. It was during his reign that a unified Russian state was formed under Moscow's rule. The Novospassky Monastery was just one of the numerous churches and monasteries built during the prosperous time of Ivan's reign.

You enter the monastery through the Bell Tower Gate, which was erected in 1786. If you look carefully you can trace the frescoes that once decorated the inside walls of the archway. The entire monastery is, sadly, in a state of disrepair. It has been under reconstruction for more than a quarter of a century. It was recently returned to the Orthodox Church, and perhaps this will result in renewed efforts to restore it. Except on Sunday and church holidays, the monastery grounds are often deserted. A stroll among its decaying buildings can therefore be a rather eerie experience.

The first thing you see as you enter the monastery grounds is the massive **Sobor Spasa Preobrazheniya** (Transfiguration Cathedral). You may notice a resemblance to the Kremlin's Assumption Cathedral, which served as its model. The Transfiguration Cathedral was built in 1642–49 by the Romanov family, commissioned by the czar as the Romanov family crypt. The gallery leading to the central nave is decorated with beautiful frescoes depicting the history of Christianity in Rus. It is worth timing your visit with a church service (daily at 5 PM) to see the interior. Even if the church is closed, the doors may be unlocked. No one will stop you from taking a quick look at the gallery walls.

In front of the cathedral, on the right-hand side, is the **Nadmogilnaya Chasovnya** (Memorial Chapel), marking the grave of Princess Alekseyevna Tarankova, the illegitimate daughter of Empress Elizabeth and Count Razumovsky. She led most of her life as a nun in Moscow's St. John's Convent, forced to take the veil by Catherine the Great. During her lifetime her identity was concealed, and she was known only as Sister Dofiya. The chapel over her grave was added in 1900, almost a century after her death. Sister Dofiya's imposter played a more prominent role in Russian history than the real Princess Tarankova. A mysterious character of European origin, the impostor never revealed her true identity. She was imprisoned by Catherine the Great in St. Petersburg's Peter and Paul Fortress, where she died of consumption in 1775. Her death in her flooded, rat-infested cell was depicted in a famous painting by Konstantin Flavitsky in 1864.

None of the monastery's original 15th-century structures have survived. The present fortification wall and most of the churches and residential buildings on the grounds date from the 17th century. To your immediate right as you enter stands the small Church of St. Nicholas (1652). Directly behind the cathedral is the Church of the Sign. It was built in 1791–1808 by the wealthy Sheremetyev family and contains the Sheremetyev crypt. In the back right-hand corner, running along the fortification walls, are the former monks' residences.

Leaving the monastery through the bell-tower gates, turn right and cross the busy Sarinsky Proyezd. Walking in the direction of the river (away from the subway), you will come to a narrow street leading up a steep incline to your left (Chetvortoye Krutitskoye Lane). At the top of the hill stands the Krutitskoye Podvorye (Krutitskoye Residence). It dates back even further than the Novospassky Monastery; the first cathedral on this site was erected sometime in the 13th century. Its name comes from the word *kruta*, meaning "hill." This was originally a small monastery, of little or no defense value, but its prestige grew at the end of the 16th century, when it became the suburban residence of the Moscow metropolitan. The church and grounds were completely rebuilt, and the present structures date from this period. As monasteries go, its period of revival was short-lived; it was closed in 1788 on orders from Catherine the Great, who secularized many church buildings during her reign. In the 19th century it was used as an army barracks, and it is said that the Russians accused of setting the Moscow fire of 1812 were tortured here by Napoleon's forces. In the 20th century, the Soviets turned the barracks into a military prison. Although the buildings have now been returned to the Orthodox Church, the prison remains on the monastery grounds. There is also a police station right outside the main gate, so do not be alarmed if you are greeted by a small band of uniformed policemen as you enter.

To your left as you enter the monastery grounds is the five-domed, redbrick **Uspensky Sobor** (Assumption Cathedral), erected at the end of the 16th century on the site of several previous churches. Attached to it is a gallery leading to the **Teremok** (Gate Tower), a splendid example of Moscow Baroque. It was built in 1688–94, and its exterior decoration is the work of Osip Startsev. Except for the carved, white columns, the walls are completely covered with colorful ceramic tiles. The red, green, and white tiles—all of different sizes and shapes—are framed in the red brick of the adjoining buildings. As a result, despite the frenzy inherent in the tile decoration, the overall effect is one of a compositional whole. The gallery and Teremok served as passageway for the metropolitan as he walked from his residence (to the right of the Teremok) to the cathedral. The military prison, replete with lookout towers, is located on the opposite side of the Teremok gates.

The next monastery on the tour is best reached by subway. Return to the Proletarskaya station and take the subway one stop to the Taganskaya station. Before exiting, transfer to the connecting station on the circle line. You will come out onto Taganskaya Square.

Time Out   Taganskaya Square is home to Moscow's most renowned drama theater, the Taganka, and the area is rich in restaurants catering to theater crowds. One of the best is the **Skazka** restaurant (1 Tovarishchevsky pereulok, tel. 095/ 271–0998), an excellent cooperative specializing in Russian cuisine. As with most other restaurants in Moscow, you are best off making reservations.

Several streets intersect at this busy square. Head for Bolshaya Kommunisticheskaya, the third street to your left as you exit the subway. This is a quiet residential area; the narrow street is lined with tall birch trees and two-story apartment buildings. One block down, at No. 15, is the lovely **Church of St. Martin the Confessor**. It dates from the late 18th century and is badly in need of restoration; its cupola is rusted and trees are growing on its roof. For years the church stood empty and abandoned, but recently it was returned to the Orthodox Church, and despite its decrepit condition, daily services have been resumed here. Farther down the street, at No. 29, you find another building of historical importance, the apartment house where the theater director Stanislavsky was born in 1863.

Continue down the street until you reach **Andronevskaya Ploshchad**. Cross to the opposite side of the square and turn left onto Andronevsky Pereulok. On the left-hand side of the street there is a small park, and just beyond that lies the entrance to the **Andronikov Monastery**. The whitewashed walls of the monastery's fortification will be visible through the trees.

The Andronikov Monastery is home to the **Andrey Rublyov Museum of Ancient Russian Culture and Art**. The museum is named after the monastery's most celebrated monk, the icon painter Andrey Rublyov, who is believed to be buried here. Rublyov lived in the early 15th century, a time of much bloodshed and violence. Russia was slowly loosening the Mongol-Tatar yoke, and people lived in constant fear as the divided Russian principalities fought among themselves and against the Mongol-Tatar invaders. Rublyov's icons seem even more remarkable when viewed against the backdrop of his turbulent era. His works are amazing creations of flowing pastels conveying peace and tranquility. His most famous work, *The Holy Trinity*, is now housed in the Tretyakov Gallery (*see* Tour 7). The museum in the Andronikov Monastery, strangely enough, does not contain a single Rublyov work. Its collection of ancient religious art is nevertheless a fine one and well worth a visit. Tickets to the exhibits are sold in the office located to your immediate right and around the corner as you enter the monastery grounds. The museum is divided into three sections, and you must purchase a ticket for each. *Andronevskaya Ploshchad 10, tel. 095/278–1429. Open Thurs.–Tues. 11–6. Closed last Fri. of month.*

The Andronikov Monastery underwent extensive reconstruction in the 1950s and was refurbished again in the late 1980s. It is happily in much better condition than the Novospassky Monastery or Krutitskoye Podvorye. A stroll inside its heavy stone fortification is like taking an excursion into Moscow's past. The rumble of the city is drowned out by the loud crowing of birds overhead. The air even seems more pure here, perhaps because of the tall, old birch trees growing on the monastery grounds and just outside its walls. The Andronikov Monastery was founded in 1360

by the metropolitan Alexei and named in honor of its first
abbot, St. Andronik. The site was chosen not only for its
strategic importance—on the steep banks of the Yauza River—but also because, according to legend, it was from this
hill that the metropolitan Alexei got his first glimpse of the
Kremlin.

The dominating structure on the monastery grounds is the
Spassky Sobor (Cathedral of the Savior), erected in 1420–27
on the site of an earlier, wooden church. It rests on the mass
grave of Russian soldiers who fought in the Battle of
Kulikovo (1380), the decisive Russian victory that eventually led to the end of Mongol rule in Russia. Unfortunately,
the original interiors, which were painted by Andrei
Rublyov and another famous icon painter, Danil Chorny,
were lost to a fire in 1812. Fragments of their frescoes have
been restored, however. The cathedral is open for services
at 5:30 PM on Saturday and 9 AM on Sunday.

The building to your immediate left as you enter the monastery
is the former abbot's residence. It now houses the exhibit entitled "Masterpieces of Ancient Russian Art" from the 13th
through 16th centuries. The exhibit includes icons from the
Novgorod, Tver, Rostov, and Moscow schools. A highlight of
the collection is the early-16th-century *St. George Smiting
the Dragon*, from the Novgorod School.

The next building, to the left and across the pathway from the
Cathedral of the Savior, is the **Refectory.** Like the Novospassky Monastery, it was built during the reign of Ivan
the Great, in 1504–06. Today it houses the museum's exhibit of new acquisitions, which consists primarily of icons
from the 19th and 20th centuries. Attached to the Refectory is the Church of St. Michael the Archangel, another
example of the style known as Moscow Baroque. It was
commissioned by the Lopukhin family—relatives of
Yevdokiya Lopukhina, the first, unloved wife of Peter the
Great—as the family crypt in 1694. But there are no
Lophukins buried here; Peter had Yevdokiya banished to a
monastery in faraway Suzdal before the church was even
finished, and her family was exiled to Siberia.

The last museum exhibit is located in the former monks'
residence, the redbrick building just beyond the Church of
St. Michael. The exhibit is devoted to Nikolai the Miracle
Worker and contains icons depicting his life and work.

Leave the monastery through the main gate and return to
Andronevskaya Ploshchad. The nearest subway station is
Ploshchad Ilyicha. To reach it, turn left from the square
onto Tukhinskaya ulitsa; the subway is just one long block
away.

Excursion 1: Arkhangelskoye Estate Museum

This museum is located in the village of Arkhangelskoye, some 26 kilometers (15 miles) from Moscow. It has been closed for several years for restoration work, and no date has been set for its reopening. Check with IntourService (tel. 095/203–8954 or 095/202–9975) for updated information; if the museum does reopen, it is well worth a visit.

The estate, which includes the former palace of Prince Yusupov, is a striking group of 18th- and 19th-century buildings whose architecture artfully blends into the landscape. The main complex was built at the end of the 18th century for Prince Golitsyn by the French architect Chevalier de Huerne. In 1810, it was bought by the rich landlord Yusupov, who was at one time the director of the imperial theaters and of the Hermitage Museum. The estate became home to his extraordinary art collection.

The classical palace contains paintings by Boucher, Vigeé-Lebrun, Hubert Robert, Roslin, Tiepolo, Van Dyck, and many others, as well as antique statues, furniture, mirrors, chandeliers, glassware, and china. In the study there are portraits of royalty and nobility. The collection also includes samples of fabrics, china, and glassware, all of which were produced on the estate.

In the French Park, the avenues are lined with many statues and monuments to commemorate royal visits; there is also a monument to Pushkin, whose favorite retreat was Arkhangelskoye. In the western part, a small pavilion known as the Temple to the Memory of Catherine the Great depicts the empress as Themis, goddess of justice. The Estate Theater, on the right side of the main road, was built in 1817 by the serf architect Ivanov; it seated 400 and was the home of the biggest and best-known company of serf-actors. The well-preserved stage decorations are by the Venetian artist Pietrodi Gonzaga.

Excursion 2: Zagorsk (Sergyev Posad)

Zagorsk is located some 75 kilometers (46.5 miles) northeast of Moscow, making it a comfortable day trip. The city's chief attraction is the **Troitsa-Sergyeva Lavra** (Trinity Monastery of St. Sergius), which for 500 years has been one of the most important centers of pilgrimage in Russia. Before the revolution, the town was known as Sergyev Posad, after the monastery's founder, and in 1991 it was officially returned to its proper name. But the Soviet name of Zagorsk—in honor of a Bolshevik who was assassinated in 1919—has ironically stuck, and even today you are more likely to hear the town and even the monastery itself referred to as Zagorsk.

The city's second claim to fame is its role as a center of toy making. The world's first *matryoshka* (wooden nesting

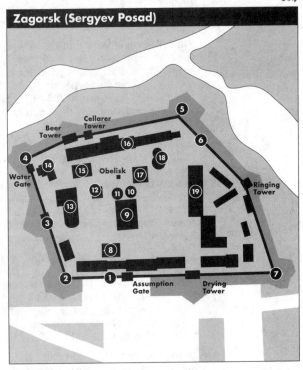

doll) was designed here at the beginning of the century, and most of the matroshkas you see for sale in Moscow and St. Petersburg originated in Zagorsk. The city even has a Toy Museum. It is rarely included on organized tours, but it is located within walking distance of the monastery, at 136 Prospect Krasnoi Armii. The museum contains a collection of toys that amused, educated, and illuminated the lives of Russian children for generations. It is well worth an hour of your time, even if your interest is only casual.

The best way to visit is on an organized tour. IntourService (tel. 095/203–8954 or 095/202–9975) and Apex Tours (tel. 095/941–8426) both offer day trips to Zagorsk. The cost is around $40–$45 and usually includes lunch in addition to a guided tour and transportation. It is also possible to visit on your own by taking the commuter train from Moscow's Yaroslavsky Vokzal (Yaroslav Railroad Station). The ride takes about two hours; tickets are purchased at the train station for rubles. This is obviously much less expensive than an organized tour, but far from hassle-free. If you choose this alternative, be sure to pack your own lunch, since Zagorsk's only full-fledged restaurant fills up fast with prebooked tourist groups, especially in the summer. You should also take care to dress appropriately for your visit to the functioning monastery. Men are expected to remove their hats, and women should wear skirts and bring something to cover their heads.

The monastery was founded in 1340 by Sergius of Radonezh, who would later become Russia's patron saint. The site rapidly became the nucleus of the small medieval settlement, and in 1550 the imposing white walls were built to enclose the complex of buildings. The monastery was a Russian stronghold during the Time of Troubles and the Polish assault on Moscow in the early 17th century, and Peter the Great took refuge here during a bloody revolt of the streltsy that took the lives of some of his closest relatives and advisors. After the Bolshevik Revolution, the monastery was closed and turned into a museum. During World War II however, in an attempt to mobilize the country and stir up patriotism, the Soviet government got the support of the Church by returning to religious purposes some of the church property that had been confiscated earlier, including the Monastery of St. Sergius. Today almost all the churches are again open for worship, and there is even a flourishing theological college here. Until the reopening in 1988 of the Danilovsky Monastery in Moscow, this monastery was the residence of the patriarch and administrative center of the Russian Orthodox Church.

The ride to Zagorsk takes you through the Russian countryside, dotted with colorful wooden cottages. As you approach the town, you see the sad and monolithic apartment buildings of the modern era. Then, peeking out above the sloping hills, the monastery's golden cupolas and soft-blue bell tower come into view.

You enter the monastery through the archway of the **Gate Church of St. John the Baptist.** It was erected in the late 17th-century and is decorated with frescoes telling the life story of St. Sergius.

One of the most important historical events in his life occurred prior to the 1380 Battle of Kulikovo, the decisive Russian victory that led to the end of Mongol rule in Russia. Before leading his troops off to battle, Prince Dmitry Donskoy sought the blessing of the peace-loving monk Sergius, a move that is generally thought to have greatly aided the Russian victory.

The dominating structure of the monastery is the massive, five-domed **Uspensky Sobor** (Assumption Cathedral) located in the center of the monastery grounds. Built in 1554–85 with money donated by Czar Ivan the Terrible, it was modeled after the Kremlin's Uspensky Sobor. This one, however, has dark-blue, star-studded domes. Its interior boasts frescoes and a 17th-century iconostasis. Among the artists to work on it was Simon Ushakov, a well-known icon painter from Moscow. The cathedral is open for morning services.

The small building just outside the Uspensky Cathedral (near the northwest corner) is the Tomb of Boris Godunov and his family. Boris Godunov died suddenly in 1605, during the Polish attack on Moscow led by the False Dmitry, the first of many impostors to claim he was the son of Czar Ivan the Terrible. The death of Boris facilitated the invaders' victory, after which his family was promptly murdered. This explains why Boris was not bestowed the honor of burial in the Kremlin normally granted to czars.

Opposite Boris Godunov's tomb is a tiny and colorful chapel built above a miracle-working fountain. According to legend, the spring here appeared during the Polish Siege (1608–10), when the monastery bravely held out for 16 months against the foreign invaders (this time led by the second False Dmitry). Towering above the monastery grounds is the five-tiered Baroque Belfry, which rises 285 feet. It was built in the 18th century to a design by the master of St. Petersburg Baroque, Bartolomeo Rastrelli.

Along the southern wall of the monastery, to your far left as you enter, is the 17th-century **Refectory and Church of St. Sergei.** The church is at the eastern end, topped by a single gilded dome. It was built at the same time as the long building of the Refectory, whose colorful facade adds to the vivid richness of the monastery's architecture. In times past, pilgrims from near and far would gather here on feast days. The pink building just beyond the Refectory is the Metropolitan's Residence.

A continual service in memorium to St. Sergei is held all day, every day in the gold-capped **Troitsky Sobor** (Church of the Holy Trinity), situated across the path from the Metropolitan's Residence. The church was built in the 15th century over the tomb of St. Sergei; over the centuries it has received many precious gifts from the powerful and wealthy rulers who have made the pilgrimage to the church of Russia's patron saint. The icons inside were created by the famous Andrei Rublyov and Danil Chorny. Ryublov's celebrated *Holy Trinity*, now on display at the Tretyakov Gallery, originally hung here; the work you see is a copy.

The vestry, the building behind the Church of the Holy Trinity, houses the monastery's **Museum of Ancient Russian Art.** It is often closed for no apparent reason, and often open only to groups, which is yet another reason to visit Zagorsk on a guided tour. The museum contains a spectacular collection of gifts presented to the monastery over the centuries. On display are precious jewels, jewel-encrusted embroideries, chalices, and incense burners. Next door to the vestry are two more museums, which are generally open to individual tourists. The first museum contains icons and icon covers, portrait art, and furniture. The other museum (on the second floor) is devoted to Russian folk art, with wooden crafted items and toys, as well as porcelain and jewelry. There is a gift shop here where you can pick up a souvenir of your visit to ancient Zagorsk.

Excursion 3: New Jerusalem Monastery

Novoierusalimsky Monastyr (New Jerusalem Monastery) is located near the town of Istra, some 55 kilometers (34 miles) northwest of Moscow. This is not the most visited place in Russia, and it is included in the standard offerings of tourist agencies only in the summer. In nice weather, it is a marvelous way to spend a day; its location in the picturesque Russian countryside—far from tourist crowds—only adds to its attraction. If you can't book a tour and are feeling adventurous, you could try an excursion on the commuter train. Trains leave from Rizhsky Vokzal (Riga Railroad Station) and take about an hour and a half. The best option of all would be to ask a Russian friend to guide your way and make a day of it in the countryside. Be sure to pack your lunch; the best you'll find in Istra is an occasional cafeteria or outdoor café. The monastery's museums are open 10–5 and are closed Monday and the last Friday of the month.

Many of the museums, monasteries, and palaces in Russia are marvels of restoration. This is particularly true of those found in St. Petersburg, for that city and its environs were almost totally destroyed by the Germans in World War II. A visit to New Jerusalem will give you an idea of exactly how miraculous their rise from the ashes has been. The monastery is being restored from the damage done to it in 1941, but the work has far to go to completion. Here you can see paintings on plaster that have almost disappeared, rooms that have no doors, walls that are on the verge of collapse. But you can also see the vision the architects and religious leaders of the day had for this early Russian monastery.

The monastery was founded in 1652 by Nikon, patriarch of the Russian Orthodox Church. It lies on exactly the same longitude as Jerusalem; and its main cathedral, Voskresensky Sobor (Resurrection Cathedral) is modeled after the Church of the Holy Sepulcher in Jerusalem. Nikon's objective in re-creating the original Jerusalem in Russia was to glorify the power of the Russian Orthodox Church and at the same time elevate his own position as head of the Church. Nikon initiated the great church reforms in the 17th century that eventually led to the *raskol* (schism) resulting in the Old Believer sects of the Russian Orthodox faith. As a reformer, he was a progressive and enlightened man, but he also lusted for power, and that eventually was his undoing. In 1658, before the monastery was even finished, the czar and the patriarch quarreled over Nikon's claim that the Church was ultimately superior to the State. Eventually Nikon was defrocked and banished to the faraway Ferapontov Monastery. He died in virtual exile in 1681 and was buried in the monastery that was supposed to have glorified his power. You can find his crypt in the

Church of St. John the Baptist, which is actually inside the Resurrection Cathedral. Ironically, the same church commission that decided to defrock Patriarch Nikon also voted to institute his reforms.

The monastery houses the Moscow Regional Museum, which contains a modest collection of prerevolutionary paintings, portrait art, porcelain, and armory. One section is devoted to the history of the monastery and its reconstruction. There is also an exhibition hall for temporary exhibits of contemporary art on the monastery grounds. Besides the Resurrection Cathedral, the ensemble of buildings inside the monastery includes the Moscow Baroque Nativity Church, the Czar's Chambers, and the modest Three-Saints Church. Nikon's three-story Hermitage is located just outside the monastery's stone walls.

If you follow the path behind the monastery leading to the river, you will reach the Architectural and Ethnographic Museum of the Moscow Region. This open-air museum of renovated Russian wooden architecture is set among the coppices on the high banks of the River Istra. Here you will find a 19th-century reconstructed peasant hut, which is particularly interesting since dwelling houses like this are still in use. A huge stove takes up much of the living space, above which the peasants slept. You will also find on the museum grounds a reconstruction of a wooden palace, a 17th-century wooden church, and a windmill, all of which have been brought from various parts of Russia.

What to See and Do with Children

The **Moscow Circus** is always a hit with children. There are two big tops: the intimate "Old" Circus at 13 Tsvetnoy Bulvar (tel. 095/200–0668), and the modern "New" Circus at 7 Vernandsky Prospect (tel. 095/930–2815). You can get tickets for both through the IPS Theater Box Office in the Metropole hotel (tel. 095/927–6728 or 095/927–6729) or IntourService (tel. 095/203–8954 or 095/202–9975).

Even children who don't know Russian will enjoy the performances of the **Obraztsov Puppet Theater** (3 Sadovo-Samotechnaya, tel. 095/299–3310). Puppetry is a particularly popular art form in Russia, and this troupe is world-famous. The theater also boasts a "puppet cuckoo clock," which comes to life every hour on the hour.

A fast elevator ride up the 364-meter (1,200-foot) **Ostankino Television Tower** (15 ul. Akademika Korolyeva, tel. 095/282–2038) is bound to thrill any child. On a clear day, the view is tremendous. The tower is open for viewing 9–7, closed Monday. Visitors are allowed in at set times (approximately every 30 minutes) in groups. Bring your passport; you'll be asked to fill out a form with all your background information, a holdover from the Soviet days. If you want, you can have lunch at the tower's rotating restaurant, Sedmoye Nebo (Seventh Heaven). The food is bland but cheap. The restaurant is open from 10 to 6:30. The set meal includes appetizer, main course, ice cream, and coffee.

Animal lovers will get a kick out of the **Durova Animal Theater** (ul. Durova 4, tel. 095/971–3047). The acting troupe at this theater (named for its founder, the famous animal trainer Vladimir Durov) is made up of cats, dogs, goats, and bears.

Winter or summer, **Gorky Park** has something for children of all ages. The Ferris wheel offers spectacular views of downtown Moscow; the amusement park has plenty of other rides that will thrill even the most jaded youngsters. In summer, excursion boats leave from the park's pier for trips around Moscow. In winter, you can join Muscovites on the crowded skating rinks or take a ride on a horse-drawn troika.

Off the Beaten Track

Donskoy Monastery The 16th-century Donskoy Monastery is a fascinating memorial to Russian architecture and art. From 1934 through 1992 the monastery housed a branch of the Shchusev Architecture Museum. Architectural details of churches, monasteries, and public buildings destroyed under the Soviets were deposited and stored inside its walls. Today the monastery is once again functioning as a religious institution, and the museum is slowly removing its exhibits from inside the churches. But the bits and pieces of demolished churches and monuments remain, forming a graveyard of destroyed architecture from Russia's past.

The monastery is situated in a secluded, wooded area in the southwest section of Moscow. You can reach it by taking the subway to the Shabolovskaya station. When you exit the subway, turn right and walk one block to Donskaya ulitsa. Turn right again and follow the street until you see the copper-topped domes of the monastery's churches above the trees to your left. Follow the path along the redbrick fortification wall until you reach the main entrance on the other side.

The monastery grounds are surrounded by a high defensive wall with 12 towers. Founded in the late 16th century, it was the last of the defense fortifications to be built around Moscow. It is situated on the site where, in 1591, the Russian army stood waiting for an impending attack from Tatar troops grouped on the opposite side of the river. According to legend, the Russians awoke one morning to find the Tatars gone. Their sudden retreat was considered a miracle, and Regent Boris Godunov ordered a monastery built to commemorate the miraculous victory. Of course, it didn't happen quite like that, but historians confirm that the Tatars did retreat after only minor skirmishes, which is difficult to explain. Never again would they come so close to Moscow. The miracle was attributed to the icon of the Virgin of the Don, which Prince Dmitry Donskoy had supposedly carried during his campaign in 1380, during which the Russians won their first decisive victory against the Tatars. The monastery was named in honor of the wonder-working icon.

When you enter through the western gates, an icon of the Mother of the Don looks down on you from above the entrance to the imposing New Cathedral. The brick cathedral was built in the late 17th century by Peter the Great's sister, Sophia. It has been under restoration for decades; services are held in the gallery surrounding the church, where the architectural exhibits were once housed. The smaller, Old Cathedral stands to the right of the New Cathedral. The attractive red church with white trim was built in 1591–93, during the reign of Boris Godunov. It is open for services.

One of the most fascinating sections of the monastery is its graveyard, where you will find many fine examples of memorial art. After the plague swept through Moscow in 1771, Catherine the Great forbade any more burials in the city center. The Donskoy Monastery, at that time located on the city's outskirts, became a fashionable burial place for the well-to-do. The small **Church of the Archangel** built against the fortification wall to your far right was the private chapel and crypt of the prominent Golitsyn family. Many leading intellectuals, politicians, and aristocrats were buried here in the 18th, 19th, and 20th centuries. Among them are the dramatist Alexander Sumarokov, the architect Osip Bove, and the philosopher Pyotr Chaadayev, who to this day receives flowers at his grave from his modern-day followers.

If you walk down to the eastern wall of the monastery, you will find remnants of the decorative stone facade of the **Cathedral of Christ Our Savior** (*see* Tour 6) which the Soviets blew up in 1931. One of the facades shows Monk Sergei of Radonezh giving his blessing to Dmitry Donskoy before he left for the decisive battle that led to the end of Tatar rule in Russia. The northern wall is lined with portals from ancient churches destroyed or flooded along the Volga to make way for a huge reservoir. As you make your way back to the main entrance, you will notice a cast-iron pedestal in the courtyard outside the New Cathedral. This is the remains of the Triumphal Arch that once stood at the end of Tverskaya ulitsa. It was destroyed in the 1930s and then, in the 1960s, a replica of the original arch was erected at the end of Kutuzovsky Prospect.

Kolomenskoye If you want to spend an afternoon in the great Russian outdoors without actually leaving the city, a visit to Kolomenskoye is a must. Situated on a high bluff overlooking the Moskva River, this estate was once a favorite summer residence of Moscow's grand dukes and czars. Today it is a popular public park with museums, a functioning church, old Russian cottages, and other attractions. Take the subway to the Kolomenskaya station on the green line; a short walk up a slight hill will bring you to the park's entrance. *39 Prospect Andropova, tel. 095/115–2713. Open Wed.–Sun. 11–5.*

As you walk up the hill to Kolomenskoye, the first sight to greet you is the striking blue domes of the **Church of Our Lady of Kazan.** The church is open for worship. A wooden palace once stood in the park opposite the church. It was built by Czar Alexei, Peter the Great's Father, and Peter spent much time here when he was growing up. Nothing remains of this huge wooden palace (Catherine the Great ordered it destroyed in 1767) but there is a scale model at the museum. The exhibits of the museum, devoted to Russian timber architecture and folk crafts, are found in the old servants' quarters, at the end of the treelined path leading from the main entrance.

Most remarkable is the **Church of the Ascension,** situated on the bluff overlooking the river. Its skyscraping tower is an example of the tent or pyramid-type structure that was popular in Russian architecture in the 16th century. The church dates from the 1530s although it was restored in the late 19th century. The view from the bluff is impressive: you can look from the 16th century across the river to the north, to the 20th-century concrete apartment houses that dominate the contemporary Moscow skyline. In summer you'll see Muscovites bathing in the river below the church, and in winter the area abounds in cross-country skiers.

Examples of wooden architecture from other parts of Russia have been transferred to Kolomenskoye, turning the estate into an open-air museum. In the wooded area near the site of the former wooden palace, you will find a 17th-century prison tower from Siberia, a defense tower from the White Sea, and a 17th-century mead brewery from the village of Preobrazhenskaya. One of the most attractive buildings to be seen in its original form is the wooden cottage where Peter the Great lived while supervising the building of the Russian fleet in Arkhangelsk. It was moved here from that northern city in 1934.

Kuskovo Palace Museum In the 18th and 19th centuries, this country estate was the Moscow aristocracy's favorite summer playground. It belonged to the noble Sheremetyev family, one of Russia's wealthiest and most distinguished (you probably arrived at "their" international airport, built on land once belonging to one of their many estates). Kuskovo is located just outside the ring road marking the city borders, but you can reach it by public transportation. Take the subway to Ryazansky Prospect and then Bus 208 or 133 six stops to Kuskovo Park. This is obviously not as accessible as Kolomenskoye, and you may find it more convenient to book a tour that would include transportation. Whatever you do, be sure to phone ahead before making the trek out here, because the estate often closes in humid weather and when it is very cold. *Ul. Yunosti 2, tel. 095/370–0160. Open Wed.–Sun. 10–4. Closed last Wed. of month.*

The land of Kuskovo belonged to the Sheremetyevs as far back as the early 17th century, but the estate acquired its present appearance in the late 18th century. Often called a Russian Versailles, it was commissioned by Prince Peter Sheremetyev, who sought a suitable place for entertaining guests in the summer. The park was created by Russian landscape artists who had spent much time in Europe studying their art. The French-style gardens are dotted with buildings representing the major architectural trends of Europe: the Dutch cottage, the Italian villa, the grotto, and the hermitage, where, in the fashion of the day, dinner tables were raised mechanically from the ground floor to the second-floor dining room.

The centerpiece of the estate is the wooden palace, built in the early Russian classical style by the serf architects Alexei Mironov and Fedor Argunov. Peter Sheremetyev owned more than 150,000 serfs, many of whom received architectural training and participated in the building of his estate. The palace, which is made of timber on a white-stone foundation, overlooks an artificial lake. It has been a museum since 1918, and its interior decorations, including fine parquet floors and silk wall-coverings, have been well preserved.

On display in the inner rooms are paintings by French, Italian, and Flemish artists, Chinese porcelain, furniture, ornaments, and other articles of everyday life from the 18th and 19th centuries. The palace also houses one of the best collections of 18th-century Russian art and contains a ceramics museum with a rich collection of Russian, Soviet, and foreign ceramics. The bedroom, with its fine canopy bed, was merely for show; the Sheremetyevs used the palace exclusively for entertainment purposes and did not actually live here. The marvelous White Hall, with its parquet floors, gilded wall decorations, and crystal chandeliers, served as the ballroom.

Ostankino Museum of Serf Art Like the Kuskovo Palace (*see above*), this museum is set in another estate belonging to the wealthy Sheremetyev family. It was commissioned by Count Nikolai Sheremetyev in the late 18th century and built by a team of serf architects. They were led by Pavel Argunov, himself a serf, who contributed much to the Sheremetyev estate in Kuskovo. There is a sad tale of love behind this magnificent estate. In 1801 Count Nikolai married Praskovia Kovalyova, a member of his serf acting troupe. The daughter of a blacksmith, Praskovia had captured the count's heart with her wit and beauty. Their marriage caused quite a scandal, and the couple withdrew from society to their newly built estate in

Ostankino. But just two years after their marriage, Praskovia died in childbirth, and the heartbroken count abandoned the estate forever. The palace was closed for restoration work in 1991; it was scheduled to reopen again in late 1993, but call first to confirm opening hours. You can reach it by taking the subway to VDNKh (All-Russian Exhibition Center, opposite the Kosmos Hotel); from there take Tram 11 or 17 to the last stop on the line. *Ul. Pervaya Ostankinskaya 5, tel. 095/286–6288.*

The Sheremetyev estate encompassed more than 2 million acres, with 150,000 serfs and an annual income of 1 1/2 million rubles. The palace's fine decorations include delicate, lacelike gilt carvings on the portals and doors, cornices, columns, and walls. Ornate crystal chandeliers hang from the painted ceilings, and the fine parquet floors are truly masterpieces of art. The stoves and fireplaces are faced with varnished tiles, marble, malachite, and bronze. There is also a fine collection of 17th- and 18th-century carvings, crystal, porcelain, and fans.

The highlight of the palace is its theater, which had its heyday in the 18th century. The company included some 200 actors, singers, dancers, and musicians, all of them serfs belonging to the Sheremetyev family. The chairs in the theater were movable so that the auditorium could be transformed into a ballroom within minutes. The devices for scenic, lighting, and sound effects were also invented by the serfs. Just outside the main entrance to the palace is the redbrick Church of the Trinity, built in 1683 by the serf architect Pavel Potekhin. The church recently reopened for services.

Sightseeing Checklist

This list includes attractions covered in the preceding tours as well as additional ones described for the first time.

Art and Architecture Museums

Andrey Rublyov Museum of Ancient Culture and Art (in the Andronikov Monastery, *see* Tour 9)

House of Artists (*see* Tour 7)

Manege Central Exhibit Hall (*see* Tour 4)

Museum of Decorative, Applied and Folk Art. This museum is similar to the Russian Folk Art Museum (*see* Tour 3), only bigger. The highlight here is the Palekh collection. *Delegatskaya ul. 3, tel. 095/921–0139; tours, 095/923–1741. Open Wed., Sat.–Mon. 10–6; Tues., Thurs. 12:30–8. Closed last Thurs. of month.*

Museum of Horse Breeding. This special curiosity grew out of a collection of paintings belonging to a stud-farm owner who was in charge of Russia's stud farms in the 1920s. On display are canvases and sculptures depicting thoroughbreds, Russian trotters, and troikas in decorative and everyday harness. The collection also includes carriages, dress harnesses, various bells, and toy horses made of china, clay, and glass. *Timiryazevskaya ul. 44, tel. 095/976–1003. Open Thurs., Sat. 10–4.*

Museum of 17th-Century Applied Art (*see* Tour 1)

Museum of 17th-Century Architecture and Art (*see* Tour 2)

Oriental Art Museum. The museum has a large collection of art from the Central Asian republics, China, India, Japan, and Africa. *12A Nikitsky Bulvar, tel. 095/202–4555. Open Tues.–Sun. 11–8.*

Ostankino Museum of Serf Art (*see* Off the Beaten Track)

Puppet Museum. This museum, located in the Obraztsov Puppet Theater, has a collection of old and modern theatrical puppets from more than 30 countries. It is open 45 minutes prior to performances. *3 Sadovaya-Samotechnaya, tel. 095/299–0904. Closed summer.*

Pushkin Museum of Fine Arts (*see* Tour 6)

Russian Folk Art Museum (*see* Tour 3)

Shchusev Architecture Museum (*see* Tour 5)

16th–17th Century Palace Chambers (in the Romanov House, *see* Tour 2)

Tretyakov Art Gallery (*see* Tour 7)

Churches, Temples, and Monasteries

Andronikov Monastery (see Tour 9)

Annunciation Cathedral (Blagoveshchensky Sobor, *see* Tour 1)

Assumption Cathedral (Uspensky Sobor, *see* Tour 1)

Cathedral of the Archangel (Arkhangelsky Sobor, *see* Tour 1)

Cathedral of Twelve Apostles (*see* Tour 1)

Church of All-Saints in Kulishki (*see* Tour 2)

Church of the Ascension (*see* Tour 4)

Church of the Deposition of the Robe (Tserkov Rispolozheniya, *see* Tour 1)

Church of the Intercession in Fili. This 17th-century church is a charming example of Moscow Baroque. It is open as a museum and used as a display hall for temporary art exhibits. It is located near the Fili subway station on the light blue line; follow the subway line (which runs above ground) when you exit the station, and it will lead you directly to the church. *Ul. Novozavodskaya 6, tel. 095/148–4552. Open Thurs.–Mon. 11–5. Closed last Fri. of month.*

Church of the Nativity (*see* Tour 3)

Church of the Resurrection (*see* Tour 3)

Church of St. Barbara (*see* Tour 2)

Church of St. George on Pskov Hill (*see* Tour 2)

Church of St. Martin the Confessor (*see* Tour 9)

Church of St. Maxim the Blessed (*see* Tour 2)

Church of St. Nicholas in Khamovniki (*see* Tour 7)

Church of St. Simon Stylites (*see* Tour 5)

Church of the Transfiguration on the Sands (*see* Tour 5)

Danilovsky Monastery. Originally founded in the 13th century and used as an orphanage by the Soviets, this monastery was returned to the Orthodox Church in the 1980s and restored for the celebrations of 1,000 years of Christianity in Rus in 1988. It is now the seat of the Patriarch of Moscow and All Russia; the Orthodox Church moved its administrative center here from the St. Sergius monastery in Zagorsk. The monastery is open on Sunday, when services are held in its Church of the Intercession. The closest subway stop is the Tulskaya station on the gray line. *22 Danilovsky Val.*

Donskoy Monastery (*see* Off the Beaten Track)

Dormition Cathedral (Uspensky Sobor, *see* Tour 1)

Epiphany Monastery (*see* Tour 2)

Ivan the Great Bell Tower (*see* Tour 1)

Ivanovsky Monastery (St. John's Convent, corner of Zabelina ul. and Maly Ivanovsky Pereulok, near the Kitai Gorod subway station). The monastery was built in the 16th century and restored in the 19th. Today it is in shambles, having been used as a prison in the Stalinist era. Among the noble women who were forced to take the veil here were Empress Elizabeth's illegitimate daughter, Princess Tarankova, and the mad serf-owner Daryia Saltykova, who was imprisoned here after she murdered 138 of her serfs, most of them young women.

Krutitskoye Residence (Krutitskoye Podvorye, *see* Tour 9)

New Jerusalem Monastery (*see* Excursion 3)

New Maiden's Convent and Cemetery (Novodevichy Monastery, *see* Tour 8)

New Savior Convent (Novospassky Monastery, *see* Tour 9)

St. Basil's Cathedral (Pokrovsky Sobor, *see* Tour 1)

Trinity Church in Nikitniki (*see* Tour 2)

Synagogue. Moscow's synagogue, located near the Kitai Gorod subway station, holds services every morning at 8. *Ul. Arkhipova 8, tel. 095/923–9697.*

Yelokhovsky Cathedral. This attractive, blue-and-gold cathedral is one of Moscow's most important churches. Until the reopening of the Danilovsky Monastery in 1988, this was the seat of the Moscow patriarch. The remains of St. Alexei, metropolitan of Moscow in the 14th century, are buried here in a shrine in front of the iconostasis. Morning and evening services are held daily. The cathedral is located a block south of the Baumanskaya subway station. *Ul. Spartakovskaya 15.*

Zachaitievsky Monastery (*see* Tour 6)

Zagorsk (Sergyev Posad, *see* Excursion 2)

Znamensky Cathedral (*see* Tour 2)

Historical Buildings and Sites

Arbat (*see* Tour 5)

Armory Palace (Oruzhenaya Palata, *see* Tour 1)

Bolshoi Theater (*see* Tour 2)

Children's World (Detsky Mir, *see* Tour 2)

Diamond Fund (Almazny Fond, *see* Tour 1)

English House (*see* Tour 2)

Friendship House (*see* Tour 5)

Gorky House Museum (*see* Tour 4)

Grand Kremlin Palace (Bolshoi Kremlyovsky Dvorets, *see* Tour 1)

GUM (*see* Tour 1)

Ivan the Great Bell Tower (*see* Tour 1)
Kitai Gorod (*see* Tour 2)
Kremlin (*see* Tour 1)
Lenin Mausoleum (Mavzolei Lenina, *see* Tour 1)
Lubyanka Prison (*see* Tour 2)
Merchant Arcade (Gostinny Dvor, *see* Tour 2)
Metropole Hotel (*see* Tour 2)
Moskva Swimming Pool (*see* Tour 6)
Ostankino Television Tower (*see* What to See and Do with Children)
Palace of Congresses (Dvorets Syezdov, *see* Tour 1)
Palace of Facets (Granovitaya Palata, *see* Tour 1)
Pashkov House (*see* Tour 6)
Pertsov House (*see* Tour 6)
Printing Yard (Pechatny Dvor, *see* Tour 2)
Pushkin Square (Pushkinskaya Ploshchad, *see* Tour 3)
Red Square (Krasnaya Ploshchad, *see* Tour 2)
Russian State Library (*see* Tour 6)
Savoy Hotel (*see* Tour 2)
Slavonic Greco-Latin Academy (*see* Tour 1)
Spasso House (*see* Tour 5)
Tchaikovsky Conservatory (*see* Tour 4)
Terem (*see* Tour 1)
Yeliseyevsky Gastronome (*see* Tour 3)

Historical Museums

Arkhangelskoye Estate Museum (*see* Excursion 1)

Battle of Borodino (1812) Panorama and Kutuzov's Hut. The battle panorama is housed in a cylindrical building that was built in 1962 to commemorate the 150th anniversary of the famous Battle of Borodino. Adjacent is Kutuzov's wooden hut, where the Russian War Council, headed by Field Marshal Mikhail Kutuzov, decided that the army would retreat from Moscow. *38 Kutuzovsky Prospect, tel. 095/148–1927 or 095/148–5676; Kutuzov's Hut, tel. 095/148–5332. Kutuzov's Hut open Sun., Tues.–Thurs., Sat. 10–5; closed last Thurs. of month. Panorama bldg. open Sat.–Thurs. 11–6.*

Central Lenin Museum (*see* Tour 2)

Central Revolution Museum (*see* Tour 3)

Central Revolution Museum, Mokhovaya Branch (*see* Tour 6)

History Museum (*see* Tour 1)

Kolomenskoye Estate Museum (*see* Off the Beaten Track)

Kuskovo Palace Museum (*see* Off the Beaten Track)

Lenin House Museum. This manor house in Leninskyie Gori, about 30 kilometers (18 miles) from Moscow, was Lenin's country retreat. The ailing Lenin died here on January 21, 1924. The rooms are furnished as they were when Lenin lived here, and there are documents and manuscripts on display. Built in 1830, the house stands in a park of 175 acres, with 150-year-old oak trees and a number of ponds; before the revolution, it was the home of the mayor of Moscow. Old motor cars stand in the garage, including Lenin's Rolls-Royce, adapted for use in heavy snow. To reach the museum, take the suburban train from the Paveletsky railway station to the Leninskaya station, and from there Bus 27 or 28. *Leninskyie Gori, tel. 095/548-9309 or 095/548-9478. Open Wed.-Mon. 10-4. Closed last day of month.*

Museum of the History of Moscow (*see* Tour 2)

Train of Mourning (1 Kozhevnicheskaya Ploshchad, tel. 095/235-2898). This memorial to Lenin is located outside the Paveletsky Railway Station. On display are the engine and carriage that brought the coffin with Lenin's body to Moscow. *Open weekdays 10-6.*

Literary, Musical, and Theatrical Museums

Chaliapin House Museum. Theodore Chaliapin, one of the world's greatest opera singers, lived in this beautifully restored manor house from 1910 to 1922. Chaliapin was stripped of his Soviet citizenship while on tour in France in 1922; he never returned to Russia again. The Soviets turned his home into an apartment building, and until restorations in the 1980s, the building contained 60 communal apartments. With help from Chaliapin's family in France, the rooms have been arranged and furnished as they were when Chaliapin lived here. The walls are covered by works of art given to Chaliapin by talented friends (such as the artists Mikhail Vrubel and Isaac Levitan). Also on display are Chaliapin's colorful costumes, which were donated to the museum by his son. When you reach the piano room, you are treated to original recordings of Chaliapin singing his favorite roles. Entrance is from inside the courtyard. English-language excursions are available. *25-27 Novinsky Bulvar, tel. 095/205-6236. Open Tues., weekends 10-6; Wed., Thurs. 11:30-6:30. Closed last day of month.*

Chekhov Museum. The museum is located in the home where Chekhov lived from 1886 to 1890. The rooms are arranged as they were when he lived here, with his personal effects on display. Also on display are manuscripts, letters, and photographs. *Sadovaya-Kudrinskaya 6, tel. 095/291-6154. Open Thurs., weekends 11-5; Wed., Fri. 2-7. Closed last day of month.*

Dostoevsky Museum. This museum devoted to the great Russian novelist is located on the grounds of the hospital where he was born and where his father worked as a doctor. *2 ul. Dostoevskovo, tel. 095/281-1085. Open Thurs., weekends 11-6; Wed., Fri. 2-7. Closed last day of month.*

Glinka Museum. This museum is devoted to the history of music, with a special emphasis on Russian composers of the 19th century. The museum contains a fine collection of musical instruments. *4 ul. Fadeyeva, tel. 095/972-3237 or 095/251-1066. Open Wed., Fri., weekends 11-6:30; Tues., Thurs. 1-7:30. Closed last Fri. of month.*

Gorky Literary Museum (*see* Tour 4)

Lermontov Museum. The museum is devoted to the poet Mikhail Lermontov and is located in the house where he lived from 1830 to 1832. *Malaya Molchanovka ul. 2, tel. 095/291-5298. Open Thurs., weekends 11-5; Wed., Fri. 2-6.*

Mayakovsky Library and Museum. This museum to Russia's great revolutionary poet is located in his former home. *3/6 Proeyzd Serova, tel. 095/255–0186. Open Tues., Fri.–Sun. 10–6; Mon. noon–6; Thurs. 1–9.*

Alexander Pushkin Apartment Museum (*see* Tour 5)

Pushkin Memorial Museum (*see* Tour 6)

Alexander Scriabin Museum (*see* Tour 5)

Leo Tolstoy House Museum (*see* Tour 7)

Leo Tolstoy Memorial Museum (*see* Tour 6)

Tretyakov Art Gallery (*see* Tour 7)

Victor Vasnetsov Museum. This house-museum was the home of the Russian artist Victor Vasnetsov from 1894 to 1926. Built by the artist himself, it is a charming example of the Russian "fairy-tale" architectural style popular at the end of the 19th century. Inside the house, Vasnetsov's paintings of Russian fairy tales are on display. *Pereulok Vasnetsova 13, tel. 095/281–1329. Open Wed.–Sun. 10–4:30. Closed last Thurs. of month.*

Monuments and Statues
Gogol Statue (*see* Tour 5)
Karl Marx's Statue (*see* Tour 2)
Monument to Alexander Pushkin (*see* Tour 3)
Monument to Revolutionary Thinkers (*see* Tour 1)
Monument to Vladimir Mayakovsky (*see* Tour 3)
Monument to Yuri Dolgoruky (*see* Tour 3)
Plevna Memorial (*see* Tour 2)
Statue of Ivan Fyodorov (*see* Tour 2)
Tomb of the Unknown Soldier (*see* Tour 1)

Parks and Gardens
Alexander Garden (Alexandrovsky Sad, *see* Tour 1)
All-Russia Exhibition Center. Better known by its old name, VDNKh (USSR Economic Achievements Exhibit), this 221-hectare (553-acre) park was designed in the late 1930s as a national showcase for the Soviet economy. A perfect example of Soviet propaganda's wishful thinking, the park's displays showed how well the centralized planning system was working, and how each of the former Soviet republics was prospering under communist rule. The park is dotted with pavilions built in the architectural styles of the different Soviet republics that were devoted to different branches of agriculture, industry, and science. Because the final and main achievement of the Soviet economy was the collapse of the Soviet Union itself, the original exhibits are slowly being closed down; many of the pavilions have been rented out to private and joint-venture enterprises as advertising display areas. The park is open daily 10–6; it is located right outside the VDNKh subway station. *Prospect Mira, tel. 095/181–9926.*

Botanic Garden of the Russian Academy of Sciences. The garden covers an area of some 360 hectares (900 acres) and has been planted in and among the original beech, oak, and spruce forests of the Moscow area. One large landscape section has nearly 3,000 species of native plants of Russia, arranged in naturally landscaped areas. More than 1,700 kinds of trees and shrubs are planted in the dendarium. The park is best reached from the VDNKh subway station (Bus 33). Alternatively, you can walk from the Botanichesky Sad (Botanical Gardens) subway station, located about a kilometer (⅝ mile) from the park's entrance.

Gorky Park (*see* Tour 7)

Izmailovsky Park. Covering almost 1,215 hectares (3,000 acres), it includes large stretches of pine forest. The former summer residence of the czars is located on its grounds, which were once a hunting preserve. The park has a fairground and an open-air theater. On weekends it is the site of a sprawling flea market, where you can pick up some great souvenirs. *17 Narodny Prospect at Izmailovsky Park subway station.*

Kolomenskoye (*see* Off the Beaten Track)

Sokolniki Park. This 619-hectare (1,530-acre) park is named after the *sokolniki* (falconers) who used to live here. The park, which includes an ancient forest, has an open-air theater, a fairground, and in winter, a skating rink. You can rent skates and cross-country skis here in the winter. *Rusakovskaya ul. 62, at Sokolniki subway station.*

Zoo. Moscow's small zoo is located near the Barrikadnaya subway station. *1 Bolshaya Gruzinskaya. Open daily 10–5.*

Scientific and Technological Museums

Central Armed Forces Museum. The exhibits of Soviet Army tanks and fighter planes date back to 1917. Of particular interest to American tourists are the pieces of the U.S. spy plane shot down over Siberia. *2 ul. Sovietskoi Armii, tel. 095/281–1880. Open Tues.–Sun. 11–6. Closed last Tues. of month.*

Cosmonaut's Museum. The museum is devoted to exploration of outer space. On display are satellites, rockets, space suits, and an audiovisual documentary. The museum is located right next to the All-Russia Exhibition Center, at the subway station VDNKh. *Alleya Kosmonavtov, tel. 095/283–7914. Open Tues.–Sun. 10–7. Closed last Fri. of month.*

Planetarium (Sadovaya Kudrinskaya 5, tel. 095/254–1838 or 095/254–0153). Showings Wednesday–Monday.

Polytechnical Museum (*see* Tour 2)

Zoological Museum (*see* Tour 4)

Shopping

The one word that probably best describes the Moscow shopping scene is "chaos." Everywhere you turn—on the streets, in the parks, in the subways and underground pedestrian walkways, in the hotels and museums—someone is trying to sell you something. There are no rules or categories, and just about anything goes. Street vendors display expensive leather Italian boots on the same shelves as canned pickles. If you're a window shopper, you're in luck. The array of goods for sale is a fascinating seminar in the transformation of the Soviet centralized economic system into a freewheeling market economy. But if you're looking to purchase something in particular, you could easily lose your mind in the jumble of shops and vendors. The situation is a far cry from a few years back, when prices were standardized throughout the city (and the country) and stores were neatly divided into categories according to the goods they sold. There were even special shops for foreigners—**Beriozka** (Birch Tree) stores—that traded exclusively in foreign currency and were far better stocked than even the biggest rubles-only department store. Until just a few years ago, it was against the law for Soviet citizens even to enter a Beriozka, not to mention shop in one.

The Beriozka store still exists, but it is no longer the exclusive domain of the foreign shopper and the only hard-currency shop in town. Under the new enterprise laws, many private and foreign-run stores have opened up, and Russians are more than welcome to shop at them. Sometimes these stores deal only in dollars, sometimes only in rubles, and sometimes in both currencies. Sometimes goods are available only for credit cards, sometimes only for cash. Traveler's checks are rarely accepted. Most state-run department stores have rented out at least one counter to a cooperative, which usually sells goods having nothing to do with the store's specialty. So you may very well find shoes for sale in a bookstore or flowers for sale in a pharmacy.

The listings below are intended to guide you through the maze of Moscow's shops. Be aware that new shops come and go, and rules change. If you are looking for something in particular, it would probably be wise to phone ahead, first to confirm that the store is still in business, and then to learn what currency it accepts (and in what form). Most stores accepting credit cards and traveler's checks will ask to see your passport to verify identity.

Before you spend a lot of money on a souvenir, think about how you would feel if you couldn't take your purchase home with you. Art objects and anything else deemed "of value to the Russian nation" are often confiscated at the border. Customs regulations are vague, change frequently, and seem to depend primarily on the whim of the individual custom official checking your bag. Keep receipts for everything purchased in a hard-currency store; theoretically, customs officials can not confiscate or impose duty on anything purchased for dollars. Sometimes just showing them a wad of hard-currency receipts is impressive enough to stop them from inquiring further.

Shopping Districts

Historically, the main shopping districts of Moscow have been concentrated in the city center, along Tverskaya Street and New Arbat (formerly Kalinin Prospect). The closest thing in Moscow to a mall is GUM (pronounced

"goom"), a series of sho
tury shopping arcade.
partment Store, is lo
from the Kremlin.

Department Stores

Besides GUM, the
town area include T
Theater Square, at
ovated Petrovsky Passage, at ιο
state-run shopping centers with a variety
shops. The selection of goods is unpredictable and consta...
ly changing, but with perseverance and luck you can pick up
an inexpensive Russian souvenir in their gift (*podarki*) sections. Petrovsky Passage also has a number of hard-currency shops.

Street Markets

For fresh fruits and vegetables, the best farmer's market in
downtown Moscow is the Tsentralny Rynok (Central Market). You might want to try some homemade pickles, pickled garlic, or *tvorog*, a Russian version of cottage cheese.
You can taste for free. If you decide to buy, be sure to bargain. As in any other crowded area, keep your eyes out for
pickpockets. *15 Tsvetnoy Bulvar. Open Mon.–Sat. 7–6,
Sun. 7–4. Transportation: Tsvetnoy Bulvar subway station.*

You can spend a whole day at Moscow's flea market in
Izmailovsky Park. Here you'll find reasonably priced souvenirs and handicrafts, as well as Soviet memorabilia, such
as army belts, gas masks, and *matryoshky* (nesting dolls)
with portraits of Soviet leaders. Munch on outdoor-grilled
shish kebab as you wander about the booths. Nearby is the
former royal residence of Izmailovo, located in an old hunting preserve. The flea market is open weekends 9–6, but it's
best to get there early. Many vendors close down their
booths by midday. *Transportation: subway to Izmailovsky
Park station on blue line (not to be confused with next stop,
Izmailovskaya station), and follow crowds as you exit.*

Ptichi Rynok (Bird Market) is on Kalitnovskaya ulitsa.
Open on Sunday only, this market offers a fascinating
glimpse of Russians and their pets. The softhearted should
be forewarned that it is very difficult to leave this place
without making a purchase. The market is bustling with individuals selling adorable, furry animals—cats, dogs, and
hamsters—as well as exotic birds and fish. *Transportation:
subway to Taganskaya station. Exit from circle-line station, and from there take any bus or trolley from
Marksistakaya ulitsa stop (across square from subway,
near purple Tagansky department store). Bus line ends at
pet market.*

The **Art Salon of the Arts Industry Institute** has an excellent selection of artwork handcrafted by the institute's students and teachers, including hand-painted trays, quilts, ceramics, and leather goods. *31 ul. Povarskaya (formerly Vorovskovo), 2nd floor, tel. 095/290–6822. Rubles only.*

Central Art Salon. This salon sells handcrafted nesting dolls, ceramics, *khokhloma* (lacquered wood), and jewelry, all made by members of the Russian Union of Artists. *6 Ukrainsky Bulvar, tel. 095/243–9458. Open Sun.–Fri. 10–2, 3–7; Sat. 11–6. Rubles only.*

The **art boutiques** inside two **Varvarka Street** churches—St. Maxim the Blessed (open daily 11–6) and St. George on Pskov Hill (open daily 11–7)—offer a fine selection of handicrafts, jewelry, ceramics, and other types of Russian native art. Because the items for sale are considered part of an exhibit, you are asked to pay a nominal entrance fee (in rubles). *Transportation: subway to Kitai Gorod station.*

Russkyie Souveniry. This state-run souvenir shop sells hand-crafted and mass-produced folk art, *palekh* boxes, and jewelry. *9 Kutuzovsky Prospect. Open Mon.–Sat. 11–2, 3–8. Rubles only.*

The **Museum Shop** at the **Central Museum of the Revolution** is good for amber, nesting dolls, and other Soviet memorabilia such as pins, postcards, and T-shirts. *21 Tverskaya ul., tel. 095/299–1695. Open Tues.–Sun. 10–5. Rubles only.*

Beriozka This chain of state-run hard-currency stores is a dying breed; there are only two major stores left. The Beriozka in the Ukraina Hotel (tel. 095/243–2180) has a good selection of dictionaries, guidebooks, and maps, mixed in with cosmetics, porcelain, and electronic goods (cash only; open Mon.–Sat. 10–8). The Beriozka at 39 Pyatnitskaya ul. (tel. 095/231–9527) now sells mostly grocery items. *Open daily 9–8. Hard currency only (cash and major credit cards).*

Books Russia's largest bookstore is **Dom Knigi** (The Book House, 26 Novy Arbat). It has a foreign-language section where you can occasionally find books in English (rubles only; open daily 11–8). **Progress**, the bookstore of Progress Publishers (26 Zubovsky Bulvar), has outdated Soviet-produced guidebooks as well as English translations of Russian classics. You'll find a good selection of postcards and maps among the private vendors on the steps outside the main entrance (right next to the Park Kultury subway stop) (rubles or major credit cards; open daily 10:30–7:30). **Zwemmers** (18 Kuznetsky Most) is a newly opened British-Russian joint-venture with a good selection of imported, English-language publications (open Mon.–Sat. 10–7, hard currency only).

Hotels are a good place to look for English-language books. The bookstore in the Radisson Slavyanksaya (tel. 095/941–8080) has a good selection of foreign magazines, including *Time, Newsweek,* and *Cosmopolitan.* Paperbacks and dictionaries are also available (hard currency only [cash]; open daily 7:30 AM–10 PM). The bookstore in the Mezhdunarodnaya Hotel (tel. 095/253–2376) stocks English-language paperbacks, guidebooks, dictionaries, magazines, and Russian-language editions of the Russian classics (hard currency only; cash or major credit cards only; open daily 9–2 and 3–8). The Kosmos Hotel has two well-stocked hard-currency bookstores, good for guidebooks and maps.

Food **Arbat Irish Store** offers an extremely well-stocked grocery store and small department store selling electronics, household goods, car accessories, and clothing (primarily jeans). The relatively reasonable prices here make for long lines, especially on the weekend. *21 Novy Arbat, 2nd floor, tel. 095/291–7641. Open daily 10–9. Hard currency only (major credit cards, cash, traveler's checks).*

The **Astro Shop** in the Kosmos Hotel has a good selection of imported grocery items. *150 Prospect Mira, tel. 095/217–0590. Open daily 9 AM–10 PM. Hard currency only (major credit cards, cash).*

Garden Ring Supermarket. This small and expensive grocery store near the Mayakovskaya subway station has an impressive selection of imported cheeses. *22 Bolshaya Sadovaya, tel. 095/209–1572. Open daily 9–9. Hard currency only (major credit cards, cash, traveler's checks).*

Tverskoi M & S. Centrally located, this store has a hodgepodge of imported food, from canned goods to ice cream. *6 Tverskaya ul., tel. 095/229–5533. Open daily 9–9. Hard currency only (cash, major credit cards).*

Sadko's has a large selection of imported grocery items, including cheese and other dairy products, alcohol, office supplies, and health and beauty products. *16 Bolshaya Dorogomilovskaya, tel. 095/243–7502. Open Mon.–Sat. 10–8, Sun. 10–6. Hard currency only (major credit cards, cash, traveler's checks).*

Men's and **Baginski Fashion,** in the Mezhdunarodnaya Hotel, has Ital-
Women's Clothing ian and German coats, boots, and shoes. *12 Krasnopresnenskaya Naberezhnaya, tel. 095/253–2697. Open Mon.–Sat. 10–8, Sun. 10–7. Major credit cards, cash.*

Benetton, on the first floor of GUM, carries sweaters, skirts, pants, and jeans. *Tel. 095/921–5065. Credit cards only.*

Rifle Jeans sells Italian jeans, jean jackets and skirts, corduroys, and sweatshirts. *10 Kuznetsky Most, tel. 095/923–2458. Open Mon.–Sat. 10–7. Hard currency only (major credit cards, cash).*

For a taste of Russian high fashion, try **Dom Mody** (House of Fashion), also known as the Zaitsev Showroom. *21 Prospect Mira, tel. 095/281–0009. Open Mon.–Sat. 10–7.*

Sports and Fitness

Participant Sports

Access to Moscow's many municipal athletic facilities is usually restricted to those holding a season pass. Most facilities also require a special "doctor's certificate" attesting to one's good health. It is possible to obtain such a certificate by visiting a Russian clinic, but this is a time-consuming process. The listings here are therefore limited to those places that are open to short-term visitors and where it is not necessary to produce a doctor's certificate.

Bowling The bowling alley at the Kosmos Hotel (150 Prospect Mira, near VDNKh the subway station, tel. 095/215–8680) is open daily 3 PM–midnight. For tickets, inquire at the service bureau off the first-floor lobby.

Fitness Centers The Radisson Slavyanskaya Hotel (2 Berezhkovskaya Naberezhnaya, near the Kiev Railway Station, tel. 095/941–8020, ext. 3260) has a nicely outfitted fitness center and a snack bar to go along with it. Its 25-meter (82-foot) pool is one of the largest of the hotel pools. The cost is $25 for unlimited use of the pool and gym. It's open daily 7 AM–10 PM. The Metropole Hotel (1/4 Teatralnyi Proyezd, tel. 095/927–6000) also has a Western-equipped fitness center. The pool here is smaller, but still large enough to satisfy lap swimmers. Unlimited use of all the facilities costs $10.

Skating If you've packed your skates, head straight for Gorky Park (9 Krymsky Val), where in winter months the park's lanes are flooded to create impromptu skating rinks. The park also has two large rinks where you can skate to piped-in Russian pop music. The park is open 10–10; the closest subway station is the Oktyabrskaya on the orange and circle lines. You can rent skates at the Sokolniki Park (62 Rusakovskaya ulitsa), near the subway station of the same name. Sokolniki Park is also open 10–10.

Swimming The huge Moskva swimming pool (37 Kropotkinskaya Naberezhnaya), built on the foundations of the former Cathedral of Christ Our Savior, has sections open to the general public. They do not require a health certificate here, and for that very reason many Muscovites refuse to use this pool, claiming the water is unclean. The outdoor pool is open winter and summer, 7 AM–10 PM. It is located directly opposite the Kropotkinskaya subway station.

Spectator Sports

Tickets for sporting events can be purchased at the sports arena immediately prior to the game or at any of the numerous theater box offices (*teatralnaya kassa*) located throughout the city. You can also ask your hotel's service bureau for assistance in obtaining tickets to sporting events, but the fee will probably far exceed the value of the ticket itself.

Horse-Racing The race course (Hippodrome) is at 22 Begovaya ul., (tel. 095/945–4516). Races are held on Wednesday and Saturday at 6 PM and on Sunday at 1 PM. Betting is in rubles. In winter troikas are sometimes raced.

Ice Hockey Ice hockey matches are held at the Central Lenin Stadium and at the Dynamo Stadium (36 Leningradsky Prospect, tel. 095/212–7092). This is Moscow's second-largest stadium, accommodating 60,000.

Soccer The Russian national sport is soccer (in Russian, *futbal*), and the city has several first-rate soccer teams, among them Spartak and Dinamo. Soccer matches are usually played at the Central Lenin Stadium (Luzhniki, tel. 095/246–5515). One of the world's largest stadiums, the Central Lenin Stadium seats 100,000 and is located right next to the Sportivnaya subway station.

Dining

The dining scene in the Russian capital has changed tremendously since the onset of *perestroika*. More than half the restaurants reviewed below were opened after 1987, the year the Soviet government passed the law on cooperatives. A cooperative is a self-financing, collectively owned business—an idea whose introduction paved the way for competition and free enterprise in Russia for the first time since the 1920s. If in the past your choices were limited to a handful of mediocre, overpriced hotel establishments, today you can pick and choose among private, state-run, and cooperative restaurants offering a wide variety of cuisines and price ranges. It is possible to eat very well and very cheaply in Moscow, but rarely do these two things go together. In the listings below we include the top-rated, newly opened foreign-run restaurants, which charge jaw-dropping prices, as well as the lingering state-run establishments, where, in exchange for fine dining, you get local atmosphere and great value. The private and cooperative restaurants fall between these two categories. The atmosphere is generally less formal than at the expensive joint ventures, and the food is much better than at the state-run restaurants.

Dining out in Moscow is an adventure that requires planning. Even if a restaurant is half-empty, you may be refused a table if you don't have a reservation. This is especially true in the evening, and sometimes it happens even during the day. You shouldn't encounter much difficulty booking a table at restaurants accepting only foreign currency. In establishments accepting both rubles and dollars, you will have an easier time if you indicate that payment will be made in hard currency. Many restaurants have a special room (and a special menu) set aside for the more lucrative foreign diner. But the pull of the dollar has both its advantages and disadvantages. Waiters and doormen prefer tips in dollars, and establishments will often insist that foreigners pay according to their higher-priced, dollar menu.

Reserve plenty of time for your meal. In Russia dining out is an occasion, and Russians often make an evening (or an afternoon) out of a restaurant meal. Often the meal is accompanied by a floor show or musical entertainment. Almost all the expensive new hotel restaurants offer a New Orleans Jazz Brunch on Sunday, when you can enjoy their haute cuisine and decor at greatly reduced prices.

Highly recommended restaurants are indicated by a star ★.

Category	Cost*
Very Expensive	over $45
Expensive	$30–$45
Moderate	$20–$30
Inexpensive	under $20

*per person, excluding drinks and service

Very Expensive

Exchange. This American steak house is located in the midwestern mall of the Radisson Slavyanskaya Hotel. The homesick American will enjoy the leafy salads and thick, juicy sirloins flown in from New York. The black-and-white interior decor makes for an elegant yet relaxed atmosphere, the perfect re-creation of America in Moscow. If you're not a meat lover, try the poached cod fillet or the chicken breast broiled to perfection in a tangy ginger sauce. The French onion soup or caesar salad makes a good starter. Order a bottle of imported wine from the extensive wine list, and top off your meal with a piece of apple pie. True to the American way, the restaurant offers a nonsmoking section. This is the ideal place to come for a well-earned break from Russian reality. *Radisson Slavyanskaya Hotel, 2 Berezhkovskaya Naberezhnaya, tel. 095/941–8020. Reservations advised. Dress: casual but neat. Hard currency only. AE, DC, MC, V. Open daily 11:30–3, 6–10:30.*

★ **Glazur.** This Danish-Russian joint venture is one of the numerous upscale establishments catering to the city's foreign community. It stands out from the pack for its subdued atmosphere and exquisite cuisine. Located in a renovated 19th-century mansion on the Garden Ring, the restaurant has an elegant interior, tastefully decorated in shades of brown and gold. The Russian and European dishes are beautifully prepared; the food, most of it imported from Belgium and Denmark, is a gourmet's heaven. The *russkaya zakuska*, a beef-gelatin salad with colorful layers of finely diced ham, chicken and tongue, makes a good starter. A specialty of the house is *baklazhany zarevshan*, a spicy Armenian mixture of eggplant, carrots, onion, and garlic. For your main course, try the *svinina à la gousar*, a pork dish served with a creamy mushroom sauce. The wine list is excellent. Top off your meal with a flaming ice cream surprise, the chef's special rendition of baked Alaska. Service is swift, friendly, and professional. The musical entertainment in the evenings varies, ranging from jazz to classical to Russian folk. *Smolensky Bulvar 12, tel. 095/ 248–4438. Jacket and tie advised. Reservations accepted. Credit cards only. AE, MC, V. Open daily noon–5, 6–midnight.*

Le Romanoff. This may be Moscow's finest gourmet experience at present. Located on the second floor of the Baltschug Hotel, this exquisitely managed restaurant offers a Russian/Continental cuisine that pleases both the eye and the palate. The menu is unique, the atmosphere is elegant, and the wine list is superb—the perfect spot for an important dinner. *Ul. Balchug 1, tel. 095/230–6500. Jacket and tie required. Reservations required. AE, DC, MC, V. No rubles.*

Metropol. The newly renovated interiors of the Metropol Hotel's grand dining hall are a stunning memorial to Russian Art Nouveau. The nearly three-story-high dining room, replete with stained-glass windows, marble pillars, and leaded-glass roof, recalls the splendor of prerevolutionary Russia. The beautifully laid tables and formally dressed waiters add to the elegance. In terms of its opulent atmosphere, the Metropol compares favorably with the Savoy (*see below*), but when it comes to the food and service, the Metropole is still stuck in the Soviet era. The pricey menu features such Russian delicacies as smoked salmon and beef Stroganoff, but the preparation is disappointing. The highlight of the week is Sunday brunch, when the restaurant puts out an impressive spread, including an array of meat and fish dishes, home-baked French pastries, and exotic fresh fruits flown in from Europe. *Teatralny Proyezd 1/4, tel. 095/927–6040. Reservations advised. Jacket and tie advised. Hard currency only. AE, DC, MC, V. Open daily 7–2, 6:30–midnight.*

Peking. The history of this Chinese restaurant reflects the ups and downs in the relations between Russia and China. Peking was first opened in 1957, but three years later, after

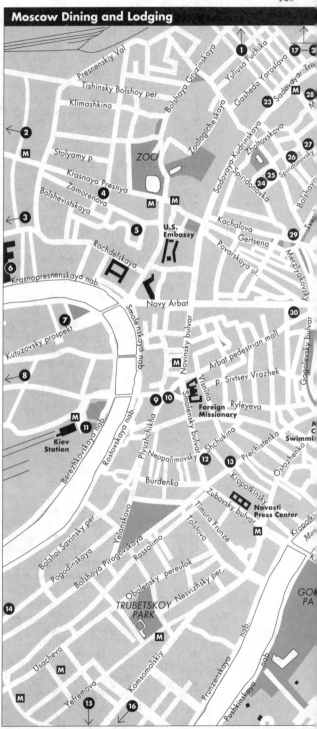

Moscow Dining and Lodging

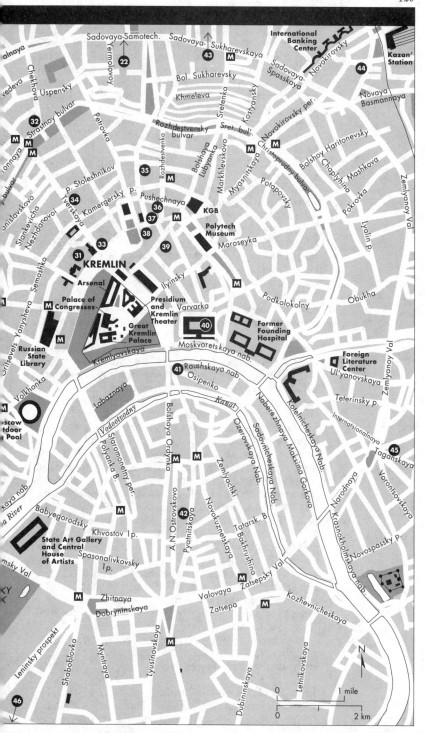

International Banking Center

Kazan' Station

Sadovaya-Samotech. Sadovaya- Sukharevskaya

22 **43** M

Novokirovsky **44**

alnaya

vedeva Chekhova Uspensky Yermolovoy

Bol. Sukharevsky Sadovaya-Spasskaya Novaya Basmannaya

Khmeleva

Sretenka Novokirovsky per.

32 Strasnoy bulvar Petrovka Rozhdestvensky bulvar Sret. bul'. Bolshoy Haritonevsky

M M M Rozhdestvenka Bolshaya Lubyanka Markhlevskovo Christoprudny bulvar Chaplyhina Mashkova

onnaya Myasnitskaya

bulvar P. Stoleshnikov **35** Potapovsky Pokrovka

nislavskovo **34** Kamergersky p. M Pushechnaya Lyalin p.

Stankevicha Tverskaya **36** Zemlyanoy Val

Nezhdanovoy **37** M KGB

Semashko **33** **38** Polytech Museum

31 **39** Maroseyka Obukha

KREMLIN Ilyinsky Podkolokolny

Arsenal M

Palace of Varvarka

M Congresses Presidium and Kremlin Theater Former Founding Hospital Foreign Literature Center

Gritsevets Yanysheva Great Kremlin Palace **40** Ul'yanovskaya

Russian State Library Kremlyovskaya Moskvoretskaya nab. Teterinsky p.

Volhonka Labaznaya **41** Raushskaya nab. Naberezhnaya Maksima Gorkovo Internatsionalnaya

M Osipenko Kolelnicheskaya Nab.

scow Vodootvodny Kanal **45**

tdoor Staromonetny per. Bolshaya Ordynka Sadovnicheskaya Nab. Taganskaya

Pool M Polyanka B. Ozerovskaya Nab. Vorontsovskaya

kaya nab. M Zemlyachki Narodnaya

Babyegorodsky Novospassky p.

a River Khvostov 1p. M **42** Novokuznetskaya Krasnokholmskaya nab.

State Art Gallery and Central House of Artists A.N.Ostrovskovo Pyatnitskaya Tatarsk. B Bakhrushina

Spasonalivkovsky Kozhevnicheskaya

msky Val 1p. Zhitnaya Valovaya Zatsepsky Val

TY M Dobryninskaya Zatsepa M

Leninsky prospekt Shaboblovka Myntraya Lyusinovskaya Dubininskaya Letnikovskaya

N

46 0   1 mile

0   2 km

the Sino-Soviet split, the Chinese chefs fled the country. The food rapidly deteriorated to diluted renditions of Chinese cuisine with a strong Russian twist. Today the Chinese chefs are back and the three huge halls have been given a face-lift, making this one of the city's most exotic places to dine. The spectacular interiors feature elaborate wood carvings, massive red pillars, and colorful papier-mâché Chinese lanterns. The food, however, is as humdrum as ever. Connoisseurs of Chinese cuisine may want to try their luck in the dollar hall, where a special hard-currency menu features imported delicacies. Dishes such as stewed shark fins and roast Peking duck come with price tags as spectacular as the interior decor. The ruble hall, where prices are much more reasonable and the food very Russian, has a lively atmosphere. It's a favorite spot for drinking and dancing with local crowds, making it difficult to book a table here—reservations must be made 10 days in advance. *Bolshaya Sadovaya 1/2, tel. 095/209–1865. Dress: casual but neat. Reservations required in ruble hall, advised in dollar hall. AE, DC, MC, V. Open daily noon–11. Expensive–Very Expensive in dollar hall, Inexpensive in ruble hall.*

★ **Savoy.** Located in the Savoy Hotel, this is perhaps the most prestigious and definitely the most luxurious restaurant in Moscow. The sumptuous interior and elegant menu are fit for a czar. The food—a mixture of Russian, Scandinavian, and French cuisine—is excellent. Ingredients are trucked in from Finland, and the Russian chef has won several international awards for his imperial creations. The restaurant features a special Czar's Menu, a re-creation of one of the 12 menus served at the coronation of Czar Nicholas II in 1896. But food aside, the real reason to come here is to see the stunning interior. With its delicate, gilded wall coverings, long mirrors, and gilded ceiling paintings, it rivals the opulence of St. Petersburg's imperial palaces. Dinner can easily run into five-digit figures; you may prefer the more reasonable prix-fixe lunch. *Ul. Rozhdestvenka 3, tel. 095/929–8600. Reservations advised. Jacket and tie required. Hard currency only, traveler's checks accepted. AE, DC, MC, V. Open daily 7:30 AM–11 PM.*

Strastnoy Bulvar 7. This is the name and address of a small but excellent restaurant located near Pushkin Square. It is a bit on the pricey side, but if intimacy and quiet conversation are in order, this is the place. The suckling pig stuffed with mushrooms and the perch with crabmeat stand out as house specialties. *Strastnoy Bulvar 7, tel. 095/299–0498. Jacket and tie advised. Reservations required. AE, MC, V, or rubles according to restaurant exchange rate.*

Inexpensive–Very Expensive

Sadko Arcade. This Swiss-Russian joint venture is actually a collection of restaurants, bars, and shops near the Mezhdunarodnaya hotel. The best restaurants in the arcade are

Trattoria (Very Expensive), with excellent Italian cuisine, and Swiss House (Expensive), which offers a succulent array of fondue dishes. Close behind are Steak House (Expensive), a good burger spot at lunchtime, and Beer House (Moderate), for Bavarian-sausage-and-strudel lovers. Pasta House (Inexpensive) accepts only rubles, and for the equivalent of about $4, patrons can enjoy an à la carte salad, pasta dish, bread, and Russian beer. *Krasnopresnenskaya Naberezhnaya, tel. 095/259–5656 for reservations at all restaurants. Jacket and tie advised. Reservations advised. AE, DC, MC, V, except Pasta House.*

Expensive

Arlecchino. Diners may think they've left Russia when they enter this art deco–style dining room and taste the imported Italian food prepared by Italian and Italian-trained Russian chefs. A quiet, sophisticated establishment, it's a popular rendezvous for foreign businesspeople. The restaurant's one banquet room seats 20. The best entrées are usually the daily veal or seafood specials, but it would be a shame to pass up the pasta. The extensive menu is complemented by an excellent wine list and dessert tray. *Ul. Druzhynnikovskaya 15 (in Kino Center), tel. 095/205–7088. Jacket and tie advised. Reservations required. AE, DC, MC, V, or rubles according to restaurant exchange rate.*

Baku. When you're tired of caviar and herring, try this rowdy joint venture named for the capital of Azerbaijan. Once a dull state enterprise, the restaurant is now under the management of a Lebanese-Azerbaijani partnership; the revised menu features exotic dishes from both countries. For a taste of Azerbaijan, try the *mutton shashlik* (shish kebab) served with a pomegranate sauce. The Beirut humus and tabuleh are also excellent. The drab interior, with its imitation marble walls, is as industrial as ever. The place turns lively after 9 PM, however, when the "variety" show featuring exotic Arab dancers begins. If you'd rather avoid the raucous late-night crowd, stop by during the day, when the menu is the same and the atmosphere as dull as the interior. *Ul. Tverskaya 24, tel. 095/299–8506. Reservations advised. Dress: casual but neat. Hard currency only. AE, DC, MC, V. Open daily 11–11.*

Kropotkinskaya 36. This was Moscow's first cooperative, and when it opened in 1987, it was known simply by its address: Kropotkinskaya 36. Since then the street has been given back its prerevolutionary name, and the restaurant has turned private. Prices have skyrocketed, and rubles are no longer accepted. As a result, it is easy these days to book a table at this favorite haunt of Moscow's expatriate community. Although you can catch the kitchen on an off day, one thing that hasn't changed is the restaurant's excellent reputation. The menu features traditional Russian dishes, but this is one place where it's worth trying herring-filled blini or Siberian meat-filled *pelmeni* (dumplings). If you're feeling adventurous, try the *govyadina po Novgorodski* for your main course. The recipe for this beef dish prepared in a honey-and-beer sauce originated in the ancient Russian town of Novgorod. The interior is elegant and intimate, with mirrored walls, yellow tablecloths, and plush auburn drapes. Discreet background music provided by the grand piano and violin soloist makes for a romantic setting. *Ul. Prechistenka 36, tel. 095/201–7500. Reservations advised. Jacket and tie advised. Hard currency only. AE, D, MC, V. Open daily noon–11.*

Panda. A relative newcomer to the Moscow dining scene, this American-style Chinese restaurant has become an overnight hit. All seafood and other hard-to-find ingredients are flown in from abroad to guarantee quality and freshness, and an award-winning Chinese cook oversees the careful preparation of each dish. The Hunan and Szechuan selections are especially delicious. Come here for an inexpensive lunch, or splurge for a large dinner with good company. Takeout orders are accepted throughout the day and evening. *Tverskoy Bulvar 3/5, tel. 095/298–6567. Reservations advised. Dress: casual. AE, DC, MC, V. No rubles.*

★ **Skazka.** The name, which means fairy tale, says it all. If you're tired of the industrial cuisine of state-run enterprises and the stuffy atmosphere of Moscow's private establishments, this cozy restaurant just off Taganka Square is a dream come true. The creative interior features darkwood carvings and long narrow windows filled with pyramid-shaped frosted glass. A soft, red light filters through the heavy glass, creating a romantic yet casual atmosphere. The service is friendly and professional, and the food is excellent. The restaurant offers traditional Russian cuisine, such as Siberian *pelmeni*—tender, meat-filled dumplings—and mushroom noodle soup, appropriately called "Like at Home with Mama." For dessert, try the house specialty, *rizhok*, a delectable layered pastry baked on the premises. Be aware that there are two menus—one for dollars and one for rubles. They are identical except that the dollar menu is more expensive. If you reserve far enough in advance, you will be allowed to pay in rubles; alcohol is available only for hard currency. The musical entertainment runs the gamut and changes every 20 minutes, from jazz to Russian folk to classical piano and violin. Although this popular restaurant was one of Moscow's first cooperatives, it still accepts rubles, keeping it somewhat accessible to local residents. *Tovarishchevsky Pereulok 1, tel. 095/271–0998. Dress: casual but neat. Hard currency and rubles. AE, MC, V. Open daily noon–5, 7–11.*

Tren-Mos. Once you get past the quintessentially stern Russian doorman guarding the entranceway, the atmosphere at this American-Russian joint venture is straight out of New Jersey. Opened in 1989 by an enterprising businessman from Trenton, the restaurant takes its name from the sister-city relationship between Trenton and the Lenin District of Moscow (Trenton-Moscow). The red, white, and blue interior is a showcase of American regalia. A portrait of George Washington peers down at dining guests, and the walls are draped in various state flags. Although the chef is French, the menu is as American as the decor. If you've been longing for a cheeseburger with fries or a sirloin steak, this is just the place for you. Quality varies, however, and the Texas chili con carne, which comes topped with tasteless grated yellow cheese, is more like a mildly spiced soup than chili. Popular with business people, the restaurant offers two dining halls and a two-tiered menu. Foreigners pay in dollars, Russians in rubles, provided they can show proof of CIS citizenship. *Komsomolsky Prospect 21, tel. 095/245–1216. Reservations advised. Jacket and tie advised. AE, DC, MC, V. Open daily noon–5 and 7–11.*

Moderate

Arkadia. Centrally located and featuring Russian, Armenian, and Georgian cuisines, this is fast becoming one of Moscow's most popular ruble-only restaurants. Outstanding jazz ensembles entertain here on a regular basis, and foreign musicians often sit in during performances. Dinner specialties include sterlet à la merchant and suckling pig *chavagach. Teatralny Proezd 3, tel. 095/926–9008 or 095/926–9545. Reservations required. Dress: casual. Rubles only.*

Atrium. Hidden away in one of the numerous and monolithic apartment buildings lining Leninsky Prospect, this popular cooperative can be a trick to find. It's a journey to get here by public transportation (three stops up the hill on a crowded trolley bus from the Leninsky Prospect subway station); the restaurant is best reached by car. Once inside, you'll wonder where you have landed. Its candlelit interiors, decorated with growling lions, armored knights, and velvet-wrapped pillars, provide a soothing change from Moscow's harried pace. Although this isn't a gourmet's paradise, the standard Russian dishes are pleasantly prepared. The appetizers and soups are excellent. Ask for *syr v testu* (garlic cheese sticks) and Staromoskovsky (Old Moscow) soup, made with a mushroom bouillon and chock-full of tender pieces of veal, chicken, and pork. For your main course, try the *zharkoye*, a veal stew served in an earthenware pot. The restaurant accepts both rubles and dollars, but alcohol is available for hard currency only. *Leninsky Prospect 44, tel. 095/137–3008. Reservations required. Dress: casual but neat. Hard currency and rubles. AE, MC, DC, V. Open daily noon–4, 6–11.*

★ **Delhi.** Moscow's only Indian restaurant was born out of the once great friendship between India and the USSR. Established as a political gesture, it opened during the 1987 Festival of India held in Moscow. Although relations between the two countries have since cooled, the restaurant continues to satisfy the cravings for authentic Indian cuisine of foreigners and local residents alike. With an Indian chef and management, the kitchen prepares excellent chicken and lamb tandoori dishes. Accompany your meal with *Nan and Tandoori roti*, crisp Indian bread baked in a tandoor. For starters, try the *subzi chaat*, diced potatoes and seasonal vegetables tossed with mint chutney and fragrant spices. Two dining rooms are available. The upscale hard-currency room is ornately decorated with silver Indian elephants and chandeliers. Classical Indian dancers provide the evening entertainment. The lively ruble room, where prices are drastically reduced (to keep it accessible to Russians), has "family entertainment." The floor show, which changes every 15 days, features magicians, jugglers, contortionists, and fire-eaters. *Krasnaya Presnya 23B, dollar room tel. 095/255–0492; ruble room, 095/252–1766. Jacket and tie advised in dollar room; casual but neat in ruble room. Reservations advised in dollar room, necessary in ruble room. Traveler's checks accepted. AE, DC, MC, V. Open daily noon–3, 6–11. Moderate in dollar room, inexpensive in ruble room.*

El Rincón Español. True to its name, this Spanish restaurant and bar is hidden in a corner of the Moskva hotel, the huge gray block towering over Manezhnaya Square. You may have to push your way past the burly doorman guarding the hotel entrance to get to the restaurant, located on the hotel's first floor (entrance facing Manezhnaya Square). The central location, reasonable prices, and lively atmosphere make this a popular watering hole with European expatriates. Wash down your Galician chicken pie or chorizo (spicy fried sausage) with a refreshing glass of San Miguel beer. The nominally Spanish menu includes several European dishes, such as French onion soup and chicken cordon bleu. Although these can be tempting, you should stick to the Spanish fare, as the European dishes tend to be bland and unimaginative. Service is polite and swift. This is one of the few restaurants in Moscow where it's possible to get a table without an advance reservation, making this a good choice for a meal on the go. *Okhotny Ryad 2, tel. 095/292–2893. Reservations accepted. Dress: casual. Hard currency only. AE, DC, MC, V. Open daily noon–12:30 AM.*

Lasagna. This small and unpretentious cooperative is situated in a historic residential district not far from the Tretyakov Art Gallery. The kitchen is mildly unpredictable, but it tries very hard to reinvent Italian cuisine using exclusively Russian ingredients. The extensive menu features such Italian specialties as ravioli, tortellini and, of course, lasagna. The pastas and breads are all homemade, and as long as you're not a connoisseur of Italian cuisine, you won't be disappointed; the quality of the food increases exponentially the longer you've been in Russia. The atmosphere is quiet and subdued. Crystal chandeliers and old-fashioned, green plush chairs help create a feeling of elegance. In the dim, candlelit setting, you'll barely notice the industrial carpeting or the seemingly incongruous modern art on the walls. Popular with local business people, this is a great place for a quiet evening of dining and conversation, a rare find in Moscow. *Ul. Pyatnitskaya 40, tel. 095/231–1085 or 095/233–1459. Reservations advised. Dress: casual but neat. Hard currency only. AE, DC, MC, V. Open Mon.–Sat. noon–1, 7–11; Sun. 3–11.*

★ **U Pirosmani.** Named for the Georgian artist Niko Pirosmani, this popular cooperative is located near the Novodevichy Monastery. Its rustic interior, with white-washed walls and wood-paneled ceilings, re-creates the atmosphere of an artist's studio. Ask for a table in the main hall, which affords picturesque views of the 16th-century monastery across the pond from the restaurant. The blackboard menu reads like a Georgian cookbook. Instead of wrestling with the decision of which of its tasty main courses to try, ask for a sampling of appetizers. The spread, which includes lobio, satsivi, and *gruzinskaya kapusta* (a spicy, marinated red cabbage), will be enough to feed the hungriest tourist. The kitchen also serves delightful *khinkali*, Georgian meat dumplings. Order a bottle of Georgian wine to accompany your meal, and top it all off with a sweet Georgian pastry, baked on the premises. Although the restaurant is very popular and often crowded, service is astonishingly good by local standards. *Novodevichy Prospect 4, tel. 095/247–1926. Dress: casual. Rubles accepted for food, dollars accepted for alcohol. AE. Open daily noon–4, 6–10:30. Moderate–Inexpensive.*

Inexpensive

Aragvi. This state-run restaurant specializing in the spicy cuisine of former Soviet Georgia has been a tourist trap for years. The kitchen is a bit unpredictable, but the gorgeous interiors, with elaborately painted walls and colorful mosaics, make up for the hit-or-miss food. A safe bet is the chicken *satsivi*, served in a walnut and coriander sauce, or the *lobio*, butter beans in a spicy sauce. The so-called Marble Hall, with its high ceilings and wall paintings depicting ancient Georgia in the spirit of socialist realism, features loud and lively Georgian musical entertainment. For solitude and relatively smoke-free dining, reserve one of the private rooms on the second floor, a favorite haunt of Lavrenti Beria, Stalin's henchman. The friendly waiters are only too eager to accept your dollars—you get a better deal in rubles. Cognac, champagne, and a limited selection of Georgian wine are available. *Ul. Tverskaya 6, tel. 095/229–2906. Reservations advised. Dress: casual. No credit cards. Open daily noon–1.*

Margarita. This café, named after the heroine of Mikhail Bulgakov's famous novel *Master and Margarita*, is in one of Moscow's quainter neighborhoods. Always patronized by a mixed crowd of Russians and foreigners, Margarita's combines a slightly offbeat, rustic atmosphere with a simple, inexpensive menu. The service is uncommonly fast, making it an excellent bet for a quick lunch. Try the stuffed-tomato appetizer, the soup of the day, and the Russian pot pie for a can't-miss meal. *Malaya Bronnaya 28, tel. 095/299–6534. Reservations advised. Dress: casual. Rubles only.*

Moskovskye Zory. This log-cabin restaurant between Pushkin Square and Mayakovsky Square is a great place for a quick, delicious lunch. It's a tiny eatery and has just a few tables, which are decked with red tablecloths. The owner is especially friendly to Americans. The dependably tasty offerings are usually limited to two types of traditional Russian soup, salad, and a few main courses. German beer and Georgian wines are usually available. Avoid the coffee at dessert time. *Maly Kozikhinsky Pereulok 11, tel. 095/299–5725. Reservations required. Dress: casual. Rubles only.*

Praga. Centrally located on Arbat Square, in a handsome prerevolutionary building, this state-run restaurant was once one of Moscow's finest dining establishments. Radical changes in the capital's restaurant scene have left the staff here nostalgic for the days when lines formed outside its doors and it took a good connection or a bribe to land a table. Although it's named for the Czech capital, the restaurant has never offered anything but standard Russian cuisine, the quality of which has fallen to new lows in recent years. The menu is huge but the availability of dishes limited. Standard offerings include beef Stroganoff and chicken Tabaka (roasted spring chicken). What keeps the place in business is its lovely interiors. A grand marble staircase with heavy brass railings leads you to the elegant second-floor dining halls, where gilded ceilings, parquet wooden floors, and brass chandeliers create an Old World atmosphere. Double-check your bill carefully. The waiters here were spoiled by years of corruption and have been known to add extra items to the check. *Ul. Arbat 2, tel. 095/290–6191. Reservations advised. Jacket and tie advised. Cash only (rubles or dollars). Open daily noon–11:30.*

Rossiya. Popular with tourists and black marketeers, this state-run enterprise is located on the 21st floor of the gigantic Rossia hotel. The interior, with green metal ceilings and orange polyester curtains, corresponds perfectly with the hotel's cement-and-steel construction. Live Russian pop music day and night makes for a festive atmosphere, but the food—traditional Russian fare—is just barely above average. Service is slow and impersonal, and the English-language menu only causes confusion, since it rarely corresponds to the items actually available. The one and only reason to book a table here is the location: the restaurant offers unrivaled views of the Kremlin and Red Square. Unfortunately, you may have to peer through dirty windows at the magical site below. *Ul. Varvarka 6, tel. 095/298–4133. Dress: casual. Reservations required. Cash only (rubles or dollars). Open daily 1–4:30, 7–11.*

Slavyansky Bazar. Located in a domed market building, this huge state-run enterprise dates back to 1870, when it opened as Russia's first full-service restaurant. The food—standard Russian fare—is only average, but the fun atmosphere and historical setting are worthy compensation. Although a bit run-down today, before the revolution this was a prestigious, first-class restaurant; memorial plaques honoring the famous patrons of the past line the walls. Don't be talked into one of the dingy private rooms on the second floor, because all the action takes place in the huge main hall. It was here, over a long dinner, that Stanislavsky and Nemirovich-Danchenko came up with the idea for the Moscow Art Theater. Russian folk ensembles provide the entertainment on a stage set up to re-create a quaint Russian village. The waiters, all dressed in peasant blouses, will offer you a high-priced set dinner, but you're better off sticking with the extensive appetizer menu. Join the locals and wash down your caviar-filled blini with a shot of vodka. *Ul. Nikolskaya 13, tel. 095/921–9853; group reservations, 095/ 921–1872. Reservations advised. Dress: casual. Rubles only. Open daily noon–4, 6–10.*

Ukraina. This state-run restaurant in the Ukraina Hotel has traditionally catered to tourist groups. In recent years it has become a popular night spot with young and restless Russians, who come here in the evenings for the positively tasteless erotic floor show. During the day, however, the only entertainment is an occasional Russian folk ensemble. The Stalinesque decor takes you back to the 1950s, with orange taffeta curtains, heavy chandeliers, massive marble pillars and, for good measure, Ukrainian embroidered tapestries draping the walls. The menu, like the decor, is a reflection of the former Soviet Union. Traditional Ukrainian dishes such as chicken Kiev and borscht are featured side by side with Russian and other national cuisines of the former Soviet republics. Bow-tied waiters offer polite and friendly service. Although the food is heavy and bland, the restaurant remains popular with foreigners and Russians alike thanks to its extremely reasonable prices. This is a good place to spend a rainy afternoon over a bottle of wine and a long lunch. *Kutuzovsky Prospect 2/1, tel. 095/243–4732. Reservations advised. Dress: casual but neat. Rubles only. Open daily noon–4:30, 6–midnight.*

Uzbekistan. As its name indicates, this restaurant specializes in the spicy cuisine of the Central Asian republic of Uzbekistan. It's long been a popular stop with tourists, but its reputation is much better than it deserves. Opened in 1949, the restaurant is a relic of the Stalinist era, when the great "friendship" of the numerous ethnic groups caught inside the borders of the Soviet Union was celebrated by opening restaurants specializing in the national cuisine of the various republics (the Aragvi and Ukraina restaurants opened under similar circumstances). The decor—high ceilings, massive pillars, ornate wood carvings, and fancy chandeliers—is a uniquely Soviet mix of Stalinism and traditional Central Asian decoration. The house specialty—*manty* (rubber dumplings filled with mystery meat and served with a thick glob of sour cream)—are just barely edible. The kitchen does a better job with the *plof* (pilaf) and *lagman* (meat and noodle soup). The restaurant makes up for the bland cuisine with its colorful atmosphere and lively entertainment. If you're looking to mingle with the locals, you can join them here for a shot or two (or three) of vodka. *Ul. Neglinnaya 29, tel. 095/924-6053. Reservations advised. Dress: casual but neat. Rubles only.*

Yakimanka. A band sings Western music in heavy Russian accents as diners lounge on sunken couches before low, candlelighted tables in the back room or sit at conventional tables—also lighted by candles—in the front room. This exotic bit of central Asia in Moscow is a good spot for a relaxing evening meal. Sample Yakimanka's grape leaves stuffed with meats, rice, and garlic, or try the pilaf with beef and vegetables. Don't miss the pickled-garlic appetizer. *Ul. Bolshaya Polyanka 2-10, tel. 095/238-8888. Reservations required. Dress: casual. Rubles or hard currency.*

Lodging

For a city with a population of more than 10 million, the number of hotels available to the foreign tourist in Moscow is amazingly small. But compared with what was happening just a few years back, the situation has significantly improved. In the past, foreign tourists were more or less told where to stay by the monolithic state-run tourist agency, Intourist. Requests for specific hotels were ignored, and tourists would often find out where they were staying only after arrival at the airport. Thankfully, the days of complete disrespect for the consumer are over. Not only can you choose your hotel today, but you actually have something to choose from. Since 1990, a dozen new hotels have opened in Moscow, most of them under foreign management. A new entity—the luxury hotel—has been introduced in great numbers.

The hotel reviews are grouped according to the price categories outlined below. With just one exception, the hotels in the Very Expensive and Expensive categories are all newly opened, foreign-run joint ventures where service and accommodations are far superior to those at the Soviet-built hotels in the Moderate and Inexpensive categories. If you are visiting on an organized tour arranged through IntourService (Intourist's successor), you are most likely to land in one of the old Intourist hotels: Belgrade, Kosmos, Intourist, or Ukraine. Quality of service and accommodations varies widely at these establishments; pack your patience and be ready to roll with the punches.

All prices are quoted in U.S. dollars; hotels always require payment in foreign currency and do not normally accept rubles.

Highly recommended lodgings are indicated by a star ★.

Category	Cost*
Very Expensive	over $350
Expensive	$215–$265
Moderate	$100–$170
Inexpensive	under $65

All prices are for a standard double room for two, excluding service charge.

Very Expensive

Baltschug Kempinski. Situated on the banks of the Moskva River, opposite the Kremlin and Red Square, this newly opened, five-star hotel boasts extraordinary views—and prices, too. Long in a state of disrepair, the 19th-century building, once an aristocratic apartment house, has been completely reconstructed. The modern interiors sparkle, but they lack the distinct character of prerevolutionary Russia found in comparably priced hotels, such as the Metropole or the Savoy. The spacious rooms are done in a stately red and cream and are equipped with every modern amenity. The Swiss management has thought of some nice touches, like bathroom slippers, perhaps to encourage guests to stay home and enjoy the picture-postcard views across the river. The location is central but not particularly convenient: the hotel is not accessible by public transportation, and the city's main attractions are on the other side of the river. Make sure you specify that you want a room with a view; otherwise you could end up staring at the grim factory bordering the eastern side of the hotel. *Ul. Balchuga 1, tel. 095/230–6500, fax 095/230–6502. From outside Russia, tel. 007–501–230–9500, fax 007–501–230–9502. 202 room with bath, 32 suites. Facilities: 3 restaurants, café, nighttime bar, 24-hr room service, cable TV with CNN and BBC, complimentary minibar, fitness center with sauna and 20-meter pool, business center, hard-currency shops. Traveler's checks accepted. AE, DC, MC, V.*

★ **Metropol.** Originally built in 1899–1903 by William Walcott, this lavish, first-class hotel reopened in 1991 after five years of extensive renovations. Now operating as a British-Russian joint venture, the Metropol is a member of Inter-Continental Hotel groups. Its posh interiors have been the site of many historic events. Lenin spoke frequently in the assembly hall of the building, and in 1918–19 the Central Committee of the Russian Republic met here under its first chairman, Yakov Sverdlov (for whom the square outside the hotel was named until 1991). Today the hotel is one of Moscow's most elegant, with outstanding service and amenities. The nicely appointed rooms feature hardwood floors, Oriental rugs, large closets, and modern furnishings. All the suites are furnished with authentic antiques, and the two presidential suites come with private saunas.

The location, opposite the Bolshoi Theater and a five-minute walk from the Kremlin, can't be beat. *Teatralny Proyezd 1/4, tel. 095/927–6000, fax 095/975–2355. From outside Russia, tel. 7501–927–1000, fax 7501–927–1010. 328 rooms with bath, 75 suites. Facilities: 4 restaurants, 2 bars, 24-hr room service, in-room movies and cable TV television with CNN and MTV, satellite telephone, fitness center with sauna and swimming pool, travel agent, theater-ticket agency, conference facilities. Traveler's checks accepted. AE, DC, MC, V.*

Olympic Penta. Opened in 1991 under German management, this was one of Moscow's first joint-venture hotels. It was built by a Finnish contruction team, and everything here is imported, down to the last doorknob. The rooms are large and fully equipped with all the modern amenities. The hotel's fitness center is one of the best in town. Service is good, although the European-trained Russian staff has been known to let its Soviet upbringing rear its ugly head. The location—near the Olympic Sports Stadium—is far from the city's tourist attractions, but the subway is just a 10-minute walk away. *Olympisky Prospect 18/1, tel. 095/971–6301 or 095/971–6101, fax 095/230–2597. 490 rooms with bath, 10 suites. Facilities: restaurant, café, beer hall, bar, 24-hour room service, minibar, cable TV, satellite telephone, fitness center with sauna and 22-meter pool, gift shops, car service, conference facilities. Traveler's checks accepted. AE, DC, MC, V.*

Palace. With an interior that lives up to its name, the Palace has all the makings of a true five-star establishment. This new arrival on the Moscow hotel scene opened in February 1993, and some services, such as the hotel's business center, are still not fully operational. However, at press time (fall 1993), the management was confident that all services would be functioning smoothly by the end of the year. The second-floor bar is open for business, as is the adjoining seafood restaurant, Anchor. Located on one of Moscow's major avenues, the Palace is just five minutes by car from the Kremlin. *A Marco Polo hotel. Ul. Tverskaya 49, tel. 095/956–3152, fax 095/956–3151. 199 rooms, 21 suites. AE, DC, MC, V.*

★ **Savoy.** This luxury hotel combines the opulence of the turn of the century with every modern amenity. It was originally built in 1912, in connection with celebrations commemorating the 300th anniversary of the Romanov Dynasty. Used as a tourist-class hotel (under the name Berlin) by the Soviets, it was completely renovated in the late 1980s and now operates as a Finnish-Russian joint venture. Its gorgeous interiors, replete with gilded chandeliers, ceiling paintings, and polished redwood paneling, bring back the glory and glitz of prerevolutionary Russia. The decor is complemented by friendly and efficient service. Although the rooms are slightly small (a legacy of Soviet remodeling), they are nicely appointed with pretty, rose-colored wallpaper and matching upholstery. One of the gilded suites con-

If we renamed ourselves Latviasaintpetersburgmoscow-estoniakievlithuanian Airlines you might forget we fly to Scandinavia.

You'd probably have trouble pronouncing it anyway. But considering how close Scandinavia is to the Baltic States and the Commonwealth of Independent States, it makes sense that Scandinavian Airlines flies there. A convenient connection in Stockholm or Copenhagen, and you'll be comfortably on your way to wherever business or vacation takes you.

Thanks to SAS, getting to this part of the world is easier than ever. For reservations or information, call your travel agent, or SAS at 800-221-2350. And please remember we fly beyond Scandinavia. We'd prefer not to make our name longer.

SCANDINAVIAN AIRLINES

Scandinavian Airlines, the natural choice to the Baltic Countries.

SCANDINAVIAN AIRLINES

tains a piano purchased especially for Luciano Pavarotti when he stayed here while performing at the Bolshoi Theater. Popular with visiting dignitaries, the hotel is centrally located, just off Theater Square and within walking distance of the Kremlin. *Ul. Rozhdestvenskaya 3, tel. 095/929–8500 or 095/929–8558, fax 095/230–2186. 86 rooms with bath, 29 suites. Facilities: restaurant, 2 bars, 24-hr room service, satellite telephone, cable TV with CNN, minibar, business center, excursion and travel bureau. Traveler's checks accepted. AE, DC, MC, V.*

Expensive

★ **Aerostar.** The Aerostar, not to be confused with the run-down Aeroflot Hotel next door, is a Russian-Canadian joint venture between Aeroflot and IMP Group Limited. Opened in 1992, the hotel was originally commissioned for the 1980 Olympics but never completed. The Canadian team has worked wonders with the austere Soviet design, transforming it into a first-rate, Western-style hotel. The lobby areas are bright and cheery, and the rooms are nicely appointed, with European furnishings and redwood paneling. In a move unusual for Russia, the hotel has nonsmoking rooms available. The rooms on the northeast side look out onto the Petrovsky Palace, a striking, crenelated redbrick palace where the czars would break their journey between St. Petersburg and Moscow. Service is excellent, and business travelers find the location—halfway between the city center and Sheremetyevo International Airport—very convenient. Tourists, though, may find the city's major attractions are too far away. Many of the city's expatriates are making the trek out here to eat at the hotel's Taiga Restaurant. The house specialty is fresh lobster flown in from Nova Scotia, and on Sunday the restaurant features a lavish champagne brunch. *Leningradsky Prospect 37, tel. 095/155–5030, fax 095/155–6614 or 095/200–3286. 386 rooms with bath, 31 suites. Facilities: 2 restaurants, 2 bars, 24-hour room service, international TV programming including CNN and BBC, satellite telephone, gift shop, fitness center, business center, exchange bureau, excursion bureau, car rental, conference facilities. Traveler's checks accepted. AE, DC, MC, V.*

Mezhdunarodnaya. Its name translates as "International," but foreign residents have dubbed it "the Mezh." Until the opening of the Radisson Slavyanskaya Hotel, this huge complex was the center of international business in Moscow. It was built by the American financier Armand Hammer in 1980. Its atrium lobby and indoor mall were once an oasis for foreign shoppers who came here for the hotel's first-class restaurants and well-stocked hard-currency stores. But times are changing in Russia, and the best enterprises have moved out to more exciting premises. The shops still charge exorbitant prices, but their shelves are looking depressingly bare. Its restaurants and late-night bars are frequented by prostitutes who search for the businessmen who have escaped to the Radisson. The rooms here are bigger than at the Radisson, but the views are no better and the Italian furnishings have definitely seen better days. The hotel is located near the city center but far from the subway, and there is only one city bus that stops anywhere near the hotel. At these high rates, you're better off in one of the city's numerous newly built foreign-run hotels. *Krasnopresnenskaya Naberezhnaya 12, tel. 095/253–1391 or 095/253–1392, fax 095/253–2051. 530 rooms with bath. Facilities: 5 restaurants, 6 bars, hard-currency shops and grocery store, service bureau, fitness center with pool and sauna, minibar, in-room movies. Traveler's checks accepted with commission. AE, DC, MC, V.*

Presnya. Once the exclusive domain of the Communist Party, this modest hotel has been renovated by an Austrian firm and transformed into a Western-style hotel. It's located in a quaint residential district in the city center not far from Patriarch's Pond. Renovations are still not complete, and plans are under way to expand the small fitness center, retile the bathrooms, and replace the remaining plywood. Service is friendly and efficient, the atmosphere quite and subdued. The standard-size rooms are clean and pleasant. The main attraction here is the quiet and central location, a rare find in Moscow. *A Marco Polo hotel. Spiridonovsky Pereulok 9, tel. 095/202–0381, fax 095/230–2704. 68 rooms with bath. Facilities: restaurant, lobby bar, room service, minibar, cable TV, fitness center with sauna, business center, gift shop, car service, conference facilities. Traveler's checks accepted. AE, MC, V.*

Pullman Iris. Under French management, this new hotel is located in a bleak residential district on the northwest outskirts of town, adjacent to the world-famous Fyodorov Eye Institute. The hotel hoped to attract foreign patients, but their numbers are not as great as anticipated, and the hotel is operating far below capacity. Its distant location is unfortunate, because this is one of the finest of the new foreign-run hotels in Moscow. The spacious rooms are cheery and bright, with lots of closet space and large bathrooms. The views are quite dismal, though, since the hotel is surrounded by monotonous high rises. There are few shops or restaurants of any interest to the tourist in the area. The hotel's own French restaurant, however, is fast earning an excellent reputation among the city's foreign community. Complimentary shuttle service is provided to guests, making it easier to enjoy the city's attractions. Buses run hourly to Red Square, and five times daily to the Sovincenter. *Korovinskoye Shosse 10, tel. 095/488–8000, fax 095/906–0105; from outside Russia, 095/220–8000, fax 095/220–8888. 195 rooms with bath. Facilities: 2 restaurants, bar, 24-hour room service, minibar, satellite telephone, cable TV, fitness center with swimming pool, car service, complimentary shuttle service to city center, excursion bureau, gift shop. Traveler's checks accepted. AE, DC, MC, V.*

★ **Radisson Slavyanskaya.** This American-Russian joint venture is Moscow's answer to New York's World Trade Center. Designed with the frustrated business traveler in mind, the hotel offers every modern amenity in a no-nonsense, efficient atmosphere. Its huge, two-story lobby is lined with first-class restaurants and shops. Among the offices opened here are a full-fledged travel agency and a full-service bank. Everything you might want or need is located inside the hotel, and as long as you never look out the window, you'll never even know you are in Moscow. You have to wonder what they were thinking when they chose the location; the hotel is situated right next door to the crime-ridden Kiev Railway Station, notorious for its pickpockets and Gypsy community. A protective wall and the guards posted at the hotel's main entrance keep the uninvited from wandering in. The rooms are nicely appointed but small; the views are dismal. This is a good choice for long-term visitors who favor comfort and service over character and who don't want or need any contact with the real Moscow. *Berezhkovskaya Naberezhnaya 2, tel. 095/941–8020, fax 095/941–8000; fax from outside Russia, 7502–224–1225. Reservations may be made through Radisson Hotels in U.S, tel. 800/333–3333. 407 rooms with bath, 24 suites. Facilities: 2 restaurants, café, lobby bar, fitness center with 25-meter lap pool, 24-hr room service, satellite telephone, minibar, cable TV with CNN, hard-currency shops, exchange bureau, car rental, excursion bureau, conference facilities. Traveler's checks accepted. AE, DC, MC, V.*

Moderate

Belgrade II. Built in 1975 as one of two twin towers (the other is now the Zolotoye Koltso), this hotel is a typical Brezhnev-era high rise. It belongs to IntourService (formerly Intourist), so tours booked through this agency have a good chance of landing here. The hotel's main advantage is its central location, near the subway and the Arbat. The interior decor is unimaginative, and the hotel has the same institutional feeling as the Intourist (*see below*). The rooms could definitely use some sprucing up, and renovations are underway to replace the cheap, plywood furnishings and worn industrial carpeting. IntourService also plans to add a fitness center and swimming pool. But until the renovations are complete, you are better off somewhere else. You can get similar accommodations at half the price at the Zolotoye Koltso across the street. *Smolenskaya Ploshchad 8, tel. 095/248–1676. 487 rooms with bath. Facilities: 2 restaurants, 2 snack bars, 2 bars, exchange bureau, excursion bureau. AE, DC, MC, V.*

Intourist. Centrally located at the bottom of Tverskaya ulitsa and a stone's throw from the Kremlin, this aging skyscraper is a popular destination with tourist groups. Unfortunately, its super location also attracts a seedy-looking mob of taxi drivers, Gypsies, and black marketeers, whose constant presence outside the hotel's main entrance makes coming and going a rather unpleasant experience. Its smoke-filled lobby features the usual drab decor, although the gift and souvenir shops are better stocked than most. The hotel staff, when they aren't busy taking personal phone calls, are receptive and relatively helpful. The interior has remained basically unchanged since the hotel opened in 1970, which is obvious from the poor condition of the rooms. Although they all come with telephone and television, the stained furnishings, worn carpeting, and monotone polyester curtains make the rooms seem more appropriate to a dormitory. Despite the drawbacks, the rates here remain relatively high. This is mostly due to the hotel's prime location, which is the only reason to stay here. *Ul. Tverskaya 3, tel. 095/203–0131. 443 rooms with bath. Facilities: 3 restaurants, 7 snack bars, casino, excursion bureau. DC, MC, V.*

★ **Kosmos.** This huge, 26-story hotel was built by the French for the 1980 Olympics. It is French-equipped and furnished, but years of heavy tourist traffic have dulled its shine. Service varies wildly, with large groups getting preference over individual tourists. The slot machines and late-night bars attract unsavory types, including plenty of prostitutes, but the rooms themselves are adequate and clean. Overall, service and accommodations here are far superior to those at the Intourist Hotel, another popular destination with tourist groups. Its spacious, two-story lobby is reminiscent of a mall, full of well-stocked, hard-currency stores and shops. The hotel is located across the street from the former USSR Economic Achievements Exhibit, an elaborate park designed in the 1930s as a national showcase for the Soviet economy. The location is far from downtown, but there's a subway stop right across the street. *Prospect Mira 150, tel. 095/217–0785 or 095/217–1649, fax 095/215–7180. 1,777 rooms with bath. Facilities: 4 restaurants, 8 bars, swimming pool, sauna, bowling alley, hard-currency grocery store. AE, MC, V.*

Novotel. If you need a room near the Airport, this is the place to stay. Professional soccer teams visiting from other European countries patronize Novotel because of its few distractions. The rooms and beds are comfortable, the hallways are quiet, and the price is right. In addition, the staff is eager to please, and the modern facilities are well maintained. *Sheremetyevo II Airport, tel. 095/578–9401 or 095/578–9110, fax 095/578–2794. 155 rooms, 40 suites. AE, DC, MC, V.*

Sovietskaya. Massive jade pillars, marble walls, and heavy brass chandeliers make for an elegant atmosphere in this palatial hotel. They say it was Beria's favorite, and the Communist Party's Central Committee used to get first dibs on the choicest rooms. Now it is open to anyone willing to pay the inflated rates, and as a result the hotel is practically empty. The building is just four stories high, and you can walk up to your room along an impressive marble staircase whose red carpeting could have been laid out for a czar. The rooms are spacious and clean, with velveteen-upholstered furniture (circa 1952) and huge bathrooms. If you pine for the bad old days of totalitarianism, you'll feel right at home, but if you're looking for the amenities of the modern age, you won't find them here. The hotel is poorly equipped to deal with tourists, and it doesn't even have an excursion bureau. There are no hard-currency shops, not to mention a fitness center, and the hotel's one restaurant is open only for breakfast. But the rooms come with refrigerators (as well as telephone and television) so you can stock up on supplies in town. The location (halfway to the airport) is a drawback, but the subway is within walking distance. *Leningradsky Prospect 32, tel. 095/250–7255 or 095/250–7253, fax 095/250–8003. 80 rooms with bath. Facilities: restaurant (breakfast only). AE, DC, MC, V.*

Soyuz. Yugoslav-built in 1980, this hotel on the northwest outskirts of town has an interesting avant-garde design. Its distant location keeps its rates in the Moderate category, but the service and atmosphere here far outrank those of similar hotels closer to the city center. The rooms were recently renovated by an Austrian company and come with modern furnishings and cheery, flowery wallpaper. Some of the rooms have views of the Moskva River, where in summer Muscovites come in droves to swim and sunbathe. The lobby area, too, is bright and cheery, with lots of windows and plants. The public areas and rooms are spotless by local standards, but the location is a serious drawback. The hotel is convenient only to the Sheremetyevo Airport (15 minutes away). The closest subway stop—Rechnoy Vokzal, the last stop on the green line—is a 20-minute bus ride away, and it can take more than an hour to reach the city center by car. *Ul. Levoberezhnaya 12, tel. 095/457–2088, fax 095/457–2096. 154 rooms with bath. Facilities: restaurant, bar, snack bar, exchange bureau. AE, DC, V.*

★ **Ukraina.** This imposing skyscraper on the banks of the Moskva River is one of the seven Stalin Gothics. The interior is not as monumental as at the Leningradskaya (*see below*), but the red carpeting, high ceilings, and colorful socialist-realist ceiling paintings are definite throwbacks to the Stalinist era. The rooms are worn but relatively clean in a city where standards of cleanliness are low. Redwood and oak furnishings and fancy chandeliers create an atmosphere of faded elegance. The door locks were recently replaced with electronic, magnetic-strip locks. The old tradition of floor attendants has been retained here, and you can find a hotel staff member on every floor. The hotel is situated across the river from the "White House" (the Russian Parliament Building), which allows some great views from the higher floors. This is a central location, but the subway is a good 10-minute trek away. A plus here is the well-stocked Beriozka store and the German-run joint-venture restaurant, tucked away on the third floor.

Kutuzovsky Prospect 2/1, tel. 095/243–2596; reservations, 095/243–3030; fax 095/243–3092. 1,010 rooms with bath. Facilities: 2 restaurants, 6 snack bars, 3 bars, Beriozka, sauna. AE, DC, MC, V.

Inexpensive

Leningradskaya. This Soviet fortress is another of Moscow's seven Stalin Gothic skyscrapers. Its awe-inspiring, monumental interior features high ceilings, red carpets, and heavy bronze chandeliers. A faded gem of the Stalinist era, the hotel is often used to house Russian parliament members. The rooms are modestly furnished but surprisingly clean and well maintained. Ask for a room high up—the views from the lower floors are strictly industrial. The location is relatively central but not exactly convenient. The hotel stands at a busy intersection, right across from the Leningrad, Kazan, and Yaroslav railway stations. To reach the subway you have to dash across the highway and then make your way through the rather unsavory crowds that live at the train station. Nevertheless, the reasonable rates here make this is a good choice for budget-minded travelers. Just be sure to pack plenty of patience; the hotel staff long ago wearied of their jobs. *Ul. Kolanchovskaya 21/40, tel. 095/975–3032, telex 411 659 GLORSU. 346 rooms with bath. Facilities: restaurant, 2 snack bars, casino, Beriozka, exchange bureau. AE, DC, MC, V.*

Molodyozhnaya. Its name translates as "youth," and the hotel has traditionally catered to groups of young people traveling under the auspices of Sputnik (the Soviet youth tourist agency). It was built for the 1980 Olympics and features the typical drab decor of a Brezhnev-era high rise. The cement-and-steel lobby is decorated with a mosaic depicting happy proletariat youth. The rooms are standard size and adequate, provided you are not a stickler for cleanliness. The decor is standard Soviet fare—heavy on the plywood and polyester. The location on the outskirts of town is far from the city's tourist attractions, but there's a subway stop within walking distance. This is one of the best of the inexpensive hotels, and definitely the most easily accessible. The three- and five-person suites are a real deal in this overpriced city. *Dmitriovskoye Shosse 27, tel. 095/210–4565, fax 095/210–4311. 600 rooms with bath. Facilities: restaurant, 4 bars, Beriozka. No credit cards; cash only.*

Mozhaiskaya. The hotel's distant location, just beyond Moscow's Ring Road, helps keep it in the inexpensive category. It's a 30-minute bus ride to the subway and another good 40 minutes from there to the city center. Even by car it's an hour's drive. Built in 1971, the hotel is in poor condition and there are no redeeming qualities to make up for its inconvenient location. The lobby features plywood paneling, cheap mosaics of the Kremlin, and thick clouds of cigarette smoke. The rooms are rather dismal, with more plywood and a depressing red-and-brown decor. About half of the rooms come with a telephone, and some have a working television set. Unless you're on a tight budget, stay elsewhere. *Mozhaiskoye Shosse 165, tel. 095/447–3434. 297 rooms with bath. Facilities: restaurant, snack bar, sauna, excursion bureau, hard-currency shop. AE, DC, MC, V.*

Rossiya. Pack your compass and map if you're staying here, because negotiating the seemingly endless corridors from one end to the other of this huge hotel is a cartographer's nightmare. The mammoth building is one of Europe's largest hotels, able to accommodate up to 6,000 guests. Opened in 1967, it once numbered among the Soviet Union's finest hotels, but service and accommodations have rapidly sped downhill in recent years. All the rooms come with television and telephone, but there's no guarantee they'll work. Cockroaches (and worse) are also not unheard of. As with the Intourist, the main reason to stay here is the location: the views of the Kremlin and Red Square are stupendous (ask for a room on the west side). Deteriorating conditions have forced the hotel to reduce its rates, making this one of the best bargains in downtown Moscow. Popular with parliamentary delegates, the hotel often closes its doors to the general public when the Russian Congress is in session. *Ul. Varvarka 6, tel. 095/298–1567. 2,800 rooms with bath. Facilities: 8 restaurants, 20 snack bars, 2 bars, pool and sauna, exchange bureau. Traveler's checks accepted. AE, MC, V.*

Sevastopol. This is a huge complex comprising four 16-story high rises. Although the hotel is far from the city's tourist attractions, the subway is close by. Rates here are lower than at the Mozhaiskaya, but standards of cleanliness are higher and the rooms are in slightly better shape. The green stucco walls give the place an institutional feeling more appropriate to a dormitory than a hotel. The rooms come with the same plywood furnishings as at the Mozhaiskaya, but the televisions usually work and the closets are bigger here. For tourists on a budget who don't mind roughing it a bit, this is a bearable if far from luxurious option. *Pervaya Bolshaya Yushuniskaya ul., reservations tel. 095/318–0918; Bldg. 1, tel. 095/119–8182; Bldg. 2, tel. 095/318–4972; Bldg. 3, 095/318–6483; Bldg. 4, 095/318–8371. 2,588 rooms with bath. Facilities: 9 restaurants, 8 snack bars, bar, casino, sauna, excursion bureau. DC, MC, V.*

Zolotoye Koltso. Formerly the Belgrade II, this hotel offers the best deal for your money in a downtown location. It's situated across from the imposing Ministry of Foreign Affairs, close to the subway and the Arbat. The rooms are very basic, with narrow twin beds, mismatched upholstery, and worn industrial carpeting. All the singles and suites come with telephone and television, which you'll find only sporadically in the doubles. Standards of cleanliness are higher here than at the Belgrade, the hotel's twin across the street. Some of the rooms come with pleasant views of the Moskva River. Service is friendly, and there's an attendant on every floor. Considering its location, the rates are reasonable, and you can get an entire suite here for less than the price of a single at the nearly identical Belgrade. *Smolenskaya Ploshchad 5, tel. 095/248–6843; reservations, 095/248–7395, fax 095/248–7395. 460 rooms with bath. Facilities: 2 restaurants, café, 2 bars, casino, business center, excursion bureau. AE, DC, MC, V.*

The Arts and Nightlife

The Arts

Moscow is famed for its rich cultural life. The city boasts more than 60 officially registered theaters, with new ones opening all the time. Except at the most renowned theaters, such as the Bolshoi, tickets cans be obtained for rubles at the theaters themselves, or at the numerous theater box offices (*teatralnaya kassa*) scattered throughout the city. If you're intimidated by the language barrier, you can avail yourself of the IPS Theater Box Office in the Metropol Hotel (tel. 095/927–6728 or 095/927–6729), IntourService (tel. 095/203–1493) or the service bureau in your hotel. The prices are highly inflated ($30–$45 for the Bolshoi), but they can often get tickets to sold-out performances. Another alternative is to purchase a ticket from a scalper immediately prior to the performance. Scalpers will ask for $10 to $25, but there is no guarantee that you'll get a seat with a view.

The English-language newspaper *Moscow Times* publishes a schedule of cultural events for the coming week every Friday. Details of cultural events can also be found in the newspaper's quarterly magazine, *The Moscow Guide.*

Art Galleries With the end of the state's monopoly, a whole new art scene has surfaced. Numerous private galleries have opened in the past few years, and new ones are opening all the time. The Friday edition of the *Moscow Times* carries a review of the current exhibits. For opening hours, check with the galleries themselves; some are open only by appointment. A partial listing of galleries includes: A-3 Gallery, 39 Starokonyushenny Pereulok, tel. 095/291–8484; Art Moderne Cultural Center, 39 Bolshaya Ordynka, tel. 095/233–1551; Contemporary Art Center, ulitsa Bolshaya Yakimanka 6, tel. 095/238–4422; First Gallery, 7 Strasnoy Bulvar, in the restaurant Strasnoy 7, tel. 095/299–0498; Mars, 32 Malaya Filyovskaya ulitsa, tel. 095/146–2029; Red Art, 25/1 Proyezd Serova, tel. 095/924–2236; Today Gallery, 35 Arbat, tel. 095/241–0209; Moscow House of Artists, 11 Kuznetsky Most, tel. 095/925–4264.

Drama Even if you do not speak Russian, you might want to explore the intense world of Russian dramatic theater. The partial listings below cover Moscow's major drama theaters.

Chekhov Moscow Art Theater, or MKhAT (Kammergersky Pereulok 3, tel. 095/229–8760 or 095/290–5128). Founded in 1898 by the celebrated actors and directors Konstantin Stanislavsky and Vladimir Nemirovich-Danchenko, this theater is famous for its productions of the Russian classics, especially those of Chekhov. An affiliated, modern Moscow Art Theater with a seating capacity of 2,000 is located at 22 Tverskoy Bulvar.

LenKom Theater (Ul. Chekhova 6, tel. 095/299–9668). This youth theater presents new plays by young authors.

Maly Theater (Teatralnaya Ploshchad 1/6, tel. 095/923–2621). This was Moscow's first dramatic theater; it is famous for its staging of Russian classics, especially those of Ostrovsky.

Mossoviet Theater (Bolshaya Sadovaya 19, tel. 095/200–5943). This spot is good for contemporary drama.

Taganka Theater (Taganskaya Ploshchad, tel. 095/272–6300). This is the best known of Moscow's avant-garde and experimental companies. Performances sell out far in advance.

Satire Theater (Triumfalnaya Ploshchad 2, tel. 095/299-6305). This theater specializes in satirical comedies, such as Mayakovsky's *The Bathhouse* and *The Bedbug*.

Sovremmenik Theater (Chistoprudny Bulvar 19A, tel. 095/921–6473). This is one of Moscow's youngest theaters, with an experimental repertoire and company of young actors.

Vakhtangov Theater (Arbat 26, tel. 095/241–0728). Named after Stanislavksy's pupil Evgeny Vakhtangov, this is an excellent traditional theater, good for contemporary dramas.

Yermolova Theater (Tverskaya ul. 5, tel. 095/203–7952). The repertoire here varies from the Russian classics to modern, Western plays.

Music Moscow's musical life is particularly rich; the city has a number of symphony orchestras, as well as song-and-dance ensembles. Moiseyev's Folk Dance Ensemble is well known in Europe and America, but the troupe is on tour so much of the year that when it performs in Moscow, tickets are very difficult to obtain. Other renowned companies include the State Symphony Orchestra and the Armed Forces Song and Dance Ensemble. Except for tickets for special performances, tickets are easily available at dirt-cheap prices.

Glinka Music Museum (Ul. Fadeyeva 4, tel. 095/972–3237). This is one of many small concert halls scattered throughout the city.

Kolonny Zal (Pushkinskaya ul. 1, tel. 095/292–4864) This is also called the Hall of Columns and holds chamber-music and symphony concerts.

National Academy of Music (Ul. Paliashvili 1, tel. 095/290–6737). The academy is highly recommended for student productions of chamber music, symphony concerts, and operas.

Tchaikovsky Concert Hall (Triumfalnaya Ploshchad, tel. 095/299–6446). This huge concert hall with seating for more than 1,600 is home to the State Symphony Orchestra.

Tchaikovsky Conservatory (Ul. Gertsena 13, tel. 095/229–8183). The acoustics of this magnificent concert hall are excellent, and portraits of the world's great composers hang above the high balcony. Rachmaninoff, Scriabin, and Tchaikovsky number among the famous composers who have worked here. There is also a Small Hall, usually reserved for chamber-music concerts.

Scriabin Apartment Museum (Ul. Vakhtangova 11, tel. 095/241–1901.) Performances are held in a small concert hall located in the apartment building where the composer Alexander Scriabin lived. Concerts are usually held on Wednesday and Friday evenings.

Soviet Army Hall (2 Ploshchad Kommuny, tel. 095/281–5550). This theater is home to the Armed Forces Song and Dance Ensemble.

Opera and Ballet   **Bolshoi Opera and Ballet Theater** (Teatralnaya Ploshchad, tel. 095/292–9986). The Bolshoi's ballet company is justly world-famous, and its orchestra is also outstanding. The gilded, 19th-century auditorium is itself a sight to behold. Unfortunately, restoration plans are currently in the works, and the theater may close in the near future.

Kremlin Palace of Congresses (in the Kremlin, tel. 095/926–7901 or 095/929–7726). The Bolshoi and other opera and ballet troupes hold regular performances in this modern concert hall where the Soviet Communist Party congresses were once held. Entrance is through the whitewashed Kutafya Gate, near the Manege.

Operetta Theater (6 Pushkinskaya ul., tel. 095/292–0405). Come here for classical and modern works.

Pokrovsky Chamber Musical Theater (Leningradsky Prospect 71, tel. 095/198–7204). This experimental theater stages interesting productions of Russian classics.

Stanislavsky and Nemirovich-Danchenko Musical Theater (Ul. Pushkinskaya 17, tel. 095/229–8388). This offers classical and modern operas, ballets, and operettas.

Nightlife

Moscow's nightlife has exploded in the past few years. These days just about anything goes and many clubs and bars feature erotic floor shows that rival those of Times Square. You may find the entertainment in poor taste, but put it in perspective: Moscow's wild nightlife is more than anything a reaction to 70 years of being told "no."

As a foreigner, you should take special precautions at night. Press reports on increased crime exaggerate the situation, but foreign tourists are crime targets. Use common sense and make arrangements for the trip home before setting out. Keep in mind that the more you drink, the more vulnerable you become.

Bars and Lounges All the major hotels have their own bars and nightclubs. The lobby bars in the Savoy and Metropole hotels feature glitzy, prerevolutionary decor and a soothing atmosphere. The top-floor bar of the Baltschug Hotel offers magical views of the Kremlin. At the other end of the spectrum are the bars of the old Intourist hotels (Belgrade, Kosmos, Intourist), where the atmosphere ranges from sleazy to scary. Be forewarned that hard-currency prostitution is a thriving business in these places.

Some favorite new bars with Moscow's expatriate community are the Irish-run Shamrock Bar (Novy Arbat 19, tel. 095/291–7641) and the American Tren-Mos Bar (Ostozhenka ul. 1/9, tel. 095/202–5722). If you want to mix with the locals, check out Peter's Place (72 Zemlyanoy Zal, tel. 095/298–3248), a lively bar with dancing and a floor show.

Casinos Moscow has a serious case of casino fever. Numerous casinos, both upscale and back-alley, have opened in the past few years. It all makes perfect sense: people spend money in an inflationary environment, and Russia has one of the world's highest inflation rates. The gem of the bunch is **Casino Royal** (Begovaya ul. 22, tel. 095/945–1410), in the elegant Hippodrome, built for Nicholas I in 1834. Dress is formal and there's a $10 entrance fee. Betting is in U.S. dollars. The casino offers complimentary car service from all the major hotels and is open daily 8 PM–4 AM. The **Savoy, Mezhdunarodnaya, Leningradskaya,** and **Ukraina** hotels all have their own casinos. The **Alexander Blok** (tel. 095/255–9323), a ship moored permanently near the Mezhdunarodnaya Hotel, has three casinos. Minimum bets start at $10. The state-run **Arbat** restaurant (29 Novy Arbat, tel. 095/291–1172) has a ruble casino but a dollar entrance fee; it's open daily 8 PM–4 AM.

Discos **Nightlife** (Tverskaya ul. 17, tel. 095/229–4165). This Swedish-Russian joint venture was Moscow's first authentic disco. The music starts at 9 PM and continues through the wee hours of the morning. There is a $15 entrance fee and a dress code (no jeans). For all-night dancing and carousing, check out the brazen **Red Zone** (39 Leningradsky Prospect), located in the skating arena of the Army Central Sports Club (TsSKA). This is one of the hottest new spots for drinking and dancing, but if bared flesh makes you blush, better to go elsewhere. There is a $15 entrance fee, and the club is open Tuesday–Sunday 11 PM–6 AM.

Jazz and Rock Rock concerts are usually held in the city's sports stadiums; for listings of upcoming concerts, check the Friday edition of the *Moscow Times*. Some of the new clubs to open up in recent years include Arbat Blues Club (Pereulok Aksakova 11, Bldg. 2, tel. 095/291–1546); Rock Land Club (Izmailovsky Bulvar 39/11, tel. 095/163–8140), with a ruble cover charge (men pay more); and Victoria Club (tel. 095/237–0709). Owned by the Russian rock star Stas Namin, the latter is better known as the Hard Rock Cafe. It's at the Zelyony Teatr (Green Theater) in Gorky Park.

3 St. Petersburg

By Juliette
Shapland

St. Petersburg, born in the heart of an emperor, is Russia's adopted child. So unlike the Russian cities that came before it, St. Petersburg—with its strict geometric lines and perfectly planned architecture—is in many ways too European to be Russian. And yet it is too Russian to be European. A powerful combination of both East and West, of things Russian and things European, St. Petersburg is, more than anything, a city born of the passion of its founder, Czar Peter the Great, to bring an unwilling Russian nation into the fold of Europe and into the mainstream of history.

Founded less than 300 years ago as the grand, new capital of the budding Russian empire, St. Petersburg was built to face Europe, with its back to the reactionary Moscow. It did not arise but was forcibly constructed, stone by stone, under the direction and according to the exacting plans of Peter the Great, for whose patron saint the city is named. Covering more than 100 islands and crisscrossed by more than 60 rivers and canals, it has become known as the Venice of the North. Even in today's dark days of economic poverty and political uncertainty, its imperial palaces sparkle in the cold light of the Russian winter; in the long days of the northern summer the colorful facades of its riverside estates glow gently, in perfect harmony with the dark blue waters of the Neva River.

Water plays an enormous role in the city's life. Because much of St. Petersburg lies practically at sea level, there is often the danger of flooding, at times severe. This occurred in 1824 (the subject of Pushkin's poem "The Bronze Horseman"), in 1924, and again as recently as 1984. Half of the River Neva—a very short one of only 74 kilometers (46 miles)—is within the city's boundaries. The river divides into four arms as it reaches the Gulf of Finland: the Great and Little Neva, and the Great and Little Nevka. Together with numerous affluents, they combine to form an intricate delta. From late November to early March, the Neva River freezes solid enough to bear the weight of pedestrians. While winters are long and dark, between mid-June and early July the city falls under the spell of the White Nights. During the summer, twilight lasts no more than 30 to 40 minutes, giving the city's streets and canals an unusual charm.

The history of St. Petersburg is integrally linked to the turmoil of war and revolution that has plagued the Russian nation. In the 19th century, the city stood witness to the struggle against czarist oppression. Here the early fires of revolution were kindled, first in 1825 by a small band of starry-eyed aristocratic officers, the so-called Decembrists, and then by organized workers' movements in 1905. The full-scale revolutions of 1917 led to the demise of the Romanov dynasty, the foundation of the Soviet Union, and the end of the city's role as the nation's capital. But the worst ordeal by far came during World War II, when Leningrad withstood a 900-day siege and blockade by Nazi forces. Nearly 650,000 people died of starvation, and more than 17,000 were killed in air raids and by indiscriminate shelling.

St. Petersburg has had its name changed three times during its brief history. With the outbreak of World War I, it became the more Russian-sounding Petrograd. After Lenin's death in 1924, it was renamed Leningrad in the Soviet leader's honor. Today, with the latest Russian revolution, its original name has been restored. A sign of the changing times is that—for the first time—the city's residents were given a choice in the matter. Many people opposed the change, primarily because memories of the siege of Leningrad and World War II became an indelible part of the city's identity. But for all the controversy surrounding its name, many residents refer to the city simply—and affectionately—as Peter.

Essential Information

Important Addresses and Numbers

Tourist Information
Because St. Petersburg has no official visitor's office or central location for dispensing tourist information, the major hotels have established tourist offices for their guests. These offices, which provide a wide variety of services, will help you book individual and group tours, make restaurant reservations, or purchase theater tickets. Even if you are not a hotel guest, you are usually welcome to use these facilities, provided you are willing to pay the hefty fees (charged in foreign currency only) for their services.

Consulates
United States (15 Furshtatskaya [formerly Petra Lavrova], tel. 812/274–8235, 812/274–8568, or 812/274–8689). **Canada** (3 ul. Yakubovicha; open Mon. and Thurs. 9–1). **British Consulate** (5 Ploshchad Proletarskoi Diktatury, tel. 812/119–6036).

A word of warning: Phone lines to the U.S. Consulate are constantly busy. It may take hours of persistent dialing to get through.

Emergencies
Police (tel. 02, Russian speakers only), **ambulance** (tel. 03, Russian speakers only).

Hospitals and Clinics
Medical facilities in St. Petersburg leave a lot to be desired. Poorly equipped and short on supplies, the average hospital is likely to scare even the most seasoned traveler. The **American Medical Center,** which opened a clinic in Moscow in the early 1990s, now has an office in St. Petersburg (77 Fontanka, tel. 812/119–6101; open weekdays 8:30–6, Sat. 10–2). The center offers diagnostic, laboratory, and X-ray facilities, as well as a pharmacy. Payment must be made with hard currency (MasterCard, Visa, or cash). **St. Peters-**

burg Polyclinic No 2. (22 Moskovsky Prospect, tel. 292–62–72; open weekdays 9–9, Sat. 9–3) has been around for years but has recently gone private, and while care is still far below Western standards, the facilities are clean and foreign medicines are available. A doctor is on call 24 hours a day (tel. 812/110–1102).

If you are unfortunate enough to be hospitalized while in St. Petersburg, you will probably be placed in **Hospital No. 20** (21 ul. Gastello, tel. 812/108–4808 or 812/108–4066).

Dentists Several private dental practices have recently opened in St. Petersburg. In an emergency, you could ask your hotel for a referral, or try one of the following private clinics: **St. Petersburg Polyclinic No. 2** (22 Moskovsky Prospect, tel. 812/292–6272), **Dental Polyclinic No. 3** (12 21aya liniya, tel. 812/213–7551 or 812/213–5550), or **Normed** (12/15 ul. Tverskaya, tel. 812/110–0206).

Where to Change Money **Vneshekonombank,** 29 Bolshaya Morskaya, off Nevsky Prospect and not far from the Astoria Hotel (tel. 812/314–6059); **St. Petersburg Bank,** 70/72 Fontanka, Room 73 (tel. 812/315–4300); **Industry and Construction Bank,** 38 Nevsky Prospect (tel. 812/110–4703).

All major hotels also have exchange bureaus, which are generally open from 9 AM to 6 PM with an hour's break for lunch in the afternoon. In today's strained economic atmosphere, just about everybody wants to exchange their rubles for your dollars, and new exchange bureaus pop up daily. You are probably best off using your hotel or one of the established banks listed above. For safety reasons, avoid changing money on the street, no matter how tempting or persistent the offers.

English-Language Bookstores For English-language publications, try St. Petersburg's largest bookstore, **Dom Knigi** (The Book House), at 28 Nevsky Prospect. The selection is nothing to write home about, but it's still the biggest bookstore in town. A limited selection of outdated English-language guidebooks on various parts of the former Soviet Union is available at **Akademkniga** (57 Liteiny Prospect) and **Iskusstvo** (16 Nevsky Prospect). American and British paperbacks, newspapers, and magazines are on sale in hotel gift shops.

Late-Night Pharmacies Most pharmacies in St. Petersburg close by 8 or 9 PM. However, **Apteka No. 6** (22 Nevsky Prospect, tel. 812/311–2077) has a pharmacist on call 24 hours a day.

Drugs and medicines are in short supply in Russia, and pharmacies are generally poorly stocked. In a jam, you might try the recently opened **Pharmacy Damaian** at the St. Petersburg Polyclinic No. 2 (22 Moskovsky Prospect, tel. 812/292–62–72; open 9 AM–8 PM). It offers a wide selection of Western medicines and personal-hygiene products.

Travel Agencies **American Express** operates an office in the Grand Hotel Europe (1/7 ul. Mikhailovskaya, just off Nevsky Prospect, tel.

812/315–7487), where you can replace lost traveler's checks
and credit cards or take out a cash advance (in traveler's
checks only). The office does not have an automated teller
machine, and due to limited availability of cash, it is not always possible to cash your traveler's checks for dollars.
Open weekdays 9–5.

Arriving and Departing by Plane

Airports and St. Petersburg is served by two airports, **Pulkhovo I** (do-
Airlines mestic) and **Pulkhovo II** (international), located just 5 ki-
lometers (3 miles) apart and 12 kilometers (7 miles) south of
downtown St. Petersburg. The runways of the two
Pulkhovos interconnect, so it's possible you could land at
Pulkhovo I and taxi over to Pulkhovo II.

Pulkhovo II has been under reconstruction for several
years. A new departures terminal opened in spring 1992,
but at press time no date had been set for the opening of the
new arrivals terminal. The small building that has been
serving as a "temporary" arrivals terminal for several
years now is ill equipped and unsuited to its purpose. There
is just one luggage conveyor belt to serve all of the arriving
flights, so be ready for a long wait—and a lot of pushing and
shoving—to get your bags. Be prepared to carry your own
luggage as well: there are no luggage carts for rent, and
assistance with your baggage is available only after you
have passed through customs.

Aeroflot (tel. 812/104–3444) offers direct flights to more
than 20 countries out of Pulkhovo II. International airlines
maintaining offices in St. Petersburg include **Czech Air** (tel.
812/315–5264), **Delta** (tel. 812/311–5819), **Finnair** (tel. 812/
315–9736), and **Lufthansa** (tel. 812/314–4979). **KLM** (tel.
812/104–3440) has an office at Pulkhovo II.

Between the Municipal bus No. 13 will take you to the Moskovskaya sub-
Airport and way stop at the edge of town, but the service is unreliable
Downtown and inconvenient. If you have any luggage, the only realistic way to reach downtown St. Petersburg is by car. If you
are traveling with a tour package, all transfers will have
been arranged. Independent tourists are advised to make
advance arrangements for transfers from the airport.
There are plenty of taxis available, but for safety reasons
non-Russian speakers should not pick up a cab on their own.
Foreign tourists, especially arriving passengers at train
stations and airports, are prime crime targets. Cab fare
from the airport will depend entirely on your negotiating
skills; the range is $10 to $50. The airport is about a 40-min-
ute ride from the city center.

Arriving and Departing by Car, Train, Bus, and Boat

By Car   You can reach St. Petersburg from Finland via the Helsinki–St. Petersburg Highway through the border town of Vyborg. To reach Moscow, take the Moscow–St. Petersburg Highway, which leaves the city near the Varshavsky (Warsaw) Railroad Station, close to Izmailovsky Cathedral.

A word of warning about driving in St. Petersburg: Be aware of occasional long lines and periodic gas shortages at fueling stations, the risk of car theft, and the lack of repair shops and replacement parts. Add to this the poor road conditions and maintenance, and you may very well decide against driving to St. Petersburg.

By Train   Train travel is by far the most convenient and comfortable mode of travel in Russia. St. Petersburg has several train stations, the most important of which are **Finlandsky Vokzal** (Finland Station), for trains to Finland; **Moskovsky Vokzal** (Moscow Station), at Ploshchad Vostania, off Nevsky Prospect, for trains to Moscow and points east; **Varshavsky Vokzal** (Warsaw Station) for trains to the Baltic countries; and **Vitebsky Vokzal** (Vitebsk Station) for trains to Ukraine and points south. All the major train stations have a connecting subway stop, so they are easily reached by public transportation.

There are several trains daily from Moscow to St. Petersburg, the most popular of which is the **_Red Arrow_**, a night train that departs Moscow at 11:55 PM and arrives in St. Petersburg at 8:25 AM the next day. During the day travelers prefer the high-speed **_Avrora_**, which makes the trip in less than six hours. There are two trains daily to and from Helsinki; the trip takes 6½ hours.

For information on train arrival and departure schedules, call 812/168–0111. Train tickets may be purchased through the tourist bureau in your hotel or at the ticket office at 24 Kanal Griboyedova (off Nevsky Prospect, adjacent to the Kazan Cathedral). Tickets for anything other than same-day departures are _not_ for sale at the train stations.

A note on train travel: You must travel on an Intourist train ticket or risk being fined by the railway. As a foreigner you pay a special price for train travel and, in return, usually get above-average service (the best trains are reserved for foreign tourists).

Long-distance travelers should be aware that trains often lack heat and hot water, a result of feuds between rail administrations in different republics. To avoid discomfort, be sure to bring along some drinking water whenever traveling by train. You are also advised to have your own supply of toilet paper.

By Bus The Russian firm **Sovavto St. Petersburg** (tel. 812/298–1352) offers daily departures to Helsinki from the following hotels: Astoria, Grand Hotel Europe, Pulkhovskaya, Sovietskaya, and St. Petersburg. The Finnish bus company **Finnord** (tel. 812/314–8951) offers daily service to Vyborg, Lakhti, and Helsinki, leaving from the Sovietskaya Hotel.

By Boat Cruise ships of the Baltic Line call at St. Petersburg. Cruises are available from Stockholm and Helsinki. For information on schedules and fares, contact their Helsinki office: 6 kluuvitaku, SF-00100, Helsinki, tel. 358/90–665755.

Getting Around

Although St. Petersburg is spread out over 650 square kilometers (150 square miles), most of its historic sites are concentrated in the downtown section and are best explored on foot. Most of the historical sites are not well served by the extensive public transportation system, so be prepared to do a lot of walking.

By Subway Although St. Petersburg's metro does not boast the elaborate design and decoration of the Moscow subway, its beauty and convenience still astound. And despite current economic hardships, St. Petersburg has managed to maintain efficient service. The only drawback to the system, which is simple to use and inexpensive as well, is that the stops tend to be far apart.

To use the subway, you must purchase a token (available at stations) and insert it upon entering into the slot at the turnstile. Due to shortages, however, there is currently a limit of two tokens per customer, and lines are sometimes long. Stations are deep underground, and the escalator ride is long. The fare is the same regardless of distance. Alternatively, you may purchase a pass valid for the entire month and good for transport on all modes of city transportation. The cost is insignificant and well worth the convenience. The subway operates from 5:30 AM to 1 AM and is best avoided during rush hours.

By Bus, Tram, and Trolley Surface transportation operates on the honor system: Upon entering, you validate your ticket by canceling it using one of the machines on the wall of the vehicle. You can purchase strips of tickets at subway stops and kiosks throughout the city or from the driver after you have boarded. The ticket is valid for one ride only; if you change buses you must pay another fare. Buses, trams, and trolleys operate from 5 AM to 1 AM, although service in the late evening hours and on Sundays tends to be unreliable.

St. Petersburg has an elaborate surface transportation system, but in contrast to the subway, service has greatly deteriorated in recent years. Vehicles tend to be dilapidated and extremely overcrowded during rush hours. People with claustrophobia should avoid them. In the last years of the Soviet

St. Petersburg Metro

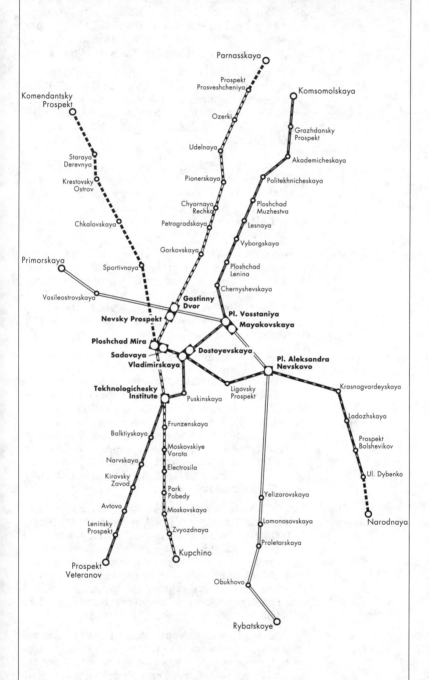

regime, Russia depended on Hungary for buses, but in today's economic order, they are no longer forthcoming. It is not uncommon to ride a bus with holes in the ceiling and doors that will not close due to constant overcrowding, or that keels to the side when turning corners like a sailboat on rough seas.

By Taxi Although taxis roam the city quite frequently, it is far easier—and certainly safer—to order a cab through your hotel. Fares vary according to the driver's whim; you are expected to negotiate. Foreigners are always charged much more than Russians, and tourists tend to be gouged. If you speak Russian, you can order a cab by dialing 312–00–22. There is sometimes a delay of several hours, but usually the cab arrives within 20–30 minutes. If you order a cab this way, you pay the official state fare, which turns out to be very reasonable in dollars, plus a fee for the reservation. Drivers will appreciate and expect a tip of at least 20%. If you hail a cab on the street, expect to pay in dollars only; fares generally begin at $5 for tourists.

Tourists should take the same precautions when using taxicabs in St. Petersburg as in Moscow.

Guided Tours

A host of private tour agencies have arisen in the past few years, primarily because tourism is seen as an easy source of foreign currency. Keep in mind that whatever the price quoted for a tour, it may very well be negotiable. In addition to the private agencies, every major hotel has a tourist bureau through which individual and group tours can be booked.

St. Petersburg Travel Company (formerly Intourist) maintains excursion bureaus in all the major hotels. Group or individual excursions are available to all of the major sites and suburban palaces. City tours start daily at 10 AM. Excursions depart from the Astoria Hotel. For more information, call the service bureau at the Astoria, tel. 812/210–5046.

The newly formed joint-stock company **Artika** offers individual and group tours in and around St. Petersburg on just about any subject. It can also make arrangements for travel to other cities within the CIS. *163 Obukhovskoi oborony Prospect, tel. 812/262–2568.*

Exploring St. Petersburg

Highlights for First-Time Visitors

Alexander Nevsky Lavra (*see* Tour 4)
Field of Mars and **Russian Art Museum** (*see* Tour 5)
Hermitage Museum (*see* Tour 1)
Nevsky Prospect (*see* Tour 4)
Palace Square and the **Winter Palace** (*see* Tour 1)

Peter and Paul Fortress (*see* Tour 3)
St. Isaac's Cathedral and **Decembrists' Square** (*see* Tour 2)
Summer Gardens (*see* Tour 5)

Tour 1: Palace Square, the Winter Palace, and the Hermitage Museum

Numbers in the margin correspond to points of interest on the St. Petersburg map.

The best place to begin your tour of St. Petersburg is **Dvortsovaya Ploshchad** (Palace Square), where the city's imperial past has been preserved in all its glory and splendor. A stunning ensemble of buildings and open space, Palace Square combines several seemingly incongruous architectural styles in perfect harmony. Besides being one of the world's most magnificent squares, it is also a site of great historical significance. It was here on Bloody Sunday in 1905 that the last Russian czar's fate was sealed after palace troops opened fire on peaceful demonstrators, killing scores of women and children. It was across Palace Square that the Bolshevik revolutionaries stormed the Winter Palace in their successful attempt to overthrow Kerensky's provisional government in October 1917, an event that led to the birth of the Soviet Union. Appropriately, it was also here on Palace Square that, during the tense days of the 1991 August coup, citizens held all-night vigils to demonstrate their support for perestroika and democracy.

The centerpiece of Palace Square is the **Aleksandrovskaya Kolonna** (Alexander Column), a memorial to Russia's victory over Napoleon. Measuring 25 meters (82 feet) from the pedestal to the top, the Alexander Column was commissioned by Nicholas I in memory of his brother, Czar Alexander I, and was designed by August Ricard de Montferrand. The column was cut from a single piece of granite and, together with its pedestal, weighs more than 650 tons. It stands in place by the sheer force of its own weight; there are no attachments affixing it to the pedestal. In 1832 the column was erected by 2,000 soldiers and 400 workmen, using an elaborate system of pulleys and ropes. The column is crowned by an angel (symbolizing peace in Europe) crushing a snake, an allegorical depiction of Russia's victory over Napoleon.

Bordering Palace Square is the **Zimny Dvorets** (Winter Palace), formerly the residence of the czar, built in the lush style of Russian Baroque. Created by the Italian architect Bartolomeo Francesco Rastrelli at the behest of Empress Elizabeth I, the Winter Palace stretches from Palace Square to the Neva River embankment and was the fourth royal residence on this site. The present palace was commissioned in 1754, when Russian Baroque was in vogue, but by the time of its completion in 1762, both the fashion and the empress had changed. After assuming power, Catherine the Great left the exterior unaltered, but the interiors were redesigned in the neoclassical style of the day. In 1837 the interiors were revamped once again after the palace was gutted by fire. The Winter Palace contains more than 1,000 rooms and halls, the most celebrated of which include the Gallery of the 1812 War, where portraits of Russian commanders who served against Napoleon are on display, the Great Throne Room, richly decorated in marble and bronze, and the Malachite Hall, designed by the architect Alexander Bryullov and decorated with malachite columns and pilasters. Before the 1917 Revolution, the Winter Palace served as the main royal residence and was used for ceremonial occasions, grand balls, and receptions. Today it is part of the Hermitage Museum and is open to the general public.

To the east of Palace Square is the huge inverted circle of the **Glavny Shtab** (General Staff Building), whose form and size lend Palace Square its unusual shape. During czarist rule the building served as military headquarters and also housed the ministries of foreign affairs and finance. Created by the architect Carlo Giovanni Rossi, and built in the neoclassical style between 1819 and 1829, the General Staff Building is actually two structures connected by a monumental archway. The passageway created by the arch leads from Palace Square to St. Petersburg's main thoroughfare, Nevsky Prospect. The arch supports an impressive 10-meter (33-foot) bronze sculpture of a victory chariot, created by the artists Vasily Demut-Malinovsky and Stepan Pimenov and commemorating Russia's victory in the war against Napoleon.

The **Shtab Gvardeiskovo Korpusa** (Headquarters of the Guard Corps), to the left of the General Staff Building, serves as an architectural buffer between the neoclassical General Staff Building and the Baroque Winter Palace. Designed by the architect Alexander Bryullov and built between 1837 and 1843, this modest building is noteworthy for the very fact that it easily goes unnoticed. Instead of drawing attention to itself, it leads the eye focus to the other architectural masterpieces bordering each side of Palace Square. Bryullov's creation was considered the ultimate tribute to the field of architecture. In his restraint he deferred to the masters who came before him; instead of disturbing the beauty they created, Bryullov used his talent to enhance it.

No matter what your plans while in St. Petersburg, make sure you set aside at least half a day for a visit to the ❷ **Ermitazh** (Hermitage Museum). The museum includes the lavish Winter Palace as well as the various buildings that once housed the art galleries of the czars. The present museum acquired its name from the original Hermitage, which was attached to Catherine the Great's private apartments in the Winter Palace. Built between 1764 and 1775, the orig-

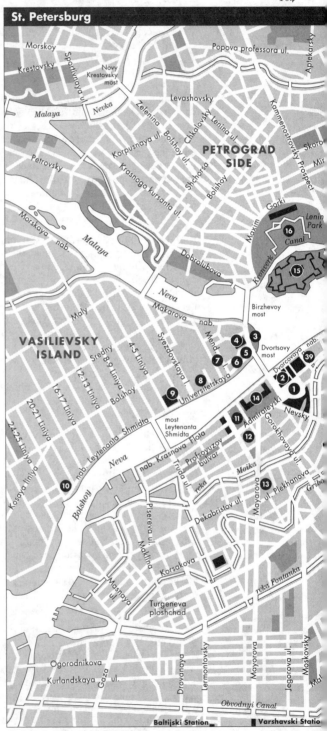

inal Hermitage was used as a retreat (hence the name) and quickly filled up with masterpieces collected from all over the world. This section of the Hermitage Museum is now known as the Little (*maly*) Hermitage. It is attached to the Great (*bolshoi*) Hermitage, which was built in 1783 to house the overflow of art from the Little Hermitage and also contained conference chambers for the czar's ministers. Attached to the Great Hermitage by an arch straddling the Winter Canal is the **Hermitage Theater** (1783–1787), created for Catherine the Great by the Italian architect Giacomo Quarenghi. Yet another addition, the New Hermitage, was added between 1839 and 1852; it became Russia's first public museum, although admission was by royal invitation only. *36 Dvortsovaya Naberezhnaya, tel. 812/311–3420. Open Tues.–Sun. 10:30–6.*

Today's Hermitage Museum contains one of the world's richest repositories of art. It was created out of czarist treasures and private collections, then confiscated and nationalized by the Soviet government after the 1917 Bolshevik Revolution. With more than 400 exhibit halls, the Hermitage cannot possibly be seen in a single day. It has been estimated that in order to spend one minute on each object on display, a visitor would have to devote an entire year to the endeavor. Official guided tours tend to be rushed, and you will probably want to return on your own.

It is best to begin your tour around 11:30 AM, when the early morning crowds have dispersed. During peak tourist season, you may encounter long lines at the museum entrance. If you want to avoid the hours-long wait, go to the head of the line and walk innocently past the guard. If you make it clear that you are a foreign tourist, the guard may assume that you have strayed from your group tour and allow you to enter. Once inside, buy a ticket and be on your way—if you make it past the guard you will not be harassed further. Be aware, however, that as a foreigner you will be expected to pay a higher entrance fee.

When you first enter the Hermitage you will most likely be overwhelmed by the lavish interiors of the former Winter Palace. The museum's main route takes you to the second-floor galleries by way of the **Jordan Staircase**, a dazzling creation of marble, granite, and gold. Although the museum is divided into eight distinct sections, they are not clearly marked. The floor plans that are available, labeled entirely in Russian, are not terribly useful. All of this makes it easy to get lost in the mazelike complex of the Hermitage, but do not despair. Special assistants placed throughout the museum will be happy to point you in the right direction; do not be shy about asking for their help.

The first section of the museum covers prehistoric times, showing the discoveries made on former Soviet territory, including examples of Scythian relics and artifacts. Section two is devoted to the Asian republics, the Caucasus, and their peoples. Ancient Greece and Rome are the subjects of section three, where the so-called Venus of Taurida (in Room 109) and Greek vases (Rooms 129–131), also found on former Soviet territory, are on display. Section four concentrates on Russian history and culture. Western European art is covered in the fifth and sixth sections. The seventh section contains riches from ancient Egypt, Babylon, Assyria, Byzantium, China, and Japan. The last section is devoted to medals and decorations, both Russian and foreign.

The sixth and seventh sections are of particular interest to most art lovers. To mention just a few highlights—there are two Leonardos: *Madonna with Flowers* (also known as the *Benois Madonna*) and *Madonna Litta* (in Room 214); two Raphaels: *Madonna Connestabile* and *Holy Family* (in Room 229); and Michelangelo's *Crouching Boy* (in Room 229). Titian is represented by eight fine canvases (Rooms 219 and 221). The Hermitage also boasts a fine collection of Spanish art, of which only a portion is currently on display due to ongoing museum renovations. Works by El Greco, Velázquez, Zurbarán, and Goya are temporarily on display in Rooms 143–146. In Room 246 one can see Flemish art of the 17th century, including a splendid self-portrait by Van Dyck. The Hermitage has more than 40 canvases by Rubens (Room 247) and 25 Rembrandts, including *Danae* and *The Prodigal Son* (Room 254). French art is also well represented by Poussin's *Landscape with Polyphemus*, Watteau's *Capricious Woman*, and Houdon's statue of Voltaire (Rooms 273–278). Many works of late-19th- and early 20th-century art, amassed with great foresight by rich Moscow merchants, are now in the Hermitage: Degas and Renoir are in Room 320, Monet and Cézanne (including *The Banks of the Marne*) are in Rooms 319 and 318, respectively. Van Gogh is in Room 317. There are 35 paintings by Matisse (Rooms 346–348), including *The Dance*. Picasso, in his various blue, pink, and cubist periods, can be seen in Rooms 344 and 345. British art is well represented by many paintings of Sir Joshua Reynolds, Thomas Gainsborough, and William Morris (Rooms 298–302).

Time Out The **Literary Café** at 18 Nevsky Prospect (tel. 812/312–6057) is a short walk from the Hermitage Museum. Although the menu is standard Russian fare, with hearty soups and heavy meat dishes, the café stands out for its pleasant atmosphere and 19th-century decor; live chamber music further adds to the Old World atmosphere. In 1837 the beloved Russian poet Alexander Pushkin was served his last meal here before setting off for his fatal duel. Reservations are almost always essential, so you should call ahead. To reach the café, walk across Palace Square, through the arch of the General Staff Building, and then take a left onto Nevsky Prospect. It's at the end of the block, at the corner of the Moika river canal (Naberezhnaya reki Moiki) and Nevsky Prospect. *Open daily noon–5 and 7–10.*

Possibly the most prized section of the Hermitage—and definitely the most difficult to get into—is the **Osobaya Kladovaya** (Special Collection), sometimes referred to as the Zolotaya Kladovaya (Gold Room). This spectacular collection of gold, silver, and royal jewels is well worth the hassle and expense of admission. Entry is restricted to groups of 17, which must book in advance. The easiest way to join one of these groups is through your hotel's tourist bureau, which may be able to attach you to a prebooked tour at a cost of about $25 per person. Alternatively, private tours for up to three people are available for around $70 through the St. Petersburg Travel Company (formerly Intourist). The third option is to join a Russian-language tour, at a cost of $12. You must call ahead to reserve a spot (tel. 311–3725, open 10:30–3:30); tours are usually booked to capacity, and the rule limiting 17 people into the collection is strictly observed.

The collection is divided into two sections. The first section, covering prehistoric times, includes gold and silver treasures recovered from the Crimea, Ukraine, and Caucasus. The second section, truly mind-boggling with its dazzling array of ornate and jewel-encrusted pillboxes, miniature clocks, and cigarette cases, covers the Renaissance through the 1917 Revolution.

Tour 2: Vasilievsky Island and the Left Bank

Vasilievsky Ostrov, the largest island in the Neva Delta, was one of the first areas of the city to be developed. It is a popular residential area, with most of its historical sites contained on its eastern edge. The island's western tip, facing the Gulf of Finland, houses the city's main sea terminals. The island is also home to the city's most renowned academic institutions, including the St. Petersburg branch of the Academy of Sciences, St. Petersburg University, the Repin Art Institute (formerly St. Petersburg Academy of Arts), and the city's oldest institution of higher learning, the St. Petersburg Institute of Mining Technology.

Peter the Great's original plans for the island called for a network of canals, intended to transport goods from the main sea terminal to the city's commercial center at the opposite end of the island. These plans to re-create Venice never materialized, although some of the smaller canals were actually dug (and later filled in). These would-be canals are now streets, and are called "lines" (*liniya*). Instead of names, they bear numbers and run parallel to the island's three main thoroughfares: the Great, Middle, and Small Avenues (Prospects).

③ Begin your tour of Vasilievsky Island at its easternmost point, known as the **Strelka** (arrow or spit). It is most easily reached by crossing the **Dvortsovy Most** (Palace Bridge), off Palace Square, or by taking Trolley 1 or 7 from any stop on Nevsky Prospect. The Strelka affords a dazzling view of the Winter Palace and the Peter and Paul Fortress (*see* Tour 3, *below*) and reveals the city's triumphant rise from a swamp outpost to a metropolis. Seen against the backdrop of the Neva, the brightly colored houses lining the embankment seem like children's toys—the building blocks of a bygone aristocracy. They stand at the water's edge, supported not by the land beneath them but almost by the panorama of the city behind them. Gazing at this architectural wonder, you start to understand the power of Peter the Great's vision for his country. The view is also revealing because it makes clear how careful the city's founders were to build their city not despite the Neva but around and with it. The river's natural ebb and flow accords perfectly with the monumental architecture lining its path.

As you stand in Pushkin Square, as the park on the Strelka is called, you will notice two red columns, known as the **Rostralnyie Kolonny** (Rostral Columns). Erected in honor of the Russian fleet between 1805 and 1810, their name comes from the Latin *rostrum*, meaning "prow." Modeled on similar memorials in ancient Rome, the columns are decorated with ships' prows, with sculptures at the base depicting Russia's main waterways, the Dneiper, the Volga, the Volkhov, and Neva rivers. Although the columns originally served as lighthouses—until 1855 this was St. Petersburg's commercial harbor—they are now lit only on special occasions.

The group of buildings facing the Neva opposite Pushkin Park once served the busy harbor that was here. Of particu-
④ lar interest is the **Voenno-Morskoy Muzey** (Central Naval Museum), which until the mid-19th century was the city's main stock exchange (*birzha*). Erected in 1804–10 and, like the Rostral Columns, designed by the Swiss architect Thomas de Thomon, the neoclassical Stock Exchange was modeled on the Greek temple at Paestum. The museum's collection dates from the reign of Peter the Great. Starting in 1709, in accordance with his orders, a miniature replica was made of every ship built in Russian shipyards. The museum itself was established in 1805. Moved into the former stock exchange building in 1940, the museum's collection contains a 3,000-year-old dugout found on the bottom of the Bug River, as well as Peter the Great's personal belongings, including his first boat and the ax he used to build it. *4 Pushkin Sq., Vasilievsky Ostrov, tel. 812/218–2501 or 812/218–2502. Open Wed.–Sun. 10:30–4:30. Closed last Thurs. of month.*

Flanking both sides of the Stock Exchange and lending balance to the architectural ensemble of the spit are two virtually identical buildings in the Greek classical style. These former warehouses, originally intended to serve the city's busy port, also house museums: the **Dokuchayev Soil Museum** (of interest only to soil specialists and now closed for repairs) and the **Zoologichesky Muzey** (Zoological Museum). The prize of this museum's unusual collection, which contains over 40,000 species, is a stuffed mammoth recovered from Siberia in 1901. Scientists believe it roamed the earth some 44,000 years ago. *1 Universitetskaya Naberezhnaya, tel. 812/218–0112. Open Sat.–Thurs. 11–5. Closed holidays.*

Farther north along the embankment is the former **Customs House.** Constructed in the 19th century in the same style as the warehouses, it is now known as the **Pushkin House** and holds a special place in the heart of the Russian people. Here valuable manuscripts and original works by some of Russia's most beloved authors are stored in special archives maintained by the Academy of Sciences' Institute of Russian Literature. At one time the institute also maintained a public museum displaying original manuscripts as well as the personal effects of such Russian literary giants as Gogol and Tolstoy. The building's state of disrepair has forced the institute to close the museum and severely restrict access to its archives.

Continue along the **Universitetskaya Naberezhnaya** (University Embankment), which leads away from the Strelka on the south side of the Stock Exchange. With the Neva River to your left, the first building you will encounter is the so-called **Kunstkamera.** A fine example of Russian Baroque, painted bright azure with white trim, the building stands out from the surrounding classically designed architecture. Its playful character seems to reflect its beginnings; it was originally commissioned in 1718 to house Peter the Great's collection of curiosities, gathered during his travels. Completed by 1734, the Kunstkamera (from the German *Kunst,* meaning "art," and *Kammer,* meaning "chamber") was destroyed by fire in 1747 and almost entirely rebuilt. Today it houses the Museum of Anthropology and Ethnography, whose holdings include Peter's original collection, a truly bizarre assortment of oddities ranging from rare stones to preserved human organs. The museum is enormously popular, so purchase entrance tickets early in the day. *3 Universitetskaya Naberezhnaya, tel. 812/218–1412. Open Sun.–Thurs. 11–4. Closed last Thurs. of month.*

Next to the Kunstkamera stands the original building of the Russian Academy of Sciences. Erected on strictly Classical lines in 1783–89, it is considered to be Quarenghi's grandest design, with an eight-column portico, a pediment, and a double staircase. The academy, founded in 1724 by Peter the Great and known as the Imperial Academy of Sciences until the 1917 Revolution, had its administrative offices transferred to Moscow in 1934. The building now houses the St. Petersburg branch of the Russian Academy of Sciences and is not open to the public.

Continue along the embankment, crossing Mendeleyevskaya Liniya (Mendelyev Line) and passing an imposing statue of the 18th-century Russian scientist Mikhail ⑦ Lomonosov. You will come to the main campus of **St. Petersburg University,** whose name has changed as often as the city's. One of Russia's leading institutions of higher learning, with an enrollment of over 20,000, St. Petersburg University was founded by Alexander I in 1819. Its campuses date from the time of Peter the Great. The bright red Baroque building to your immediate right is the so-called **Twelve Colleges Building,** whose name comes from the governmental administrative bodies established during Peter's reign. Designed by Domenico Trezzini and completed 16 years after Peter's death, in 1741, the building was transferred to the university at the time of its establishment and today houses the university's library and administrative offices. The building is not open to the public, but no one will stop you from looking around.

The next building in the university complex is the **Rector's Wing,** where, as the plaque on the outside wall attests, the great Russian poet Alexander Blok was born in 1880. The building was originally commissioned in 1727 as a palace for Peter the Great's grandson, who ruled only briefly. Completed in 1761, the building was later given to the University.

Farther up the embankment, at the corner of Syezdovskaya Liniya, is the grandest building of old St. Petersburg, the ⑧ **Menshikovsky Dvorets** (Menshikov Palace). Alexander Menshikov, St. Petersburg's first governor, is one of Russian history's more flamboyant characters. A close friend of Peter the Great, Menshikov rose from humble beginnings as a street vendor and reportedly got his start when he sold a cabbage pie to Peter the Great—or so the legend goes. Eventually becoming one of Russia's most powerful statesmen, Menshikov was famous for his corruption and political maneuvering. His palace, the first stone building in St. Petersburg, was at the time of its completion in 1720 the city's most luxurious building. Although only a portion of the original palace has survived, it easily conveys a sense of Menshikov's inflated ego and love of luxury. Particularly noteworthy is the tilework in the restored bedrooms, whose walls and ceilings are completely lined with handcrafted ceramic tiles. After Peter's death and Menshikov's exile to Siberia in 1727, his palace was turned over to a military training school and was significantly altered over the years. In June 1917 it served as the site for the First Congress of Russian Soviets. Neglected until 1967, when badly needed restoration work was launched, the Menshikov Palace is today a branch of the Hermitage Museum. In addition to the restored living quarters of the Menshikov family, there is an exhibit devoted to early 18th-century Russian culture. *15 Universitetskaya Naberezhnaya, tel. 812/213–1112. Open Tues.–Sun. 10:30–4:30.*

As you leave Menshikov Palace, crossing Syezdovskaya Liniya, you'll come upon a small square to your right, opposite the embankment. This is **Rumantsev Square,** established in honor of the 18th-century general who led Russia to victory in the Russo-Turkish wars of 1768–74. The obelisk, designed by Vikenty Brenna, originally stood in the Field of Mars (Marsovo Pole) and was moved to its present site in 1818. The new site was chosen for its proximity to the military school in the former Menshikov Palace, where Rumantsev once studied.

Another notable building farther up the embankment is the
❾ **Repin Institute of Painting, Sculpture, and Architecture.** Built between 1764 and 1788 and designed by Alexander Kokorinov and Vallin de la Mothe, the structure is a fine example of early Russian classicism. The sculptures above the main entrance on the embankment portray Hercules and Flora. This was originally the home of the Russian Academy of Arts, which was founded here in 1757 by Elizabeth I but moved to Moscow in 1947. The institute maintains a public museum of graduation works from the original Academy. Also on display is an interesting collection of copies created by the institute's students, who worked directly from the original works of art. The institute's many famous graduates included Ilya Repin (1844–1930), for whom it is now named. *17 Universistetskaya Naberezhnaya, tel. 812/213–6496. Open Wed.–Sun. 11–6.*

Directly in front of the Academy of Arts stands one of St. Petersburg's landmarks, the famous Egyptian Sphinxes. It took more than a year to transport the granite statues from Egypt to St. Petersburg, where they arrived in 1832. Recovered at Thebes in 1820, the statues weigh more than 23 tons and date from the era of Pharaoh Amenhotep III (ca. 1417–1379 BC), whose face is supposedly depicted on the sphinxes. The special quay of granite, built to support the statues, affords one of the finest views of old St. Petersburg.

Time Out If you want a rest and a bite to eat at a popular local establishment, try **Lukamore** (2/19 13-aya Liniya, tel. 812/218–5900). It's a short walk (four blocks) up the embankment from the Academy of Arts and is located on the corner of the 13th Line and the embankment. If you arrive before the lunch crowds, which begin around 1 PM, you will probably be seated without a wait. The cuisine is far from gourmet, and the café's dark lighting creates a rather dismal atmosphere. This is the real St. Petersburg, though, and despite gloomy appearances, a few items on the menu are worth trying. The *griby v smetane* (mushrooms in creme sauce) is good and

MCI brings Europe and America closer together.

Call the U.S. for less with MCI CALL USA.®

It's easy and affordable to call home when you use MCI CALL USA!

- Less expensive than calling through hotel operators
- Available from over 80 countries and locations worldwide
- You're connected to English-speaking MCI® Operators
- Even call 800 numbers in the U.S.†

†Regular MCI CALL USA rates apply to 800 number calls.

Spend your
vacation
touring
castles.
Not train
stations.

Vacation Cars. Vacation Prices. Wherever your destination in Europe, there is sure to be one of more than 1,000 Budget locations nearby. Budget offers considerable values on a wide variety of quality cars, and if you book before you leave the U.S., you'll save even more with a special rate package from the Budget World Travel Plan.℠ For information and reservations, contact your travel consultant or call Budget in the U.S. at **800-472-3325.** Or, while traveling abroad, call a Budget reservation center.

THE SMART MONEY IS ON BUDGET.®

We feature Ford and other fine cars.   *A system of corporate and licensee owned locations.*

filling, as is the borscht. Since this is a state-run restaurant, whose patrons are predominantly Russian, you should expect the slow and inattentive service typical of such enterprises. *Open daily 11–4. Rubles only.*

At this point you may conclude your tour of Vasilievsky Island by crossing the **Most Leytenanta Shmidta** (Lieutenant Schmidt Bridge), which will take you across the Neva and back toward the city center. Built in 1842–50, this was the first stationary bridge to connect Vasilievsky Island with the left bank of the Neva; it was renamed in honor of the naval officer who was a leader of the Black Sea Fleet mutiny during the 1905–07 Revolution.

If time permits, however, you may choose to continue your tour of Vasilievsky Island to the end of the embankment, at the corner of 21 liniya, to see the **Gorny Institut** (Institute of Mining Technology). It can be reached either by walking or by taking any of the trams that stop at the corner of 11 liniya and the embankment. Founded in 1773 by Catherine the Great, this is St. Petersburg's oldest institution of higher learning. The present building in the Neoclassical style was built between 1806 and 1811 by Andrei Voronikhin, architect of the Kazan Cathedral on Nevsky Prospect. The main entrance is supported by 12 Doric columns and is lined with statues designed by Demut-Malinovsky and Pimenov (creators of the sculpture above the General Staff Building). The institute boasts an unusual museum of precious stones and minerals, including a piece of malachite weighing over a ton and an iron meteorite. *2 21-aya Liniya, tel. 812/218–8605 or 812/218–8681. Open weekdays 9–6.*

Lieutenant Schmidt Bridge takes you to the left bank of the embankment, which at this stretch is called *naberezhnoye Krasnovo Flota*, in honor of the Red Fleet. Before the 1917 Revolution it was called the English Embankment, as this was the center of the city's English community. Here one finds some of St. Petersburg's finest aristocratic estates. Take a left off the bridge and follow the embankment to No. 28, formerly the mansion of Grand Duke Andrei Vladimirovich Romanov. Today this is a state-run Wedding Palace, where secular ceremonies are perfunctorily performed with assembly-line efficiency.

Continue down the embankment with the Neva River on your left until you reach another of St. Petersburg's landmarks, the *Medny Vsadnik* (*Bronze Horseman*) in **Polshchad Dekabristov** (Decembrists' Square). The square was the scene of dramatic events on December 14, 1825, when, following Alexander I's death, a group of aristocrats launched a rebellion on the square in an attempt to overthrow the new czar, Nicholas I. Their coup failed miserably, and those who were not executed were banished to Siberia. Although the Decembrists did not bring significant change to Russia, their attempts at liberal reform were much touted by the Soviet regime as proof of deep-seated revolutionary fervor in Russian society. In 1925 the square, previously known as Senate and, before that, Petrov Square, was renamed in their honor.

The centerpiece of the square is the statue the *Bronze Horseman,* which was erected as a memorial from Catherine the Great to her predecessor, Peter the Great. The simple inscription reads, "To Peter the First from Catherine the Second, 1782." The clever empress may have been trying to insinuate that she was Peter's descendent but she was of German origin and of no relation whatsoever. Created by the French sculptor Etienne Falconet, the statue depicts Peter astride a rearing horse that symbolizes Russia, trampling a serpent that represents the forces opposed to his reforms. (The serpent actually provides an additional point of support for the horse balanced on its two legs). The statue was immortalized in a poem of the same name by Alexander Pushkin, who wrote that the czar "by whose fateful will the city was founded beside the sea, stands here aloft at the very brink of a precipice, having reared up Russia with his iron curb."

Decembrists' Square was once called Senate Square for a reason: To the west stands the building of the former Senate, Russia's highest judicial and administrative body before the 1917 Revolution. Designed by Carlo Rossi and built between 1829 and 1834 along Classical lines, the golden yellow building balances the architectural ensemble of Decembrists' Square, which is bordered to the east by yet another Classical structure in golden yellow, the **Admiralty** (*see below*). The former Senate building houses the Historical State Archives and is not open to the public.

⑫ Behind the *Bronze Horseman* stands **Isaakievsky Sobor** (St. Isaac's Cathedral), whose enormous gilded dome seems to burst upon the skyline like a metal balloon. Of the grandest proportions, St. Isaac's is the world's third-largest domed cathedral. Its beauty is a matter of taste: Some consider the massive design and highly ornate interior to be excessive, while others revel in its opulence. Commissioned in 1818 by Alexander I to celebrate his victory over Napoleon, it took more than 40 years to build. The French architect Montferand devoted his life to the project and died the same year the cathedral was finally consecrated, in 1858. The interior is lavishly decorated with malachite, lazulite, marble, and other precious stones and minerals. Gilding the dome required 100 kilos (200 pounds) of gold. The church can hold up to 14,000 worshipers. After the 1917 Revolution it was closed for services and in 1931 was opened as a museum. Since 1990, occasional services have resumed, and talk is mounting of its eventual return to the Orthodox Church. During the city's blockade during World War II the gilded dome was painted black to avoid being targeted by enemy fire. Despite efforts to protect it, the cathedral nevertheless suffered heavy damage, as bullet holes on the columns on the south side attest. The dome balcony, open to those who are willing to make the climb, offers a spectacular view. *1 Isaakievskaya Ploshchad, tel. 812/315–9732. Admission for foreigners: $8. Open Mon., Tues., Thurs.–Sun. 11–6.*

In the center of St. Isaac's Square stands a statue of Czar Nicholas I (1825–55). Unveiled in 1859, the Nicholas Statue was commissioned by the czar's wife and three children, whose faces are engraved on its base. It was designed, like St. Isaac's Cathedral, by Montferand. The statue depicts Nicholas I mounted on a rearing horse whose hind legs actually serve as the statue's support. The engravings on the base describe the main events of the czar's reign, such as the Decembrists' uprising and the opening ceremonies of the St. Petersburg–Moscow railroad line.

On the opposite side of the square, directly across from St. Isaac's Cathedral, is the building of the St. Petersburg City **⑬** Council. Commonly referred to as **Mariinsky Dvorets** (Maria's Palace), it was completed in 1844 for the eldest and favorite daughter of Czar Nicholas I. The roof is still adorned with Soviet regalia, although the banner flying proudly above it is the newly reclaimed Russian flag. Since this is a working governmental building, access to the public is restricted; group tours, however, can be arranged by special request. *3 Isaakievskaya Ploshchad, tel. 812/319–9443. Excursion fee for foreigners: $3.*

The Nicholas Statue and the Mariinsky Dvorets are separated by the **Siniy Most** (Blue Bridge), so called because of the paint on its underside. The bridge, which spans the Moika River, is so wide (116 meters, or 328 feet) and so short that it seems not to be a bridge at all but, rather, a continuation of St. Isaac's Square.

Time Out   The **Astoria Hotel,** on the east side of the square, is one of St. Petersburg's most luxurious. Don't be intimidated by the regal dress of its doormen. Take the lobby elevator to the fourth floor and you will encounter an oasis for the weary traveler. The self-service café (open daily 7–4 and 5–10), offers coffee and tea, imported beverages, and a variety of light snacks, from smoked salmon to cream-filled pastries. Prices are in rubles, and you are welcome to stay as long as you like. If this café is closed, try the third-floor café, which operates for dollars.

⑭ The final stop on your tour of the left bank is the **Admiralty,** which can be reached by returning to the Neva embankment and heading east along the river, in the direction of Palace Square and the Hermitage. The Admiralty is the city's architectural center, its golden spire one of St. Petersburg's most renowned emblems. The first shipyard was built on this site in 1704 and was designed to function as part of the city's defenses. A moated fort containing a well-protected wharf was also here. The present Admiralty, erected between 1806 and 1823 to a design by Andrei Zakharov, was a shipbuilding center until the 1840s. The building is adorned with Classical sculptures that glorify Russia's naval power. The famous gilded spire, topped by a weathervane shaped like a vessel, can be seen from various parts of the city. Since 1925 the Admiralty has belonged to the Higher Naval Academy and is not open to the public.

Tour 3: Peter and Paul Fortress and the Petrograd Side

⓯ This tour takes you to where the city began, the **Petropavlovskaya Krepost** (Peter and Paul Fortress). The fortress was erected in just a year's time, from 1703 to 1704, to defend St. Petersburg in the Great Northern War against Sweden. It was never used for its intended purpose, however, since the Russian line of defense quickly moved farther north. Instead, it was a political prison under the czarist regime. The fortress is located on Zayachy Ostrov (Hare Island), almost directly across the Neva from the Winter Palace. Cut off from the north by the moatlike Kronverk Canal, Hare Island is connected by a footbridge to **Troitskaya Ploshchad** (Trinity Square, sometimes still referred to by its Soviet name, Kirov Square) on Petrogradsky Ostrov (Petrograd Island). This section, which actually consists of a series of islands, is commonly referred to as the **Petrogradskaya Storona** (Petrograd Side) and is one of the city's earliest residential areas. Trinity Square, named for the church that once stood here (demolished in 1934), is the city's oldest square. You can reach Hare Island from central St. Petersburg by crossing the **Troitski Most** (Trinity Bridge) from the Palace Embankment. It is also easy to reach by subway; the closest station is Gorkhovskaya. After exiting the station, walk through the small park in front of you, heading in the direction of the Neva. The fortress will emerge through the trees to your right.

Cross the footbridge and enter the fortress through **Ioannovskyie Vorota** (Ivan Gate), the main entrance to the outer fortification. Once inside, you will need to stop at the ticket office, which is inside the outer fortification wall (the ticket booth to your immediate left sells only theater tickets). Although entry to the fortress grounds is free, you must buy tickets here for the exhibits. Without them you will be sent back to the ticket office. *Trinity Square, tel. 812/238-4540. Admission for foreigners: $2 in rubles. Open Thurs.–Tues. 11–6. Closed last Thurs. of month.*

Entrance to the inner fortress is through the **Petrovskyie Vorota** (Peter's Gate). Designed by the Swiss architect Domenico Trezzini, it was built from 1717 to 1718. Its decoration includes the double-headed eagle of the Romanovs and a wooden bas-relief depicting the Apostle Peter casting down Simon Magus. The allegory was meant to inspire confidence in Peter the Great's impending victory over Charles XII of Sweden, which did not come until 1721.

After passing through the Peter Gate, the first building to your left is the **Inzhenerny Dom** (Engineer's House), which was built from 1748 to 1749. It is now a branch of the Museum of the History of St. Petersburg (as are all exhibits in the fortress) and contains temporary exhibits on the city's prerevolutionary history. Next to the Engineer's House stands the **Vakhta** (Guardhouse), built in 1743 and later reconstructed. Today it houses administrative offices of the museum and is not open to the public.

As you continue your walk away from the Peter Gate, you will soon come to the main attraction of the fortress, the **Petropavlovsky Sobor** (Cathedral of Sts. Peter and Paul). Constructed between 1712 and 1733 on the site of an earlier wooden church, it was designed by Domenico Trezzini and later embellished by Bartolomeo Rastrelli. It is highly unusual for a Russian Orthodox church. Instead of the characteristic bulbous domes, it is adorned by a slender gilded spire whose height (121 meters, or 400 feet) made it the city's tallest building. The spire is identical to that of the Admiralty across the river, except that it is crowned not by a weathervane but by an angel bearing a golden cross. The spire remained the city's highest structure—in accordance with Peter the Great's decree—until 1962, when the television tower was erected, greatly marring the harmony of the city's skyline.

The interior of the cathedral is also atypical. The Baroque iconostasis, designed by Ivan Zarodny and built in the 1720s, is adorned by freestanding statues. Another uncommon feature is the pulpit. According to legend, it was used only once: in 1901, to excommunicate Leo Tolstoy from the Russian Orthodox Church. Starting with Peter the Great, the cathedral served as the imperial burial grounds. You can identify Peter's grave, to the far right as you face the iconostasis, by the czar's bust on the railing. Nearly all of Peter's successors were buried in the cathedral as well, with a few notable exceptions: Peter II, Ivan IV, and the last czar, Nicholas II, who was executed with his family in Ekaterinburg in 1918. In 1992, in recognition of Russia's imperial past, the most recent Romanov pretender, Grand Duke Vladimir, was bestowed the honor of burial in the Peter and Paul Fortress, although not in the royal crypt.

You may exit the cathedral through the passageway to the left of the iconostasis. This leads to the adjoining **Usypalnitsa** (Grand Ducal Crypt), built between 1896 and 1908. It contains an exhibit on the architectural history of the fortress.

As you leave the cathedral, you will notice a small Classical structure to your right. This is the so-called **Botny Dom** (Boathouse), built in 1762–66 to house Peter the Great's first boat. The boat has since been moved to the Central Naval Museum on Vasilievsky Island, and the building is not open to the public. The wooden figurine on its roof is meant to symbolize navigation.

Across the cobblestone yard, opposite the entrance to the cathedral, stands the **Monetny Dvor** (Mint), which dates from 1716. The present building was erected between 1798 and 1806. The mint is still in operation, producing coins, medals, military decorations, and *znachki*, Russian souvenir pins.

The pink-and-white building to your left as you exit the cathedral is the **Komendantsky Dom** (Commandant's House). Erected in 1743–46, it once housed the fortress's administration and doubled as a courtroom for political prisoners. The Decembrist revolutionaries were tried here in 1826. The room where the trial took place is now part of the temporary exhibits, which deal with the history of St. Petersburg from its founding in 1703 to 1917.

Take the pathway to the left of the Commandant's House (as you are facing it), and you will be headed right for the **Nevskyie Vorota** (Neva Gate), built in 1730 and reconstructed in 1787. The gate leads out to the **Komendantskaya Pristan** (Commandant's Pier), which affords a splendid view of St. Petersburg. From here you may step down to the sandy beach, where even in winter hearty swimmers enjoy the Neva's arctic waters. In summer the beach is lined with sunbathers, standing up or leaning against the fortification wall (supposedly this allows for a more even tan). As you walk through the passageway of the Neva Gate, notice the plaques on the inside walls recording flood levels reached by the Neva. The most recent plaque was erected after the flood of September 25, 1975, when the river rose 2.8 meters (9¼ feet) above normal.

The Peter and Paul Fortress is probably best known for the prominent political prisoners it has housed. One of the first prisoners to be confined in its dungeons was Peter the Great's own son, Alexei, who was tortured to death in 1718. The czar himself allegedly supervised the torture, imposed for Alexei's treasonous behavior. The dungeons in the Alexeivsky Bastion, which were known as the Secret House, held the writers Dostoevsky and Chernyshevsky. In 1872, when opponents of autocracy grew too numerous for the Secret House, a new prison was built in the Trubetskoi Bastion. Open to the public as a museum, the prison is in the southwest corner of the fortress; turn left as you exit the Neva Gate and walk the length of the fortification wall. The museum can be identified by the diagonal stripes on its door and by the iron gate enclosing the entranceway. Aside from a few exhibits of prison garb, the only items on display are the cells themselves, restored to their chilling, prerevolutionary appearance. Among the revolutionaries held here were some of the "People's Will" (*narodnoye volye*) terrorists, who assassinated Alexander II in 1881, as well as Lenin's elder brother Alexander, executed for his role in the assassination attempt on Alexander III. Leon Trotsky and Maxim Gorky were detained in the fortress after the 1905 Revolution. The last prisoners were apparently the sailors who mutinied against the communist regime in Kronstadt in 1921. The prison was opened as a museum and memorial to its former inmates in 1925.

One more building connected to the fortress but outside its ⓰ walls is the horseshoe-shaped **Artilereysky Muzey** (Artillery Museum), located north of the Kronverk Canal, on the bank opposite the fortress. As you leave the fortress via the Ioannovskyi footbridge, the museum will be visible to your left. The building once served as the city's arsenal and was turned over to the Artillery Museum in 1872. The museum itself dates from the days of Peter the Great, who sought to present the entire history of weaponry, with a special emphasis on Russia. Today the Artillery Museum is the main army museum of St. Petersburg. The exhibit on the Soviet (now Russian) army focuses on World War II. A relic from the Bolshevik Revolution is the Austin armored car from the turret of which Lenin made his first public speech at the Finland Station on his return from exile in April 1917. Also on display are prerevolutionary artillery, arms, uniforms, and medals. *7 Park Lenina, tel. 812/232–0296. Open Wed.– Sun. 11–6.*

Time Out | If you have walked all the way over to the Artillery Museum, you may as well walk a bit farther and try out St. Petersburg's floating café, the **Petrovsky**. It is located on a ship permanently moored in the Kronverk Canal, just south of the Artillery Museum. The upper deck contains a full-fledged restaurant that never seems to have any available tables. Down below, however, is an intimate café where you can enjoy a cup of strong coffee, pastry, or even a shot of cognac. *3 Naberezhnaya Mytninskaya. Open daily noon–4.*

Return now to Trinity Square. At the northern edge of the square, at the corner of Bolshaya Dvoryanskaya ulitsa and Kamennostrovsky Prospect, stands the former mansion of Mathilda Kshesinskaya, a famous ballerina and onetime mistress of the last Russian czar, Nicholas II. Built in the style Moderne in 1905, the mansion served as Bolshevik committee headquarters in the months leading up to the October Revolution. In 1957 it was turned into the Museum of the Great October Socialist Revolution and was renamed ⓱ the **Russian Political History Museum** in 1991. It offers temporary exhibits on Russian political movements, both before and after the 1917 Revolution. One hall contains an interesting collection of wax figures, showing victims and perpetrators of violence in Russian history, including Alexander II, who was assassinated by terrorists, and Stalin, who was responsible for millions of deaths. The mansion itself is interesting as well, simply because it gives you a sense of prerevolutionary St. Petersburg and the lifestyle of its aristocracy. *2/4 Bolshaya Dvoryanskaya, tel. 812/ 233-7052. Open Fri.-Wed. 10-6.*

Not far from the Kshesinskaya Mansion is St. Petersburg's
⑱ only **Mechet** (Mosque). As you leave the mansion, take a right, and then turn right again onto Kronversky Prospect. It's hard to miss the brightly painted azure domes peaking out above the trees. Built in 1910–14 to serve St. Petersburg's Muslim community, the Mosque was designed after the Gur Emir in Samarkand, where Tamerlane is buried. *7 Kronversky Prospect, tel. 812/233-9819. Services daily at 1:30.*

Head back now in the direction of the Neva River. When you reach the waterfront, turn left onto Petrovskaya Naberezhnaya (Petrov Embankment). You will soon come
⑲ upon the **Domik Petra Pervovo** (Peter the Great's Cottage). Built in just three days' time in May 1703, the cottage was home to Peter the Great during construction of the Peter and Paul Fortress. It is made of wooden logs painted to resemble bricks. Inside, 18th-century furniture is on display, arranged as it might have been in Peter's day, as well as some of Peter's personal effects. The stone structure enclosing the cottage was erected in 1784 by Catherine the Great to protect it from the elements. The cottage consists of just three rooms whose ceilings are surprisingly low— considering that Peter the Great was 6 feet 6 inches tall. *6 Petrovskaya Naberezhnaya, tel. 812/232-4576. Open Wed.-Mon. 10-6. Closed last Mon. of month and in humid weather.*

In the courtyard in front of the cottage stands a bronze bust of Peter the Great. The sculptures of the Shchi-Tsza (Lion-Frogs) flanking the pier on the embankment side were brought to Russia from Manchuria in 1907.

Continue walking east along the embankment. At the corner of Petrovskaya and Petrogradskaya embankments, where the Great Nevka meets the Neva River, stands a blue-and-white building in the style of Russian Baroque. This is the **Nakhimov Academy of Naval Officers,** which was a high school before the 1917 Revolution. Although the architectural style is from Peter's era, the building was built in 1912.

Permanently moored across from the Nakhimov Academy
⑳ is the cruiser *Avrora.* Launched in 1903, it fought in the 1904–05 Russo–Japanese War as well as in World War II, but it is best known for its role in the Bolshevik Revolution. At 9:40 PM on October 25, 1917, the cruiser fired a shot signal-

ing the storming of the Winter Palace. A cherished relic in the Soviet era, the *Avrora* was carefully restored in the 1980s and opened as a museum. Although the revolution it launched is now under fire itself, the cruiser is still a favorite place to bring children, and on weekends you may encounter long lines. On display are the crew's quarters and the radio room used to broadcast Lenin's victory address. *4 Petrogradskaya nab., tel. 812/232–4266. Open Tues., Wed., Fri.–Sun. 10:30–4.*

Across the river from the *Avrora* stands the **St. Petersburg Hotel.** Before 1992 it was named the Leningrad, which was probably a more appropriate name since the hotel clearly belongs to the Soviet era. Built in the monotonous style of a Brezhnev-era high rise, the concrete-and-steel structure seems horribly out of place among the prerevolutionary architecture lining the embankment.

From here you can return to your starting point by retracing your steps along the embankment. If you want to see more of the Petrograd Side's residential areas, you can take the longer route back via Bolshaya Dvoryanskaya ulitsa. Walk down to the bridge to your left (as you face the cruiser *Avrora*) and turn left onto Bolshaya Dvoryanskaya. This will take you back to Trinity Square. From here the Trinity Bridge is to your left and the Gorkhovskaya subway stop a short walk to your right.

Tour 4: Nevsky Prospect and the Alexander Nevsky Lavra

We turn now to the inner city and St. Petersburg's most famous avenue, **Nevsky Prospect.** Laid out in 1710, this is one of the city's oldest streets. It begins at the Admiralty at its northwestern end and runs in a perfectly straight line to the Moscow Railway Station, where it curves slightly. The second section of the avenue, known as **Stary (Old) Nevsky,** ends at the Alexander Nevsky Lavra. Just short of 5 kilometers (3 miles) long, the avenue was originally conceived in the early master plan of St. Petersburg as the Great Perspective Road, and for a time was even called the Nevsky Perspektiv.

"There is nothing finer than Nevsky Prospect, not in St. Petersburg at any rate, for in St. Petersburg it is everything . . ." wrote the great Russian author Nikolai Gogol more than 150 years ago. Today it is clearly not as resplendent as it was in the 1830s, when fops and their ladies strolled along the elegant avenue or paraded by in horse-drawn carriages. It is, however, still the center of everything and still the main thoroughfare. In many ways Nevsky Prospect is a perfect reflection of today's two-tiered economy. It is lined with buildings scarred by years of neglect and caked in dust and grime. A large portion of the once-glorious architecture is hidden behind rickety scaffolding. But here and there are beautifully renovated facades that hint at how the city might look if only it could afford the costly restoration work.

Nevsky Prospect boasts the city's finest hotels and shops, but it also attracts all the problems of its ravaged economy. It is the favorite gathering place of homeless children, whose dirty faces and pitiful looks evoke sympathy but whose tricks may easily catch you off guard and without a wallet. The street is also roamed by bands of colorfully dressed Gypsy women and children, who can smell a tourist miles away. Unfortunately, a stroll down today's Nevsky Prospect requires some caution. As in any large city, you need to use common sense.

㉒ Start at the relatively peaceful **Alexander Nevsky Lavra** (monastery), which is at the southeastern end of Nevsky Prospect. It can be reached by taking the subway to the Ploshchad Alexandra Nevskovo Station. The entrance to the Lavra is across the square from the subway exit. The monastery complex includes the Church of the Annunciation, converted under the Soviets into the Museum of Urban Sculpture, the Holy Trinity Church, a theological seminary, and several cemeteries. Entrance to the monastery grounds is free, but you must purchase a ticket for the two most interesting cemeteries and the museum. The ticket office is outside the monastery, to the right of the main gate. *1 Ploshchad Alexandra Nevskovo, tel. 812/274–0409 or 812/277–1716. Open Fri.–Wed. 11–6.*

The word *lavra* in Russian is reserved for a monastery of the highest order, of which there are just four in all of Russia and Ukraine. Named in honor of St. Alexander Nevsky, this monastery was founded in 1710 by Peter the Great. Prince Alexander of Novgorod (1220–1263), the great military commander and a beloved national hero, went down in history for halting the eastward drive of the Germans and Swedes. Peter chose the site for the monastery, thinking that this was where the prince had fought the battle in 1240 that earned him the title Alexander of the Neva (Nevsky). The famous battle actually took place some 20 kilometers (12 miles) away, however. Alexander Nevsky was buried in Vladimir, and in 1724, on orders of Peter the Great, his remains were transferred to the monastery that was founded in his honor.

Entrance to the monastery is through the archway of the elegant **Gate Church,** built by Ivan Starov in 1783–85. The walled pathway is flanked by two cemeteries, whose entrances are located a short walk down the path. To the left lies the older Lazarus Cemetery. The list of famous people buried here reads like a catalogue of St. Petersburg architecture and includes Quarenghi, Rossi, Voronikhin, and Thomas de Thomon. The cemetery also contains the tombstone of the father of Russian science, Mikhail Lomonsov.

The **Tikhvin Cemetery,** on the opposite side, was the final resting place of a number of St. Petersburg's great literary and musical figures. The grave of Fyodor Dostoevsky, located in the northwestern corner, is easily identified by the tombstone's sculpture, which portrays the writer with his flowing beard. Continuing along the path you'll soon reach the composers' corner, where Rimsky-Korsakov, Mussorgsky, Borodin, and Tchaikovsky are buried.

Having pondered St. Petersburg's cultural legacy, return to the path and cross the bridge spanning the quaint **Monastyrka Canal.** As you enter the monastery grounds, the Church of the Annunciation greets you on your left. The red-and-white rectangular church was designed by Domenico Trezzini and built between 1717 and 1722. The Museum of Urban Sculpture inside contains models of St. Petersburg's architectural masterpieces, as well as gravestones and other fine examples of memorial sculpture. The great soldier, Generalissimo Alexander Suvorov, who led the Russian army to numerous victories during the Russo-Turkish War (1768–74), is buried here under a simple marble slab that he purportedly designed himself. It reads simply: "Here lies Suvorov."

Continuing along the same path, you'll reach the monastery's main cathedral, the **Troitsky Sobor** (Trinity Cathedral), which was one of the city's few functioning churches during the Soviet era. Designed by Ivan Starov and completed at the end of the 18th century, it stands out among the monastery's predominantly Baroque architecture for its monumental Neoclassical design. Services are held here daily, and the church is open to the public, although it closes between 2 and 5 in the afternoon for housekeeping. The magnificent interior, with its stunning gilded iconostasis, is worth a visit. The large central dome, adorned by frescoes designed by the great architect Quarenghi, seems to soar toward the heavens.

Return now to Alexander Nevsky Square. From here you can either walk the entire length of Nevsky Prospect or take the subway one stop to Mayakovskaya Station. The avenue's most interesting architecture is concentrated in
㉓ this northern section, which begins at **Ploshchad Vosstaniya** (Insurrection Square). The street is lined with almost every imaginable shop, from fruit markets to art salons to bookstores. A stroll here is not a casual affair, however, for Nevsky is almost always teeming with bustling crowds of shoppers and street artists. Budding entrepreneurs, who sell their wares on the sidewalk on folding tables, further obstruct the flow of pedestrian traffic. Here you will also see an increasingly rare sight, the old men of the Great Patriotic War (the Russian name for World War II) still proudly wearing their medals.

Heading west (left) as you exit the subway, after three blocks you'll reach the **Fontanka (Fountain) River** and one of

② the city's most beautiful bridges, the **Anichkov Most** (*most* means "bridge"). The four colossal bronze groups of horse tamers were cast to a design by Peter Klodt. The sculptures, erected between 1839 and 1841, show different phases in the process of horse training. The bridge was named for Colonel Mikhail Anichkov, whose regiment built an earlier, wooden version of the bridge in the early 18th century. At that time this marked the city limits. The guards posted here at night served much the same purpose as today's border guards at Pulkhovo Airport, carefully screening those entering the city. As you cross the bridge, pause for a moment to look back at the colorful Baroque building on the corner of Nevsky and the Fontanka. The highly ornate, bright red mansion belonged to the wealthy nobleman Prince Beloselsky-Belozersky. Built by Stackenschneider in the 1840s, the building housed the local Communist Party headquarters during the Soviet era. Today it is the setting for classical music concerts. The interiors have unfortunately been largely destroyed and are not nearly as magnificent as the facades.

On the far side of the Fontanka stands the **Anichkov Palace,** named for the same colonel whose regiment built the bridge. It was built by Empress Elizabeth for her lover Alexei Razumovsky between 1741 and 1750. As if to continue the tradition, Catherine the Great later gave it to one of her many favorites, Grigory Potemkin. An able statesman and army officer, Potemkin is famous for his attempts to fool Catherine about conditions in the Russian south. He had fake villages put up along the banks of the Volga River for her to view as she passed by during her 1787 tour of the area. The term "Potemkin village" has come to mean any impressive facade that hides an ugly interior—a phrase put to good use during the Soviet era.

The Anichkov Palace was originally designed by Mikhail Zemtsov and completed by Bartolomeo Francesco Rastrelli. The building has undergone a number of changes, and little remains of the elaborate Baroque facade. This was once a suburban area, which explains why its main entrance faces the Fontanka rather than Nevsky, where there is only a side entrance. Today it houses the Youth Palace (once the Pioneer Palace), which offers all sorts of activities for young people.

The next stop is **Ploshchad Ostrovskovo** (Ostrovsky Square), named for the famous Russian playwright and created by Carlo Rossi. The square is dominated by the **②** **Pushkin Theater,** originally named the Alexandra Theater (for the wife of Nicholas I) and built in Empire style between 1828 and 1832. Six Corinthian columns adorn the Nevsky facade. Apollo's chariot dominates the building, with statues of the muses Terpischore and Melpomene to keep him company. In the small garden in front of the theater stands the **Catherine Monument,** which shows the empress towering above the principal personalities of her reign. Depicted on the pedestal are Grigory Potemkin, Generalissimo Suvorov, the poet Gavril Derzhavin, and others who made her reign so famous. Among the bronze figures is the Princess Dashkova, who conspired against her sister's lover, who just happened to be Catherine's husband, Peter III, to help the empress assume the throne.

Before moving beyond Ostrovsky Square, step around to the back of the Pushkin Theater, where the amazing **ulitsa Zodchevo Rossi** begins. The proportions of this extraordinary street are perfect. It is bounded by two buildings of exactly the same height, its width (22 meters, or 72 feet) equals the height of the buildings, and its length is exactly 10 times its width. A complete view unfolds only at the end of the street, where it meets Lomonosov Square. The perfect symmetry is reinforced by the identical facades of the two buildings, which are painted the same subdued yellow and decorated with impressive white pillars. One of the buildings is the famous **Vaganova Ballet School** (founded in 1738), whose pupils included Karsavina as well as Pavlova, Nijinsky, and Ulanova.

Back at Ostrovsky Square, take note of the Neoclassical building to your left, on the west side of the square. This is the **Saltykov-Shchedrin Library,** Russia's largest after the State Library in Moscow. Opened in 1814 as the Imperial Public Library, it was Russia's first built for that purpose and today is known fondly as the "Publichka." Its holdings number over 20 million books, and the library claims to have a copy of every book ever printed in Russia. The building comprises three sections. The main section, on the corner of Nevsky Prospect and Sadovaya ulitsa, was designed by Yegor Sakolov and built between 1796 and 1801. The wing nearest you, built between 1828 and 1832, was designed by Carlo Rossi as an integral part of Ostrovsky Square. True to the building's purpose, the facade is adorned with statues of philosophers and poets, including Homer, Vergil, and the Roman goddess of wisdom, Minerva.

You may want to cross Nevsky at this point to peek inside the **Yeliseyevsky Food Emporium** (No. 56), today officially called Gastronome No. 1. It is located directly across the street from the Catherine Monument. Built at the turn of the century for the merchant Yeliseyev, it is decorated in the style of early Art Nouveau, with colorful stained-glass windows, gilded ceilings, and brass chandeliers. Before the 1917 Revolution it specialized in imported delicacies, but today its stocks differ little from any other state-run grocery store.

Taking up the entire block on the other side of the street is ❷⑥ the huge **Gostinny Dvor** (Market Arcade or Bazaar), St. Petersburg's answer to the GUM department store in Moscow. Started by Rastrelli in 1757, it was not completed until 1785, by Vallin de la Mothe, who was responsible for the fa-

cade with its two tiers of arches. It was completely rebuilt
in the last century, when it housed some 200 general-pur-
pose shops that were far less elegant than those in other
parts of the Nevsky. The bazaar remained the city's main
shopping area until alterations in the 1950s and 1960s
turned most of its little boutiques into St. Petersburg's
largest department store. Sections of the store are still
operating, but a large portion of Gostinny Dvor has been
gutted for what Russians call "capital" repairs.

Time Out The **Konditorei** on the other side of Nevsky Prospect, at No.
40, offers a soothing place to take a break. The wood-paneled interior and parquet ceilings have been restored to
their original, prerevolutionary appearance. Coffee, ice
cream, and scrumptious cakes are available (for hard currency only) in a no-smoking environment. If you're looking
for something more substantial, try the German restaurant
and bar next door.

Set back from the street on the other side of Nevsky, at
Nos. 40–42, is the blue-and-white **Armenian Church,** built
by Velten between 1771 and 1780. A fine example of the early Classical style, the church has sadly fallen into disrepair
and is closed for restoration work. At the corner of
Mikhailovskaya ulitsa is the recently renovated **Grand Europe Hotel** (*see* Tour 5). Across the street, at No. 33, stands
the **Gorodskaya Duma,** the building of the former city hall.
The tower held signaling devices for sending messages between the Winter Palace and Peterhof, the summer residence of the czars.

Continuing farther on the other side of the street, you'll
reach the Catholic **Church of St. Catherine** (Nos. 32–34),
built between 1762 and 1783 in a mixture of Baroque and
Classical styles by Vallin de Mothe and Rinaldi. The grave
of the last king of Poland (and yet another lover of Catherine the Great), Stanisław Poniatowski, is here. On the far
corner of this block, just before you reach the subway entrance, is the St. Petersburg Philharmonic's **Glinka Hall.**

Cross the short Kazan Bridge over Griboyedov Canal (actually a river), and you'll come to the city's largest bookstore,
㉗ which still goes by its generic Soviet name **Dom Knigi** (the
Book House). Before the revolution, the building housed
the offices of the Singer Sewing Machine Company, whose
distinctive globe trademark still adorns the roof. Here one
finds Russians in a favorite pursuit, buying and perusing
books. The store also contains a wonderful collection of
books and maps.

Across the street from Dom Knigi is one of the city's finest
㉘ buildings, the **Kazansky Sobor** (Kazan Cathedral). Erected
between 1801 and 1811 to a design by Andrei Voronikhin, it
is approached by a semicircular colonnade modeled on St.
Peter's in Rome. The huge cathedral is surmounted by a

high (80 meters / 260 feet) dome set on a drum with 16 pilasters and 16 windows. On the Nevsky side the frontage has niches with colossal statues of St. John the Baptist and of saints prominent in Russian history: Vladimir, Alexander Nevsky, and Andrei. The bronze doors are copies of the Baptistry's in Florence, and the interior has even more statues. The cathedral was completed just before Napoleon's invasion of Russia, and it was here that Field Marshal Kutuzov prayed before taking command. His statue and that of his predecessor (and successor) in the same war, Prince Barclay de Tolly, stands at the end of the colonnade. Kutuzov's grave is in the crypt of the northern chapel.

After the 1917 Revolution, the cathedral—conceived as the Orthodox rival to Rome's St. Peter—was closed down. In 1932 it was turned into the Museum of Religion and Atheism, presenting the history of religion from the Marxist point of view. With the recent religious revival, the museum dropped the 'Atheism' from its name and reorganized its displays; the new exhibit is devoted to Russian church art. Services have also been resumed in the cathedral. *2 Kazanskaya Ploshchad, tel. 812/312–0495 or 812/312– 3586. Open Mon., Tues., Thurs.–Sat. 11–5; Sun. 2–6. Church services Mon.–Sat. at 9 AM and 6 PM, Sun. and holidays at 10 AM.*

Continuing one block down Nevsky, you'll reach the **Lutheran Church,** which is set back from the street on the right-hand side. Designed by Alexander Bryullov, its rounded arches and simple towers owe much to the Romanesque tradition. Farther down, at No. 20, is the **Dutch Church,** yet another reminder of the religions that coexisted in old St. Petersburg.

Return now to the other side of the street. As you cross the little bridge spanning the Moika Canal, look back at the magnificent green building overlooking the embankment. This is the former **Stroganov Palace,** completed in 1754. Similar in style to the bright red Beloselsky-Belozersky Mansion near Anichkov Bridge (*see above*), this palace is an outstanding example of Russian Baroque and one of Rastrelli's finest achievements. The interior was ravaged by fire at the end of the 18th century, but the outside remained intact. While it was owned by the Stroganovs, the palace housed one of the great private art collections now in the Hermitage.

On the last few blocks of Nevsky Prospect are several buildings of historical importance. No. 18, on the right-hand side, is the **Literary Café** (formerly the Café Wulf et Béranger). Popular with writers and poets, it was here in 1837 that Alexander Pushkin ate his last meal before setting out for the duel that killed him. Farther down, at No. 14, is one of the rare buildings on Nevsky Prospect built *after* the Bolshevik Revolution. The blue sign on the facade dates from

World War II and the siege of Leningrad. It warns pedestrians that during air raids the other side of street is safer.
The city was once covered with similar warnings; this one
was left in place as a memorial.

The golden building of the Admiralty marks the end of
Nevsky Prospect. To return to the subway, take Trolley
Bus 1, 5, 7, or 14 one stop to Nevsky Prospect Station. Since
trolley buses on Nevsky are notoriously overcrowded, you
might prefer to walk.

Tour 5: From the Square of the Arts to the Field of Mars

This tour takes you through the streets and squares of inner
St. Petersburg. Start at **Ploshchad Iskusstv** (Square of the
Arts formerly Mikhailovskaya Ploshchad), which can be
reached from the Nevsky Prospect subway stop. The first
building to catch your eye will be the newly renovated
Grand Hotel Europe on the corner of Nevsky and Mikhailovskaya ulitsa. Built in the 1870s and given an Art Nouveau
look in 1910, the hotel is one of St. Petersburg's most elegant. Its shiny new facade stands out among the dust-cov-
ered buildings lining Nevsky Prospect, giving you a sense
of what St. Petersburg might have looked like today had it
not been so sorely neglected by the Soviet regime.

To get to the square itself, walk to the end of the short Mikhailovskaya ulitsa. This plaza was designed by Carlo Rossi
to complement the **Mikhailovsky Dvorets** (Mikhailovsky
Palace) to the north. The Mikhail (Michael) for whom everything in the area seems to have been named was the younger brother of Alexander I and Nicholas I, Grand Duke
Mikhail (1798–1849). His palace, also designed by Rossi,
was built between 1819 and 1825 in the style of a nobleman's
town house, with a principal residence and two service
wings. In front of the central portico with its eight Corinthian columns lies a large courtyard enclosed by an attractive railing in the Art Nouveau style. Added later (in 1903), a
product of another architectural era, the railing functions
somewhat like a picture frame: Beautiful in itself, it never
distracts from the work of art it encloses.

In 1896 Nicholas II turned the palace into a museum in hon-
or of his father, Alexander III, who took a special interest
in Russian art. Today it is the **Russky Muzey** (Russian Museum). Officially known as the *Gosudarstvenny Muzey
Russkovo Isskustva* (State Museum of Russian Art), this
museum holds a collection next in importance to that of the
Tretyakov Gallery in Moscow. Like many Russian museums, its holdings were greatly enhanced after the 1917
Revolution, when private art collections were confiscated
by the Soviet government. Today the museum displays
some outstanding icons (Rooms 1–4, on the second floor),
including the 15th-century *Angel Miracle of St. George and*

the Dragon and many works by Andrei Rub
Ushakov. Seventeenth- and 18th-century Ru
are well represented, but most important ‹
19th century, such as the seascape painter Aıvazovsky's
Ninth Wave (Room 15) and the huge canvases of Ilya Repin,
including his *Volga Boatmen* (Rooms 33–35, on the first
floor). There are many fine portraits of Valentin Serov,
among them the beautiful *Countess Orlova* (Room 71), and
Vrubel's strange *Demon* (Room 66). Painters of the World
of Art movement—Bakst, Benois, and Somov—are here,
too (mainly in Room 68). There are some fine examples of
20th-century Russian art as well, including works by Kandinsky and Malevich (Room 79), and Altman's striking portrait of the poet Anna Akhmatova (Room 77). Due to
ongoing renovations, certain rooms of the museum may be
closed. *4/2 Inzhenernaya ulitsa, tel. 812/314–3448. Open
Mon. 10–5, Wed. and Fri.–Sun. 10–6, Thurs. 10–8.*

The building next to the Russian Museum, which deceptive-
ly appears to be a wing of the Mikhailovsky Palace, houses
the **Ethnography Museum.** It contains fascinating collections of applied art, as well as displays depicting the
lifestyles of various nationalities in the 19th and 20th centuries. There are also displays covering the various ethnic
groups of the former Soviet republics. *4/1 Inzhenernaya
ulitsa, tel. 812/219–1174 or 812/219–1676. Open Tues.–
Sun. 11–6. Closed last Fri. of month.*

Return now to the Square of the Arts, which Carlo Rossi
spent some 15 years creating. To your right, with old-fash-
❸❶ ioned lanterns adorning its doorways, is the **Maly Teatr**
(Little Theater). This is also a Rossi creation, although it
was later rebuilt by Albert Cavos. Like everything else
around the square, it was once named the Mikhailovsky
Theater. Before the 1917 Revolution, French companies
performed here so often that it was more commonly referred to as the French Theater. Today it is St.
Petersburg's second most important theater for opera and
ballet after the Mariinsky (Kirov).

The building next to the Maly, yet another of Rossi's creations, was built in the 1820s for the Golenshishchev-Kutu-
zov family. It has been under reconstruction for years now,
but it used to house (and presumably will again) a museum
devoted to the artist Isaak Brodsky, who lived here from
1924 until his death. *3 Ploshchad Iskusstv, tel. 812/314–
3658.*

Another notable example of Carlo Rossi's architectural
style is the facade of the former **Nobles' Club,** on the southeastern side of the square, at the corner of Mikhailovskaya
❸❷ ulitsa. The building is now the home of the St. **Petersburg
Philharmonic,** which is named for the Soviet composer
Dmitri Shostakovich. Its main concert hall, with its impressive marble columns, has been the site of many famous
performances. On August 9, 1942, when the city was

completely blockaded by German forces, Shostakovich's Seventh Symphony, the *Leningrad* Symphony, was premiered here. The statue in the middle of the square is of Pushkin reading his poetry.

Time Out The **Grand Hotel Europe,** back on Mikhailovskaya ulitsa, has a lovely mezzanine café, where you can relax and enjoy a nice, strong cup of coffee or a steaming hot chocolate. While you're at it, take a peak at the beautifully renovated Art Nouveau lobby, replete with stained-glass windows and authentic antique furnishings.

Leave the Square of the Arts now, turning left (as you face the Mikhail Palace) onto Inzhenernaya ulitsa. Walk down to the canal, named for the writer Griboyedov, and to your right you will see a highly ornate and colorful church in the ❸❸ Old Russian style. This is **Khram Spasa na Krovi** (Church of the Savior on the Spilled Blood), built at the turn of the century by Alexander III, on the spot where his father (Alexander II) had been killed by a terrorist's bomb on March 1, 1881. Against the background of St. Petersburg's graceful, European-inspired architecture, the church's highly ornate design seems somehow frenzied and misplaced. It was designed by the architect Alfred Parland, who was trying to re-create St. Basil's in Moscow. The church has been under reconstruction for more than 15 years and is not open to the public.

To the right of the church lies a small park known as the **Mikhailovsky Sad** (Mikhailovsky Gardens). Walk through the gate and follow the path in front of you. Bordering the park to your right is the garden facade of the elegant Mikhail Palace. A short walk through the pleasant park, which was redesigned by Rossi in the 1830s, will bring you to Sadovaya ulitsa.

The bright red-orange castle towering before you across ❸❹ the street is the **Inzhenerny Zamok** (Engineer's Castle). The history of this fiery medieval-looking building is linked to the life and death of Paul I, one of Russian history's more demented and pathetic figures. Paul grew up in the shadow of his powerful mother, Catherine the Great, whom he despised. He held her responsible for the death of his father, who was murdered in the aftermath of the coup that put Catherine on the throne. By the time Paul himself became czar, he had developed a paralyzing fear of being murdered, as his father had been before him. According to Paul, shortly after he succeeded his mother, the Archangel Michael appeared to him in a dream and told him to build a church on the site of his birthplace. The paranoid czar proceeded to build not only a shrine but an impenetrable fortress to protect him from the multitude of enemies he so feared. Out of spite for his mother, he collected stone and building materials for his castle from palaces she had erected. The castle was protected by the Fontanka and Moika rivers to the north and east, while to the west and south, moats (since filled in) were dug. The castle was accessible only by the drawbridges, which were brought up at night. But all his careful planning did Paul little good: On March 11, 1801, just 40 days after moving in, he was murdered in his castle—suffocated by a pillow. Historians speculate that his son Alexander I knew about the plans to murder him and perhaps even participated.

After Paul's murder, no one in the royal family wanted to live in the castle, and it stood empty for more than 20 years. In 1823 it was turned over to the Military Engineering Academy, hence its present name. One of the academy's more famous pupils was the future novelist Fyodor Dostoevsky, who studied here from 1838 to 1841. It still functions as an engineering institute and is therefore not open to the public.

During Paul's brief occupancy he pursued his favorite pastime in the square to your right, drilling troops. He also had a statue erected here to Peter the Great. Sculpted by Bartolomeo Carlo Rastrelli (the great architect's father), it shows the czar as a Roman emperor crowned with a laurel wreath. Its formality contrasts with the simplicity of Falconet's *Bronze Horseman*. Catherine disliked the statue and had it put in storage, but Paul—always looking for ways to spite his mother—had it reerected. The inscription, "To the Great Grandfather from the Great Grandson—1800," is a clumsy paraphrase of his mother's tribute to Peter the Great at the foot of the *Bronze Horseman*.

Walk around to the opposite side of the castle, where the salmon pink facade stands out from the red-orange brick on the other side. This is exactly as it was in Paul's day, for in accordance with the laws protecting the castle as a historical monument, its original appearance has been preserved.

A short walk across the bridge spanning the Moika brings **㉟** you to the **Letny Sad** (Summer Garden). The Summer Garden was yet another brainchild of Peter the Great, who wanted to create a Russian Versailles. When it was first laid out in 1704–12, the garden was planned in a regular, geometric style, decorated with statues and sculptures collected from all over the world and with trees imported from various parts of Russia and abroad. Pavilions, ponds, and an intricate network of fountains completed Peter's European garden, which was bordered on all sides by rivers and canals. The fountains were fed by the nearby Fontanka (in Russian, little fountain); they were destroyed in the 1777 floods and were never restored. In the 18th and 19th centuries the Summer Garden was the center of the city's social life. Today the Letny Sad is as popular as ever, although the formal gardens have given way to a landscaped park.

Among the 80 or so statues that have survived is *Peace and Abundance*. Sculpted by Pietro Barrata in 1722, it allegorically depicts Russia's victory over Sweden. The statue of Ivan Krylov, the "Russian La Fontaine," on the path just off the main alley, was sculpted by Peter Klodt and unveiled in 1855. Scenes from his fables, including "The Fox and the Grapes," appear on the pedestal. As in many other St. Petersburg parks, the sculptures are protected against severe weather by wooden covers from early fall to late spring.

In the southeastern corner of the gardens stands the **Letny Dvorets,** Peter I's Summer Palace. Built by Domenico Trezzini, the two-story building is remarkably simple in design. The walls are of stucco-covered brick and are painted primrose yellow. Opened as a museum in 1934, the Summer Palace has survived without major alteration. There are several other attractive buildings in the Summer Garden, including the **Coffee House** (rebuilt by Rossi in 1826) and the **Tea House** (by I. L. Charlemagne in 1827). The magnificent railing on the Neva side of the park was built between 1770 and 1784 to a design by Yuri Felton. The pink granite pillars supporting the railing are decorated with vases and urns. The light grillwork linking the pillars seems suspended in the air.

36 Continuing west along the embankment, in the direction of the Hermitage, you'll reach **Suvorovskaya Ploshchad** (Suvorov Square). In the center stands a statue in the Classical style of the great military commander, Alexander Suvorov. Designed by Kozlovsky and unveiled in 1801, the statue is more a glorification of military valor than a likeness.

37 From here a splendid panorama opens up onto **Marsovo Pole** (Field of Mars). Peter the Great drained the marsh that was once here and used the area for parades and public celebrations. The field acquired its present name around the beginning of the 19th century, when it became the site of great military parades. Following the February and October revolutions of 1917, the field was turned into a burial ground for victims of both revolutions and the ensuing civil war. The massive granite **Monument to Revolutionary Fighters,** in its center, was unveiled on November 7, 1919. The monument's eternal flame was lit on the 40th anniversary of the October Revolution.

The impressive facade bordering the west side of Marsovoye Pole is the former **Barracks of the Pavlovsky Guards Regiment,** built in 1817–19, to commemorate the regiment's victories in the War of 1812. In the distant background, to the east, you can see the fiery facades of the Engineer's Castle. The architecture to the south, between Marsovoye Pole and the Neva, dates from the end of the 18th century and shows the change from Baroque to Classical style. The **Mramorny Dvorets** (Marble Palace) is a case in point. Designed by Arnoldo Rinaldi, it was built between 1768 and 1785 for one of Catherine's foremost favorites, Grigori Orlov, but was not completed until after his death. The name derives from the pale-pink marble facing. The sides are strictly Classical, while the main frontage, which faces inward to the forecourt with its columns, is vaguely Baroque. For most of the Soviet era, the Marble Palace housed the city's obligatory Lenin Museum. Today its exhibits have been completely revamped, and on display are portraits of members of the Romanov dynasty—yet another sign of the changing times. Even if you're not interested in the museum, step inside the courtyard for a full view of this impressive facade. *7 Millionnaya ul., tel. 812/312–9196. Open Wed.–Mon. 10–6.*

The street leading west from the Marble Palace (to your right as you exit the palace courtyard) is **ulitsa Millionnaya** (Millionaire's Street). Before the 1917 revolution this was St. Petersburg's most prestigious street, and even today its facade conveys a sense of bygone elegance. A short walk down this splendid street brings you to the **Zimnaya Kanavka** (Winter Ditch), a touch of Venice in this northern city. As you cross the canal, look to your right. The canal is crossed by an arched bridge whose curved shape is repeated in the archway above it. The arched passageway is part of the Hermitage complex and connects the Great Hermitage to the Hermitage Theater. Just past the canal you'll come to the New Hermitage, with its massive granite Atlantes supporting the portico. The street ends at Palace Square. To reach Nevsky Prospect and the subway, you'll can take a shortcut through the Triumphal Arch of the General Staff Building, which will lead you via Bolshaya Morskaya ulitsa to Nevsky Prospect.

Excursion 1: Petrodvorets

Several extraordinary palaces are located in the suburbs of St. Petersburg. Following the 1917 Revolution, these former summer residences of the czars were nationalized and turned into public museums. They can all be reached by commuter trains (*elektrichka*), but the simplest way to see the palaces is to book an excursion (available through the St. Petersburg Travel Company or other tourist agencies). The cost is reasonable and covers transportation, guided tour, and admission fee.

During World War II and the siege of Leningrad, most of the suburban palaces were occupied by enemy forces and used as army barracks or stables. At the end of the war, what little remained of the former palaces was burned and looted by the retreating German troops. Museum workers had managed to evacuate much of the art housed in the palaces before the German occupation, but for the most part the original interiors were lost forever. Painstaking restoration using pieces of fabric, pictures, and written descriptions has returned the palaces to their former splendor, although some renovation work is still ongoing.

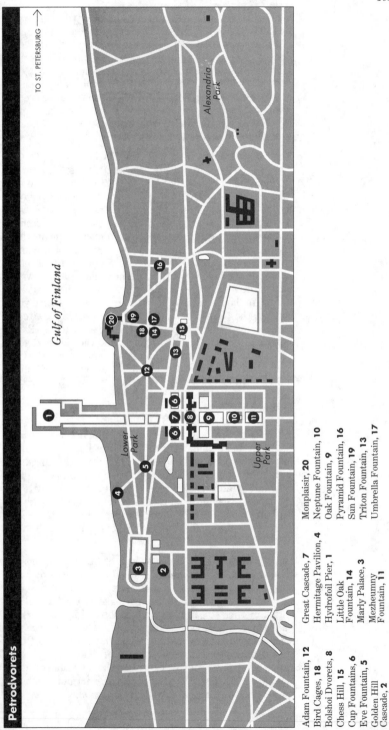

Petrodvorets

TO ST. PETERSBURG →

Gulf of Finland

Lower Park

Upper Park

Alexandria Park

Adam Fountain, **12**
Bird Cages, **18**
Bolshoi Dvorets, **8**
Chess Hill, **15**
Cup Fountains, **6**
Eve Fountain, **5**
Golden Hill
Cascade, **2**

Great Cascade, **7**
Hermitage Pavilion, **4**
Hydrofoil Pier, **1**
Little Oak
Fountain, **14**
Marly Palace, **3**
Mezheumny
Fountain, **11**

Monplaisir, **20**
Neptune Fountain, **10**
Oak Fountain, **9**
Pyramid Fountain, **16**
Sun Fountain, **19**
Triton Fountain, **13**
Umbrella Fountain, **17**

An organized excursion to any of the suburban palaces will take at least four hours. If you travel on your own, it's likely to take up the entire day. Although you'll encounter an occasional cafeteria or café, there are few eating places, so pack a lunch or bring a snack with you.

Of all the palaces you will see in Russia, one that will make a distinct and lasting impression is **Petrodvorets,** situated on the shores of the Baltic Sea, some 29 kilometers (18 miles) from St. Petersburg. Petrodvorets, originally called Peterhof, is more than just a palace: It is an imperial playground replete with lush parks, monumental cascades, and gilded fountains. Its history, both glorious and tragic, in many ways parallels the history of the Russian nation. Built by what might properly be called slave labor, Petrodvorets was for centuries accessible only to Russia's upper crust. In 1918 the young Soviet government turned this former summer residence of the czars into a public museum, thus giving the people a chance to enjoy the fruits of their ancestors' labor. But then came World War II and the German occupation, during which the palace and its magical parks were utterly destroyed. Years of excruciating restoration work, conducted by professional restorers, art historians, and craftsmen, have brought back the palace's former splendor and playful origins. Before-and-after photographs on display at the palace help the visitor to understand why Russians take such pride in this glorious seaside estate.

Petrodvorets is best visited in summer; a winter visit can be quite disappointing. From late September to early June the fountains and cascades are closed down, acquiring the depressing look of a drained pool. You can reach the palace by commuter train from St. Petersburg, but, fog permitting, the best way to go is by hydrofoil, for then you get a panoramic first view of the grand palace overlooking the sea. Be aware that the lines to get into the palace can be excruciatingly long in the summer. You can bypass them by purchasing a spot on a guided tour for foreigners, available through St. Petersburg Travel Company (tel. 812/210–5046) and other tourist agencies. *Ul. Kominterna, town of Petrodvorets, tel. 812/427–9527. Admission for foreigners: $4 or equivalent in rubles. Great Palace open Tues.–Sun. 10–5. Closed 1st Tues. of month. Transportation: commuter train from Baltisky Vokzal (Baltic Station) to Novy Petergof Station, approximately 40 min from St. Petersburg. From station take Bus 351, 352, or 356 to Dvorets. In summer, hydrofoils to Petrodvorets leave from pier outside Hermitage Museum approximately every 20 min. Ride takes about ½ hr.*

Like the city of St. Petersburg, the complex of parks and palaces at Petrodvorets was masterminded by Peter the Great, who personally drew up the first plans. Many of the fountains were based on his ideas. If you travel by hydrofoil, you will arrive at the pier near the Lower Park, a for-

mal Baroque garden in the French style adorned with statues, fountains, and cascades. Peter's playful spirit is still
very much evident here. The fun-loving czar had hidden water sprays built into trees and tiny plazas. They come to life
with great surprise for the unsuspecting visitor and offer
entertainment to squealing children who race through the
showers on hot summer days.

Also located in the Lower Park (east of the pier) is the oldest building at Petrodvorets, the **Monplasir** (literally "My
Pleasure"). This is where Peter the Great lived while over-
seeing the construction of the main imperial residence. As
was often the case with Peter, he greatly preferred this
modest Dutch-style villa to more extravagant living quarters. One of its most interesting rooms is the **Lacquered
Study,** decorated with replicas of panels (the originals were
destroyed during World War II) painted in Chinese style.
Next door is the so-called **Catherine Wing,** built by Rastrelli
in the mid-18th century. The future Catherine the Great
was staying here at the time of the coup that overthrew her
husband and placed her on the throne. Another famous
structure, to the left of the pier as you face the sea, is the
Hermitage. This two-story pavilion gives new meaning to
the concept of a movable feast. The building is equipped
with a device that would lift the dining table—diners and
all—from the ground floor to the private dining room
above.

A short walk up the path through the Lower Park leads you
to the centerpiece of Petrodvorets, the famous **Great Cascade.** Running down the steep ridge separating the Lower
Park and the Grand Palace towering above, the cascade
comprises three waterfalls, 64 fountains, and 37 gilded
statues. The system of waterworks has remained virtually
unchanged since 1721. The ducts and pipes, which convey
water over a distance of some 20 kilometers (12 miles), work
without pumping stations: The water flows downhill, while
the fountains operate on the principle of communicating
vessels. The centerpiece of the waterfalls is a gilded Samson rending the jaws of a lion from which a jet of water
spurts into the air. The statue represents the Russian victory over the Swedes at Poltava on St. Samson's day. The
present figure is a meticulous replica of the original, which
was carried away by the Germans.

Crowning the ridge above the cascade is the magnificent **Bolshoi Dvorets** (Great Palace). Little remains of Peter's original two-story house, built between 1714 and 1725 under the
architects Leblond, Braunstein, and Machetti. The building was altered considerably and enlarged by Peter's
daughter Elizabeth. She entrusted the reconstruction to
her favorite architect, the Italian Bartolomeo Rastrelli,
who transformed the modest residence into a sumptuous
blend of medieval architecture and Russian Baroque. Before you begin your tour of the palace interiors, pause for a

moment to enjoy the breathtaking view from the marble terrace. From here a full view of the Lower Park unfolds, stretching from the cascades to the Gulf of Finland.

An integral part of visiting any museum-palace in Russia are the autocratic *babushki* who now control them. In this, Petrodvorets is no exception. No matter how annoying, they deserve respect, for they have survived the 900-day siege of Leningrad, witnessed the palaces' destruction, and seen its nearly miraculous rise from the ashes. As you enter the palace, you will be given tattered shoe covers to protect the highly polished floors as you walk through the splendid halls. One cautionary note: On most occasions flash photography is not allowed, although for a fee, fast film and videotaping are. Sometimes the babushki aren't aware of the difference. So hang on tight to your equipment to avoid having it confiscated by an overzealous custodian of Peter's treasures.

The palace's lavish interiors are primarily the work of Rastrelli, although several of the rooms were redesigned during the reign of Catherine the Great in accordance with the architectural style of her day, Neoclassicism. Of Peter's original design, only his Dubovy Kabinet (Oak Cabinet) survived the numerous reconstructions. The fine oak panels (some are originals) lining the walls were designed by the famous French sculptor Pineau. The entire room and all its furnishings are made of wood, with the exception of the white marble fireplace, above which hangs a long mirror framed in carved oak.

One of the largest rooms in the palace is the **Tronny Zal** (Throne Room), which takes up the entire width of the building, Classically designed, this majestic room—once the scene of great receptions and official ceremonies—features exquisite parquet floors, fine stucco ceiling moldings, and dazzling chandeliers. The pale green and dark red decor is bathed in light, which pours in through the two tiers of windows (28 in all) taking up the long sides of the room. Behind Peter the Great's throne at the eastern end of the room hangs a huge portrait of Catherine the Great. The empress, a picture of confidence after her successful coup, is shown riding a horse, dressed in the uniform of the guards regiment that supported her bid for power.

Next to the Throne Room is the **Chesmensky Zal** (Chesma Hall), whose interior is dedicated entirely to the Russian naval victory over the Turks in 1770. The walls are covered with 12 huge oil canvases depicting the battles, which were created by the German painter P. Hackert at Empress Catherine's behest. According to legend, the artist complained that he could not paint a burning ship since he had never seen one. Catherine arranged to have ships blown up for him to use as models. Such were the days of divine right.

Arguably the most dazzling of the palace's rooms is the **Audients Zal** (Audience Hall). Rastrelli created the ultimate Baroque interior with this glittering room of white, red, and gold. Gilded Baroque bas-reliefs adorn the stark white walls, along which tall mirrors are hung, further accentuating the richness of the decor.

Other notable rooms include the **Kitaiskye Kabinety** (the Chinese Study Rooms), designed by Vallin de Mothe in the 1760s. As was the fashion in Europe at the time, the rooms are ornately decorated with Chinese motifs. Finely carved black-lacquered panels depict various Chinese scenes. Between the two rooms is the **Kartinny Zal** (Picture Hall), whose walls are paneled with 368 oil paintings by the Italian artist Rotari. The artist used just eight models for these paintings, which depict young women in national dress.

After a tour of the palace interiors, a stroll through the Upper Park is in order. Located on the south side of the palace, this formal garden with its symmetrical design is far less imaginative than the Lower Park, with its playful fountains and cascading waterfalls. Its focal point is the Neptune Fountain, originally made in Germany in the 17th century and bought by Paul I in 1782. During the war the three-tiered group of bronze sculptures was carried away by the Germans. It was eventually recovered and reinstalled in 1956.

Excursion 2: Pushkin

The town of **Pushkin,** located 24 kilometers (15 miles) south of St. Petersburg, was the summer residence of the imperial family from the days of Peter the Great right up to the last years of the Romanov dynasty. Formerly known as **Tsarskoye Selo** (the czar's village), its name was changed after the 1917 Revolution, first to Detskoye (Children's) Selo and then to Pushkin, in honor of the great Russian poet who studied at the lyceum here. During the 18th and 19th centuries, Tsarskoye Selo was a popular summer resort for St. Petersburg's aristocracy and well-to-do. Not only was the royal family close by, but it was here, in 1837, that Russia's first regular railroad was opened, linking Tsarskoye Selo to St. Petersburg.

Pushkin's main attraction is the dazzling **Yekaterininsky Dvorets** (Catherine Palace), a superb example of Russian Baroque. With a facade 300 meters (985 feet) long, the exterior features a row of white columns and pilasters with gold Baroque moldings boldly set against a turquoise-blue background. Much of the palace's history and architectural design is tied to Catherine the Great, who spent much time here. But it is for the first Catherine, Peter the Great's second wife, that the palace is named. Under Empress Elizabeth, their daughter, the modest stone palace was completely rebuilt. The project was originally entrusted to

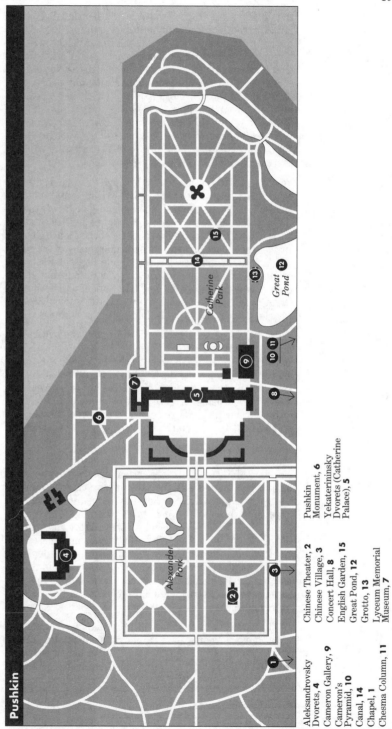

Pushkin

Aleksandrovsky
Dvorets, **4**

Cameron Gallery, **9**

Cameron's
Pyramid, **10**

Canal, **14**

Chapel, **1**

Chesma Column, **11**

Chinese Theater, **2**

Chinese Village, **3**

Concert Hall, **8**

English Garden, **15**

Great Pond, **12**

Grotto, **13**

Lyceum Memorial
Museum, **7**

Pushkin
Monument, **6**

Yekaterininsky
Dvorets (Catherine
Palace), **5**

*Catherine
Park*

*Alexander
Park*

*Great
Pond*

the Russian architects Kvasov and Chevakinsky, but in 1752 Elizabeth brought in the Italian architect Bartolomeo Rastrelli (who went on to build the Winter Palace in St. Petersburg). Although Elizabeth's successor, Catherine the Great, later had the interiors remodeled in the Neoclassical style, she left Rastrelli's stunning facade untouched. *7 ul. Komsomolskaya, town of Pushkin, tel. 812/465–5308. Admission for foreigners: $5. Open Wed.–Mon. 10–5. Closed last Mon. of month. Transportation: commuter train from Vitebsky Vokzal (Vitebsk Station) to Pushkin–Tsarskoye Selo, approximately 20 min from St. Petersburg. From station take Bus 371 or 382 to Dvorets (palace).*

You'll enter the palace grounds through the gilded gates designed by Rastrelli. To your right, a visual feast unfolds as you walk the length of the long blue-and-gold facade toward the museum entrance. Sparkling above the palace at the northern end are the golden cupolas of the Palace Church. Inside, the palace is just as spectacular; many of the rooms are famous in their own right. While little of Rastrelli's original interior remains, the many additions and alterations made between 1760 and 1790 under Catherine the Great were carried out by top architects, the Scottish Charles Cameron and the Italian Giacomo Quarenghi.

Entering the palace by the main staircase, you will see displays showing the extent of the wartime damage and the subsequent restoration work. Like Peterhof, the palace was almost completely destroyed during World War II. It was used by the occupying Nazi forces as army barracks, and as the Germans retreated, they blew up what remained of the former imperial residence. Today the palace again stands in all its glory, although the interior is still being restored.

The largest and arguably most impressive room is the **Bolshoi Zal** (Great Hall), which was used for receptions and balls. The longer sides are taken up by two tiers of gilt-framed windows. Tall, elaborately carved gilded mirrors have been placed between them. The light pouring in through the windows bounces off the mirrors and sparkles in the all-encompassing gilt, creating a sensation of spaciousness and light. The huge ceiling painting, depicting Russian military victories and accomplishments in the sciences and arts, makes the room seem even larger. It is easy to imagine the extravagant lifestyles of St. Petersburg's prerevolutionary elite.

On the north side of the State Staircase is one of the palace's most famous rooms, the **Yantarnaya Komnata** (Amber Room), so named for the engraved amber panels that once lined its walls. A gift to Peter the Great from the king of Prussia, the panels were stolen by the Nazis and presumably hidden in Kaliningrad (then Königsberg). The mystery surrounding their disappearance persists to this day. Although rumors still circulate about their rediscovery, in

1979 the Soviet government finally gave up hope of ever retrieving the original panels and began the costly work of re-
storing the room. The restoration is far from complete, but
the few restored panels—and a prewar black-and-white
photograph of the room—give you an idea of the marvelous
original interior.

Leaving the Amber Room, the next room you will come to is
the large **Kartinny Zal** (Picture Gallery), which runs right
across the building. The paintings are all from Western Europe and date from the 17th to the early 18th century. Of
the 130 pictures on display, 113 are originals.

Highlights of the other splendid rooms on the north side include the Blue Drawing Room, the Blue Chinese Room, and
the Choir Anteroom, all of which face the courtyard. They
feature fine wall coverings of pure silk. The Blue Chinese
Room, originally designed by Cameron, has been restored
on the basis of the architect's drawings. Despite its name, it
is a purely Classical interior, and the only thing even re-
motely Chinese is the Oriental motifs on the blue silk covering the wall. The fine golden-yellow silk of the Choir
Anteroom is from the same batch used to decorate the room
in the 18th century. When the postwar restoration began,
an extra supply of the original silk was discovered tucked
away in a storage room of the Hermitage.

Having savored the treasures inside the palace, you can
now begin exploring the beautiful **Yekaterininsky Park** outside, with its marble statues, man-made waterfalls and
ponds, pavilions, concert halls, and other buildings. The
park is split into two sections. The inner, formal section,
known as the French Garden, runs down the terraces in
front of the palace's eastern facade. The outer section centers around the Great Pond and is in the less rigid style of an
English garden. If you follow the main path through the
French Garden and down the terrace, you will eventually
reach Rastrelli's Hermitage, which he completed just before turning his attention to the palace itself. Other highlights of the French Garden include the Upper and Lower
Bath pavilions (1777–79) and Rastrelli's elaborate blue-
domed Grotto.

There is much to be seen in the English Garden, too. A good
starting point is the **Cameron Gallery,** which actually forms
a continuation of the palace's parkside frontage. The building is to your right as you exit the palace. Open only in the
summer, it now contains a museum of 18th- and 19th-centu-
ry costumes. The building offers the best views of the park
and its lakes—which is exactly what Cameron had in mind
when he designed it for Catherine the Great in the 1780s.
The double-sided staircase leading majestically down to the
Great Pond is flanked by two bronze sculptures of Hercules
and Flora.

From here you can turn right (south) and begin your exploration of the park. Just beyond the island in the middle of the Great Pond, which is actually an artificial lake, stands the **Chesma Column,** marking the Russian naval victory in the Aegean in 1770. At the far end of the pond is **Cameron's Pyramid,** where Catherine the Great buried her favorite dogs.

Outside the park, just north of the Catherine Palace, stands yet another palace, the **Alexandrovsky Dvorets,** a present from Catherine to her favorite grandson, the future Czar Alexander I, on the occasion of his marriage. Built by Quarenghi between 1792 and 1796, the serene and restrained Classical structure was the favorite residence of Russia's last czar, Nicholas II. The building is not open to the public.

Attached to the Catherine Palace is the **Lyceum.** Built in 1791 and originally intended for the education of Catherine the Great's grandchildren, it later became a school for the nobility. The building is now open as a museum, and the classroom, library, and Pushkin's bedroom have been restored to their appearance at the time he studied there.

Excursion 3: Pavlovsk

The imperial estate of Paul I (in Russian Pavel, hence Pavlovsk) is located some 30 kilometers (18 miles) south of St. Petersburg and only 5 kilometers (3 miles) from Pushkin and the Catherine Palace. Due to the proximity of the two towns, tours to the palaces of Pavlovsk and Pushkin are often combined. This is not recommended, however—if only because this does not allow you to do justice to either palace. The estate grounds of Pavlovsk, at that time the site of the royal hunt, were given to Paul by his mother, Catherine the Great, in 1777, upon the birth of Paul's eldest son, the future Alexander I. Construction of the first wooden buildings started immediately, and in 1782 the brilliant Scottish architect Charles Cameron began work on the Great Palace and the landscaped park. In contrast to the dazzling Baroque palaces of Pushkin and Peterhof, Pavlovsk is a tribute to the reserved beauty of Classicism. It is a popular destination with St. Petersburg residents, who come here to stroll through the 600-hectare (1,500-acre) park, with its woods, ponds, rivers, alleys, pavilions, and statues. *20 ul. Revolutsia, town of Pavlovsk, tel. 812/470-2155 or 812/470-2156. Admission fee for foreigners: $4 or the equivalent in rubles. Open Tues.–Sun. 10–5:00. Closed 1st Tues. of month. Transportation: commuter train from Vitebsky Vokzal (Vitebsk Station) to Pavlovsk, approximately 25–35 min from St. Petersburg. From station walk to palace, or take Bus 370 or 383.*

A tour of Pavlovsk begins with the **Bolshoi Dvorets** (Great Palace), which stands on a high bluff overlooking the river and dominates the surrounding park. The building is painted golden yellow and crowned with a flat dome supported by 64 bold white colonnades. Built in 1782–86 as the summer residence of Paul and his wife, Maria Fyodorovna, the original design of this strictly Neoclassical stone palace was based on a Roman villa. It was enlarged by Vincenzo Brenna in 1796–99, when a second story was added to the galleries and side pavilions. Despite a devastating fire in 1803 and further reconstruction by Voronikhin in the early 19th century, Cameron's basic design survived.

Outside the palace stands a statue of the snub-nosed Paul I, a copy of the statue at Gatchina, Paul's other summer residence. The splendid interiors, with their parquet floors, marble pillars, and gilded ceilings, were created by some of Russia's most outstanding architects. Besides Cameron, Brenna, and Voronikhin, the roll call includes Quarenghi, who designed the interior of five rooms on the first floor, and Carlo Rossi, who was responsible for the library, built in 1824. The state apartments on the ground floor include the dining room, where a 19th-century dinner service produced at the imperial porcelain factory in St. Petersburg is on display. Among the lavishly decorated state rooms on the second floor is the famous Grecian Hall, whose rich green Corinthian columns stand out against the white of the artificial marble walls. The chairs with the wild bird-winged arms were designed by the architect Voronikhin. The hall, which also served as a ballroom, linked the state rooms of Paul I to those of his wife, Maria. Her private suite, called the Hall of Peace, was designed to correspond to the Hall of War on Paul's side of the palace. The gilded stucco wall moldings are decorated with flowers, baskets of fruit, musical instruments, and other symbols of peace.

Covering over 1,500 acres, Pavlovsk's splendid park boasts numerous pavilions, tree-lined alleys, waterways, and statues. Like the palace, the park was designed by the leading architects of the day—Brenna, Cameron, Voronikhin, and Carlo Rossi. Once again, the Pavlovsk park differs greatly from those of the other imperial palaces, where the rules of geometrical design were strictly applied. Much of Pavlovsk's beauty is in its easy naturalness. Instead of the tense and cold perfection of calculated rows of trees or uniformly cropped bushes, it offers the beauty of nature, without any signs of human intervention.

The length of the park's paths and lanes is said to equal the distance between St. Petersburg and Moscow (656 kilometers [410 miles]). Since you can't possibly cover the entire territory in one day anyway, you might just want to follow your whim and see where it leads you. If you walk down the slope just behind the palace to the **Czar's Little Garden** (Sobstvennyi Sadik), you can see the Three Graces Pavilion. Created by Cameron, the 16-columned pavilion encloses a statue of the three graces. Of the numerous pavilions and memorials dotting the park, the mausoleum to the Spouse and Creator is of particular interest. Set alone on a remote and overgrown hillside toward the center of the park, it was built by Maria for her husband after he was murdered in a palace coup. The park's earliest structure is the Classical Temple of Friendship, intended to symbolize the friendship between Maria and her mother-in-law, Catherine the Great. Yet another Cameron creation, the yellow pavilion with colonnade was erected in 1782.

Excursion 4: Lomonosov

The town of Lomonosov is located on the Gulf of Finland, some 40 kilometers (25 miles) west of St. Petersburg. The former imperial estate, presently known by the same name as the town, was founded by Alexander Menshikov. A favorite of Peter the Great, Menshikov followed Peter's lead and in 1710 began building himself a luxurious summer palace on the shores of the Baltic Sea. Following Peter's death, Menshikov was stripped of his formidable political power and was subsequently exiled, leaving his summer estate only half finished. The palace reverted to the crown and was given to the ill-fated Peter III. Most of the buildings on the grounds were erected during his short reign and later, under Catherine the Great. Originally called Oranienbaum (an orangery was once attached to the Great Palace), the estate is perhaps the least extravagant of the suburban imperial palaces. It is, however, the only palace to have survived World War II intact. With its seaside location and extensive park, it is a splendid place to spend a warm summer day. *48 Prospect Yunovo Lenitsa, town of Lomonosov, tel. 812/422–3757. Open Wed.–Mon. 11–5. Transportation: commuter train from Baltisky Vokzal (Baltic Station) to Oranienbaum-1, approximately 1 hr from St. Petersburg.*

Menshikov's Great Palace is situated on a terrace overlooking the sea. The main facade is turned toward the sea, and the formal garden in front of the terrace is peopled by sculptures. Built between 1710 and 1725, it was designed by the same architects who built Menshikov's grand mansion on Vasilievsky Ostrov, Giovanni Fontana, and Gottfried Schaedel. The Great Palace has been under reconstruction for some time and is currently not open to the public.

Peterstadt Dvorets, Peter III's modest palace, is a two-story stone mansion built between 1762 and 1785 by Arnoldo Rinaldi. Its interior is decorated with handsome lacquered wood paintings. It was here, in 1762, that the czar was murdered in the wake of the coup that put his wife, Catherine the Great, on the throne.

By far the most interesting building on the estate is Catherine the Great's **Kitaisky Dvorets** (Chinese Palace), also designed by Rinaldi as her private summer residence. With a

519 M.P.H.

190 M.P.H.

75 M.P.H.

0 M.P.H.

WE LET YOU SEE EUROPE AT YOUR OWN PACE.

Regardless of your personal speed limits, Rail Europe offers everything to get you over, around and through anywhere you want in Europe. For more information, call your travel agent or 1-800-4-EURAIL.

OFFICIAL DISTRIBUTOR

Rail Europe

OF THE EURAIL PASS

All The Best Trips Start with Fodor's

Baroque exterior and a highly Rococo interior, the palace is by no means a pure example of Chinese architecture, although some of the rooms are furnished in the Rococo style. The palace is lavishly decorated, with ceiling paintings created by Venetian artists, inlaid-wood floors, and elaborate stucco walls.

On a slope to the east of the Great Palace is the curious **Katalnaya Gorka** (Sledding Hill). All that remains of the 18th-century imperial slide is the pavilion that served as the starting point of the ride. Here guests of the empress would rest and freshen up while taking turns on the breathtaking slide. Situated in an isolated section of the park and painted a soft blue with white trim, the fanciful pavilion looks like a blue-frosted birthday cake plopped in the middle of a forest.

What to See and Do with Children

A **boat ride** on the Neva or through the city's twisting canals is always a pleasant way to spend a summer afternoon. For trips through the canals, pick up a boat at the pier near Anichkov Bridge on Nevsky Prospect. Boats cruising the Neva leave from the pier outside the Hermitage Museum. *Mid-May–mid-Sept. Departures early morning–late afternoon.*

The **St. Petersburg Circus** dates from 1867. Though perhaps not as famous as the Moscow Circus, it is very popular with children. *3 Fontanka Naberezhnaya tel. 812/210–4411. Performances daily 7:30 PM; matinees on weekends.*

In summer, children delight in Petrodvorets (*see above*), the amusement park of the czars, where Peter the Great's trick fountains come to life in the most surprising ways. Located 29 kilometers (18 miles) south of the city, it can be reached by hydrofoil from the pier outside the Hermitage museum.

St. Petersburg's three puppet theaters all perform regularly for children: **Bolshoi Puppet Theater** (10 ul. Nekrasova, tel. 812/272–8215), **Puppet-Marionette Theater** (52 Nevsky Prospect, tel. 812/311–2156), and **Sharmanka** (151A Moskovsky Prospect, tel. 812/297–2666). The last is a new "cinematic" theater whose fascinating and bizarre performances may frighten very young children.

Off the Beaten Track

Chesmenskaya Tserkov Surrounded by dreary Soviet high rises in a remote residential area, this bright red, white-striped church is a delightful surprise. A rare example of pseudo-Gothic Russian architecture, it was built to accompany the Chesma Palace (across the street), which served as a staging post for the imperial court en route to the summer palaces of Tsarskoye Selo (now Pushkin) and Pavlovsk. Commissioned by Catherine the Great, the palace was built to commemorate the Russian naval victory at Chesma in the Aegean in 1770. After the Bolshevik Revolution, the palace became a home for the elderly and is not open to the public. The church, in turn, was made into a branch of the city's Naval Museum, dedicated to the battle at Chesma. In recent years, baptisms and weddings have occasionally been performed here, although regular church services have not yet resumed. Whether the museum will survive Russia's religious revival is unclear at this point. Not far from the Pulkhovskaya Hotel, the Chesma Church is within walking distance of the Moskovskaya subway stop. *12 ul. Lensoveta, tel. 812/293–6114. Open Tues.–Sun. 10–5.*

Piskaryevskoye Kladbishche The extent of the city's suffering during the 900-day siege of Leningrad becomes clear after a visit to the somber Piskaryevskoye Cemetery. Located on the outskirts of town, the field here was used as a mass burial ground for victims of cold and starvation between 1941 and 1944. The long rows of common graves are marked by a simple slab indicating only the year in which the victims died. In all, nearly 500,000 people are buried here. Inscribed on the granite wall at the far end of the cemetery is the famous poem by radio personality Olga Bergholts, which ends with the oft-repeated phrase, "No one is forgotten, nothing is forgotten." The granite pavilions at the entrance house a small museum with photographs and memoirs documenting the siege. On display is Tanya Savicheva's diary, scraps of paper on which the young schoolgirl recorded the *death* of every member of her family. The last entry reads, "May 13. Mother died. Everyone is dead. Only I am left." *74 Nepokorennykh, tel. 812/247–5716. Open daily 10–6. Transportation: Bus 123 from subway stop Ploshchad Muzhestva.*

Pushkin Apartment Museum This is where, on January 27, 1837, the beloved Russian poet Alexander Pushkin died after participating in a duel to defend his wife's honor. Reopened in 1987 after extensive renovations, the apartment/museum has been restored to its appearance at the time Pushkin lived here. Although few of the furnishings are authentic, his personal effects and those of his wife are on display. The library, where Pushkin died, has been rebuilt according to sketches made by his friend and fellow poet, Vasily Zhukovsky. A moving account leads you through the apartment and retells the events leading up to the poet's death. The museum is a short walk from the corner of Nevsky Prospect and the Moika Embankment. *12 Nab. Reki Moiki, tel. 812/311–8001. Open Wed.–Mon. 10:40–5. Closed last Fri. of month.*

Smolny Confusion abounds when you mention the Smolny. That can either mean a beautiful Baroque church or a classically designed institute that went down in history as Bolshevik headquarters in the 1917 Revolution. It doesn't help matters much that the two architectural complexes are right next door to each other, on the eastern edge of the Neva's left bank. Construction of the Smolny Convent and Cathedral began under Elizabeth I and continued during the reign of Catherine the Great, who established a school for the daughters of the nobility within its walls. The centerpiece of the convent is the magnificent five-domed **Cathedral of Resurrection,** which was designed by Bartolomeo Rastrelli and is arguably his greatest creation. At first glance, the highly ornate blue-and-white cathedral seems to have leaped off the pages of a fairy tale. Its five white onion domes, crowned with gilded globes supporting crosses of gold, convey a sense of magic and power. Begun by Rastrelli in 1748, the cathedral was not completed until the 1830s, by the architect Vasily Stasov. The cathedral is now open to the public, but few traces of the original interior have survived. *3/1 Ploshchad Rastrelli, tel. 812/271–9182. Open Mon., Tues., Thurs.–Sun. 11–6; Wed. 11–5. If a concert is being held in evening, museum closes 1 hr earlier. Transportation: Trolley Bus 5 from Ploshchad Vostaniya to Rastrelli Sq.*

The **Smolny Institute,** just south of the cathedral, is a far different structure. Designed by Giacomo Quarenghi in 1806–08, the Neoclassical building was done in the style of a large country house. The Smolny Institute will long be remembered by the Russian people as the site where Lenin and his associates planned the overthrow of the Kerensky government in October 1917. The rooms Lenin used during his time at the institute once housed a museum that, since the latest revolution, has been closed. Today the building houses the offices of the mayor of St. Petersburg. Although it is not generally open to the public, it may be possible to arrange a tour. *3/11 Ploshchad Rastrelli, tel. 812/311–3690.*

Yusupovsky Dvorets Located on the banks of the Moika River, this elegant yellow palace belonged to one of Russia's wealthiest families. It was here on a cold night in December 1916 that Prince Yusupov and others loyal to the czar spent several frustrating and frightening hours trying to kill the invincible Rasputin, the mad monk who courted the czarina during the tumultuous years leading up to the Bolshevik Revolution. When the monk did not succumb to the poison-laced cake given to him, the conspirators proceeded to shoot wildly and then dumped him—bound and gagged—into the icy waters of a nearby canal. The building now serves as a cultural center for teachers but is also open for excursions (by advance booking only). On display are the rooms in which Rasputin was killed as well as a waxworks exhibit of Rasputin and Prince Yusupov, who was forced to flee the country when the monk's murder was uncovered. *94 nab. Reki Moiki, tel. 812/311–5353. Excursion fee: $8 or equivalent in rubles.*

Sightseeing Checklist

This list includes attractions covered in the preceding tours as well as additional attractions described for the first time.

Churches, Monasteries, and Temples

Alexander Nevsky Monastery (*see* Tour 4)

Chesma Church (Chesmenskaya Tserkov, *see* Off the Beaten Track)

Church of the Savior on the Spilled Blood (Khram Spasa na Krovi, *see* Tour 5)

Mosque (Mechet, *see* Tour 3)

St. Isaac's Cathedral (Isaakievsky Sobor, *see* Tour 2)

St. Nicholas Cathedral (Nikolsky Sobor). This 18th-century Russian Baroque cathedral is surrounded by picturesque canals and green spaces. It's well worth a visit to hear the beautiful choir. *1/3 Nikolskaya Ploshchad, tel. 812/114–0862. Morning services at 7 and 10 AM.*

Smolny Convent and Cathedral (*see* Off the Beaten Track)

Historic Buildings and Sites

Admiralty (*see* Tour 2)

Anichkov Bridge (Anichkov Most, *see* Tour 4)

Engineer's Castle (Inzhenerny Zamok, *see* Tour 5)

Gostiny Dvor (*see* Tour 4)

Kazan Cathedral (Kazansky Sobor, *see* Tour 4)

Marble Palace (Mramorny Dvorets, *see* Tour 5)

Maria's Palace (Mariinsky Dvorets, *see* Tour 2)

Menshikov Palace (Menshikovsky Dvorets, *see* Tour 2)

Nevsky Prospect (*see* Tour 4)

Palace Square (Dvortsovaya Ploshchad, *see* Tour 1)

Peter and Paul Fortress (Petropavlovskaya Krepost, *see* Tour 3)

Peter I's Summer Palace (Letny Dvorets, *see* Tour 5)

Peter the Great's Cottage (Domik Petra I, *see* Tour 3)

Piskaryevskoye Cemetery (Piskaryevskoye Kladbishche, *see* Off the Beaten Track)

Rossi Street (ulitsa Zodchevo Rossi, *see* Tour 4)

Smolny Institute (*see* Off the Beaten Track)

Square of Art (Ploshchad Iskuustv, *see* Tour 5)

Strelka (Spit of Vasilievsky Island, *see* Tour 2)

Stroganov Palace (*see* Tour 4)

Winter Palace (Zimny Dvorets, *see* Tour 1)

Yelisevsky Food Emporium (*see* Tour 4)

Yusupov Palace (Yusupovsky Dvorets, *see* Off the Beaten Track)

Museums

Anna Akhmatova Literary Museum. Opened in 1989, the museum is located in the former palace of the Count Sheremetyev, which was home to the famous St. Petersburg poet for many years. *34 Nab. Reki Fontanki, tel. 812/272–4080 or 812/272–1811. Open Tues.–Sun. 10:30–6:30. Closed last Wed. of month.*

Artillery Museum (*see* Tour 3)

Avrora (*see* Tour 3

Dostoevsky Apartment Museum. The writer's last residence, where he wrote *The Brothers Karamazov. 5/2*

Kuznechny Pereulok, tel. 812/311–4031. Open Tues.–Sun. 10:30–5. Closed last Wed. of month.
Ethnography Museum (*see* Tour 5)
Hermitage Museum (Ermitazh, *see* Tour 1)
Mining Institute Museum (*see* Tour 2)
Museum of Anthropology and Ethnography (Kunstkamera, *see* Tour 2)
Pushkin Apartment Museum (*see* Off the Beaten Track)
Rimsky-Korsakov Museum. In the composer's apartment; classical concerts are occasionally held in its small concert hall. *28 Zagorodny Prospect, Apt. 39, tel. 812/113–3208. Open Wed.–Sun. 11–6.*
Russian Political Museum (*see* Tour 3)
State Museum of Russian Art (*see* Tour 5)
Zoological Museum (*see* Tour 2)

Parks and Gardens
Botanical Gardens. Founded as an apothecary garden for Peter the Great. *2 ul. Professora Popova, tel. 812/234–1764. Hothouses open Mon.–Thurs., weekends 11–3:30.*
Field of Mars (Marsovoye Pole, *see* Tour 5)
Kirovsky Park on Yelagin Ostrov (tel. 812/239–0911). Yelagin Ostrov (island) is named after its 18th-century aristocratic owner. The park covers most of the island and has an open-air theater, boating stations, and a beach. To reach the park, take Bus 71 from Petrogradskaya subway station.
Mikhailovsky Gardens (Mikhailovsky Sad, *see* Tour 5)
Primorsky Park Pobedy (Seaside Park of Victory). This beautiful park is situated on an isolated island off the coast of Finland. Biking, boating, and swimming in summer. *21 Krestovsky Prospect, tel. 812/234–2146. Tram 33, 34, 11, or 21 from Vasilieostrovsky subway station.*
Summer Gardens (Letny Sad, *see* Tour 5)
Zoo. Located near the Peter and Paul Fortress, directly behind the Gorkhovskaya subway station. *1 Park Lenina, tel. 812/232–8260. Open Tues.–Sun. 10–4.*

Statues and Monuments
Alexander Column (Aleksandrovskaya Kolonna, *see* Tour 1)
Bronze Horseman (Medny Vsadnik, *see* Tour 2)
Catherine Monument (*see* Tour 4)
Egyptian Sphinxes (*see* Tour 2)
Nicholas Statue (*see* Tour 2)
Suvorov Monument (*see* Tour 5)

Shopping

If you have come to St. Petersburg to shop, you will be disappointed. Despite valiant attempts at economic reform, shopping is still quite limited and the availability of goods, while much improved, remains highly unpredictable. Service has not improved much either since the old days of communism. A smiling clerk eager to help you is still the exception rather than the rule, even in the gleaming new private stores catering exclusively to foreign tourists. Be prepared to be the one who does the enticing, rather than the other way around.

Still, shopping here has its appeal, especially for those seeking adventure and amusement. There is no better way of getting to know St. Petersburg and the challenges facing it than to roam its streets in search of a good buy. Often the best places to shop are not stores or established shopping areas but the sidewalks and streets: In today's new entre-preneurial mood almost everyone who owns anything is out to make a sale, and the streets and subway stations are lined with kiosks overflowing with odd assortments of goods, from Russian caviar to Italian boots.

Although distinctions are easily blurred, it may prove use-ful to understand the various categories of shops in St. Pe-tersburg today. The so-called **hard currency stores,** which normally deal exclusively in dollars and other hard curren-cies, cater to the foreign community and the Russian nou-veau riche, offering primarily large-purchase items, such as stereos and washing machines. Some of these stores are now accepting rubles, too—but at a very disadvantageous exchange rate. Stores serving the tourist industry, which often accept both rubles and dollars, limit their selection to Russian souvenirs appealing to the foreign tourist. Private and cooperative stores are St. Petersburg's newest ven-tures; the selection here runs the gamut, and prices (in ru-bles) are far beyond the average Russian's budget. Finally, there are the remnants of the old regime, the run-of-the-mill state stores, where prices—and the selection of goods—tend to be rock-bottom, especially when you con-sider the advantageous exchange rate of the dollar in rela-tion to the ruble.

Shopping Districts

These days it is difficult to tell where the shops end and the streets begin, but historically St. Petersburg's main shop-ping district centers around **Nevsky Prospect** and **Gostiny Dvor** (literally, Merchant Arcade). Located smack in the center of town, at 35 Nevsky Prospect, Gostiny Dvor is easi-ly reached by subway; a station right outside its doors is named in its honor. Some sections of Gostiny Dvor are cur-rently closed due to ongoing restoration.

Department Stores

Major department stores in the downtown area include the popular **DLT** (*Dom Leningradskoi Torgovly*), just off Nevsky Prospect, at 21/23 Bolshaya Konyushennaya ulitsa, and **Passage,** at 48 Nevsky Prospect, which cater primarily to the local population. Their souvenir sections, however, are often a shopper's paradise as prices, in rubles, are sig-nificantly lower here than in the souvenir shops around ho-tels and in other areas frequented by tourists. The patient shopper may chance upon some tremendous bargains, although there is a catch: When you leave Russia you may be told that you can't take your purchases with you, or that you must pay a fine (which, it would appear, goes directly into the customs official's pocket). The only way to be absolutely sure that your purchases will be allowed to leave the country with you is to buy everything in officially sanctioned "dollar" stores and retain receipts as proof that purchases were made in hard currency.

Outside the large department stores of Nevsky Prospect, you will find clusters of individual sellers offering a variety of souvenir and art items. They spread their wares out on the sidewalks, string their paintings up along the walls of buildings, or set up makeshift booths to display their handcrafted items. There are no set prices, and you are expected to bargain. Beware, too, that you can run into the same problems at departure with goods purchased on the streets, since even if you pay in hard currency, you are not given a receipt as proof.

Specialty Stores

Art Shops Although they cater primarily to the lucrative tourist market, art shops in St. Petersburg offer items of much higher quality than what you will find on the streets. Nevsky Prospect is lined with such shops, where local artists sell their wares on commission. Before making a major purchase at these stores, be sure to ask if they will take care of the paperwork necessary to allow you to take the item out of the country. It's also a good idea to clarify whether they charge an additional fee for this service. Some of the best art shops include **Lavka Khudozhnikov** (8 Nevsky Prospect, tel. 812/312–6193); **Alivekt** (22/24 Nevsky Prospect, tel. 812/315–5978); **Arianda** (11 Konnogvardeiski Prospect, apt. 17, tel. 812/311–6867, appointment necessary); **Golubaya Gostinaya** (38 Bolshaya Morskaya ul., tel. 812/315–7414); and **Nevsky 20,** operated by the St. Petersburg Association of Free Art (20 Nevsky Prospect, tel. 812/311–7777).

Beriozka Stores The state-run dollar stores, known as *Beriozky* (little birch trees), also offer imported and Russian goods for foreign currency. The Russian-made goods here are cheaper than those found in other hard-currency stores, but the selection is increasingly limited. Apparently they are running into distribution problems as a result of economic reforms. Another drawback is that the Beriozka stores do not accept credit cards or traveler's checks. When it comes to cash, though, they aren't picky: virtually any convertible currency is accepted. The main stores are at 7/9 Nevsky Prospect (tel. 812/315–5162), 26 Bolshaya Morskaya ulitsa (tel. 812/314–6637), and 15 Morskaya Naberezhnaya (tel. 812/355–1875), across from the Pribaltiskaya Hotel and St. Petersburg's largest Beriozka. Generally open 10 AM to 8 PM,

Beriozka shops close for lunch, either from 1 to 2 or from 2 to 3.

Farmers' Markets As in Moscow, the farmers' markets are lively places where a colorful array of goods and foods are sold by individual farmers, often from out of town and sometimes from outside the Russian republic. In recent years the variety of goods available at the market (in Russian, *rynok*) has increased tremendously, as the distribution system of the old regime gradually deteriorates and the city becomes increasingly dependent on private farmers. While the tourist is not likely to make any major purchases at the farmers' market, it is fun to visit and browse. In addition to the fine cuts of meat, dairy products, and homemade jams and jellies, piles of fruits and vegetables can be found, even in winter. Try some homemade pickles or pickled garlic, a tasty local favorite. You can also find some finely knitted scarves, hats, and mittens. You are expected to bargain, and—as in any crowded area—watch out for pickpockets. St. Petersburg's most popular markets are the **Kuznechny Rynok,** 3 Kuznechny Pereulok, just outside the Vladimirskaya metro station; the **Sytny Rynok,** 3/5 Sytninskaya Ploshchad, in the Petrograd Side district, not far from the Gorkhovskaya metro station; and the huge, sprawling flea market known as **Sennoi Rynok,** Sennaya Ploshchad, at the exit from the subway station of the same name. Farmers' markets are generally open daily from 8 AM to 7 PM and usually close at 5 PM on Sunday.

Hard-Currency Stores As in Moscow, you may find it easiest to do all your shopping here. If you retain your receipt as proof that you paid in hard currency, you shouldn't have any trouble getting your purchases across the border. The souvenirs and works of "art" for sale are almost exclusively mass-produced, although occasionally hand-painted nesting dolls and *palekh* boxes appear—always at very high prices. The hard-currency store is especially good for convenience items that are difficult to find in the average Russian store. The best stores are the Irish-run **Baltic Star** stores, where the selection includes imported beer, wine, and hard liquor; foreign cigarettes; Finnish and Irish food products, including a variety of packaged cheeses, meats, and dairy products; bottled water from Ireland; cookies, candies, and other snack items; as well as health and beauty products. There are currently three such stores in St. Petersburg, all open from 8 AM to 10 or 11 at night, with no break for lunch. The largest is in the **Hotel Moskva,** across the street from the Alexander Nevsky Monastery (tel. 812/274–0012 or 812/274–0024); another is in the **Pribaltiskaya Hotel** on the western end of Vasilievsky Island and thus probably only convenient if you're staying at the hotel (tel. 812/356–4185); the third and smallest is in the **Astoria Hotel,** with its entrance on Malaya Morskaya ul., not far from St. Isaac's Cathedral (tel. 812/210–5860). The Baltic Star stores readily accept both credit cards and traveler's checks. Change is always given in dollars.

Souvenir Shops The goods available here are often mass-produced, with an arty look to appeal to the unsuspecting tourist. Prices, sometimes in rubles, sometimes in hard currency, are high by local standards and are based on world-market prices. These shops are springing up all over the city, sometimes in the most unusual spots but most often in hotels and surrounding areas. Some of the better shops include **Podarki, Suveniry,** (Bolshoi Prospect, Petrograd Side, tel. 812/232–2092); **Khudozhestvennyi Salon** (31 Nevsky Prospect, tel. 812/314–8081); **Khudozhestvennyi Promysli** (51 Nevsky Prospect, tel. 812/113–1495); and **Nasledie** (116 Nevsky Prospect, tel. 812/279–5067).

Sports and Fitness

Participant Sports

Unfortunately, athletic facilities in St. Petersburg are rather limited. As in Moscow, access to the municipal facilities is restricted and requires a special "doctor's certificate" attesting to the user's health. They are possible to get, but you'd have to spend at least a few hours at a Russian clinic to do so. The athletic facilities in the city's hotels, however, are open to nonguests and do not require a doctor's certificate.

Fitness Centers The health club in the **Grand Hotel Europe** offers a sparkling workout center, with brand-new Western training equipment, including a StairMaster. MTV keeps you entertained. Adjacent to the fitness room are a sauna and dipping pool. All this for a whopping $18 per visit, but there's no time limit. *Tel. 812/312–0072. Open weekdays 7 AM–10 PM, weekends 9–9.*

The fitness center at the **Astoria Hotel** is smaller, but its pool (10 meters) is by far the largest in the city's hotels. *Tel. 812/210–5869. Open weekdays 7:30 AM–10 PM, weekends 9–9. Fee for unlimited use of gym or pool, $13; for gym and pool, $20.*

Skating Rinks You can rent skates at the following rinks: **Moskovsky Park Pobedy** (25 ul. Kuznetsovskaya, tel. 812/298–0881; open Mon.–Fri. 2–9, Sat., and Sun. 4–9); **Tavrichesky Sad** (50 ul. Saltikova-Shchedrina, tel. 812/272–6044); and **Central Park of Culture and Rest** (4 Yelagin Ostrov, tel. 812/239–0911; open Mon.–Fri. 10-4, Sat. and Sun. 11–6).

Tennis Courts Public courts are located in the **Primorsky Park Pobedy** (Seaside Park of Victory, 9 Krestovsky Prospect, on Krestovsky Island, tel. 812/235–2146 or 812/230–1419). The park can be reached by riding Tram 21, 33, or 34 from the Vasileostrovskaya subway station.

Spectator Sports

Tickets for sporting events can be purchased at the sports arena immediately prior to the game or at one of the many theater box offices (*teatralnaya kassa*) located throughout the city: 22–24 Nevsky Prospect, 33 Nevsky Prospect, 42 Nevsky Prospect, 74 Nevsky Prospect, and 27 Sredny Prospect (Vasilievsky Island).

Basketball and Volleyball Basketball and Volleyball matches are held at **Yubilieny Sports Palace** (18 Prospect Dobroluybova, tel. 812/238–4122) and **Zimny Stadium** (2 Manezhnaya Ploshchad, tel. 812/315–5710). St. Petersburg's basketball team *Spartak* also sometimes hold games at the **Mozhaisky Military Sports Complex** (15 Zhdanovskaya ul).

Hockey and Volleyball Matches are held at the **Yubilieny Sports Palace** (18 Prospect Dobrolyubova, tel. 812/238–4122).

Soccer International matches are held at the **Lenin Stadium** (2-g Petrovsky Ostrov, tel. 812/238–4003) and at the **Kirov Stadium** (1 Morskoi Prospect, Krestovsky Ostrov, tel. 812/235–5435 or 812/235–5494).

Dining

In the age-old rivalry between Moscow and St. Petersburg, the capital is definitely winning when it comes to dining out. For such a large city, St. Petersburg's restaurant scene is unfortunately fairly limited. But if you look back into the not-so-distant past, when the best you could do was a large and rowdy state enterprise in one of the city's foreign hotels, it quickly becomes clear that things are getting better in St. Petersburg. Not only is there a vast array of newly opened cooperative and private restaurants, often specializing in the cuisine of the former Soviet republics, but there are also several first-class foreign enterprises serving imported food. If you are visiting St. Petersburg on an organized tour, chances are that after a few days of the same grisly meat and heavy sauces of typical hotel cuisine, you will be ready for the adventure that dining out can bring.

Landing a table in a good restaurant is not done on a whim: You must plan ahead. Reservations are almost always essential, especially in the evening, and you'll have better luck if you ask your hotel or tour guide for help—the best meals are often still had through connections. Keep in mind that dining out is an all-night affair. Most restaurants feature live entertainment, and eating out means not only a meal but drinking and dancing as well. Although you may find it in poor taste, the entertainment usually entails loud music, colorful light shows, and scantily clad dancers. Few restaurants offer no-smoking sections.

As with the shopping scene, St. Petersburg's restaurants can be divided roughly into categories based on the currency they accept and the clientele they seek to serve. Foreign-run enterprises aim at the growing foreign community and its tourist industry. Private and cooperative restaurants, which often accept both dollars and rubles, are far more expensive—and usually of much better quality—than the state-run restaurants operating exclusively in rubles. Whatever restaurant you choose, it is very likely to be beyond the budget of the average Russian, so you are not apt to meet many "typical" residents by eating out. You will, however, most likely encounter young Russian entrepreneurs, often still disparagingly referred to by their Soviet label of black marketeers.

Highly recommended restaurants are indicated by a star ★.

Category	Cost*
Very Expensive	over $40
Expensive	$25–$40
Moderate	$10–$25
Inexpensive	under $10

per person, excluding drinks and service

Very Expensive

★ **Europe.** This elegant restaurant in the Grand Hotel Europe is in a category all of its own. It offers luxury and fine dining of a kind that St. Petersburg has not seen since the 1917 Revolution. The breathtaking interior, complete with stained-glass roof and private balconies, seems fit for a czar. But then, so do the prices. The menu, which features European and Russian cuisines, is exotic by local standards, which may explain why all the ingredients for this restaurant are shipped in from Sweden. For starters, try the fresh goose liver, served with a honey-and-wine sauce. The main dishes vary, but a highlight is the fillet of salmon, filled with cream cheese and served with a wine-and-herb sauce. If you're not up for an opulent dinner, you may enjoy the popular Sunday morning jazz brunch. Don't think about it too long, though, because tables book up fast, especially in the summer. *1/7 Mikhailovskaya ul., in Grand Hotel Europe, tel. 812/312–0072. Reservations advised. Jacket and tie required at dinner. AE, MC. Hard currency only. Breakfast Mon.–Sat. 7–10, dinner daily 6–11, Sun. brunch 10–3.*

Venice. Situated among the gloomy high rises of Vasilievsky Island, this Italian-Russian joint venture is easy to spot: It's the only building in the area that isn't dominated by the color gray. Its distant location makes it truly convenient

St. Petersburg Dining and Lodging

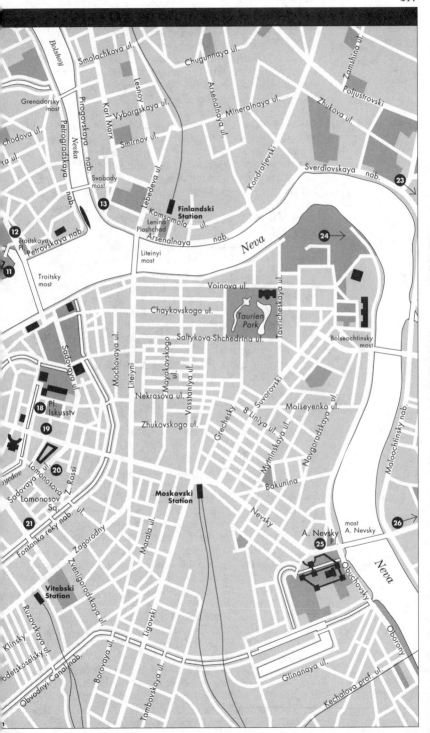

only for those already staying at the Pribaltiskaya Hotel, for whom the immaculate and snazzy interior is a welcome change of pace. The service, provided by formally dressed waiters, is rather pretentious and stiff, but the food is a delight. With an Italian chef and imported ingredients (right down to the flour and salt), the kitchen produces authentic pasta and Italian meat dishes. The computerized menu changes weekly depending on shipments, but standard offerings include Alfredo-style egg noodles and a tangy lasagna. The wide selection of Italian and other imported wines is unusual for St. Petersburg. Attached to the restaurant is an inexpensive pizzeria, which operates for rubles and is very popular with foreign students staying in the university dormitory across the street. *21 ul. Korablestroitelei, tel. 812/352–1432. Reservations advised. Jacket and tie advised. AE, DC, MC, V. Hard currency only. Open noon–midnight.*

Expensive

Angleterre. This pretty restaurant off the main lobby of the Angleterre Hotel offers average food at above-average prices. Though it advertises European cuisine, the unimaginative menu is dominated by standard Russian dishes, such as borscht, herring, and steak fillet with mushrooms. Considering the prices, which are outrageous by local standards, the food is a disappointment. What the restaurant lacks in culinary delights, however, it makes up for in atmosphere. The all-white interior is lit by crystal chandeliers and has views through the glass walls onto the exquisite lobby. The quiet piano music in the background brings back the hotel's better days at the turn of the century. The restaurant also offers a popular buffet breakfast, which comes with all the blini you can eat for a more reasonable $8. *39 Bolshaya Morskaya ul., tel. 812/210–5829. Reservations advised. Dress: casual but neat. AE, MC, V. Hard currency only. Open daily 7:30 AM–11:30 PM.*

Brasserie. This restaurant on the first floor of the Grand Hotel Europe is the perfect place for a refreshing Caesar salad or a regular hamburger with fries. The exotic menu—try the garlicky snails with tomato bread—features a plat du jour. The casual, relaxed atmosphere is combined with the hotel's efficient and excellent service: Nothing about the Brasserie will remind you of the stormy world of Nevsky Prospect just outside its doors. Come here when you need a break from Russian reality. *1/7 Mikhailovskaya ul., tel. 812/312–0072. Reservations accepted. Dress: casual but neat. AE, MC. Hard currency only. Open weekdays 11–11, weekends 3–11.*

★ **Vostok.** It's a long but pleasant ride out to this Indian joint venture, located in the picturesque Primorsky Park Pobedy (Seaside Park of Victory, not to be confused with the Victory Park on Moskovsky Prospect). The restaurant offers two halls and two menus, one for dollars and one for rubles.

In either, the authentic Indian food is worth the trip, although you get better service for dollars. For vegetarians weary of the meat-dominated Russian cuisine, the *dal makhani* (lentils cooked in butter and cream) or *sabs samosa* (fried vegetable pastries) offer a welcome change of pace. The kitchen also serves excellent chicken and mutton dishes, such as *murg chaat*, tender chicken marinated and barbecued in a tandoor and served with a spicy mint chutney sauce, or *achaar goshi*, slow-cooked lamb marinated in herbs and spices. The downstairs hall, open night and day, offers drab decor and few distractions. In the evening, the upstairs hall, a remodeled theater, offers a nightly cabaret and/or authentic Gypsy music and dance. The slanting floor and long booths lined up in rows allow every table a bird's-eye view of the stage below. Reservations aren't necessary during the day, but it's a good idea to call ahead of time anyway. Have your driver wait or come back for you after your meal—it's easy to get stranded on this isolated island. *Primorsky Park Pobedy, tel. 812/235–5984. Reservations advised. Dress: casual during day. Jacket and tie required at dinner. AE, DC, MC, V. Dollar menu is expensive; ruble menu is inexpensive. Open daily 1 PM–4:30 AM.*

Moderate

Bubovny Valet. Tucked away on a side street off Bolshoi Prospect in the Petrograd Side district, this modest private restaurant is run by former employees of Intourist. Although the restaurant claims to offer European cuisine, the menu is dominated by standard Russian dishes. The decor is pretentious and cold, but the food is well prepared and served by courteous waiters in formal dress. For appetizers, you can't go wrong with the blini, little pancakes served with black or red caviar. Another recommended Russian appetizer is the *griby v smetane* (mushrooms baked in creme sauce). Their excellent soups include *solyanka*, a spicy thick stew made with vegetables and meat or fish, and borscht. The dessert menu features fruit mousse and a rich Russian favorite, *Krem so smetanoi*, which is simply cream with sweetened sour cream (and countless calories). Beverages, alcoholic and nonalcoholic, are available only for hard currency (cash). The closest subway station is Petrogradskaya. *32 ul. Lenina (Shirokaya), tel. 812/230–8830. Reservations advised. Dress: casual but neat. No credit cards. Open daily noon–midnight. No credit cards. Rubles only (except for beverages).*

Chaika. This lively, smoke-filled restaurant and bar is popular with Hotel Europe staff and other expatriates. A German-Russian joint venture, it offers good, hearty food and great German beer. The interior is right out of Germany, and the food, except for such Russian delicacies as caviar, is dominated by dishes like frankfurters with sauerkraut. It's a great place to come on a rainy day for a piping hot bowl of French onion soup or Hungarian goulash.

The patrons are almost exclusively foreigners, who come here for a relaxing break from the frustrations of Russian life. *14 Kanala Griboyedova, tel. 812/312–4631. Reservations not accepted. Dress: casual. Open 11 AM–5 AM. No credit cards. Hard currency only; traveler's checks accepted.*

Chopsticks. It doesn't seem quite fair that in addition to St. Petersburg's best accommodations, finest restaurant, and hippest bar, the Grand Hotel Europe also lays claim to the city's best Chinese food. With Chinese chefs and authentic ingredients (supplies are imported), Chopsticks is in a league of its own. The Oriental decor combines with the hotel's renowned efficiency and service to produce an almost otherworldly experience. If you crave American-style Chinese food, this is a gold mine. But if you're looking for a taste of the real St. Petersburg, you won't find it here. *1/7 Mikhailovskaya ul., tel. 812/312–0072, ext. 6391. Reservations accepted. Dress: casual but neat. AE, MC. Hard currency only. Open daily noon–3, 6–11.*

Na Fontanke. This restaurant's reputation rests on its status as St. Petersburg's first cooperative. When it opened in 1988, it met with immediate and resounding success, in large part because it faced little competition. Even though Na Fontanke is no longer the only place in town, reservations are still essential and are best made several days in advance. Although the restaurant is right on the Fontanka (hence its name), there are no tables with a view of the city's canals: As in most Russian restaurants, all the windows are heavily draped. The one small dining room is elegantly decorated in blue and gold. The food is uninspired, but what it lacks in originality it makes up for in presentation. The prix fixe dinner includes an array of Russian appetizers (cold cuts, herring, mushrooms in cream sauce in a pastry shell), a main course, ice cream, and coffee. Alcoholic beverages are available for hard currency (cash) only. The nightly entertainment is a fascinating—if loud—extravaganza of authentic Gypsy music and dance. This is not the place for intimate dining and conversation. *77 Fontanka, tel. 812/310–2547. Reservations required. Dress: casual but neat. No credit cards. Rubles only (except for beverages). Open daily 1–5, 8–11:30.*

★ **Petrostar.** This is yet another newly opened private restaurant aiming to create an exclusive image. The sign on the door—BY INVITATION ONLY—scares the casual customer away. The staff, however, would welcome a foreign visitor, who probably wouldn't understand the warning anyway, since it's in Russian. The Petrostar (Peter Star) actually comes close to achieving the high level of fine dining that it cultivates. Tuxedo-clad waiters provide polite and friendly service. The interior has been carefully remodeled (a beer hall occupied the space) in the tradition of "Old St. Petersburg." The main dining hall features wood-paneled ceilings, airy white drapes (which actually let the sunshine in), and cast-iron wall lamps. Entertainment in the evening varies but sometimes includes an excellent, authentic Gypsy performance ensemble. The Petrostar proudly specializes in Russian and Ukrainian cuisines. Cold appetizers include black and red caviar, crab, and Georgian *satsivy* (spicy chicken in walnut sauce). The mushroom soup is excellent, and don't overlook the hot appetizer *pekantnaya* (ham slices stuffed with garlic and cheese). For your main course, try the excellent *Kievskaya kotleta* (chicken Kiev); the Petrostar's is about the best in the city. And best of all, when you're done with your meal, the staff will help you hail a cab home—a splendid service on a dark St. Petersburg winter night. *30 Bolshaya Pushkarskaya ul., tel. 812/232-4047. Reservations required. Jacket and tie advised. No credit cards. Rubles only. Open daily 11-11.*

Sadko. This lively, well-decorated restaurant and bar is yet another eating establishment of the Grand Hotel Europe. But here all the pomp and circumstance of the fancy new hotel are missing. Check your tie at the door and sit down for a refreshing (imported) draft beer and pizza. The blackboard menu, which changes daily, offers Western-style bar food, such as hamburgers, spare ribs, and pasta. The good food, fun atmosphere, and nightly entertainment, which features both top performers and up-and-coming new bands, make this one of the hottest spots in town for foreign tourists and students. The prices are reasonable enough to make it affordable for a few Russians as well. *1/7 Mikhailovskaya ul. (separate entrance from Grand Hotel Europe), tel. 812/210-3667. Reservations accepted. Dress: casual. Hard currency only. AE, MC. Open daily noon-midnight.*

Shvabsky Domik. You can tell the food here is authentic by the crowds of German expatriates who keep coming back for the schnitzel and wurst. The simple decor, with heavy wood paneling and long wooden benches, makes for a relaxed and pleasant atmosphere. The waitresses, all in German national dress, aim to please and offer a pleasant change of pace from the usual harried service. Unlike most restaurants in St. Petersburg, advance reservations aren't necessary. Combine that with the quick service and location—right outside the Krasnogvardeiskaya subway station—and this becomes a good stop for a quick meal on those days when you haven't planned ahead. A German-Russian joint venture, the restaurant specializes almost exclusively in German cuisine, with a few Russian appetizers like blini with caviar or cabbage soup thrown in for variety. The kitchen produces its own homemade pretzels, the *Shvabski Brezel*. Wash down your sausage and sauerkraut with a cold mug of refreshing German draft beer. *28/19 Krasnogvardeivsky Prospect, tel. 812/528-2211. Reservations accepted. Dress: casual. AE, DC, MC, V. Hard currency only. Open daily 11 AM-2 AM.*

Inexpensive

Austeria. This state-run restaurant inside the Peter and Paul Fortress dates from the reign of Peter the Great. Formerly an officer's club (hosteria), the restaurant offers Russian cuisine in an 18th-century setting. Handcrafted, cast-iron chandeliers provide the lighting, while the thick stone walls and fully draped windows create the somber atmosphere appropriate to a fortress. The cooking isn't exactly gourmet, but the appetizers and soups are consistently good, and prices are very reasonable. For starters, try the *Petrovsky shchi* (cabbage soup), served in a crock topped by a pastry shell. The kitchen does a good job with the St. Petersburg fillet, a local favorite served with a creamy mushroom sauce. Since this restaurant is state-run, many items on the menu may not be available when you visit. The restaurant is rarely crowded, but since it closes for private parties or tourist groups, it's best to call ahead. It's located inside the fortress's outer fortification wall, a short walk to your left after entering through the Ivan Gate. The cast-iron sign above the entrance can be easy to miss. *Peter and Paul Fortress, tel. 812/238–4262. Reservations advised. Dress: casual but neat. No credit cards. Rubles only. Open daily noon–5, 6–1.*

★ **Dom Arkhitektorov.** Previously open only to members of the Architecture Union, this little-known restaurant is located in a beautiful 18th-century mansion just off St. Isaac's Square. The dazzling interior features carved oak paneling, ceiling paintings, brass chandeliers, and gilded window frames. Its astounding beauty has somehow remained a secret, and unlike other elegant dining establishments, the place is not swarming with tourists. The cuisine, unfortunately, is far less appealing than the decor. The kitchen offers simply prepared meat and fish appetizers, as well as standard Russian dishes. The house specialty, *Myaso po Arkhitektorsky*, is a beef dish baked in a mayonnaise sauce and topped with thinly sliced potatoes. This is obviously not gourmet food, but with interiors like these it doesn't matter. If you're nice to the friendly waitresses, they may let you take a peek upstairs at the oak-paneled library and gilded ballroom. *52 ul. Bolshaya Morskaya, tel. 812/311–0531 or 812/312–5085. Reservations advised. Dress: casual but neat. No credit cards. Rubles only. Open Mon.–Sat. noon–4, 5–10.*

Fortesia. This was one of St. Petersburg's first joint-venture restaurants, and the staff let success go to their head: Service tends to be cold and patronizing. The kitchen theoretically specializes in Belgian and Russian cuisines, but the menu is dominated by unimaginatively prepared Russian dishes. Despite the drawbacks, the restaurant remains very popular, thanks to its proximity to the Peter and Paul Fortress and its cozy atmosphere. The deafening "musical" entertainment found in most St. Petersburg restaurants is happily missing. As long as you don't have your heart set on fine Belgian cooking, this is a good place for a quiet evening of dining and conversation. Stick to the simpler dishes: It's hard to go wrong with caviar-filled blini or grilled sturgeon. Some items, such as caviar and alcoholic beverages, are available for hard currency only (cash). *7 Bolshaya Dvoryanskaya ul., tel. 812/233–9468. Reservations advised. Dress: casual. No credit cards. Rubles and dollars. Open daily noon–5, 7–11.*

Hebei. This private enterprise in the Petrograd Side district recently joined the ranks of the city's Chinese restaurants. The colorful wood carvings and Chinese lanterns adorning the entranceway make it hard to miss among the gloomy apartment buildings lining Bolshoi Prospect. The restaurant is located one flight up (bypass the dingy looking "Korean" café on the first floor). The interior, apart from highly ornate ceiling decorations and a few Chinese lanterns, is typical of any Russian restaurant: wallpaper painted to look like brick, plastic-covered windows imitating stained glass. What it lacks in atmosphere, however, it makes up for in friendly service and reasonable prices. The chefs are Chinese, but the dishes are predominantly Russian-oriented, with ingredients from the local markets. An exception is the *Svetnyie Macaroni*, clear rice noodles imported from China and prepared with Chinese spices and whatever vegetables are in season. For your main course, try the house specialty, *Kura po Hebeiski* (Hebei chicken), or *Govyadino po Gunbao*, strips of beef prepared with soy sauce and vegetables (a real delicacy in these parts). *61 Bolshoi Prospect, tel. 812/233–2046. Reservations accepted. Dress: casual. No credit cards. Rubles only. Open daily 1–10.*

Metropole. Centrally located near Gostinyi Dvor and just off Nevsky Prospect, this faded, state-run restaurant was once one of St. Petersburg's finest. Today it faces stiff competition, and the kitchen is having trouble keeping up with the city's foreign-run joint ventures. The menu offers standard Russian fare, such as chicken Kiev and fried perch. The selection of *zakuski* (hors d'oeuvres) is good, but the main courses tend to be heavy on the sauces and fried potatoes. Where the Metropole has the city's shiny new cooperatives beat is in atmosphere. Opened in 1898, it's the city's oldest restaurant, and its atmosphere can't be reproduced with modern decor—no matter how tasteful. Although it has clearly seen better days, the marble pillars, ceiling moldings, and crystal chandeliers still exude a sense of faded elegance. For a price, you can reserve one of the private balcony rooms (which accommodate up to 30 people) overlooking the main dining hall. Russian pop bands provide nightly entertainment. If you want to mingle and dance with the locals, ask for a table in the main hall. There is a limited selection of wine—but plenty of Russian vodka and champagne. Except for the unpleasant reception you might get from the grouchy man guarding the front door, service here is pleasant, although typically slow. *22 ul.*

Sadovaya, tel. 812/310–1845. Reservations advised. Dress: casual but neat. No credit cards. Rubles only. Open daily noon–midnight.

Saigon Neva. Don't be fooled by the name—you'll find nothing but Russian cooking at this pleasant restaurant located just a block off St. Isaac's Square. And don't be fooled by the finely remodeled interior. The Vietnamese partners in this newly opened private restaurant pulled out at the last minute, but the Saigon Neva opened its doors anyway. It's a lovely, quiet place in which to take a break from the hustle and bustle of downtown St. Petersburg. The menu is standard Russian fare. The varying selection of main dishes, although pleasantly prepared, are heavily laden with french fries and oily vegetables. The appetizers and soups are better. Try the house specialty, *Griby po Domashnemy* (homestyle mushrooms), served with a heavy sauce inside light pastry shells. If you like squid, you'll enjoy the *Stolichnyi Salat,* prepared with onions and radishes in a mayonnaise base. The chicken soup comes with a tasty open-faced grilled cheese sandwich. Where the Saigon Neva is ahead of the competition is in its soothing atmosphere, complete with background music that's quiet enough to allow conversation. *33 ul. Plekhanova (Kazanskaya), tel. 812/315–3772 or 812/314-9301. Reservations accepted. Dress: casual. No credit cards. Rubles only. Open daily 1–11.*

Tbilisi. One of St. Petersburg's first cooperatives, the Tbilisi was immediately besieged by hungry crowds eager for a decent restaurant, and it made it into just about every guidebook on the city. Today it is definitely the worse for wear. In addition to the thick clouds of smoke, its shady clientele makes for a seedy atmosphere, especially in the evenings. During the day, however, it's a great place to try some Georgian food (it's named after the capital of the former Soviet republic), provided loud music doesn't curb your appetite. Despite the rowdy crowds, the service is friendly. The food is much better than the atmosphere and reasonably priced. The *lobio* (butter beans in a spicy sauce), satsivy, and *kharcho* (a spicy meat soup) are the best in town. Lobio, served warm, is also available as a main course and is highly recommended. Don't forget to order *lavash* (Georgian bread) and *khachapuri* (cheese-filled fried dough). Georgian wine and German beer are available for hard currency (cash); cognac and Soviet champagne (when available) are sold for rubles. Located near the Gorkhovskaya metro station. *10 Sytninskaya ul. tel. 812/ 232–9391. Reservations advised. Dress: casual. No credit cards. Open daily noon–10. Rubles only (except for some alcoholic beverages).*

★ **Tete-à-Tete.** As its name suggests, this exclusive private restaurant, which has just one small dining room, specializes in French cuisine. Tables are available only by advance booking, and the front door is bolted shut to keep unwanted customers from entering "off the streets." (If you have a reservation, ring the bell.) Although the chef is clearly not from Paris, the kitchen does a credible job of producing French dishes with locally procured ingredients. For starters, try the rich and creamy onion soup, or the *julienne s gribami*, served in a cream sauce with mushrooms and onions. The French menu also features *myaso po Milanski*, grilled beef wrapped inside a cheese omelet and served with a heavy mushroom cream sauce. The classically designed interior suits the restaurant's exclusive image well. In the evenings, the grand piano tucked away in the corner provides light background music. The fully draped windows and dim lighting further add to the intimate atmosphere. *65 Bolshoi Prospect, near Petrogradskaya metro station, tel. 812/232–7548. Reservations required. Jacket and tie required. No credit cards. Open daily 1–5, 7–midnight. Rubles only.*

Lodging

St. Petersburg's hotel industry has undergone some major changes in recent years. Until the late 1980s, all of the city's hotels were controlled by Intourist, the Soviet tourist agency that enjoyed a monopoly over the tourist trade. Rates for foreign tourists were standardized, and there were few distinctions in service and facilities from one hotel to the next. Perestroika—and St. Petersburg's sudden rise in popularity as a tourist destination—changed all this. The influx of tourists prompted foreign contractors to launch major renovation projects, and two of the city's most prestigious hotels, the Grand Hotel Europe and the Astoria Hotel, have recently reopened after major reconstruction.

The choices are still limited, however. There are few inexpensive hotels catering to foreign tourists. The least expensive way to visit the city is through a tour operator. But if you are on an organized tour, you are not likely to land in one of the newly renovated hotels. Most U.S. and British tour operators are taking advantage of deeply discounted rates available to them at the old Intourist standbys and usually place groups at the Moskva, the Pribaltiskaya, the Pulkhovskaya, or the St. Petersburg (formerly Leningrad). These hotels were built in the late 1970s and early '80s, and offer similar facilities. The service, though mildly unpredictable, is perfectly acceptable—provided you are not expecting royal treatment.

All prices are quoted in dollars; hotels always require payment in foreign currency and do not accept rubles.

Highly recommended lodgings in each price category are indicated by a star ★.

Category	Cost*
Very Expensive	over $200
Expensive	$140–$200
Moderate	$65–$140
Inexpensive	under $65

All prices are for a standard double room for two, excluding service charge.

Very Expensive

Astoria. Reopened in 1991 after major reconstruction, the Astoria is actually two hotels: It interconnects with the Angleterre, where the poet Sergei Yesenin committed suicide in 1925. Originally built in the style Moderne in 1910–12, it was one of St. Petersburg's most renowned hotels before the 1917 Revolution. Its renovation by Finnish contractors was bitterly opposed by many residents, as plans called for the complete destruction of the original building where Yesenin died. The contractors won out, and their renovations produced a fine hotel: Not a trace of St. Petersburg's dusty streets can be found. The splendid interior has been decorated using antiques retrieved from various museums. Adding to the hotel's attraction is its convenient location in the heart of downtown St. Petersburg, directly across the street from St. Isaac's Cathedral and a 10-minute walk from the Hermitage. The lackluster service, however, is disappointing, and standards of efficiency have a long way to go. The Astoria still boasts some of the city's highest room rates: Its three-room deluxe suite, with private sauna, goes for $600 a night, even in the off-season. *39 Bolshaya Morskaya ul., tel. 812/315–2676, 812/210–5010, or 812/210–5020, fax 812/315–9668. 436 rooms with bath. Facilities: 2 restaurants, 2 cafés, beer hall, nightclub, fitness center with pool and sauna, business center with satellite telephone, excursion bureau, hard-currency shops.*

★ **Grand Hotel Europe.** This five-star hotel is without question the finest in town. Reopened in 1991 after extensive renovations, it offers all the elegance of prerevolutionary St. Petersburg along with every modern amenity. Its stunning Baroque facade has been carefully restored, while the Art Nouveau interior, with its stained-glass windows and authentic antique furniture, brings back the past glory. (Some people complain because the original interior was largely destroyed during renovations.) The hotel is operated as a Russian-Swedish joint venture and is managed by Reso Hotels of Sweden. The Russian staff has been carefully trained in European standards of excellence, and the service shines. The Swedish management has thought of everything: 24-hour room service, direct-dial international telephone, mail service via courier to Helsinki, and satellite TV and radio, with CNN and MTV programming. The central location can't be beat: Nevsky Prospect, the Hermitage, and the Square of the Arts are all within walking distance. If money is no object, this is the place to stay. *1/7 Mikhailovskaya ul., tel. 812/113–8066, fax 812/311–4465. 211 standard rooms with bath, 17 junior suites, 18 terrace rooms, 23 penthouse suites, 26 2-room suites, 4 executive suites, 2 deluxe suites. Facilities: 4 restaurants, café, bar, nightclub, sauna, health club, banquet and conference facilities. Traveler's checks accepted. AE, MC.*

Expensive

Olympia. The Olympia is actually a Swedish ocean liner permanently moored at St. Petersburg's sea passenger terminal, situated on the western edge of Vasilievsky Island. Swedish-managed (by the same firm that operates the luxurious Grand Hotel Europe), the hotel offers excellent service and all the modern amenities of a three-star Western hotel. Although the ocean liner recently underwent renovations (in Sweden) that doubled the size of the cabins, the accommodations are still cramped. The interior decor is unimaginative, and following renovations, every room now has two sides that mirror each other, with two tiny, identical bathrooms. With its low ceilings and brass railings lining the corridors, you never forget you're on a ship, although it rarely rocks, even in windy weather. Unusual for Russia, the hotel offers several no-smoking rooms. The isolated location is a drawback, but the hotel offers its guests complimentary shuttle service on the hour to the more centrally located Grand Europe Hotel. *Ploshchad Morskoi Slavy, tel. 812/217–8054, satellite tel. 873/137–0316, satellite fax 873/137–0317. 146 rooms with shower. Facilities: restaurant, 2 bars, satellite TV and telephone, sauna and fitness center, conference facilities, limited excursion bureau, mail service via courier to Finland. AE, DC, MC, V.*

Pribaltiskaya. Swedish-built but Soviet-designed, this huge 16-story skyscraper is popular with tourist groups. Opened in 1978, it was formerly the city's most luxurious hotel and still offers the best service and accommodations of the old Intourist hotels. The rooms are clean and all come with cable television (including CNN and MTV). The modest furnishings are adequate, although slightly worn. The major drawback is the location: Far out on the western tip of Vasilievsky Island, the hotel is a good 20-minute drive to downtown St. Petersburg, and the closest subway station is several bus stops away. The predominantly residential area offers rows and rows of benumbing Soviet-era high rises— but very few shops and restaurants. If you can stand the isolation, the views of the Gulf of Finland are phenomenal, especially at sunset (ask for a room on the western side of the hotel). Another plus is the hotel's well-stocked "Baltic Store" hard-currency shop, where you can pick up bottled water, imported snack foods, and a fairly recent copy of the

International Herald-Tribune or *USA Today. 14 ul. Kor-
ablestroiteli, tel. 812/356–4135 or 812/356–5112, fax 812/
356–0094. Facilities: 11 restaurants, 10 snack bars, 5 bars,
bowling alley, sauna with dipping pool, banquet and conference facilities, hard-currency shop, excursion bureau,
exchange bureau. Traveler's checks accepted. AE, V, MC.*

★ **Pulkhovskaya.** Opened in 1981, this Finnish-built hotel has
withstood heavy tourist traffic, and its attractive Scandi-
navian-designed interior has been surprisingly well maintained. Accommodations are on the same level as the
Pribaltiskaya (*see above*), although the rooms are slightly
cleaner and more attractive. Service is friendly and efficient by local standards. Unusual for a Russian hotel, the
curtains and bedspreads actually match the upholstery;
and the bathrooms, complete with Finnish plumbing, are
relatively large. The outdated telephone system, which
continually disabled all the room phones, should be working
soon. Again, the disadvantage here is location. The hotel is
convenient only to the airport; the subway is a 10-minute
walk away, and the ride into town takes at least 20 minutes.
But in contrast to the Pribaltiskaya's surroundings, the
area around the Pulkhovskaya has plenty of shops and even
a restaurant or two. The views, though, are dismal: You
have a choice of gloomy high rises and smokestacks or the
severe, very Soviet, Victory Square monument outside the
hotel's main entrance. *1 Ploshchad Pobedy, tel. 812/264–
5122, from abroad 812/264–5844, fax 812/264–6396. 850
rooms with bath, telephone, TV, refrigerator. Facilities: 2
restaurants, 6 snack bars, 6 bars, 2 saunas and dipping
pool, business center, excursion bureau, gift and souvenir
shops. AE, DC, MC, V.*

Moderate

Moskva. The unimaginative and depressing decor at this
huge, aging hotel is yet another prime example of Brezhnev-era design. Formerly one of the city's best hotels, the
Moskva now ranks among the most dismal of the old
Intourist standbys. Store up on patience before checking
in, because the lackluster service can make even paying
your bill a frustrating experience; the desk clerks spend
more time at lunch and on the phone than they do serving
guests. The dreary rooms and public areas show obvious
signs of neglect, but the hotel management is slowly beginning to make renovations. Electronic-strip locks are to be
installed soon, which should provide a sense of security
from the seedy mobs hanging out at the main entrance. Despite the drawbacks, the hotel has its advantages. It is located literally on top of the subway and faces the entrance
to the 18th-century Alexander Nevsky Monastery. Another plus is the hard-currency Baltic Star store, where you
can supplement the hotel restaurant's bland cuisine with
imported crackers and salami. Rates are on the low end of
the Moderate category. *2 Ploshchad Alexandra Nevskovo,*

tel. 812/274–2051 or 812/274–2052, fax 812/274–2130. 770 rooms with bath. Facilities: restaurant, 7 snack bars, 5 bars, excursion bureau, exchange bureau (traveler's checks accepted), business center, souvenir and gift shops. AE, DC, MC, V.

★ **Okhtinskaya.** The location, directly across the river from the Baroque Smolny Sobor, is great for views but terribly inconvenient if you ever plan on going anywhere by public transportation. St. Petersburg's museums and tourist attractions are all on the other side of the river, and the subway is several bus stops away. Canadian-built and opened in 1991, the hotel is now run as a French-Russian joint venture. Service is unusually friendly, and the rates are extremely reasonable for this overpriced city. Although the interior features the usual marble-and-chrome decor, the public areas are cheery and bright and, most important, devoid of the ubiquitous slot machines. The rooms are clean and well appointed, with imported furnishings and pretty, flowered wallpaper. While almost all the rooms come with balconies, only the suites have full baths. Unfortunately only one room on every floor faces the cathedral, but the views of the urban landscape on this side of town are more refreshing than most. *4 Bolsheokhtinsky Prospect, tel. 812/ 227–4438, fax 812/227–2618. 204 rooms with bath or shower. Facilities: 2 restaurants, snack bar, 2 bars, sauna, hard-currency gift shop, grocery store. AE, DC, MC, V.*

★ **St. Petersburg.** Formerly called the Leningrad, this aging luxury hotel offers both the best and worst views of contemporary St. Petersburg. While the rooms overlooking the Neva have magnificent vistas of the city's waterfront architecture, rooms on the opposite side face the half-completed cement skeleton of the hotel's forthcoming addition (construction has been halted due to lack of funds). The hotel has also been slow to repair the damage to its top stories caused by a 1991 fire, and only the first five floors are currently open to guests. While this is definitely not the luxury hotel it once was, if you can land a waterfront room, it is the only place to stay during the White Nights. The Finnish-decorated interior is faded and the furnishings are a bit worn, but the rooms and public areas are clean. The lobby offers an array of hard-currency stores, including souvenir and gift shops. The location, however, is good only for the views. The Finland Train Station and subway are within walking distance, but the route is unpleasant and takes you along a busy highway. *5/2 Vyborskaya Naberezhnaya, tel. 812/542–9411, fax 812/248–8002. 410 rooms with bath. Facilities: 2 restaurants, 3 snack bars, 3 bars, sauna with dipping pool, excursion bureau, exchange bureau, business center, shops, conference facilities. DC, MC, V.*

Sovietskaya. The name says it all: This is a Soviet hotel with the typically slow and disgruntled service of a state-run enterprise. Yet another concrete-and-steel monstrosity, the hotel is in an attractive section of downtown St. Petersburg. While the location allows for some good views of St.

Petersburg's canals, it's a long walk to just about any-where, including the subway. There are two buildings, both built in the late 1960s, but the "newer wing" was recently remodeled. All rooms in both wings are relatively clean and have decent views. But accommodations in the "new" wing are generally in better shape and come with Finnish furnishings (and higher rates). The hotel was originally intended for foreign tourists, but not until recently could a foreigner legally book a room here. Someone discovered—after the hotel was built—that some rooms had a bird's-eye view of the once "secret" dockyards of the Admiralty. Luckily things have changed since then, although the hotel staff hasn't seemed to notice. *43/1 Lermontovsky Prospect, tel. 812/259–2552 or 812/259–2652, fax 812/251–8890. 1,099 rooms with bath. Facilities: 3 restaurants, café, 4 snack bars, 3 bars, sauna with dipping pool, business center, excursion bureau. No credit cards.*

Inexpensive

★ **Gorny.** This unusual hotel is actually a renovated dormitory belonging to the wealthy St. Petersburg Institute of Mining (Gorny Institute). The rooms on the lower floors are reserved for foreign students studying Russian at the institute, while the upper floors have been painstakingly renovated to meet hotel standards. Although the building itself, a typical modern high rise, is far from luxurious, the rooms are clean and nicely appointed, with German furnishings and imported decor. All the rooms are actually suites, with kitchen facilities available at the end of the corridor. The only drawback here is location: the western tip of Vasilievsky Island. The Gorny will, however, provide local transportation as needed (for an additional fee). This is a good choice for budget-minded tourists who want to get closer to real life in Russia without really experiencing the hassles that go along with it. No one on the staff speaks English all that well, but you can fax in English for a reservation. *15 Morskaya Naberezhnaya, Bldg. 3, tel. 812/218–8605 or 812/218–8681, fax 812/218–5463. 50 rooms with bath. Facilities: 2 cafés. Traveler's checks accepted. No credit cards.*

Karelia. Situated in a gloomy residential area dominated by monotonous and crumbling high rises, this former Intourist hotel is a prime example of Brezhnev-era architecture. Built for the 1980 Olympics, it looks a lot older than its years. The lobby, decorated with gaudy, socialist-realist paintings depicting an outdated Leningrad, is dismal and smoky. Service, however, is surprisingly friendly, and the rates are the best in town. The double and triple rooms (no singles available) are adequate and relatively clean, and the friendly floor attendants willingly address complaints. While the decor is less than attractive (bedspreads, curtains, and carpets are all different colors), the furnishings have been imported from Finland, and the beds are more comfortable than most. Some rooms come with television, and all come with telephone and balcony (and dreary views). For tourists on a budget who don't mind long excursions on the city's unreliable trolley buses, the hotel offers bearable if far from luxurious accommodations. But if you're not counting your rubles, stay elsewhere. *27/2 ul. Tukhachevskovo, tel. 812/226-3515, fax 812/226-3511. 430 rooms with bath or shower. Facilities: restaurant, 5 snack bars, 3 bars, casino, disco, excursion bureau, business center with satellite telephone and fax, sauna. Traveler's checks accepted. AE, DC, MC, V.*

The Arts and Nightlife

The Arts

St. Petersburg's status as Russia's cultural capital is well deserved; its cultural life is one of the city's top attractions. Except for the most renowned theaters, tickets are easily available and ridiculously inexpensive. You can buy them at the theaters themselves and at theater kiosks (*teatralnaya kassa*) located throughout the city. For performances at the Mariinsky Theater (better known in the West by its Soviet name, Kirov) and the Maly Theater of Ballet and Opera you have two choices: Pay the inflated rates charged by hotel excursion bureaus (which start at $42 for the Kirov) or buy a ticket from a scalper outside the theater just before the performance. The second route is invariably cheaper, although there's no guarantee that your seat will have a view of the stage.

Even if you're not staying at the Astoria Hotel, you're welcome to use their service bureau (tel. 812/210-5046) for booking theater tickets. Most hotels post performance listings in their main lobby. The quarterly English-language magazine *Petersburg News* also carries theater and concert listings.

Special musical performances are usually organized for the White Nights' Festival, held in the last two weeks of June. After that, most major theaters close down for the summer and start up again in mid-September.

Concerts Classical music can be enjoyed all over the city. The famous **St. Petersburg Shostakovich Philharmonic** (2 ul. Mikhailovskaya, tel. 812/311-7333) offers excellent performances in its concert hall on the Square of Arts, located in a former Nobleman's Club. Concerts are also given in the Philharmonic's **Maly Zal imeni Glinki** (Little Glinka Hall) around the corner (30 Nevsky Prospect, tel. 812/311-8333). One of St. Petersburg's best-kept secrets is its lovely **Glinka Kapella Choral Hall** (20 Nab. Reki Moiki, tel. 812/314-1058), where not only choral recitals but also symphonic, instrumental, and vocal concerts are held. The theater dates from the 1880s, and many famous musicians, including Glinka and Rimsky-Korsakov, have performed here.

For a relaxing evening of classical music in a prerevolutionary setting, try one of the concert halls in St. Petersburg's mansions and palaces. Performances are held regularly in the **Beloselsky-Belozersky Palace** (41 Nevsky Prospect, tel. 812/311–1384), **Mathilde Kshessinskaya's Mansion** (4 ul. Bolshaya Dvoryanskaya, tel. 812/233–7052), and the **Smolny Cathedral and Convent** (3 Ploshchad Rastrelli, tel. 812/542–0942).

Other major concert halls include the **Oktyabrski Bolshoi Concert Hall** (6 Ligovskii Prospect, tel. 812/277–7400) and the **St. Petersburg Music Hall** (1 Ploshchad Lenina, tel. 812/542–9422).

Opera and Ballet The world-renowned **Mariinsky Theater of Opera and Ballet** (1/2 Teatralnaya Ploshchad, tel. 812/114–4344) is not to be missed. Its elegant blue-and-gold auditorium has been the main home of the Russian ballet since the 1880s. The lesser-known **Maly Theater of Opera and Ballet** (1 Ploshchad Iskusstv, tel. 812/314–3758) also offers outstanding performances but at much lower prices. Operas are usually sung in Russian, and the repertoire is dominated by Russian composers.

Theater St. Petersburg also offers some excellent dramatic theaters, but performances are almost exclusively in Russian. Even if you can't understand the dialogue, you may want to visit the famous **Bolshoi Drama Theater** (Nab. Reki Fontanki, tel. 812/310–9242) or Russia's oldest theater, the elegant **Pushkin Drama Theater** (2 Ploshchad Ostrovskovo, tel. 812/312–1545), where the repertoire is dominated by the classics.

Nightlife

Compared with Moscow, which is bursting at the seams with hot new night spots, St. Petersburg borders on tame. Although discos and bars pop up spontaneously here and there, nightlife still centers on restaurants and hotels. Many restaurants offer musical entertainment and dancing for their guests; check the dining listings for details.

A note about security: Though media reports on increased crime in Russia exaggerate the situation, foreigners in this economically strapped country are easy prey for robbery and muggings. Use common sense and stay away from the sleazy bars and clubs where prostitution thrives and black marketeers use their earnings to reach a drunken bliss. If you plan to spend the evening outside your hotel, make arrangements for the trip home before setting out. Although there are virtually no after-dark hours during the White Nights, a late-evening stroll down Nevsky Prospect may be an invitation to trouble.

Bars and Lounges All the major hotels have bars and nightclubs, but except for the Astoria and Grand Hotel Europe, the local clientele is often of questionable intention and the atmosphere tends to get sleazy as the night wears on.

One of the hottest spots in town is **Sadko** (Grand Hotel Europe, 1/7 ul. Mikhailovskaya, tel. 812/210–3667). Nightly entertainment features top performers, such as the zany Sergei Kuriyokin, and a Russian reggae band. The crowds are mostly foreign tourists and students, with only a few very rich Russians mixed in—but that's par for the course in the current two-tiered economy and the price you pay for security. The hotel's Swedish management rid the place of the mafia thugs who hung out here by instituting a hard-currency-only policy.

Vostok, an Indian restaurant located in the faraway Primorsky Park Pobedy (*see* Dining, *above*), stages a musical cabaret as well as a wild extravaganza of Gypsy music and dance (cover charge: $10).

Casinos The casino fever that has taken Moscow by storm hasn't quite hit St. Petersburg yet. The Astoria Hotel has plans to open a casino soon, and the floating Olympia Hotel may open theirs again as well. Both **Vostok** (*see above*) and **Nevskye Melodyie** (*see below*) have casinos attached to their restaurants.

Discos The nightclub on the fifth floor of the **Grand Hotel Europe** (tel. 812/210–3667) offers two dance floors, as well as a dazzling view of St. Petersburg's rooftops (jacket and tie required; cover charge: $10).

The Russian-Swedish joint venture **Nevskye Meldoyie** (62 nab. Sverdlovskaya, tel. 812/227–2676) has a hopping dance floor, an all-night casino, and an erotic floor show that is definitely a matter of taste. This night spot is extremely popular with St. Petersburg's nouveaux riches.

Jazz The one and only place to hear Russia's top jazz musicians is the St. Petersburg **Jazz Philharmonic Hall** (27 Zagorodny Prospect, near the Pushkinskaya metro station, tel. 812/164–8565). Regular performances by the world-renowned **Leningrad Dixieland Band** and **David Goloshchyokin's Ensemble** make this a favorite night spot. Serious jazz lovers will enjoy the fantastic atmosphere in this turn-of-the-century building, originally commissioned as an exhibit hall for the porcelain-factory owner Kuznetsov. Black-and-white photographs of Dizzy Gillespie and other American jazz greats cover the walls. Light sandwiches and beverages are available for rubles and hard currency. The hall opens at 7 PM, and concerts begin at 8. Reserve a table in advance; performances sell out fast (the ticket office is open Mon. 2–7, Tues.–Sun. 2–8). On Monday the mike is open for freewheeling jam sessions.

4 Kiev

By Juliette
Shapland

Think of your trip to Kiev as a time machine that will hurl you back into the earliest pages of Russian history. Kiev (in Ukrainian, Kiyv) is known as the Mother of Russia, for it was here, around the end of the 9th century, that Russian civilization began. Although it is a bustling modern metropolis—the capital of a newly independent Ukraine—the city's identity is closely tied to its ancient past and founding role in the development of Russian culture. Between the 10th and 12th centuries Kiev flourished as the capital of Rus, as the lands of the Eastern Slavs were then known, and was an important cultural, political, and economic center. Its gradual decline began in the late 1100s, ending abruptly in 1240, when the city was razed to the ground by Mongol invaders. Since that time, Kiev has been the capital of an independent nation for only brief periods. Freed from the Mongol yoke in the 14th century, it fell under the rule of the Lithuanians and then the Poles. In 1654, choosing the lesser of two evils, Ukraine joined the Russian empire.

Much of what is known of Kiev's early history comes from the *Primary Chronicle*, written in the 11th–12th centuries by monks at Kiev's Monastery of the Caves. According to the chronicles, "There were three brothers . . . Kii lived upon the hill where the Borich trail now is; and Shchek dwelled upon the hill now named Shchekovitza; while on the third resided Khoriv, after whom this hill is named Khorevitsa. They built a town and named it Kiev after their oldest brother." Archaeological findings confirm that there was indeed a settlement called Kii around the end of the 6th century, and the hills still exist. You will see them and the golden domes of Kiev's ancient churches rising above the green expanses that carpet the hilly terrain and vast plains.

The city has seen its full share of violence and bloodshed, which, along with its ancient glory, is an essential key to understanding today's Kiev. In the aftermath of the Bolshevik Revolution and the ensuing civil war, Kiev saw bitter fighting, which pitted brother against brother. The city suffered heavy losses and was nearly destroyed again during World War II, when it was captured and held by German forces for almost 800 days. Its most recent tragedy came in 1986, when the Chernobyl nuclear power reactor, just 104 kilometers (65 miles) north of the city, exploded, spewing radioactive materials into the air and into the city's water supply. Scientists affirm that Kiev is now safe for visitors, but residents will feel the effects of the accident for decades to come.

Kiev straddles the wide Dnieper River. To the east lie the steep hills of Old Kiev, while to the west you will find the newly developed regions of the low-lying left bank. The political and industrial center of modern Ukraine, Kiev displays both the tranquillity of its ancient past and the frenzy of a newly independent nation grappling with the political and economic problems inherited from 70 years of Soviet rule.

Essential Information

Important Addresses and Numbers

Tourist Information The closest thing Kiev has to a tourist information bureau is the former Ukrainian branch of Soviet Intourist, now known as **Intourist-Kiev** (12 vul. Gospitalna, in the Hotel Intourist, tel. 044/225–3243). You can also obtain tourist information at the excursion bureaus of major hotels. The only printed materials available are outdated, Soviet-produced booklets, which are heavy on propaganda and scant on information.

Consulates **United States** (10 vul. Yuria Kotsyubinskovo, tel. 044/244–7349 or 044/244–7354), **Canada** (31 Yaroslaviv Val, tel. 044/212–2235), and **United Kingdom** (9 Desyatinna vul. tel. 044/228–0504).

Emergencies **Police** (tel. 02), **ambulance** (tel. 03). As in Moscow and St. Petersburg, you are unlikely to get an English-speaking operator if you call these emergency numbers. Medical facilities are far below world standards, and Kiev is plagued by the same shortages of basic medical supplies and equipment that afflict Moscow and St. Petersburg. In a true emergency, evacuation to Finland or Western Europe should be considered. The U.S. Embassy recommends **Polyclinic No. 1** (Kiev Research Institute of Urology and Nephrology, 5 vul. Verkhna, tel. 044/295–9438, 044/294–7107, or 044/294–4700; foreign patients are admitted in Room 335, tel. 044/296–6668). Standards here are above average, as the clinic serves the Ukrainian cabinet of ministers. They provide a wide range of services, from surgery to X-rays to private ambulances. Foreigners are charged in hard currency. If you call an ordinary ambulance (03), you will probably end up at **Polyclinic No. 14** (1/29 vul. Machnikova, tel. 044/224–7364). It enjoys a good reputation, partly because foreigners have always been sent here for treatment.

Dental care is available at **Polyclinic No. 1** (*see above*).

Where to Change Money All of the major hotels have exchange bureaus, which are generally open from 9 to 6, with an hour break for lunch. The following banks also have exchange desks: **Ukrinbank** (12a Institutskaya vul., tel. 044/291–5643), **Brockbusinessbank** (vul. 3 Shota Rustaveli, tel. 044/227–0433), and **Bank Vidrozhennya** (7a vul. Kotsubinskovo, tel. 044/225–1360 or 044/221–3069). As the value of the Ukrainian "coupon" plunges to new lows, spontaneous exchange bureaus are popping up on every corner. You're probably best off using your hotel or one of the established banks.

American Express offers Travelers Cheques built for two.

American Express® Cheques *for Two*. The first Travelers Cheques that allow either of you to use them because both of you have signed them. And only one of you needs to be present to purchase them.

Cheques *for Two* are accepted anywhere regular American Express Travelers Cheques are, which is just about everywhere. So stop by your bank, AAA* or any American Express Travel Service Office and ask for Cheques *for Two*.

English-Language Bookstores **Druzhba** (30 Khreshchatik, 044/224–0373) and **Inostran-naya Kniga** (48 Chervonoarmiiska, tel. 044/227–0088) have English-language sections, but the selection is meager, and bookshelves are usually lined with Ukrainian souvenirs. The art-book shop **Mistetstvo** (26 Khreshchatik, tel. 044/228–2526) has the best selection of the state-run stores. You'll find an occasional guidebook or art book on Kiev in street kiosks and in the cavelike passageways of the subway (a favorite spot for budding entrepreneurs). American and British newspapers and magazines (*USA Today*, *Financial Times*, *The Wall Street Journal*) are available at the lobby kiosks of the hotels Dneiper and Intourist.

Late-Night Pharmacies **Central Regional Pharmacy** 114 (Bulvard Druzhby Narodov, tel. 044/295–0481) has a pharmacist on call 24 hours a day; drugs and medicines are in short supply in Kiev. The foreign-currency pharmacies **Farma** (30 vul. Prorizna, tel. 044/228–2871) and **Pharmacy No. 20** (10 vul. Chervonoarmiiska, tel. 044/225–4398) are generally better stocked than the state-run pharmacies operating for Ukrainian coupons.

Arriving and Departing by Plane

Airports and Airlines Kiev's **Borispol International Airport** (tel. 044/295–6701), located 29 kilometers (18 miles) east of Kiev, is small and uncongested, but arrival can be frenetic. There are no conveyor belts, and an entire flight's luggage is piled up outside the airport, where you jockey with other passengers to find your bag. The international terminal was recently refurbished; but the main domestic terminal is in disrepair, with building materials strewn about the waiting area. The domestic terminal is very poorly heated, so if you are traveling in winter, be sure to dress warmly.

Some domestic flights depart from the small **Zhulyany** airport (tel. 044/272–1201 or 044/272–1202) located on the city outskirts.

Air Ukraine (tel. 044/274–9913) offers direct flights to over 15 countries, with three flights weekly to New York and two flights weekly to London. International airlines maintaining offices in Kiev include: **Balkan** (tel. 044/229–7203), **Czech Air** (tel. 044/296–7449), **Lot** (tel. 044/228–7150), and **Malev** (tel. 044/229–3661). **Finnair** and **KLM** (tel. 044/268–9023) have recently begun offering flights to Kiev. Flights within the CIS have been drastically reduced in the past year. **Aeroflot** (tel. 044/274–5223 or 5152) offers frequent service to Moscow, but there are just two flights weekly to St. Petersburg. Air Ukraine also offers limited service to other points in the CIS and is the only domestic airline.

Between the Airport and Downtown An express bus service—**Polet**—will take you to Ploshcha Peremogi in the center of town. Departures are scheduled every 20 minutes, although recent fuel shortages have resulted in last-minute cancellations. The ride takes one hour. Taxis and private cars are available, but it is wise to make advance arrangements for your transfer from the airport.

Arriving and Departing by Car and Train

By Car It is possible to drive to Kiev from Moscow (via the M4 Highway through Orel) or from Poland, Slovakia, the Czech Republic, and Hungary. Be aware, however, that roads are poorly maintained, repair shops are few and far between, and aggravated relations between Russia and Ukraine have created severe fuel shortages.

By Train Train is by far the most convenient mode of traveling to other points in the CIS. There are several overnight trains daily to and from Moscow; the trip takes about 12 hours. There is also a daily train to St. Petersburg, but the ride is 30 hours long. The train station is located at 1 Vokzalnaya Ploshcha; there's a connecting subway station (Vokzalnaya), so it is easily accessible by public transportation. For information on arrival and departure schedules, call 044/223–3306.

Interrepublic trains often lack heat and hot water—a result of feuds between rail administrations in different republics. To avoid discomfort, bring along some drinking water and light snacks. There is no official border check between Ukraine and Russia, but Russian officials occasionally check the documents of foreign passengers upon arrival in Moscow and St. Petersburg. Traveling to Russia without a valid Russian visa carries a fine of up to $300.

Getting Around

Kiev is divided into 12 districts, but most of its historical sites are concentrated in the **Verkhny Gorod** (Old Town), **Podol** and **Pechersk** districts, and along the **Khreshchatik,** the principal thoroughfare. Although the main tourist attractions are far apart, they are all easily reached by subway.

By Subway It pales by comparison with the elaborate and extensive metro of Moscow and St. Petersburg, but Kiev's subway system is efficient and well maintained. Three lines radiate from the Khreshchatik, connecting the city's historical center to the newer residential districts on the left bank of the Dnieper.

Purchase a token and insert it into the slot at the turnstile. Tokens are available at stations, but due to shortages, there is sometimes a limit on the number you can buy, and lines can be long. The fare is the same regardless of distance. If you are in Kiev at the beginning of the month, you may choose to purchase a monthly pass, good on all public transportation. They go on sale at the end of the month and are available through the first week. The cost is insignificant and well worth the convenience. The subway operates from 5:30 AM to midnight and is best avoided during rush hour, when trains can be very crowded.

By Bus, Tram, and Trolley Buses, trams, and trolleys operate on the honor system. Upon entering, you validate your ticket by canceling it, using one of the machines on the wall of the vehicle. You can purchase tickets at kiosks throughout the city (but not from the driver). The ticket is valid for one ride only; if you change buses, you must pay another fare. Buses, trams, and trolleys operate on the same schedule as the subway, although service in the late evening hours and Sundays tends to be unreliable.

Kiev has an extensive surface transportation system, but recent fuel shortages have led to cutbacks on many routes. The vehicles here are in much better condition than those in Moscow and St. Petersburg. During rush hours the word "crowded" acquires new meaning, as passengers squeeze into already jam-packed trams and trolleys.

By Taxi Taxis roam much less frequently here than in Moscow and St. Petersburg. Again, service has been affected by fuel shortages, and even if you order a taxi far in advance (tel. 058 or 082), there's no guarantee that it will show up. All the major hotels offer car service, available at inflated prices. Unfortunately, even hotel cars are not immune to the fuel shortages, so allow plenty of time when leaving for the airport. The Intourist Hotel's service bureau (tel. 044/227–9554) has the best rates ($15/hour).

Guided Tours

Intourist-Kiev (26 vul. Bogdana Khmelnitskovo, tel. 044/225–3243), the Ukrainian branch of the defunct Intourist, will arrange excursions to any site in or around Kiev. It will also assist you with travel and hotel arrangements to other cities in Ukraine.

The city excursion bureau **Slavutich** (22 vul. Sichnevovo Povstannya, tel. 044/290–8680), founded in 1988, offers excursions in and around Kiev on virtually any theme (historical, architectural, etc.). The agency can provide English-speaking guides and translators and also offers assistance in booking low-budget accommodations.

Exploring Kiev

Highlights for First-Time Visitors

Babi Yar (*see* Off the Beaten Track)
Khreshchatik (*see* Tour 1)
Monastery of the Caves (*see* Tour 4)
St. Andrew's Cathedral (*see* Tour 3)
St. Sophia's Cathedral (*see* Tour 2)

Tour 1: The Khreshchatik and Kiev's Art Museums

Numbers in the margin correspond to points of interest on the Kiev map.

This tour takes you along Kiev's main thoroughfare, the Kreshchatik, and to the city's most important art museums. It might be tempting to begin your exploration with the city's many monuments to ancient history, but the Khreshchatik is the best place to gain a sense of today's Kiev. The avenue's role as the city's cultural center and main shopping district invites comparison with St. Petersburg's Nevsky Prospect. Kievans themselves usually prefer to think of it as a Ukrainian Champs-Elysées, interspersed as it is by broad strips of green lanes and trees. As thoroughfares go, the Khreshchatik is quite short—just 1.6 kilometers (less than a mile) long. It is located in a valley and runs along the lines of a deep ditch that once occupied the site. Hills rise steeply along both sides, especially to the south. Little remains of the prerevolutionary architecture, and the street's stoic appearance owes much to the Stalinist era of Soviet architecture. The Khreshchatik was almost completely destroyed during World War II and was rebuilt at twice its original width. It is lined by monumental high rises—all virtually the same height and design—and by strips of trees and parks. The street's name may come from the dried-up riverbed that once ran through the valley. The river was called Khreschata (meaning crisscrossed), for the valley was crossed by numerous ravines. Another popular theory is that the name derives from the word *khreshchennya*, meaning "baptism." The street leads to the site in the Dnieper River where, according to legend, the people of Kiev were baptized en masse in 988.

❶ The tour begins at **Lenkomsomol Square,** at the eastern end of the Khreshchatik. If the current frenzy of name-changing continues, this square will soon be known by another name. But surely it will not be returned to its former name, Stalin's Square. You can reach it by taking the subway to **Maidan Nezalezhnosti** and heading east (right) as you exit. The square marks the end of the Khreshchatik, where the main streets branch off like the points of a star. Across from the Hotel Dnipro (on the northeastern corner) **Volodimirski Spusk** leads down to the riverbank. To the north, **vulitsa Trokh-Svyatitelska** (Three Saints Street) leads up a steep incline to the famous St. Andrew's Cathedral (*see* Tour 3, *below*). **Vulitsa Mikhaila Grushevskovo** to the south leads to the Pechersk district and the ancient Monastery of the Caves (*see* Tour 4, *below*). The rectangular, all-white structure on the northern slope of the square was built in the early 1980s to house the short-lived Lenin Museum (*see* Tour 2, *below*).

Follow the underpass below the square and cross to the opposite side. The building under reconstruction here is the

Kiev

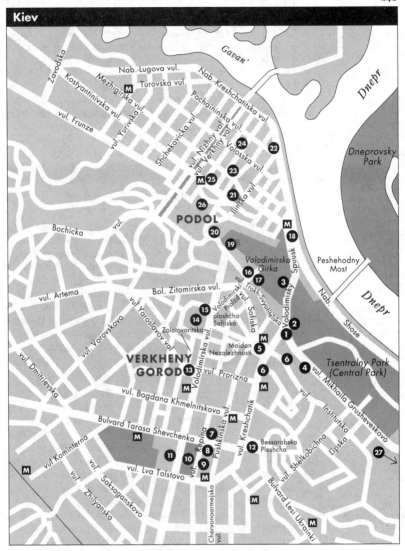

Gavan'

Dnepr

Nab.-Lugova vul.
Turovska vul.
Nab.-Kreshchattiska vul.
Zavadska
Kostyantinivska vul.
Mezhigirska vul.
Pochaininska vul.
vul. Frunze
vul. Yurivska
Shchekavicka vul.
vul. Nizhny val.
vul. Verkhny val.
Volosska vul.

Dneprovsky Park

24
22
23
25
21
Ilinska vul.
Bochicka
vul.
26
PODOL
20
19
18
M

Volodimirska Girka

Peshehodny Most

Dnepr

Bol. Zitomirska vul.
vul. Artema
vul. Yaroslavov val.
vul. Voroyskovo
Zolotovoritska
15
14
vul. Trohk-Svyatiska
vul. Volodimirski Prozd vul.
16 **17**
ploshcha Sofiiska
vul. Sofiiska
3
2
1
Volodimirsky
Spuusk
Nab.
Shose

VERKHENY GOROD
13
Maidan Nezalezhnosti
5
M
6
6
4
Tsentralny Park
(Central Park)

vul. Dmitrievska
vul. Volodimirska vul.
vul. Prorizna
vul. Bogdana Khmelnitskovo
M
vul. Mikhaila Grushevskovo
Institutska

Bulvard Tarasa Shevchenka
7
Repina
8
Pushkinska vul.
vul. Kreshchatik
12
Bessarabska Ploshcha
Lipsta
27

vul. Kominterna
11
10
9
M
vul. Lva Tolstovo
M
vul. Shelkobichna

vul. Saksaganskovo
Zhilyanska
Chervonoarmejska vul.
Bulvard Lesi Ukrainki
M

2 **Hall of Columns,** built in 1882. The former meeting place of the prerevolutionary Merchants' Assembly, it is now home to Kiev's Philharmonic Society. Climb the broad stairway to your right. When you reach the top, you will be greeted by a huge steel rainbow, the Monument Commemorating the 325th Anniversary of the Reunion of Russia and Ukraine. The union is over now, of course, but the monument remains. Below the gigantic arch are severe, proletarian figures representing Russians and Ukrainians, with a bas-relief depicting Russo-Ukrainian brotherhood. Erected in 1982, this is hands down one of the ugliest monuments ever produced in the former Soviet Union. But ignore the architecture and concentrate on the splendid view of the long bridges spanning the wide Dneiper, its islands, and the vast plains of the left bank.

Across the ravine to your immediate left is **Volodimerska Girka** (Vladimir Hill) and the **Monument to the Baptism of Russia.** The 20-meter (66-foot) monument shows Prince Vladimir—the pagan ruler who brought Christianity to Russia—dressed as a Russian warrior and holding a cross in his right hand. The pedestal, shaped like a Russian chapel, is engraved with the ancient seal of Old Kiev. Erected in 1853, the bronze statue was designed by Vasily Demut-Malinovsky, a St. Petersburg sculptor, and was cast by Peter Klodt, creator of the rearing horses adorning St. Petersburg's Anichkov Bridge.

Return now to Lenkomsomol Square and turn left (south) up vulitsa Mikhaila Grushevskovo. The attractive pink-and-purple building on the corner is the State Public Library (No. 1). The street just beyond it, to your left, leads to the main entrance to the **Central Park of Culture and Rest,** where Kiev's Dynamo Stadium is located. A few steps farther, on the opposite side of the street, stands the **4** **Museum of Ukrainian Art,** erected along the lines of an ancient Greek temple and with a six-columned portico. Its huge granite steps are flanked by a pair of growling lions. Opened in 1899, it originally housed Kiev's Museum of Antiquities and Art. In 1936 the exhibits were moved to another location, and the present museum, devoted to Ukrainian art from the 12th to early 20th centuries, was opened. *6 vul. Mikhaila Grushevskovo, tel. 044/228–6482. Open Mon.–Thurs., weekends 10–6.*

The museum's 21 halls house a wonderful collection of Ukrainian paintings, sculptures, and drawings as well as religious art. The rich collection of icons, located on the first floor, includes the 12th-century St. George with scenes from his life and the 14th-century Virgin Hodegetria, brought here from the town of Lutsk. The 18th-century Intercession is interesting for its portrait of Bogdan Khmelnitsky, the hetman who led the revolt that liberated Ukraine from Polish rule. The first-floor exhibits also contain fine examples of Ukrainian portrait and landscape paintings from the 17th to the 19th century, including Vasily Tropinin's *Girl from Podolia* and Taras Shevchenko's *Self- Portrait.* Several well-known works by Nikolai Pimonenko, including his *Wedding in Kiev* and *Victim of Fanaticism,* are also on display. The second-floor exhibits are devoted to modern Ukrainian art. Strongly influenced by Soviet propaganda and the demands of socialist realism, the works here are interesting primarily as a sociopolitical statement.

Return again to Lenkomsomol Square to begin a tour of the Khreshchatik. Most of the architecture here dates from the 1950s and '60s, with a few exceptions at the beginning of the street. On the right-hand side stand the former **St. Petersburg Bank** (No. 8) and the former **Volzhsko-Kamsky Bank** (No. 10), both built at the turn of the century.

Time Out The **Konditerska** across the street (5 Khreshchatik) has a stand-up café where you can have a cup of hot cocoa and pastry. Kiev has always been known for its delicious cakes, and you will find Kievans lining up here to buy them. If you're looking for a place to sit down, you can stop by the **Dnipro Hotel,** back at the corner with Lenkomsomol Square, where—for foreign currency only—you can have a cup of coffee or a draft beer at the lobby bar.

One block west of Lenkomsomol Square, the Khreshchatik ❺ meets **Maidan Nezalezhnosti** (Independence Square). In Yaroslav's day the southeastern gates of the high defensive wall surrounding the city stood near here, at the bottom of vulitsa Zhitomirska (to your right, beyond the fountains). Until recently this broad, sprawling square was named in honor of the October Revolution. A huge, red granite statue of Lenin once stood on the terrace (to your left) across the street; only the pedestal remains.

Towering above the square on the incline behind the terrace is the **Moskva Hotel,** built in the early 1960s and designed after the Moscow original. If you're feeling energetic, climb up vulitsa Institutska, which runs alongside the hotel. Crowning the hill, at 5 vulitsa Institutska, is a prerevolutionary building with a Classical colonnade. Built by the architect Vikenty Beretti in the early 1840s, it was originally a finishing school for young ladies of the nobility. Today it is ❻ the **Palace of Culture,** one of the city's largest concert halls.

As you return to Independence Square, the next street leading up the incline is **vulitsa Karl Marx** (also due for a name change soon). The building on the corner is the **Tchaikovsky Conservatory,** a restored version of the 1899 original. The large and elaborate building on the opposite corner is Kiev's main **post office.** Walk by it with caution. In 1989 a portal suddenly collapsed, killing several passersby. Just past the post office is the shopping arcade that links the Khreshchatik with Zamkovetskaya vulitsa. The entrance is through a large arch linking the two wings of this huge building. Here you will find many boutiques and recently opened cooperatives. Built in 1914 by P.S. Andreev, this is another of the rare buildings on the Khreshchatik that survived World War II more or less intact.

The next block contains several large department stores and administrative buildings, including the imposing Office of the President of Ukraine. At the end of the block, one of the city's few surviving statues of Lenin marks the beginning of **Bulvard Tarasa Shevchenka,** named in honor of the 19th-century Ukrainian poet and artist. Walk two blocks up the boulevard, and on your right, at the corner with vulitsa ❼ Repina, is the **Taras Shevchenko State Museum.** If you have spent any time in Ukraine, you have probably heard about this beloved national hero. Born into serfdom in 1814, he became one of the nation's greatest artists and poets, as well as a leader in the fight against serfdom. A member of the secret Society of Sts. Cyril and Methodius, which opposed serfdom, he was arrested in 1847 and spent more than 10 years in internal exile. At the age of 16 he had gone to St. Petersburg, where he quickly gained recognition for his artistic abilities, despite his lack of formal training. Art critics encouraged him to enter the St. Petersburg Academy of Arts, but first he had to purchase his freedom from his owner. The artist Karl Bryullov came to his aid, auctioning his portrait of the Russian poet Vasily Zhukovsky and donating the proceeds to Shevchenko. The portrait is now one of the museum's 4,000 exhibits. Also on display are more than 800 literary and artistic works by Shevchenko, as well as many of his personal effects. *12 Bulvard Shevchenko, tel. 044/ 224–2556. Open Tues.–Sun. 10–6.*

Turning left onto vulitsa Repina, you'll come to Kiev's ❽ **Russian Art Museum,** one of the largest repositories of Russian art outside Moscow and St. Petersburg. The building was built in the 1880s and belonged to the wealthy Tereshchenko family. The museum was founded in 1922 on the basis of the Tereshchenko collection and other private collections confiscated and nationalized by the Soviet government. The splendid interiors were designed by Robert Friedrich Meltzer, known for his work in the Winter Palace in St. Petersburg. The fine collection includes masterpieces from the 12th to the 20th century. *9 vul. Repina, tel. 044/ 224–6218. Open Mon., Tues. noon–8; Wed., Fri.–Sun. 10–6.*

The permanent exhibits are on the second floor; the gallery on the first floor is reserved for temporary exhibits. Tickets for the two sections are sold separately. The outstanding collection of religious art is contained in the first two galleries on the second floor. Here you'll find icons from the Novgorod, Rostov-Suzdal, and Moscow schools, including a 12th-century icon from Novgorod of the Russian saints Boris and Gleb. Russian 18th-century portrait art is also represented by Vasily Borovikovsky's *Portrait of Vera Arsenyeva* as well as by Dmitry Levitsky's *Unknown Woman in Blue* and his portrait of Catherine the Great. Most important is the museum's extensive collection of works from the 19th century, such as Vasily Tropinin's *The Gamblers*, Vasily Perov's *God's Fool*, and Victor Vasnetsov's *Three Tsarevnas of the Underground Kingdom*. There are also many fine landscapes by Isaac Levitan and the seascape painter Ivan Aivazovsky. The World of Art Movement (*Mir Isskustva*) is represented by works of Serov, Korovin, and Benois. The last exhibit hall contains an interesting display of 18th–20th century china, porcelain, and glass, including plates produced in Petrograd in the early 1920s.

Just a few doors down the street is yet another important ❾ art museum, the **Museum of Western and Oriental Art.** Like the Russian Museum, it was founded after the Bolshevik Revolution on the basis of a private collection. It is housed in the former mansion of the well-known archaeologist Bogdan Khanenko, who started the collection in the 1870s. The holdings include a rich collection of Corinthian and Attic painted vases from the 3rd to 4th century, found in digs in the Black Sea area, as well as terra-cotta statuettes (400 BC) and Roman sculptural portraits of the 2nd century. There are also several Byzantine icons dating from the 6th and 7th centuries. The section devoted to Western European art includes works featuring Italian Renaissance and Baroque art and the works from the golden age of Spanish Art. Velázquez's *Portrait of the Infanta Margarita*, a highlight of the collection, was a study for a large formal portrait now housed in Madrid's Prado. Flemish and Dutch schools of the 15th–18th centuries are also represented. Unfortunately, the museum was closed in 1993 for major restoration work and is not scheduled to reopen again until at least 1998. Its holdings may be moved to other locations; for information, call the museum. *15 vul. Repina, tel. 044/ 224–6162 or 044/225–0206.*

❿ Bordering vulitsa Repina to the north is **Taras Shevchenko Park.** In its center stands a statue of the Ukrainian classical writer, erected in 1939 on the 125th anniversary of his birth. It replaced an earlier statue of the deposed Russian czar, Nicholas II. On the opposite side of the park, on ⓫ vulitsa Volodimirska, stands the bright red building of **Kiev University** (also known as Shevchenko University), Ukraine's most prestigious institution of higher education. Built in 1837–43, this is another Classical structure created by Vikenty Beretti. The long central facade is adorned by an eight-columned portico in the Ionic style. Completely destroyed during World War II, the building has been restored to its original appearance. According to legend, the building acquired its unusual color in 1901, when Czar Nicholas II ordered it doused in bright red in retaliation against rebellious students who refused to comply with the draft. The color was supposed to embarrass them and intimidate others.

To the south (to your left as you face the university) vulitsa Volodimirska intersects with **vulitsa Lva Tolstovo** (Lev Tolstoy Street). Turn left at the corner and walk to the end of the street. The street ends at **Ploshcha Lva Tolstovo** (Ley Tolstoy Square), where it intersects with vulitsa Chervonoarmiiska.

Time Out You can join Kievans enjoying the benefits of capitalism at the new joint-venture **Penguin Ice Cream Shop** at 21 vulitsa Chervonoarmiiska. It's stand-up only (although you'll occasionally spot a patron or two perched on the windowsills) and offers a wide assortment of ice cream.

If you continue down vulitsa Chervonoarmiiska, you come out at the western end of the Khreshchatik. Here, on Bessarabska Ploshcha, you will find Kiev's first indoor market, the **Kriti Rynok.** Designed by Heinrich Gay and completed in 1910–12, the market was established on this site for Bessarabian (Moldovan) merchants who came to trade in Kiev. Today it is Kiev's most important market, and inside the domed building you'll find rows of private farmers selling fruit and vegetables, as well as an occasional Ukrainian souvenir. Your tour of the Khreshchatik area ends here; to reach the subway you can either walk down the street to Maidan Nezalezhnosti or return to Lev Tolstoy Street, where there is a subway station of the same name.

Tour 2: St. Sophia's and the Upper Town

This tour takes you through the hilly section of the **Verkhny Gorod** (Upper Town), also known as Old Kiev, where you will find the few surviving monuments of Kiev's ancient past. The tour begins at the **Zoloti Vorota** (Golden Gate), located just outside the subway station of the same name. As you exit the subway, you'll face the back side of the Golden Gate. In Yaroslav's day they served as the main entrance into the city, which was surrounded by a high defensive wall. Of the original gates, only the two parallel walls supporting the main entrance remain. The reconstructed version before you was completed in 1982, to coincide with celebrations of the city's 1,500th anniversary. Today the pavilion houses a museum of ancient Russian architecture, which is open only in summer. *48A Yaroslaviv Val, tel. 044/ 224–7068. Open Mar.–Nov., Mon.–Wed. and Fri.–Sun. 10–6.*

Built in 1037 by Yaroslav the Wise, the original Golden Gate, inspired by the gates of Constantinople, was famous throughout Europe. It was covered by beaten gold and other precious metals and topped by a tiny Church of the Annunciation. According to legend, it was through the Golden Gate that Batu Khan entered the city after the Mongols captured Kiev in 1240. Four centuries later, in 1648, Bogdan Khmelnitsky (the Cossack hetman who led the Ukrainian liberation movement), rode triumphantly through these gates after freeing the city from its Polish captors.

⑭ We will follow the path of Yaroslav and his contemporaries, down the road leading to the city's oldest church, **Sofiisky Sobor (St. Sophia's Cathedral).** Walk down vulitsa Zolotovoristska, which begins directly across the street from the entrance to the Golden Gate. Bear right at the end of this short street, and you will come out onto vulitsa Volodimirska; the entrance to St. Sophia's is just a few steps to your left. Today the complex of buildings and churches that make up St. Sophia's is a museum. In addition to the cathedral itself, on display are models of ancient Ukrainian and Russian towns, as well as local archaeological discoveries. You'll enter the complex through the Southern Gate Tower; follow the path directly in front of you to reach the cathedral entrance. Tickets are sold at the kiosk on the corner to your right, just before you reach the cathedral. *24 vul. Volodimirska, tel. 044/228-6152. Open Mon.–Wed., Fri.–Sun. 10-6.*

Dedicated in 1037, St. Sophia's (also known as the Cathedral of Holy Wisdom) was built by Prince Yaroslav the Wise in gratitude for winning a battle against the Pechenegs, an invading tribe from the east. Prince Yaroslav, the Peter the Great of Kievan Rus, looked not west but south for inspiration, basing his cathedral on the Hagia Sophia of Constantinople. Over the centuries, the Cathedral of St. Sophia acquired an importance far exceeding its religious role: It was not only the seat of the metropolitan but also the center of political and social life in Kievan Rus. It housed the nation's first library, whose rich collection included manuscripts from Europe and Greece. It was the site of cultural events, and it was here that princes were crowned and foreign ambassadors received.

At first glance you may wonder how the cathedral's helmet-like cupolas could possibly adorn the city's oldest church. The church was reconstructed on several occasions, and its present exterior owes much to the era of Ukrainian Baroque. The original design, strongly influenced by Byzantine architecture, also contained elements of Ukrainian wooden architecture. The huge, five-aisled church originally had 13 cupolas and was built in the shape of a Greek cross. The main cupola in the center represented Christ; the surrounding cupolas depicted the 12 Apostles. After the death of Yaroslav (who is buried inside) in 1054, the northwestern tower was added and a vault was built for his tomb. Badly damaged during the Mongol invasion and further destroyed by the Poles and Lithuanians, the cathedral lay in ruins until after the reunification of Ukraine and Russia in 1654, when restoration began. In the early 18th century, on orders from Peter the Great, the cathedral was reconstructed and the six additional domes (for a total of 19) were added.

In contrast to the exterior, much of the 11th-century interior has been preserved. It is richly decorated with mosaics and frescoes, many of which date from the 11th and 12th centuries. One curious feature of the fresco work is the use of secular subjects. An example of this can be found in the spiral staircase of the southwestern tower, to your left as you enter the 18th-century narthex. Although the stairway is sealed off, you can peek through the iron grid for a glimpse of everyday life in Kievan Rus: The frescoes depict hunting scenes, wild animals, court jesters, and musicians. The spiral staircase of the towers, whose entrance was once located outside the cathedral, led to the choir loft, where Yaroslav and his family sat during services.

Continue now to the central nave, whose walls, ceilings, and pillars are decorated with colorful mosaics and frescoes. You will be immediately struck by the golden glow of the central dome. Peering down at you is an 11th-century mosaic of Christ as the Pantokrator; his portrayal as Father, Son, and Holy Ghost was influenced by Byzantine traditions. The vault of the main apse is adorned by a beautiful mosaic of the Orant Virgin. Because this mosaic has survived centuries of abuse and reconstruction intact, it has become known as the Indestructible Virgin. The magnificent gilded iconostasis in front of the altar was erected in 1747; it was partially dismantled in the 19th century, and only the lowest of the three original tiers remains.

In addition to religious themes, the frescoes include portraits of Yaroslav and his family. Considering that Yaroslav was alive when they were painted, the portraits are highly unusual for church decoration. A portrait of his four daughters, including Anna, the future queen of Henry I of France, are on the southern wall, while four of his sons are depicted on the northern wall. Fragments of portraits of Yaroslav himself and his wife, Irina, their eldest daughter, Elizabeth (later queen of Norway), and their eldest son, Vladimir, are on the western wall.

Yaroslav's marble sarcophagus is in the northeast chapel, to the left of the central nave as you face the iconostasis. The tomb, which weighs six tons, dates from the 5th or 6th century. It was brought from Greece, and its carved decoration includes such early Christian symbols as palms, cypresses, fishes, and grapevines.

Leaving through the side exit, walk around to the back of the cathedral. To your left stands a four-story, stone bell tower, painted azure with white trim. This is a fine example of Ukrainian Baroque; the lush ornamentation includes the double-headed eagle of the Romanov dynasty. Measuring 76 meters (249 feet), the bell tower was erected between

1744 and 1752; the fourth story and gilded cupola were added in 1852.

Turn right now, heading back in the direction of the main entrance to the cathedral grounds. To your left, just before you reach the ticket booth, is the 18th-century refectory, which houses archaeological and architectural displays. Its finds include the sarcophagus of Princess Olga, which once stood in the 10th-century Tithe Church (*see* Tour 3, *below*) destroyed by the Mongols. The model panoramas of Kiev in the 10th–12th centuries will give you an idea of what the city looked like before it was razed to the ground by Mongol invaders.

Time Out If you're not disturbed by the obligatory cats on the window-sills, you can sit down and have a coffee or hot cocoa at the **Kulinaria** on the corner of Volodimirska and Reitarska vulitsa (to your right as you exit the cathedral through the southern gate). The coffee is very sweet and heavily diluted with milk. Pastries and cakes are sometimes available, as well as sausages and champagne.

As you leave the St. Sophia complex, turn left onto Volodimirska vulitsa. The street opens onto **St. Sophia Square,** which until recently was named in honor of Bogdan Khmelnitsky, whose equestrian statue stands in the square's center. Khmelnitsky (1595–1657) led the Ukrainian people in the war of liberation against Poland and later pushed for reunification with Russia. The statue stands on this site where the residents of Kiev gave their hero a triumphant welcome. Paid for primarily by public conscription, it was designed by a well-known St. Petersburg sculptor, Mikhail Mikeshin, and was erected in 1888. The hetman bestrides a rearing horse that towers above a red-granite pedestal. In the distance above the trees, to your far left, is St. Andrew's Cathedral (*see* Tour 3, *below*).

Follow the street running down the right-hand side of the square, with the statue to your left and a small strip of park to your right. Before you leave the square, pause for a moment for another look at St. Sophia's, whose massive bell tower and helmet-shaped cupolas dominate the square. You are now on **Volodimirskii Proizd;** the strip of park bordering the street to your right is dotted with sculptures of pagan gods. Walk the length of the street, approximately three blocks, and you will come to **Mikhailivska Ploshcha (St. Michael's Square).** This square was also recently renamed; under the Soviets it was named in honor of the Soviet Union's third president, Mikhail Kalinin.

Bordering the square to your left is the massive, very Soviet structure of the former Central Committee of the Ukrainian Communist Party. It was built in 1937, and its cold and severe facade recalls the dark days of Stalinism. Today it houses governmental offices of the newly independent Ukraine. The square takes its name from the Mikhailovsky-Zlatoverkhy Monastery (St. Mikhail Monastery of the Golden Roof), founded on this site in 1051; its cathedral, built by Prince Sviatopolk in 1108, was the city's second most important house of worship after Sofiisky Sobor. It survived the brutal Mongol invasions and the years of Polish and Lithuanian rule—but not the Soviets: In 1936 it was destroyed to make way for the Central Committee building. St. Mikhail was considered the city's patron saint, and many Kievans find a connection between the monastery's destruction and such disasters that have struck the city as the wartime German occupation and the Chernobyl nuclear accident. Now that the monastery is being restored, it is hoped that Kiev's patron saint will spare the city from further misfortune.

Turn right off the square, onto vulitsa Trokh-Svyatitelska (Three Saints' Street). At the left-hand corner (with your back to the square) stands the 18th-century **Refectory,** the only building of the 11th-century monastery to have been spared destruction. The stone church, with its single wooden cupola, was built in 1712. Like many churches in the former Soviet Union, it was turned into a museum after the Bolshevik Revolution. Little remains of its original interior, and, like the rest of the monastery, the building is being restored. With the recent religious revival, the museum was closed and the refectory now belongs to the Ukrainian Orthodox Church. Services are held daily at 7 AM and 5 PM.

Continue on Three Saints' Street, walking away from St. Michael's Square. The street soon turns down a steep incline, which ends at Lenkomsomol Square. To your right as you head down the steep hill is the Catholic **Church of St. Alexander** (1817–1842), currently under reconstruction by Polish contractors. To your left, at the bottom of the hill, was Kiev's obligatory but short-lived Lenin Museum, erected in 1982. In 1991, the museum was closed and converted into the **Ukrainina Dim** (Ukrainian cultural center). It contains temporary displays on Ukrainian culture, from food to dress. *2 Khreshchatik. Open Tues.–Sun. 11–6:30.*

The square marks the beginning of Kiev's main thoroughfare, the tree-lined Khreshchatik (*see* Tour 1, *above*). The subway is just one block away, to your right as you enter the square from Three Saints' Street.

Tour 3: St. Andrews Cathedral and the Podol

This tour takes you to the magnificent **Andreyivsky Sobor** (St. Andrew's Cathedral), situated on a high bluff overlooking the Dnieper, and then down the steep incline to the **Podol,** the old trading quarter, on the lower right bank. Although settlement of the Podol dates from Kiev's earliest days, none of the original architecture survives; the Mongol invasion obliterated the original wooden settlement. Rebuilt in the 17th and 18th centuries, the Podol burned to the ground in 1811 after a three-day fire. Its charm today lies in the rectangular pattern of its streets, lined with 19th-century apartment buildings and trading arcades, and the glorious views of towering St. Andrew's Cathedral on the bluff above.

18 Begin your tour at the **Ploshcha Poshtova** subway stop. To reach the bluff on which St. Andrew's sits, you can take the funicular (cable car), built in 1905. Its entrance is at the bottom of the hill, just outside the subway. The ride up gives you an excellent view of the city. When you reach the top, walk straight to the square ahead of you and take a right onto vulitsa Desyatinna, which will lead you directly to St. Andrew's. As you walk down the street, do not be surprised if you run into protesters carrying signs. Leonid Kravchuk, president of Ukraine, lives at No. 8.

Vulitsa Desyatinna is named for the **Desyatinna Tserkva** (Tithe Church) that once stood at the end of the street. Founded in 989 as the Church of the Holy Virgin, it became known as the Tithe Church because Prince Vladimir the Great gave one-tenth of his income toward its maintenance. During the Mongol invasion, women and children took refuge inside its massive stone walls. But the roof collapsed under the weight of the fiery blows, killing everyone inside. If you turn left at the end of the street and walk a few hundred feet up vulitsa Volodimirska, you will find the outline of its foundation, which was been reconstructed with red quartz.

To your right as you reach the end of vulitsa Desyatinna
19 stands **St. Andrew's Cathedral.** A fine example of Ukrainian Baroque, its green, blue, and gold cupolas light up the skies above Kiev's sweeping hills and gently flowing Dnieper. Designed by the Italian architect Bartolomeo Rastrelli, who built so many of St. Petersburg's masterpieces, it is one of his few buildings to have survived intact with no reconstruction or significant damage. Its site, on the highest point of Old Kiev, was allegedly chosen because it was here that the Apostle Andrew, who first preached the Gospel in Kievan Rus, erected a cross.

The church was built at the behest of Peter the Great's pious daughter Elizabeth, who visited Kiev in 1744. Construction of the monumental cathedral proved a complicated task due to the hilly terrain—the foundation is 15 meters (50 feet) deep—and was completed in 1752. The church was not consecrated until 1767.

St. Andrew's stands on a platform reached by a broad flight of steps. The proportions are perfect, and the elegant interior is monumental and striking. The three-tiered iconostasis, whose red-velvet background accentuates the gilded wooden carvings and sculptures, is the work of the Russian painter Alexei Antropov and the Ukrainian artist Grigory

Levitsky. The church is, for the time being, still open as a museum. *33 Andriivsky Uzviz, tel. 044/228–5861. Open Mon., Tues., Thurs.–Sun. 10–6; May–Sept., also Wed. noon–8.*

When you are done basking in the glories of St. Andrew's, walk a few steps down the incline. To your right a twisting flight of iron steps will take you to a lookout platform nicknamed *Uzdikhalnitsa* or "gasp." The fantastic view of the Dnieper, the plains to the east, and the Podol below will probably make you gasp, too. The first sloping hill to your left is **Zamkova Gora,** also known as Kiselyovka Mount. It is believed that this is the hill mentioned in the ancient chronicles in connection with Kii, who with his two brothers founded the city of Kiev around the end of the 6th century.

Time Out Andriivski Uzviz, the steep street leading down into the Podol, is lined with cafés and art salons. This is the heart of Kiev's artist community. **Svitilitsa,** at No. 13A, is a popular hangout for writers and artists. Join them for some Turkish coffee or a shot of vodka. Pastries and small sandwiches are also available. The interior is reminiscent of a peasant cottage, with Ukrainian embroidery, a tile stove, and wooden picnic tables.

No. 13 Andriivski Uzviz, on the right, was the Bulgakov family home. Mikhail Bulgakov, the renowned Russian writer whose satirical works were long suppressed by the Soviet regime, lived here from 1906 to 1916 and again in 1918 and 1919. For years the house stood unmarked, but today it houses the **Bulgakov Museum,** with the writer's personal effects and family photos. The young museum plans to restore the rooms to their appearance when Bulgakov lived here. *13 Andriivskii Uzviz, tel. 044/416–5254. Open Mon., Tues., Thurs.–Sun. 10–6.*

When you reach the bottom of the hill, turn right onto Borichiv tik and then left onto vulitsa Andriivska. At the end of this short street is busy vulitsa Petra Sagaidachnovo; at this point you can turn right to return to the subway at Poshtova Ploshcha, just a few blocks away. To continue your excursion through the Podol, however, turn left. This busy shopping district is very different from the Khreshchatik, which is dominated by the monumental architecture of the Stalinist era. Before the revolution, the Podol was inhabited by merchants and craftsmen. A stroll through its quaint, narrow streets gives you a sense of Old Kiev.

㉑ After one long block, the broad **Kontraktova Ploshcha** (Contract Square) opens up on the left-hand side of the street. Here, at No. 4, is the **Gostinny Dvir** shopping arcade. Originally built in 1809, it was destroyed in the 1811 fire and rebuilt in 1833 by the prominent Ukrainian architect Andrei Melensky. The arcade is similar to Moscow's

GUM and St. Petersburg's Gostiny Dvor, but much smaller. The small statue in the square's garden, just beyond the arcade, is of the 18th-century Ukrainian poet and philosopher Grigory Skovoroda. At the far corner of the square stands the **Kontraktovy Dom** (Contract House), which lends the square its name. An interesting example of the Classical style, it was built in 1817 expressly as a headquarters for negotiating and signing agreements. It is currently under reconstruction, but hidden beneath the scaffolding are four impressive Doric portals.

Cross vulitsa Sagaidachnovo and backtrack slightly to the north end of Contract Square. Turn left onto vulitsa Illinska, heading in the direction of the river. Three blocks down the street, at the corner of vulitsa Pochaininska (just before you reach the harbor), stands the 17th-century ㉒ **Illinska Tserka** (St. Elias Church). Its history actually dates from Kiev's earliest days. According to legend, the first wooden church built on this site was erected by Askold (Rurik), the Kievan prince who was murdered by his rival from Novgorod, Prince Oleg, in 882. The present stone church, which holds services daily at 5 PM, was built in 1692.

Now return to Contract Square and turn right onto vulitsa Spaska, which begins across the street from the Contract House. The rectangular building on the right-hand corner (2 ㉓ vul. Spaska) is the former **Kievo-Mogilianksa Academy.** It was founded in the late 17th century inside the walls of the now destroyed Bratsky Monastery. In 1701 Peter the Great turned it into the Kiev Academy, which became one of the largest and most prestigious institutions of higher learning in all of Russia and Ukraine. Many famous scholars worked here, including the Russian scientist Mikhail Lomonsov, the composer Dmitry Bortnyansky, and the Ukrainian philosopher Grigory Skovoroda. Today the building houses a branch of the central library of the Ukrainian Academy of Sciences.

Continuing down vulitsa Spaska, you'll see a 19th-century yellow-brick building with a rectangular tower in a side street to your left. Formerly a fire station, the building is ㉔ now the **Chernobyl Museum.** Opened on April 25, 1992, on the sixth anniversary of the Chernobyl accident, the museum houses a somber exhibit depicting the accident and its horrifying aftermath. On display are the personal effects of the young soldiers who died as a result of their heroic efforts to put out the fire. Above the exhibit hangs a clock, permanently set at 1:23 AM, the time the explosion occurred. A reminder of the secrecy that shrouded the event is found in the display case containing newspaper clippings from around the time of the accident. The first official announcement by Soviet authorities, not issued until April 29, consists of just three short lines: "An accident occurred at the Chernobyl Atomic Power Plant. Measures are being taken to rectify the damage. The injured are being cared for." Other exhibits contain photos of Kiev's May Day celebrations and parade, after which residents were instructed to stay indoors and close their windows tightly. Another display contains graphic photos of the dying, as well as mutilated animals and children born after the accident. Plans are underway to expand the museum and to supplement the displays with videos and documentary films. Entrance and guided tours (in Russian or Ukrainian) are free. *1 Provulok Zhorevii, tel. 044/417–5422. Open Mon.–Sat. 10–6. Closed last Mon. of month.*

Time Out If you're up for some hearty Ukrainian cooking, stop by the **Spadshchina** (8 vul. Spaska, tel. 044/417–0358), just one block to your right off Kontraktova Ploshcha. Ask for a table in the back room, where you can rest in a comfy private booth. The specialty is *Kotleta Spadshchina*, fried chicken rolled in bread crumbs. The *vareniki*, filled with potatoes or cabbage, are also homemade. *Open daily noon–5, 6–11. Ukrainian coupons only.*

Return again to Kontraktova Ploshcha and turn right onto Mezhigirska vulitsa (the continuation of vulitsa Petra Sagaidachnovo). A short walk down this block of decaying buildings brings you to vulitsa Khoreva. Turn left and walk one block. At the corner of Kostyantinivska vulitsa stands an 18th-century, white-stone building. This was **Peter the Great's headquarters** in 1706, when he prepared his attack on the Swedes, who had advanced to within 40 kilometers (25 miles) of Kiev. The building is not open to the public.

Continuing up vulitsa Khoreva, will you reach the oldest surviving building in the Podol, the **Nikolai Pritiska Tserka** (Pritisko-St. Nicholas Church). The modest, white-stone church, which bears just one cupola, was built in 1631 and is similar in design to Ukrainian wooden cathedrals. Closed during the Soviet era, it was recently returned to the Ukrainian Orthodox Church and is open for services on Saturdays at 9 and 5, and Sundays at 10.

Turn left onto vulitsa Pritisko-Mikilska, and a few steps will bring you to the **Florivski Monastir** (St. Flor's Convent). The area may be swarming with uniformed soldiers, because directly across the street is the headquarters of the Ukrainian National Guard. The convent, whose history dates from the 16th century, miraculously survived the antireligious campaigns of the Stalin era and remained open under Soviet rule. Enter the convent through the bell-tower gates, designed by Andrei Melensky (who also built the shopping arcade on Contract Square) in the 1830s. To your right stands the **Voznesenska Tserka** (Church of the Ascension), the convent's main cathedral and the only functioning church left on its territory. Built in 1732, it suffered severely in the Podol fire of 1811, when the original iconostasis was destroyed. Tourists are not overly appreciated here, so to avoid a bitter scolding from the elderly women at prayer, leave your camera in your bag and your hands outside your pockets. To the right of the cathedral is a well at which you will see people lining up with glass jars. The water, which comes from an underground spring, is thought to have medicinal powers.

Just outside the convent walls, to your left as you exit through the bell tower, stands Kiev's very first **apothecary**, which dates from 1728. Restored to its original appearance, the building contains a functionary pharmacy, as well as a museum devoted to the history of medicine. The unusual exhibits, obviously compiled during the Soviet era, include a room decorated with authentic church icons and devoted to the "Christian Era" of medicine. The museum is open only for group excursions, which can be arranged by calling in advance (you'll have to provide your own interpreter). *7 vul. Pritisko-Mikilska, tel. 044/416–2437. Open Tues.– Sun. 9–4.*

To reach the subway again, retrace your steps to Peter the Great's house. Turn right onto vulitsa Kostyantinivska. The entrance to the subway station Kontraktova Ploshcha is just a few steps away, on the left-hand side of the street.

Tour 4: Monastery of the Caves and World War II Museum

㉗ If time permits, set aside an entire day for the fascinating **Kievo-Pecherska Lavra (Monastery of the Caves)**. It is not only a functioning monastery, with miles of mazelike underground tunnels containing numerous churches and ancient crypts, but also houses some of Kiev's richest museums. Among them are the Museum of Historical Treasures (the Ukrainian equivalent to Moscow's Armory or the Gold Rooms in the Hermitage), the Museum of Ukrainian Decorative and Applied Art, and the Museum of Ukrainian Books and Printing.

A *lavra* is a monastery of the highest order. The Monastery of the Caves received this honored title in 1598, but its history goes back much farther. It was founded in 1051 by a monk named Antony and his follower, Theodosius. They chose this hilly site, on the banks of the Dnieper, for its natural caves (in Ukrainian, *pechery*, hence the name). The monks lived in underground cells and were also buried in them. The cool temperatures and humid atmosphere of the caves allowed their bodies to mummify; even today their bodies remain almost perfectly preserved. At the time of the monastery's foundation, this appeared to be a miracle, enhancing the monastery's prestige in a land where Christianity had been adopted less than a century earlier.

From the 11th to the early 13th century, the Pechersky Monastery was the ecclesiastical center of the Orthodox Church in Kievan Rus. Like the city of Kiev, its demise came with the Mongol invasion of 1240. Its religious life revived in the 15th century, but it wasn't until the 18th centu-

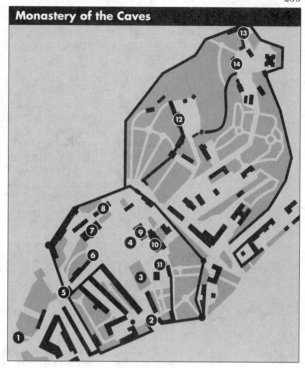

Monastery of the Caves

ry that the monastery began to prosper again. It became the site of imperial pilgrimages, and Peter the Great financed much new construction. Many of its churches as well as the surrounding fortification wall, date from this time. By the mid-18th century the monastery was so wealthy that it owned several villages, 80,000 serfs, and three glassworks. It suffered the same fate as many churches after the Bolshevik Revolution; in 1927 it was closed and converted into a museum. With the advent of perestroika and the religious revival in Russia and Ukraine, the monastery was returned to the church in 1987, on the anniversary of 1,000 years of Christianity in Rus. Parts of the grounds are still functioning as a museum, but the two sets of caves and their many churches are once again open for worship.

The monastery is situated on two hills divided by a shallow valley; it has two distinct sections. The **Verkhnya Lavra** (Upper Lavra) is situated on the highest hill and is surrounded by its own fortification wall. On the lower hill across the gully lies the Territory of the **Dalnyie Pechery** (Distant Caves). The **Blizhnyie Pechery** (Near Caves) are located in the gully between them. The two sets of caves are connected by a wooden passageway. To reach the monastery, take the subway to Arsenalna Station. When you exit, cross the street and take Trolley Bus 20 two stops. You will see the whitewashed walls of the fortification across the street. Walking south, follow the wall until you reach the entrance, a few hundred feet down the street. *21 Sichnevovo Povstannya, tel. 044/290-6646. Open Wed.-Mon. 9:30-6.*

Before you begin your excursion of the monastery, you may want to stop by the **Tserka Spas-na-Berestove** (Church of the Redeemer in the Birchwood), located just outside its walls. Follow the road directly across the street from the trolley bus stop, running along the northern edge of the fortification walls. The road will lead you directly to the church. It was built in the early 12th century by Prince Vladimir Monomakh as a burial place for the princes of Kiev. The founder of Moscow, Yuri Dolgoruky, was buried here in 1157. The church is built in the characteristic style of the time: a cross dome with six pillars. Its eastern wing, which faces the Dnieper, was added in 1640-44. In 1947, on the 800th anniversary of the founding of Moscow, a marble sarcophagus was installed here in memory of Yury Dolgoruky. It was recently returned to the Ukrainian Orthodox Church; it is open for viewing daily 9:30-1:30 and 2-6.

Continuing to the monastery, you will enter the grounds of the Upper Lavra through the archway of the **Trinity Gate Church,** which is crowned by a gilded cupola. Built in 1108, it once doubled as a watchtower. The majestic blue-and-gold exterior dates from the 18th century. The interior is decorated with colorful frescoes and a beautiful wooden iconostasis.

The ticket office is in the long building to your left as you enter; here you will buy tickets for all the exhibits and museums on the monastery's territory, except for the Museum of Historical Treasures, the Bell Tower, and the Caves, where you will purchase a candle in lieu of a ticket. Opposite the ticket office is another long white building, the former Monks' Dormitories. This building houses small exhibits of Ukrainian icon painting (17th-19th centuries), portraits from the Kiev Monastery (18th-19th centuries), and religious manuscripts. They are interesting, but if you are short on time, pass them by, for there is much to see. The passageway to your left, just before the ticket office, leads to the St. Nicholas Church, which houses an exhibit of 17th-century Western European graphic art. *Exhibits open Wed.-Mon. 9:30-6, with 30-min lunch break between 12:30 and 2.*

To your right, just past these exhibits, is the **Velika Lavskra Dzvinitsa** (Great Belfry). Great is the right name for it; in its day it was Russia's tallest structure. The present belfry, which reaches a height of 96.5 meters (317 feet), was built in the 18th century to replace a wooden version that had burned down in 1718. It was designed by the German architect Gottfried Schädel, who was dispatched from St. Petersburg. Each of the four tiers is of a different design, with Doric columns on the second level, Ionic on the third, and

Corinthian on the fourth. It is now under reconstruction, but you can purchase a ticket from the construction workers (as a sign of the capitalist times, the belfry is open to visitors at their initiative), who will give you a guided tour. From the top you'll get a marvelous view of the monastery, the rolling hills, and the Dnieper. But the wooden stairs are somewhat rickety, and every once in a while a piece of sky comes shining through the holes.

Bearing right past the Bell Tower, you will come to the ruins of the **Uspensky Sobor** (Assumption Church). Built in the 11th century, this huge stone cathedral was, like St. Sophia's, influenced by Byzantine architecture. It became a center of ecclesiastical learning and was the monastery's most important cathedral between the 11th and the 13th centuries. Like the rest of the monastery, it was destroyed during the Mongol invasion and rebuilt in 1470. The restored church, which burned in the same fire of 1718 that took the Bell Tower, was rebuilt again in the 1720s. The church was destroyed for the last time during World War II, when it was blown up by the Nazis.

The pathway to your left, opposite the ruins, leads to the five-domed **Vsikhsvyatska Tserka** (All Saint's Church), which was built over the northern gate at the end of the 17th century. Its ornate design is considered a pure example of Ukrainian Baroque. Like the Trinity Gate Church, it also served as a watchtower on the fortification wall.

After you cross the pathway, the building on the corner is the "Economic Wing"; at the window to your left, just beyond the entrance to the building, tickets are sold to the **Museum of Historical Treasures.** The museum is located in the building next to it (to the right), which formerly housed the monastery's bakery. The museum is not open to groups, but if you are patient, after a short wait enough people will gather to form a group tour. If you call ahead, you can request a tour in English. *Tel. 044/290–1396. Open Wed.– Mon. 10–4:30 (lunch break 1–1:45).*

The tour begins on the second floor, with the museum's collection of Scythian gold found in archaeological digs along the coast of the Black Sea. The highlight of the collection is a massive gold chest ornament, decorated with scenes from everyday Scythian life in the 4th century BC. One of the rooms contains the tomb of a Scythian princess and her baby, found in an ancient settlement in the Black Sea area. The skeletons of the princess and her child are arranged as they were buried, surrounded by gold and priceless jewelry. The museum's coin collection includes the first metal coins produced in Kievan Rus, which were introduced in the 10th century.

Next door, in an adjoining building (to your left as you exit), is the **Museum of Ukrainian Books and Printing.** It is housed in the monastery's former printing shop, where

Russia's first printing press was established. The collection includes manuscripts dating from the 12th century and features ornately designed, jewel-encrusted volumes. *Open Wed.–Mon. 10–6.*

Turn left onto the pathway as you exit the museum's courtyard and walk straight out to the *vidovaya* (lookout) platform. It shoots off to the side of the main pathway and offers a spectacular view.

As you leave the platform, turn left and climb back up the hill, in the direction of the Great Bell Tower. To your left is the **Refectory Church,** built at the end of the 18th century and attached to the Metropolitan's House. The church is open for viewing as a museum, but it is also a functioning church (services at 7 AM and 5 PM). It's worth a quick look inside; the gilded interiors were designed by the Russian architect Alexei Schusev. Outside the church are the graves of the Cossack leaders Ivan Iskra and Vasily Kochubei, who were executed by Ivan Mazepa in 1708.

The former Metropolitan's House now contains the **State Museum of Ukrainian Folk Art.** The entrance is to your left, a few steps up the path from the Refectory Church. Its extensive exhibits are housed on two floors and date from the 16th to the 20th century. An entire room is devoted to folk dress and another to bedspreads. Also on display are embroidered linens, handicrafts, pottery, wood carvings, and ceramics. A highlight of the collection is the *krashanki,* delicately painted Easter Eggs. *Tel. 044/293–9442. Open Wed.–Mon. 10–5:45.*

The last stop on the tour of Upper Lavra museums is the fascinating exhibit of "microminiatures," miniature art so tiny that it can be seen only with a microscope. This is a strange place for an exhibit of art that clearly belongs to the modern age of technology (its establishment here was probably the decision of a Soviet bureaucrat), but it is interesting all the same. The creator of the work is Nikolai Syadristy, a contemporary artist who has received many awards for his unusual medium. The works on display include a portrait of Ernest Hemingway engraved on a pear seed; a glass portrait of the Russian balalaika virtuoso Vasily Andreyev (complete with balalaika and case), which is set inside a poppy seed; and the world's tiniest book (0.6 sq. mm.), which is engraved with Taras Shevchenko's portrait. The entrance to the exhibit is across the pathway from the Metropolitan's House, to your left as you exit the museum. *Open Wed.–Mon. 10–6.*

Time Out There is a small café located in the same building as the ticket office, back at the entrance to the Upper Lavra. If it's closed, you can walk up the street to the Salyut Hotel (10 Sichnevovo Povstannya), which has a coffee shop on the first floor (open 8–11 and 2–8:30).

You will leave the exhibit via the courtyard exit. Bearing left, return to the pathway. Keeping the Great Bell Tower to your left, start down the hill. Just past the viewing platform, the road twists and curves down a steep incline. Walk through the iron gates marking the boundary of the Upper Lavra, and soon the road shoots off to your left, leading down to the **Blizhnyie Pechery (Near Caves)**. The entrance to the Near Caves, which are also sometimes called St. Anthony's Caves, is right next to the **Krestovozdvizhenska Church** (Church of the Exaltation of the Cross). Instead of a ticket, you'll purchase a candle from the monk outside the entrance. The passageways of the caves run about ½ kilometer (⅓ mile), but the visitors' route does not take you into every nook and cranny. Inside there are 73 tombs and three underground churches. Icons and fragments of 18th-century frescoes cover the walls. Many important historical figures are buried here, including Antony, the monastery's founder; Nikon and Nestor, the monks who authored the *Primary Chronicle*; Alimpy, a renowned icon painter; and other revered monks. The caves are open every day but close when it rains, due to flooding. Sometimes they reopen after just a few hours, so it may be worth waiting around.

To reach the **Dalnyie Pechery (Distant Caves)**, follow the covered gallery, which begins across the courtyard from the Church of the Exaltation of the Cross. If the passageway is closed you can take the longer route, walking back up the hill to the path along the Upper Monastery fortification wall. Turn left, and keep walking until you reach the second road branching off to the left. It will lead you to the territory of the Distant Caves, also known as St. Theodosius' Caves; the entrance is through the **Annozachatievska Church** (Church of the Conception of St. Ann). Again, you will purchase a candle from the monk at the entrance. These caves are the older of the two; they contain 47 tombs and another three churches, all of which date from the 12th century. Unless you are an expert in early Russian church history, you don't need to be particular about which set of caves you see. (Sometimes these caves are open when the Near Caves are closed.) The experience, which can be rather spooky, is similar in both. You'll follow a twisting path through the cool interiors of the underground labyrinth. Often the only light comes from your candle. Along the way you'll see the mummified monks, buried in the cells where they prayed during their lifetime.

To reach the trolley bus again, walk back up the hill to the road along the fortification wall of the Upper Lavra. Continue climbing the incline as it leads up the hill to your left; at the top you will find the stop for Trolley Bus 20, which will take you back to the subway (three stops).

You may want to stop by the **Museum of World War II**, located on the hillside to the south of the monastery (to your left). This museum is topped by a gigantic steel statue called *Mother Russia*. It is 72 meters (236 feet) high, and it dwarfs the monastery domes on the riverbank. Its construction was controversial; it is a gaudy, oversize structure typical of the wasteful spending of the Brezhnev era. It looks very strange and inappropriate after an excursion through the ancient monastery, but it, too, is representative of Kiev's past—albeit more recent.

The museum contains several sections, the most recent of which is devoted to the Afghan War (in the building to your right as you walk down the terrace leading to the *Mother Russia* statue). The building is surrounded by an open-air museum of Soviet artillery, planes, helicopters, and military jeeps. The somber exhibits display the uniforms and medals of the war dead, as well as their letters home and the death notifications sent to their families. Soviet propaganda photographs of smiling Afghan children hang on the walls. Russian pop songs written about the war in Afghanistan add to the emotional effect. *33 vul. Sichnevo Povstannya, tel. 044/295–9452. Open Tues.–Sun. 10–5.*

The exhibit to World War II, located in the base of the statue, has also recently been updated. The theme of the museum is the devastating effect of war on children. The main exhibit shows how children suffered during World War II, with photos and letters from Ukrainian children deported to Germany, as well as the concentration-camp garb of babies. Recent additions to the museum cover the ethnic wars now raging in various parts of the former Soviet Union, with photos of crying children in Armenia, Georgia, and Azerbaijan. Among them is a photo of a machine-gunned ABC book and a melted doll. The central dome of the statue is inlaid with a huge mosaic, which is eerily reminiscent of a religious icon. The mosaic is in the shape of a five-pointed red star with the words USSR—VICTORY. *33 vul. Sichnevovo Povstannya. tel. 044/295–9457. Open Tues.–Sun. 10–5.*

Excursion: Folk Architecture Museum

This open-air museum is set in a vast field dotted with cottages, windmills, and wooden churches. Located near the village of Pirogova, it is a lovely place to spend a hot summer day. A visit in winter, however, or on one of Kiev's wet and rainy spring days, can be dispiriting: the buildings are far apart and a visit involves a lot of walking along dirt (or muddy) roads. The museum administration organizes a variety of festivals and special events throughout the year, including Ukrainian Independence Day (August 24) and the festive Ivan Kupallo Day (June 6), a celebration of midsummer night that dates back to Kiev's pre-Christian era. The 17th-century wooden church transferred here from the village of Doroginka now holds services on church holidays, and weddings are occasionally performed here. To find out what's going on, call the museum. You can reach it by public transportation, although a guided excursion is advised, since there are few signs in English explaining the exhibits. Both Kiev Intourist and the Slavutich excursion bureau (*see* Guided Tours in Essential Information, *above*) offer tours. To reach the museum, take the subway to Lybedskaya. From there take Trolley Bus 11 to the VDNKh stop and transfer to Bus 24. *Village of Pirogova, tel. 044/266-2416, 044/266-5542, or 044/266-5783. Open winter, Thurs.-Tues. 10-4; summer, Thurs.-Tues. 10-5.*

The museum occupies a territory of 120 hectares (297 acres), and its nine sections cover various regions of Ukraine from the 18th–20th centuries. Each section re-creates a Ukrainian village, with thatch-roof whitewashed cottages, windmills, wells, and wooden churches, most of which were brought here from the region on display. The cottages are furnished and arranged to show how people actually lived. On display are authentic household objects, including wooden utensils and cast-iron pots, embroidered linens, and wooden furnishings. The last section shows the architecture and lifestyle typical of a modern Ukrainian village.

What to See and Do with Children

A ride up Kiev's **cable car** (*Funikuler, see* Tour 3, *above*) will give any child a thrill. The cars run on the same schedule as the subway, and the cost is the same as the fare for a ride on a subway, except on Sunday, when rides are free.

There is no better way to spend a hot summer day than **cruising** the **Dnieper.** Excursion boats ply the river from late spring to early fall, leaving from pier No. 3 at the River Passenger Terminal (subway Ploshcha Pochtova).

The **Kievsky Circus** (1 Ploshcha Peremogi, tel. 044/216–3856) has been a favorite outing for children since 1959. Further details and tickets are available at hotel information desks.

All children will enjoy Kiev's two puppet theaters: **City Puppet Theater** (16 vul. Lunacharskovo, tel. 044/517–4237 or 044/517–0269) and the **Republican Puppet Theater** (13 vul. Rustaveli, tel. 044/225–0246).

Kiev's **Zoo** (32 Prospect Peremogi, tel. 044/274–1180) is easy to reach by subway (Politekhnicheska Station). It's open all year (daily 9–4, closed Mon.), though it keeps shorter hours in the winter.

Off the Beaten Track

Askold's Grave This memorial to Kiev's ancient past is located in a picturesque park not far from the Park of Glory and World War II Tomb of the Unknown Soldier. Askold (also known as Rurik) was the legendary Varangian (Viking) prince who ruled Kiev during the second half of the 9th century. According to the ancient chronicles, he was murdered by the Novgorodian Prince Oleg, who seized Kiev in 882. Legend has it that Askold was buried on this hillside site overlooking the Dnieper River. A wooden church, dedicated to St. Nicholas, was built above his tomb but was later moved to the Monastery of the Caves. In 1810 a small Classical rotunda church was built on the gravesite to a design by the architect Andrei Melensky, and in 1936 a colonnade was added to protect it. You can reach Askold's grave by taking the subway to Arsenalna Station and walking south (left as you exit the subway) until you reach Dneprovskii Spusk, which slopes off to your left. Follow the road down the incline, and the rotunda will appear in the distance to your left.

Babi Yar There was a time when Babi Yar was just another pretty ravine on the outskirts of town. World War II changed that. In September 1941, the German occupying forces ordered Kiev's 33,700 Jewish residents to gather their belongings and march to Babi Yar. Thinking they would be transported to another location, the men, women, and children did as they were told and lined up along the edge of the ravine. Nazi firing squads proceeded to execute them, and their bodies toppled into the ravine below. Throughout the Nazi occupation Babi Yar was used for mass killings. In all, over 100,000 people were killed here, including partisans and members of the Soviet underground. In 1976 a monument was erected on the site, with the official cumbersome title of **Monument to Soviet Citizens, Soldiers, and Officers, Prisoners of War, Who Were Tortured and Killed by the Nazi Invaders in 1941–43.** Although Soviet officials denied for decades that Jews had been a specific target of the Nazis, the dramatic monument—crowned by the figure of a young mother—is a moving testament to their suffering. To reach Babi Yar, take Trolley Bus 16 or 18 from Maidan Nezalezhnosti (No. 16 stops across the street, at the bottom of vulitsa Zhitomirska; No. 18 stops at the bottom of Sofiska vulitsa). The trip takes 30–40 minutes; Babi Yar is located just past the tall television tower.

Kirilovska Tserkva (St. Cyril's Church) Even if you are sated with church architecture, the trip to this magnificent 12th-century cathedral, located at the northwestern end of the Podol, is well worth it. Inside, more than 800 square meters (8,600 square feet) of medieval frescoes have been preserved. The church was once attached to the St. Cyril Monastery, founded in 1140 by Vsevolod II, prince of Chernigov, a pretender to the Kievan throne. Sviatoslav Vsevolovich, a hero in the ancient Russian epic, *The Lay of Igor's Campaign*, was buried here in 1194. Badly damaged during the Mongol invasion, the church has been rebuilt several times. Its present Baroque exterior dates from the 18th century, when it was reconstructed by Alexander Beretti. Restoration of the frescoes was entrusted to the art historian Adrian Prakhov. Among his apprentices was Mikhailo Vrubel, at that time an unknown artist from St. Petersburg. Vrubel's distinctive brush is evident in the paintings on the marble altar screen and in the figures of the Holy Virgin and St. Cyril on the iconostasis. Like many churches in the Soviet Union, St. Cyril's was closed after the Bolshevik Revolution and opened as a museum in 1929. To reach the church, take Trolley Bus 18 from Maidan Nezalezhnosti (the trolley bus stops across the street, at the bottom of vulitsa Sofiskaya) to the stop Stadion Spartak. The ride takes about 40 minutes. *103 vul. Frunze, tel. 044/435–2123. Open Mon.–Thurs., weekends 10–5:30.*

Mariinsky Dvorets (Maria's Palace) If you are coming from St. Petersburg, this lovely blue-and-cream-colored palace will probably bring back memories of the imperial summer estates, and with good reason. Like St. Andrew's Cathedral (*see* Tour 3, *above*), the palace was commissioned by Empress Elizabeth during her 1744 visit to Kiev. It was designed by her favorite architect, Bartolomeo Rastrelli, and was built between 1750 and 1755 under the direction of the Moscow architect Ivan Michurin. Styled after Rastrelli's Razumovsky Palace in Perovo (near Moscow), it is a lovely mixture of Ukrainian and Russian Baroque. The main building faces an open courtyard surrounded by an elaborate wrought-iron fence. Corinthian columns and sculptures adorn the main entrance. The park facade is even more impressive: Balustrades decorated with vases and sculptures of lions lead majestically down to the formally landscaped park, also designed by Rastrelli. Unfortunately, only the main facade is open for viewing: The building now houses offices of the Ukrainian government and is closed to the public.

Before the 1917 Revolution, the palace was used as the residence for visiting members of the imperial family. It has undergone many reconstructions. In 1819 the upper, wooden floor of the main building burned. It was rebuilt in the 1870s, in preparation for an impending visit from Czar Alexander II and his wife, Maria, for whom the palace is now named. Severely damaged during World War II, it has been faithfully restored to its original appearance. To reach the palace, take the subway to Arsenalna Station. When you exit, do not cross the street. Take Trolley Bus 20 one stop. The palace is a short walk to your left through a small park.

Volodimirsky Sobor (St. Vladmir's Cathedral) Commissioned in 1862, this elaborate neo-Byzantine cathedral was supposed to have been finished in time for the 900th anniversary of Russia's conversion to Christianity. A series of construction problems delayed its completion, and the celebrations (in 1888) came and went before the cathedral was finally consecrated in 1896. Construction was begun by Ivan Strom and finished by Alexander Beretti, with several other architects working on the cathedral in the meantime. Frequent changes in design resulted in a diversity of styles. The highly ornate exterior is a strange and not particularly attractive mix of Baroque and Byzantine; the interiors, however, are splendid, with frescoes, icons, and murals created by some of Russia's most prominent artists. The work was supervised by the art historian Professor Adrian Prakhov, who was also in charge of the restoration of St. Cyril's Church (*see above*). Among the historical figures depicted are Prince Vladimir (the pagan ruler who brought Christianity to Russia), Princess Olga, Alexander Nevsky, and Monk Nestor (coauthor of the *Primary Chronicles*). *20 Bulvard Tarasa Shevchenka, across from Universitet subway station. Services Mon.–Sat. 9 AM, 6 PM; Sun. 7 AM, 10 AM, 6 PM.*

Sightseeing Checklist

This list includes attractions covered in the preceding tours as well as additional attractions described for the first time.

Churches, Monasteries, and Convents

Church of the Redeemer in the Birchwood (*see* Tour 4)

Church of the Tithe (Desyatinna Tserkva, *see* Tour 3)

Monastery of the Caves (Kievo-Pecherska Lavra, *see* Tour 4)

Pritisko-St. Nicholas Church (Nikolai-Pritiska Tserkva, *see* Tour 3)

Refectory Church of Mikhailovsky-Zlatoverhy Monastery (*see* Tour 2)

St. Alexander's (*see* Tour 2)

St. Andrew's Cathedral (Andreyivsky Sobor, *see* Tour 3)

St. Cyril's Church (Kirilovska Tserkva, *see* Off the Beaten Track)

St. Elias's (Ilinska Tserkva, *see* Tour 3)

St. Flor's Monastery (Florivskii Monastir, *see* Tour 3)

St. Nicholas's (House of Organ and Chamber Music, *see* Arts and Nightlife)

St. Sophia's Cathedral (Sofiisky Sobor, *see* Tour 2)

St. Vladmir's Cathedral (Volodimirsky Sobor, *see* Off the Beaten Track)

Vydubetsky Monastery. Founded in 1070 by Prince Vsevolod, this monastery was largely destroyed by a landslide in the 15th century. A section of St. Michael's Cathedral (1077–88) remains, including a fragment of a 12th-century fresco of the Last Judgment. Also on the monastery grounds is St. George's Church (1696–1791), a five-domed masterpiece of Ukrainian architecture. You can reach the monastery by tram from Arsenalnaya or Dneiper subway stations. *5 km (3 mi) s. of Monastery of the Caves, on bank of Dnieper.*

Historical Buildings and Sites

Askold's Tomb (*see* Off the Beaten Track)

Babi Yar (*see* Off the Beaten Track)

Contract House (Kontraktovy Dom, *see* Tour 3)

Gostinni Dvir (*see* Tour 3)

Kievo-Mogilianska Academy (*see* Tour 3)

Kiev University (*see* Tour 1)

Kriti Rynok (*see* Tour 1)

Maria's Palace (Mariinsky Dvorets, *see* Off the Beaten Track)

Zoloti Vorota (Golden Gate, *see* Tour 2)

Monuments and Statues

Bogdan Khmelnitsky Monument (*see* Tour 2)

Magdeburg Law Column. Designed by the Ukrainian architect Andrei Melensky, this monumbent was completed in 1808 and honors Kiev's right to self-government (which it lost in 1835). *In Khreshchaty Park, at bottom of Volodimirska Girka.*

Monument to the Baptism of Russia (*see* Tour 1)

Monument Commemorating the 325th Anniversary of the Reunion of Russia and Ukraine (*see* Tour 1)

Monument to the Dynamo Soccer Team (at the Republican Stadium, *see* Spectator Sports)

Mother of Russia Monument (*see* Tour 4)

Nikolai Shchors Monument. A commander in the Red Army and hero of the civil war, Shchors is shown mounted on a bronze horse. The statue stands at the intersection of Shevchenko Boulevard and vulitsa Kominterna, at the bottom of a steep incline.

Skovoroda Monument (*see* Tour 3)

Taras Shevchenko Monument (*see* Tour 1)

Tomb of the Unknown Soldier of World War II. An eternal flame burns in memory of soldiers lost during the war. *In Vechnoi Slavy (Eternal Memory) Park, 1 trolley-bus stop s. of Arsenalna subway station.*

Museums

Apothecary Museum (*see* Tour 3)

Bulgakov Museum (*see* Tour 3)

Chernobyl Museum (*see* Tour 3)

Folk Architecture Museum (*see* Excursions)

Historical Museum. The museum's extensive exhibits cover the history of Kiev from prehistoric times to the present. The section on Kievan Rus is particularly interesting. Also on display are examples of Ukrainian folk art from the 17th to the 20th century. *2 vul. Volodimirska, tel. 044/228–4864 or 044/228–2924. Open Mon., Tues., Thurs.–Sun. 10–6.*

History of Kiev Museum. Situated in the Klovsky Mansion, this museum was designed in the 1750s by the serf-architect Stepan Kovnir. *8 vul. Pilila Orlika, tel. 044/293–6071. Open Mon.–Thurs., Sat., Sun. 10–5. Closed last Thurs. of month.*

Lesya Ukrainka Museum. This is a memorial museum to the well-known Ukrainian poetess Lesya Ukrainka. *97 vul. Sagaidachnovo, tel. 044/220–1651. Open Mon.–Sat. 10–5.*

Museum of Historical Treasures (*see* Tour 4)

Museum of Ukrainian Books and Printing (*see* Tour 4)

Museum of Ukrainian Folk Art (*see* Tour 4)

Museum of Western and Oriental Art (*see* Tour 1)

Russian Art Museum (*see* Tour 1)

Shevchenko Memorial Museum. The personal effects and literary manuscripts of Taras Shevchenko are on display in the house where the Ukrainian writer lived in 1846. *8a*

Shevchenko Pereulok, tel. 044/228–3511. Closed for renovations at least until summer 1994.

Shevchenko State Museum (*see* Tour 1)

Ukrainian Art Museum (*see* Tour 1)

Ukrainian Cultural Center (Ukrainina Dim, *see* Tour 2)

World War II Museum (*see* Tour 4)

Zoological Museum. *15 vul. Institutska, tel. 044/224–1915 or 044/224–1613. Open Mon., Tues., Fri.–Sun. 10–5.*

Parks and Gardens
Kiev has miles of parkland. The right bank of the Dnieper is lined with a series of adjoining parks, beginning with **Volodimirska Girka** (*see* Tour 1), which runs into **Khreschatyi Park.** That in turn runs into the **Park of Askold's Grave,** which later becomes the **Vechnoi Slavy (Eternal Memory) Park.** The entrance to Khreschatyi Park is at Lenkomosol Square; Eternal Memory Park can be reached by taking the subway to Arsenalna Station. From there it is one stop south on any trolley bus.

Academy of Sciences Botanical Garden. This park is situated on the banks of the Dnieper River and covers 180 hectares (445 acres). It can be reached by tram from the Arsenalna and Dnieper subway stations.

Fomin Botanical Garden. This park in the center of town was laid out in 1841. It is named after Alexander Fomin, a botanist and director here in the 1920s. The entrance is near the Universitet subway station.

Gidro Park. This pretty park on an island near the left bank is a popular spot in summer for boating and bathing. To reach it, take the subway to the Gidro Park Station.

Trukhanov Island. There are several parks with outdoor recreational facilities on this island in the Dnieper. The beach is crowded with sunbathers in summer. You can reach the island via the pedestrian footbridge, south of the main river terminal (Ploshcha Poshtova subway station).

Zoo (*see* What to See and Do with Children)

Shopping

Kiev is far from being a shopper's paradise. To avoid frustration and disappointment, think of shopping here as a way to acquaint yourself with the challenges facing Ukrainian citizens as their government tries to reform the economy after 70 years of Soviet rule. The old classification of stores by what they sell has been thrown out, and the stores themselves are in a state of disarray. Economic "reform" allows people to resell goods purchased in state-run stores—an activity that was once considered to be a capital crime. As a result, the streets are lined with makeshift kiosks offering a hodgepodge of goods, from caviar to nylons. Every subway station has several bookstands, where the selection is much better than it is in even the largest bookstores (you may even come across a book in English). The shopping center has traditionally been and remains the Khreshchatik, although you'll probably find more for sale in the streets than in the huge department stores along its path.

There are two categories of shops: those operating for Ukrainian "coupons" and those that accept only foreign currency. The coupon was originally introduced in 1990 as a ration card. When prices in Russia and other republics started escalating, they remained relatively stable in Ukraine. To prevent people from buying up all of Ukraine's goods for resale in other republics, the government started paying Ukrainians in coupons instead of rubles. At first the "coupon" applied only to basic consumer goods and grocery-store items, but over time more and more stores stopped accepting rubles. Eventually the coupon acquired the status of a national currency. But the value of coupons, which look more like Monopoly money than rubles, plummets daily, and they are barely worth the paper they are printed on. Goods for sale for coupons are usually incredibly inexpensive, thanks to the advantageous exchange rate against the dollar.

Department Stores

One of Kiev's largest department stores is located just off the Khreshchatik (2 vul. Bogdana Khmelnitskovo, tel. 044/224–9505 or 044/224–7218). The huge **Ukraina** department store (1 Ploshcha Peremogi, tel. 044/274–6017 or 044/274–5047) is close to the Libid Hotel. To reach it, take any bus or trolley bus heading down the hill from the Universitet subway station.

Hard-Currency Stores

The newer dollar stores sell a wide variety of goods. Their stocks are often a very strange mix of foodstuffs and large consumer items, such as imported TVs, VCRs, or even cars. The old Soviet tradition of naming a store by what it sold ("Fruit" or "Milk") continues today, and many of the new private stores call themselves by what they sell. Others simply give themselves a "prestigious," foreign-sounding name (like *Shop*), which gives little indication of their wares. If you're looking for something in particular, it's a good idea to call ahead. A store that sells primarily snack foods will often have the AA batteries you're looking for, while a store specializing in electronic goods may not.

Candor (vul. Spaska, tel. 044/416–1308) sells shoes, boots, cosmetics, TVs, washing machines, batteries, bottled water, coffee and tea, cigarettes, and liquor.

Slavuta (14 vul. Gorkhovo, tel. 044/227–8464) is a hard-currency grocery with a good selection of imported foods, including frozen pizza, spaghetti, cereal, crackers, bottled water, coffee, canned goods, wine, beer, and alcohol. AE credit cards and traveler's checks are accepted.

So, you're getting away from it all.

Just make sure you can get back.

AT&T Access Numbers
Dial the number of the country you're in to reach AT&T.

*ANDORRA	19◊-0011	GERMANY**	0130-0010	*NETHERLANDS	06◊-022-9111
*AUSTRIA	022-903-011	*GREECE	00-800-1311	*NORWAY	050-12011
*BELGIUM	078-11-0010	*HUNGARY	00◊-800-01111	*POLAND¹◆²	0◊010-480-0111
BULGARIA	00-1800-0010	*ICELAND	999-001	PORTUGAL¹	05017-1-288
CROATIA¹◆	99-38-0011	IRELAND	1-800-550-000	ROMANIA	01-800-4288
*CYPRUS	080-90010	ISRAEL	177-100-2727	*RUSSIA¹ (MOSCOW)	155-5042
CZECH REPUBLIC	00-420-00101	*ITALY	172-1011	SLOVAKIA	00-420-00101
*DENMARK	8001-0010	KENYA¹	0800-10	SPAIN	900-99-00-11
*EGYPT¹ (CAIRO)	510-0200	*LIECHTENSTEIN	155-00-11	*SWEDEN	020-795-611
*FINLAND	9800-100-10	LITHUANIA◆	8◊196	*SWITZERLAND	155-00-11
FRANCE	19◊-0011	LUXEMBOURG	0-800-0111	*TURKEY	9◊9-8001-2277
*GAMBIA	00111	*MALTA	0800-890-110	UK	0800-89-0011

Countries in bold face permit country-to-country calling in addition to calls to the U.S. *Public phones require deposit of coin or phone card. **Western portion. Includes Berlin and Leipzig. ◊Await second dial tone. ¹May not be available from every phone. ◆ Not available from public phones. ²Dial "02" first, outside Cairo. ¹Dial 010-480-0111 from major Warsaw hotels. ©1993 AT&T.

Here's a travel tip that will make it easy to call back to the States. Dial the access number for the country you're visiting and connect right to AT&T **USADirect**® Service. It's the quick way to get English-speaking operators and can minimize hotel surcharges.

If all the countries you're visiting aren't listed above, call THE **i** PLAN™ 1 800 241-5555 before you leave for a free wallet card with all AT&T access numbers. International calling made easy—it's all part of **The i Plan.**℠

AT&T

Fodor's Travel Guides

Available at bookstores everywhere, or call 1–800–533–6478, 24 hours a day.

U.S. Guides

Alaska

Arizona

Boston

California

Cape Cod, Martha's Vineyard, Nantucket

The Carolinas & the Georgia Coast

Chicago

Colorado

Florida

Hawaii

Las Vegas, Reno, Tahoe

Los Angeles

Maine, Vermont, New Hampshire

Maui

Miami & the Keys

New England

New Orleans

New York City

Pacific North Coast

Philadelphia & the Pennsylvania Dutch Country

The Rockies

San Diego

San Francisco

Santa Fe, Taos, Albuquerque

Seattle & Vancouver

The South

The U.S. & British Virgin Islands

The Upper Great Lakes Region

USA

Vacations in New York State

Vacations on the Jersey Shore

Virginia & Maryland

Waikiki

Walt Disney World and the Orlando Area

Washington, D.C.

Foreign Guides

Acapulco, Ixtapa, Zihuatanejo

Australia & New Zealand

Austria

The Bahamas

Baja & Mexico's Pacific Coast Resorts

Barbados

Berlin

Bermuda

Brazil

Brittany & Normandy

Budapest

Canada

Cancun, Cozumel, Yucatan Peninsula

Caribbean

China

Costa Rica, Belize, Guatemala

The Czech Republic & Slovakia

Eastern Europe

Egypt

Euro Disney

Europe

Europe's Great Cities

Florence & Tuscany

France

Germany

Great Britain

Greece

The Himalayan Countries

Hong Kong

India

Ireland

Israel

Italy

Japan

Kenya & Tanzania

Korea

London

Madrid & Barcelona

Mexico

Montreal & Quebec City

Morocco

Moscow & St. Petersburg

The Netherlands, Belgium & Luxembourg

New Zealand

Norway

Nova Scotia, Prince Edward Island & New Brunswick

Paris

Portugal

Provence & the Riviera

Rome

Russia & the Baltic Countries

Scandinavia

Scotland

Singapore

South America

Southeast Asia

Spain

Sweden

Switzerland

Thailand

Tokyo

Toronto

Turkey

Vienna & the Danube Valley

Yugoslavia

Shop (4 Kontraktova Ploshcha, in the Podol Shopping Arcade, tel. 044/416–3221) stocks Italian and Austrian shoes, winter coats, children's clothing, TVs, VCRs, stereo equipment, and snack foods (coffee, tea, peanut butter, bottled water).

Victoria Shop (7 Pritsko Mikhilska, in the Podol, tel. 044/417–4331) carries a small selection of wine, TVs, kitchen appliances and accessories, shoes, clothing, snack foods, souvenirs and blown glass.

Wrangler and Lee (46 vul. Gorkhovo, tel. 044/227–3667) stocks Wrangler and Lee shirts, jeans, jackets, sweatshirts, and running shoes.

Kashtan Stores

In Russia, the state-run stores catering to tourists and operating only for dollars are called Beriozkas (birch tree). Ukraine has its own national version of these stores, also named for a tree: *Kashtan* (chestnut). There are just two left, and their stocks are dwindling rapidly. The largest Kashtan store (24/25 Bulvard Lesi Ukrainki, tel. 044/295–5569) sells souvenirs, snacks, and clothing. The other (2 Bulvard Shevehenka, tel. 044/224–4572) has started accepting coupons; only the small section on the second floor, where jewelry is sold, accepts dollars.

Specialty Stores

Art Shops and Galleries This is one area where Kiev has lots to offer. **Andriivskii Uzviv,** the twisting and winding street leading down the steep incline from St. Andrew's Cathedral, is lined with art shops and galleries that sell works in all price ranges. Even if you're not in the market for Ukrainian art, you'll enjoy browsing.

Gonchari (10A Andriivskii Uzviz, tel. 044/416–1298) has a wide selection of pottery, including teapots of all shapes and sizes, teacups, chess sets, and ceramic animals.

Gallery Taras (4 Kontraktova Ploshcha, in the Podol Shopping Arcade, tel. 044/416–2531) sells contemporary paintings and a small selection of Ukrainian handicrafts.

Gallery Triptych (34 Andriivskii Uzviz, tel. 044/416–4453), owned by an association of well-known Kievan artists, sells paintings, handcrafted jewelry, embroidered vests, pottery, graphic art, and textiles.

Tvorchistvo (34A Andriivskii Uzviz, tel. 044/228–3953) sells handcrafted Ukrainian souvenirs at very reasonable prices.

Souvenir Stores The state-run **Ukrainian Souvenir** (23 vul. Chervonoarmiiska, tel. 044/224–8516) has a surprisingly good selection of Ukrainian woodcrafts, tablecloths, bedspreads, and embroidered blouses. **Slavuticha** (32 Khreshchatik) has a much smaller selection of these items. When you're visiting the Monastery of the Caves, you might want to stop by the **Ukrainian Folk Art Shop** (Building No. 5 in the Upper Lavra, tel. 044/290–1249).

Street Markets

Kiev's largest farmers' market is the **Kriti Rynok** on Bessarabska Ploshcha at the western end of the Khreshchatik. Inside the domed building you'll find rows of private farmers selling fresh fruit and vegetables, cheeses, and fine cuts of meat; Ukrainian souvenirs are occasionally sold. Be aware that you are expected to bargain. For a glimpse of Ukrainian capitalism at work, check out the **Dvorec Sporta** (vul. Chervonoarmiiska, Dvorec Sporta subway station). On weekends the stadium is transformed into a huge flea market where you'll find everything that's not in the stores—from jeans to laundry detergent to meat grinders and kitchen utensils.

Sports and Fitness

Participant Sports

If you're a fitness fanatic, you'll have a hard time in Kiev, especially in winter. None of the major hotels has a fitness center. The Intourist Hotel's small pool, attached to its sauna, is too small to satisfy lap swimmers.

Access to Kiev's public indoor athletic facilities is restricted, just as it is in Moscow and St. Petersburg. The prerequisite "doctor's certificate" attesting to your good health would probably take more time to obtain than you plan to spend in Kiev. If you are visiting in summer, you're in luck, since the outdoor facilities are open to everyone.

Boating and Swimming You can rent boats at Kiev's **Gidro Park,** which is easily reached by subway (Gidro Park Station); there is also a nice beach here. The most popular beach by far is on **Trukhanov Island,** which is connected to the right bank by a pedestrian footbridge (south of the main river terminal, Ploshcha Poshtova subway station).

Skiing and Skating In winter you can rent skates and cross-country skis at the park on Trukhanov Island.

Tennis There are public tennis courts in the park on Trukhanov Island.

Spectator Sports

Tickets to athletic events are sold at the sporting arena prior to the game, but popular events, especially soccer games, sell out far in advance. You may want to ask your hotel excursion bureau for assistance in obtaining tickets. Kiev's main **ticket office** for sporting events is at 16 Chervonoarmiiska vulitsa (tel. 044/225–3258 or 044/224–8234).

Hockey Hockey is second in popularity only to soccer among Kievans. The home team, Kievskii Stroitel, plays at the **Dvorec Sporta** (Palace of Sport, tel. 044/212–5313) at the Central Stadium on vulitsa Chervonoarmiiska. The season is from October through March.

Soccer Soccer is a national pastime, and Kiev's Dynamo team is the most popular in the former Soviet Union; it has won several Soviet and European championships. You can watch them in action from March through September at the **Central Republican Stadium** (3 vul. Mikhaila Grushevskovo, tel. 044/229–9533). The stadium, which seats 100,000, was built in 1941 but was not opened until after World War II. There is a monument here in honor of the Dynamo Soccer Team, which was forced to play against the Nazis—and then was shot for winning.

Dining

Compared with St. Petersburg and Moscow (not to mention Western Europe), dining in Kiev is, simply put, provincial, and before Ukraine's declaration of independence in 1991 the situation was downright bleak. Although Ukraine was always considered the breadbasket of the Soviet Union, its capital had only a handful of decent restaurants, located primarily in hotels catering to foreign tourists. The cuisine here differs little from the bland, meat-laden dishes offered in the state-run hotels of Moscow and St. Petersburg. The overall situation in Kiev is slowly improving, however. The establishment of several foreign embassies and the influx of Western businesspeople have led to several joint ventures. But if you're looking for traditional Ukrainian cuisine, you're not likely to find it in these places. The menus tend to cater to the city's growing expatriate community, which long ago had its fill of chicken Kiev. Prices, too, are high, not only because there are more foreigners than restaurants but also because many of the supplies are often imported.

As in Moscow and St. Petersburg, dining out requires planning. Reservations are almost always essential in the evenings and are advised even during the day. Most restaurants close in the afternoon for a "dinner break," and some are open only in the evenings. You are unlikely to meet "typical" Kiev residents by dining out. The current inflation rate and plummeting value of the Ukrainian coupon make a restaurant meal a luxury that few Kievans can afford.

Like their languages, the cuisines of Russia and Ukraine differ only slightly; both concentrate on meat-and-potato dishes, usually served with heavy sauces. Mushrooms, served in a variety of forms, are a favorite in both countries. Both Russians and Ukrainians love to smother their dumplings and potatoes with *smetana*, a rich sour cream. Despite these similarities, Ukrainian cuisine does have its specialties. One is the famous *Kievskaya kotleta* (chicken Kiev), which is very tricky to make. If prepared correctly, a fountain of butter spurts out of the fried chicken breast when pierced with a fork. Another Ukrainian specialty is *vareniki*, boiled dumplings filled with *tvorog* (a sweet cottage cheese), potatoes, mushrooms, or cabbage. Ukrainian *borscht*, beet soup served with a huge dollop of smetana, is usually accompanied by *pampushki*, hot rolls dripping in garlic butter.

Highly recommended restaurants are indicated by a star ★.

Category	Cost*
Very Expensive	over $50
Expensive	$35–$50
Moderate	$15–$35
Inexpensive	under $15

per person, excluding drinks and service

Very Expensive

El Dorado. If you'd rather be anywhere but in Kiev, seek out this ritzy new restaurant and bar, tucked away in a cellar off Bessarabska Square. Its snazzy, modern decor features a high-tech lighting system that re-creates a starlit night through the restaurant's crystal-studded ceiling. The Ukrainian owner (who just happens to own the spiffy new car dealership directly above the restaurant) caters to Kiev's foreign business community and its fat expense accounts. Not only are the chef, bartender, and manager all German, but so are all the supplies (with the exception of the caviar and sturgeon). The menu features traditional European cuisine, such as smoked duck breast and roasted lamb. The prix fixe dinner, a mere $85, changes weekly and includes appetizer, soup, main course, and dessert. Although the business-oriented clientele can make for a rather stuffy atmosphere, things turn lively after the kitchen closes. Unlike most establishments in Kiev, the bar stays open until the last patron leaves. *13 Chervonoarmiiska vul., tel. 044/225–5007. Reservations advised. Jacket and tie advised. AE. Hard currency only: American Express traveler's checks or cash. Lunch daily noon–2, dinner daily 7–10:30, bar open daily until 2 AM. No Sun. lunch.*

Kiev Dining and Lodging

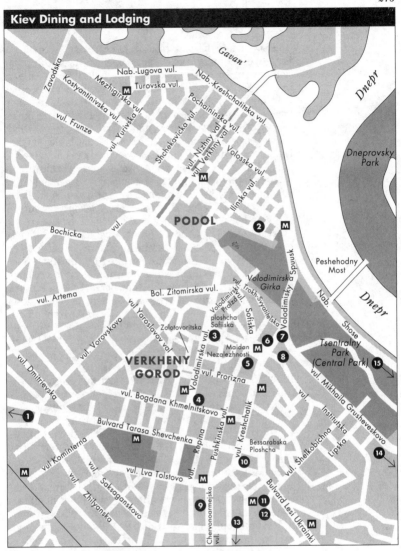

Dining
Apollo, **6**
Dnipro, **7**
El Dorado, **10**
Gostinny Dvir, **2**
Italia, **5**
Maksim's, **4**
Skhodi, **3**
Slavuta, **9**

Lodging
Bratislava, **15**
Dnipro, **7**
Intourist, **11**
Libid, **1**
Mir, **13**
Moskva, **8**
Rus, **12**
Salyut, **14**

Expensive

★ **Apollo.** One of the new restaurants catering to the city's foreign community, this recently opened Swiss-Ukrainian joint venture is quickly setting the standard for fine dining in Kiev. The beautifully restored interior, with ceiling paintings from the 19th century, Greek statues, and high-back wooden chairs, creates an elegant atmosphere far removed from the hustle and bustle of the nearby Khreshchatik. The service, like the interior, is elegant, and the formally dressed waiters have clearly been trained to meet European standards of excellence. Thanks to its Swiss partners, the restaurant imports 80 percent of its supplies, allowing it to offer truly European cuisine. For starters, try the Quiche Lorraine, prepared in a light cream sauce and served in a delicate pastry shell, or the creamy broccoli soup. The light mushroom omelet makes for a nice break from meat-laden Ukrainian cuisine. But if you're a meat lover, you won't be disappointed by the steak fillet, served with melted cheese and mushrooms and accompanied by Italian green noodles. The dessert menu features fruit salad—a rare find in this city—made of mango, kiwi, pineapple, and bananas. On Sundays the restaurant offers a popular champagne brunch. *15 Khreshchatik, in arcade, tel. 044/229-0437. Reservations advised. Jacket and tie advised. AE, DC, MC, V. Hard currency only. Open daily noon-3, 5-11; bar open until 1 AM.*

Italia. When you've had your fill of chicken Kiev, come to this newly opened Italian-Ukrainian joint venture for anything but Ukrainian cuisine. Centrally located just a block off the Kheshchatik, the restaurant offers a taste of Western Europe in a post-Soviet setting. The no-frills atmosphere is haunted by the state-run "dietetic cafeteria" that once occupied the space. Although watercolors of faraway Italy decorate the walls, the modest decor, disco lighting, and simple furnishings place you firmly in the former Soviet Union. The extensive menu offers several kinds of pizza, a wide variety of traditional meat dishes, as well as spaghetti, lasagna, and other pasta dishes. Choose a bottle of imported Italian wine from the impressive wine list, and top off your meal with a strong espresso and Italian ice. *8 vul. Prorizna, tel. 044/224-2054. Reservations advised. Dress: casual but neat. No credit cards. Hard currency only. No traveler's checks. Open daily 1 PM-2 AM.*

Moderate

★ **Maksim's.** Among the very first of Kiev's cooperatives, this intimate restaurant, directly across from the opera house, is just the place for a quiet, late-night dinner. The tastefully remodeled cellar, with its low-brick ceilings and candlelight atmosphere, is perfectly suited to Kiev's ancient history. The menu changes daily and features traditional Ukrainian dishes. The restaurant specializes in cooking to the exact specifications of its clients, and you are expected to make your wishes known when placing your reservation. Ask for *Maksim Zharkoye*, a tasty beef stew prepared with plums, mushrooms, and potatoes and served in a clay pot. Another house specialty is Ukrainian vareniki. If you show up without a reservation, your choices may be limited, but with advance notice Maksim's can provide an impressive array of appetizers, ranging from pickled garlic and fresh vegetables to caviar-filled blini. Car service is also available. *21 vul. Bogdana Khmelnitskovo, tel. 044/224–1272 or 044/224–7021. Reservations advised. Jacket and tie required. No credit cards. Open Mon.–Sat. noon–midnight. Ukrainian coupons, Russian rubles, or hard currency (cash only).*

Slavuta. This modest Ukrainian-Finnish joint venture is another favorite of Kiev's expatriate community. The restaurant offers frozen pizza and other prepackaged meals—microwaved to perfection—in a low-key, casual setting. The dark interior, with imitation stained-glass windows and trompe l'oeil brick walls, seems right out of a latter-day Monastery of the Caves. Compared to the city's other hard-currency establishments, the prices are reasonable, and the restaurant's central location keeps the crowds coming back. *14. vul. Gorkhovo, tel. 044/227–6484. Reservations advised. Dress: casual but neat (no jeans). AE. U.S. dollars or German marks. Open daily noon–midnight.*

Inexpensive

Dnipro. Centrally located at the eastern end of the Khreshchatik, on the second floor of the Dnipro Hotel, this used to be the best restaurant in town. With the recent opening of cooperatives and Western-run joint ventures, it now faces some stiff competition, but it's still the best of the hotel restaurants. Heavy chandeliers, high ceilings, and the view onto Lenkomsomol Square make for a relatively pleasant atmosphere. The service is polite and formal although a bit slow. The kitchen offers a wide selection of standard Ukrainian and Russian dishes, but only half the items listed are ever available at any time. The food is not particularly imaginative, and the main courses come loaded with greasy fried potatoes. As is often the case, the appetizers and soups fare much better, and the restaurant serves an excellent Ukrainian borscht, chock-full of fresh vegetables. *1/2 Khreshchatik, tel. 044/229–8160. Reservations accepted only in person and only for same day. Dress: casual but neat. No credit cards. Ukrainian coupons. Open daily 8–noon, 1–5, 6–11.*

★ **Gostinny Dvir.** Located in the heart of the Podol, in the 19th-century merchant's arcade, this lively restaurant specializing in traditional Ukrainian cooking is the perfect place to top off a day of sightseeing. The interior is warm and inviting, with high arched ceilings decorated with Roman motifs and brass chandeliers. The friendly waitresses, dressed in colorful Ukrainian costumes, will insist that you eat every bite—which shouldn't be too hard, because the food is excellent. Start off with a spicy bowl of Ukrainian borscht, which comes with *pampushki*, piping hot rolls topped with finely diced garlic and dripping with garlic butter. The *Gribi v Smetanoi Souci*, the local version of mushrooms in cream sauce, is a tasty appetizer. For your main course, try the house specialty, *Vareniki z Kartopleyu*, boiled dumplings filled with potatoes and topped with crisp, butter-fried onions. The slightly sweet *Varenki z Sirom* come filled with tvorog. Reasonable prices make this restaurant accessible to local residents, so you won't be completely surrounded by foreigners. *4 Kontraktova Ploshcha, tel. 044/416–6876. Reservations advised. Dress: casual but neat. No credit cards. Open daily noon–5, 7–11. No Mon. dinner. Ukrainian coupons only.*

Skhodi. Better known by its Russian translation, *Lesnitsa*, this popular private restaurant gets its name from the long stairway leading down into its dark premises, formerly used as an all-purpose storage room by the Ukrainian Architecture Union. Although a modest attempt has been made to pretty it up with wall mirrors and fake flowers, the dust still hasn't settled. But what the restaurant lacks in modern decor, it makes up for in lively atmosphere and friendly service. The dishes are all prepared from products purchased daily at the local markets. The menu features traditional Ukrainian fare, such as chicken Kiev and *Kievskii Bitok*, fried pork rolled in flour and served with a plate of vegetables and french fries. For starters, try the *Salat Kashtan*, a mayonnaise-based salad made of finely diced roast beef, pickles, hard-boiled egg, peas, and carrots. The borscht, while tasty, is slightly heavy on the fat. Except for the grouchy coat-check clerk, the service shines. For local color and wholesome Ukrainian food, this is just the place. *7 vul. Borisa Grichenka, tel. 044/229–8629. Reservations advised. Dress: casual. No credit cards. Ukrainian coupons only. Open daily noon–4, 7–11.*

Lodging

The building boom that has taken Moscow and St. Petersburg by storm has so far bypassed the Ukrainian capital. Even at the height of perestroika, when the Soviet Union suddenly became a hot new destination, Kiev was never besieged with tourists. As a result, accommodations are limited to the old Intourist standbys, which are primarily of modern construction, heavy on chrome and cement, and light on character; there are no grand, prerevolutionary hotels. And although you'll find that staff members exude hospitality, the service in general is still redolent of Soviet inefficiency. But thanks to the growing demands of foreign businesspeople, improvements are slowly being made.

Intourist's monopoly on the city's hotels has been broken, and most of them are now operating as independent establishments. Rates, however, have not been reduced, primarily because of the surfeit of foreigners with deep pockets.

Tourist groups are usually placed at one of Intourist's three-star hotels: the **Libid, Rus,** or **Intourist.** Although standards here fluctuate greatly, all provide adequate accommodations. Bring your patience and be prepared for a few unexpected touches. Shower curtains and sink stoppers are not standard issue. Not all rooms come with telephone and television, but most of them have refrigerators.

All prices are quoted in U.S. dollars; with only rare exceptions, hotels require payment in foreign currency and do not accept Russian rubles or Ukrainian coupons.

Highly recommended lodgings in each price category are indicated by a star ★.

Category	Cost*
Very Expensive	$150–$180
Expensive	$115–$120
Moderate	$50–$70
Inexpensive	under $50

All prices are for a standard double room for two, excluding service charge.

Very Expensive

★ **Intourist.** Built by Polish contractors, this huge complex overlooking the gigantic sport stadium is Kiev's newest hotel. Although the dark lobby features the usual marble decor, the rooms are pleasant and nicely appointed. All of them come with refrigerator, television, and telephone, and the higher floors feature balconies with superb views of the city. Popular with businesspeople, all of the suites have been leased as offices. The business center on the first floor offers satellite communications with direct dialing abroad. The only major drawback is the hilltop location: You'll have to put on your hiking shoes to reach the subway, since the closest stop is a 10-minute trek down the steep hill. *12 Gospitalna vul., tel. 044/220–4144, fax 044/220–4568. 350 rooms with bath. Facilities: restaurant, foreign-currency snack bar, casino, foreign-currency souvenir shop, excursion bureau, exchange office, sauna with dipping pool. AE, DC, MC, V.*

Rus. Situated next door to the new Intourist Hotel, this high rise has smaller rooms and a less appealing interior. The bright orange walls don't quite match the faded orange curtains, and the chairs are upholstered with the same industrial carpeting material as the floors. All rooms come with telephone, television, and refrigerator. Thanks to good relations with the Intourist, guests can use the sauna next door. The views here are just as grand, and the walk to the subway just as exhausting. *4 Gospitalna vul., tel. 044/ 227–8594 or 044/220–4255, fax 044/220–4396. 477 rooms with bath. Facilities: 3 restaurants, 2 foreign-currency bars, 3 snack bars, exchange bureau. AE, DC, MC, V.*

Expensive

★ **Dnipro.** Conveniently located at the eastern end of the Khreshchatik, this recently renovated hotel is one of the city's most popular. All the major tourist sites are easily accessible by public transportation, and the Philharmonic Concert Hall is just across the street. The interior is typically unimaginative for a Soviet-built hotel, but the friendly staff does its best to brighten up the place with flowers and plants. The rooms are clean and pleasant, and all have television and telephone. The double rooms have nice views onto the square below, but the singles all face the back alley. The second-floor restaurant is the best of the city's hotel restaurants. *1/2 Khreshchatik, tel. 044/229–8287, fax 044/229–8213. 180 rooms with bath. Facilities: restaurant, 3 banquet halls, 3 foreign-currency bars, excursion bureau, exchange bureau. AE, DC, V.*

Salyut. Yet another Soviet concrete monstrosity, this circular high rise looks like a spaceship fuselage but is really one of Kiev's finest hotels. Currently under the management of an American-Ukrainian joint venture, it is extremely popular with businesspeople and is within walking distance of the Monastery of the Caves. The rooms are relatively large, and some offer glorious views of the Dnieper and the golden cupolas of the monastery's churches. The furniture is slightly worn, but the overall atmosphere is light and cheery. Throw rugs cover the industrial carpeting, and flowered wallpaper and framed dried flowers replace the usual stucco green walls. All rooms come with direct-dial telephone, cable television (including CNN), refrigerator, and balcony. Service is excellent by local standards. *10 vul. Sichnevovo Povstannya, tel. 044/290–6130. 110 rooms with bath. Facilities: restaurant, snack bar. Traveler's checks accepted. AE, MC, V.*

Moderate

Libid. If you're on a tour arranged through Intourist, you may very well land in this cement block. Although it advertises a central location, the walk to the subway is a 20-minute climb up a steep hill. Opened in the early 1970s, the hotel offers the cement-and-steel decor of Brezhnev-era architecture, with plywood furnishings and green stucco walls. Only half the rooms come with television, but they all come with industrial carpeting stained from years of overuse and undercleaning. You may also find the mob of taxi drivers hanging around the main entrance a bit unpleasant. The service doesn't exactly shine, but it certainly beats the decor and atmosphere. *Ploshcha Peremogi, tel. 044/274–4261 or 044/274–0063. 280 rooms with bath, 14 suites. Facilities: restaurant, bar, exchange bureau, excursion bureau. AE, MC, V.*

Moskva. Situated on a steep hill just off the Khreshchatik, this 16-story high-rise towers above Kiev's main thoroughfare. Although its monumental design reeks of Stalinism, the hotel was built in the early 1960s. The rooms are spacious, with high ceilings and thick walls, but the place could use some sprucing up. Nevertheless, standards of cleanliness are higher than at the Libid, and the overly friendly floor attendants will be more than willing to respond to any complaints. Some rooms come with balconies offering grand views of the city. A telephone and television in every room just about exhausts the list of modern amenities. The main lobby is lined with souvenir kiosks selling such imported goods as Polish cosmetics and American bubble gum. Slot machines in a back room off the main entrance attract a seedy crowd that fills the lobby with cigarette smoke. This is obviously not the place for luxury accommodations, but it does offer local color and a superb location. *4 Institutska vul., tel. 044/299–0347. 360 rooms with bath. Facilities: restaurant, 3 snack bars, sauna with dipping pool, excursion bureau. No traveler's checks or credit cards.*

Inexpensive

★ **Bratislava.** This low-budget hotel is a good choice if you don't mind roughing it. Although it's located on the left bank 11 kilometers (7 miles) from downtown Kiev, the metro is just a five-minute walk away, and the ride (aboveground) takes you through Gidro Park. The modest rooms come with telephone and small balconies, but no television. The hotel's official rating is lower than the Libid's, but the rooms are cleaner and the atmosphere is far more pleasant. Single accommodations are not available. *1 vul. Andreya Malyshka, tel. 044/559–7570, fax 044/558–2494. 347 rooms with bath. Facilities: restaurant with adjoining banquet halls, 2 bars, snack bar, excursion bureau. Traveler's checks accepted. No credit cards.*

Mir. Formerly owned by Sputnik, the Soviet youth tourist agency, this very basic hotel is far from the city center and not easily accessible by public transportation. Considering its super low rates, though, the accommodations are quite decent, and all rooms come with television and telephone. However, water-pressure problems make a hot shower next to impossible. The lobby's slot machines and all-night bar attract the city's gilded youth. *70 Prospekt 40-richchya zhovotnya, tel. 044/268–5600. 216 rooms with bath. Facilities: restaurant (for groups only), 3 snack bars, casino, sauna with dipping pool. Ukrainian coupons only. No credit cards.*

The Arts and Nightlife

Kiev's cultural life is as rich as its ancient past, and the city boasts numerous theaters and concert halls. Except for popular ballet performances at the elegant Opera House, tickets are easy to come by and very inexpensive. The excursion bureau at your hotel will obtain tickets for you, but if you want to avoid their fee, which is often 10 times as much as the ticket itself, go directly to the theater's ticket office or to one of the ticket kiosks scattered throughout the city. They post available tickets in the window, together with a full schedule of upcoming events.

For the latest in pop and folk music, check out the underground passageways of the subway stations on the Khreshchatik. Spontaneous performances of music and dance are given in these cavelike premises night and day, and crowds make the lively events hard to ignore.

The Arts

Concerts The **House of Organ and Chamber Music** (77 Chervonoarmiiska vul., tel. 044/269–8681, 044/269–5678, or 044/268–3186), located in the former St. Nicholas Catholic Church, which was built at the turn of the century in the German-Gothic style.

Palace of Culture (5 vul. Institutsky, tel. 044/229–1582). Kiev's largest concert hall is located in a 19th-century finishing school for daughters of the nobility.

Philharmonic Concert Hall (Volodimirsky spusk, tel. 044/228–6371). Classical music concerts are performed in the former Merchant's Hall, built in 1882.

Ukrainian Palace of Culture (103 Chervonoarmiiska vul., tel. 044/268–9050). Contemporary ballet, musicals, and operas are featured here.

Drama **Lesya Ukrainka Russian Drama Theater** (5 vul. Bogdana Khmelnitskovo, tel. 044/224–4223 or 9063). Although the theater is named for a famous Ukrainian poetess, the repertoire is strictly Russian. Foreign dramas are occasionally performed, but only in Russian.

Ivan Franko Ukrainian Theater (3 ploshcha Ivana Franka, tel. 044/229–5991). Here you'll find Ukrainian classical and contemporary dramas, but only in Ukrainian.

Opera and Ballet The **Shevchenko Opera and Ballet Theater** (50 vul. Volodimirska, tel. 044/224–7165 or 044/224–7144), built in 1901, offers fine performances of Russian and Ukrainian operas and ballets in a gilded auditorium. The **State Operetta Theater** (53/3 Chervonoarmiiska vul., tel. 044/220–8754 or 044/227–2241) stages Ukrainian musical comedies. Also try the

Tchaikovsky Conservatory Operatic Studio (11 Khreshchatik, tel. 044/229–1242).

Nightlife

As in most cities in the former Soviet Union, nightlife in Kiev is very tame, centering around the city's restaurants and hotels. The only full-fledged bars are located in hotels catering to tourists; the **Dnipro, Intourist,** and **Rus** have lively lobby bars. For late-night action, the best place is the snazzy **El Dorado** (*see* Dining), whose bar stays open until the last customer leaves. For quiet late-night conversation, the **Apollo** bar offers a rare haven from rowdy crowds in the hotel bars. Many restaurants offer nightly entertainment. The best choices for music and dance are the restaurants in the hotels **Dnipro** and **Salyut.** The city's one and only casino is the **Casino Club First,** located on the ground floor of the Intourist Hotel (tel. 044/220–1978, open 8 PM–4 AM).

Index

Personal Itinerary

Departure *Date*

Time

Transportation

Arrival *Date* *Time*

Departure *Date* *Time*

Transportation

Accommodations

Arrival *Date* *Time*

Departure *Date* *Time*

Transportation

Accommodations

Arrival *Date* *Time*

Departure *Date* *Time*

Transportation

Accommodations

Personal Itinerary

Arrival *Date*   *Time*

Departure *Date*   *Time*

Transportation

Accommodations

Arrival *Date*   *Time*

Departure *Date*   *Time*

Transportation

Accommodations

Arrival *Date*   *Time*

Departure *Date*   *Time*

Transportation

Accommodations

Arrival *Date*   *Time*

Departure *Date*   *Time*

Transportation

Accommodations

Addresses

Name	*Name*
Address	*Address*
Telephone	*Telephone*
Name	*Name*
Address	*Address*
Telephone	*Telephone*
Name	*Name*
Address	*Address*
Telephone	*Telephone*
Name	*Name*
Address	*Address*
Telephone	*Telephone*
Name	*Name*
Address	*Address*
Telephone	*Telephone*
Name	*Name*
Address	*Address*
Telephone	*Telephone*
Name	*Name*
Address	*Address*
Telephone	*Telephone*
Name	*Name*
Address	*Address*
Telephone	*Telephone*

Fodor's Travel Guides

Available at bookstores everywhere, or call 1–800–533–6478, 24 hours a day.

U.S. Guides

Alaska

Arizona

Boston

California

Cape Cod, Martha's Vineyard, Nantucket

The Carolinas & the Georgia Coast

Chicago

Colorado

Florida

Hawaii

Las Vegas, Reno, Tahoe

Los Angeles

Maine, Vermont, New Hampshire

Maui

Miami & the Keys

New England

New Orleans

New York City

Pacific North Coast

Philadelphia & the Pennsylvania Dutch Country

The Rockies

San Diego

San Francisco

Santa Fe, Taos, Albuquerque

Seattle & Vancouver

The South

The U.S. & British Virgin Islands

The Upper Great Lakes Region

USA

Vacations in New York State

Vacations on the Jersey Shore

Virginia & Maryland

Waikiki

Walt Disney World and the Orlando Area

Washington, D.C.

Foreign Guides

Acapulco, Ixtapa, Zihuatanejo

Australia & New Zealand

Austria

The Bahamas

Baja & Mexico's Pacific Coast Resorts

Barbados

Berlin

Bermuda

Brazil

Brittany & Normandy

Budapest

Canada

Cancun, Cozumel, Yucatan Peninsula

Caribbean

China

Costa Rica, Belize, Guatemala

The Czech Republic & Slovakia

Eastern Europe

Egypt

Euro Disney

Europe

Europe's Great Cities

Florence & Tuscany

France

Germany

Great Britain

Greece

The Himalayan Countries

Hong Kong

India

Ireland

Israel

Italy

Japan

Kenya & Tanzania

Korea

London

Madrid & Barcelona

Mexico

Montreal & Quebec City

Morocco

Moscow & St. Petersburg

The Netherlands, Belgium & Luxembourg

New Zealand

Norway

Nova Scotia, Prince Edward Island & New Brunswick

Paris

Portugal

Provence & the Riviera

Rome

Russia & the Baltic Countries

Scandinavia

Scotland

Singapore

South America

Southeast Asia

Spain

Sweden

Switzerland

Thailand

Tokyo

Toronto

Turkey

Vienna & the Danube Valley

Yugoslavia

Special Series

Fodor's Affordables

Caribbean

Europe

Florida

France

Germany

Great Britain

London

Italy

Paris

Fodor's Bed & Breakfast and Country Inns Guides

Canada's Great Country Inns

California

Cottages, B&Bs and Country Inns of England and Wales

Mid-Atlantic Region

New England

The Pacific Northwest

The South

The Southwest

The Upper Great Lakes Region

The West Coast

The Berkeley Guides

California

Central America

Eastern Europe

France

Germany

Great Britain & Ireland

Mexico

Pacific Northwest & Alaska

San Francisco

Fodor's Exploring Guides

Australia

Britain

California

The Caribbean

Florida

France

Germany

Ireland

Italy

London

New York City

Paris

Rome

Singapore & Malaysia

Spain

Thailand

Fodor's Flashmaps

New York

Washington, D.C.

Fodor's Pocket Guides

Bahamas

Barbados

Jamaica

London

New York City

Paris

Puerto Rico

San Francisco

Washington, D.C.

Fodor's Sports

Cycling

Hiking

Running

Sailing

The Insider's Guide to the Best Canadian Skiing

Skiing in the USA & Canada

Fodor's Three-In-Ones (guidebook, language cassette, and phrase book)

France

Germany

Italy

Mexico

Spain

Fodor's Special-Interest Guides

Accessible USA

Cruises and Ports of Call

Euro Disney

Halliday's New England Food Explorer

Healthy Escapes

London Companion

Shadow Traffic's New York Shortcuts and Traffic Tips

Sunday in New York

Walt Disney World and the Orlando Area

Walt Disney World for Adults

Fodor's Touring Guides

Touring Europe

Touring USA: Eastern Edition

Fodor's Vacation Planners

Great American Vacations

National Parks of the East

National Parks of the West

The Wall Street Journal Guides to Business Travel

Europe

International Cities

Pacific Rim

USA & Canada

WHEREVER YOU TRAVEL, *H*ELP IS NEVER FAR AWAY.

From planning your trip to providing travel assistance along the way, American Express® Travel Service Offices* are always there to help.

Moscow

American Express Travel Service
21-A Sadovaya-Kudrinskaya
70-095-69000 or
70-095-69001

St. Petersburg

American Express Travel Service
Grand Hotel Europe
1/7 Ul. Mikhailovskaya St.
812-1196006